The One Show

Judged to be Advertising's Best
Print, Radio, TV

VOLUME 17

A Presentation of

THE ONE CLUB FOR ART & COPY

THE ONE CLUB FOR ART & COPY

LEE GARFINKEL
President

MARY WARLICK
Executive Director

JIM WASSERMAN
Art Director

MARY WARLICK
Editor

KRISTIN OVERSON
Associate Editor

TODD GAFFNEY
Assistant Editor

BILL SCHWAB
Creative Director, Cover
and Divider Pages

DENNIS BLACHUT
Photographer, Cover and
Divider Pages

DESIGNERS
Front and Back Cover
Gerard Huerta/Gerard Huerta Design
Box Fabrication: Justine Fasciano • Copywriter: Josh Denberg

Divider Pages

Title Page:
Rex Peteet/Sibley Peteet
Judges and Members:
Michael Beirut/Pentagram Design
Gold, Silver and Bronze Award Winners:
Missy Wilson/Duffy Design
Best of Show:
Kit Hinrichs/Pentagram Design
Gold on Gold:
Eric Baker/Eric Baker Design Associates
Print Finalists:
Michael Mabry/Michael Mabry Design

Public Service and Political Finalists:
Alex Isley/Alexander Isley Design
Radio Finalists:
Haley Johnson/Haley Johnson Design
Television Finalists:
James Victore/James Victore Design Works
College Finalists:
Neil Powell/Duffy Design
Index:
Lana Rigsby/Rigsby Design
Digital Retouching:
Norman Solis/Dennis Blachut Studio

Published and Distributed by
ROTOVISION S.A.
Route Suisse 9 • CH-1295 Mies • Switzerland
Telephone: 22-755-30-55 • Fax: 22-755-40-72

In Association with
THE ONE CLUB FOR ART & COPY
32 East 21st Street • New York, NY 10010
Telephone: (212) 979-1900 • Fax: (212) 979-5006

Copyright © 1995 as a collection by
The One Club for Art & Copy, Inc.
All rights reserved.
No part of this book may be reproduced in any way by any means whatsoever
without express permission in writing from the owners.
First Printing
ISBN 0-929837-08-8

Production and Separation in Singapore by
ProVision Pte Ltd • Fax (65) 334-7721
Printed in Singapore by Tien Wah Press Pte Ltd

CONTENTS

THE BOARD OF DIRECTORS
PRESIDENT'S MESSAGE
JUDGES PANEL
ONE CLUB MEMBERS
1995 GOLD, SILVER AND BRONZE AWARDS   (1-81)
BEST OF SHOW
THE GOLD AWARD WINNERS ON THE GOLD AWARD WINNERS
1995 PRINT FINALISTS
- CONSUMER NEWSPAPER
    - Over 600 Lines: Single   (82-122)
    - Over 600 Lines: Campaign   (123-144)
    - 600 Lines or Less: Single   (145-175)
    - 600 Lines or Less: Campaign   (176-183)
- CONSUMER MAGAZINE
    - B/W 1 Page or Spread: Single   (184-185)
    - Color 1 Page or Spread: Single   (186-256)
    - B/W 1 Page or Spread: Campaign   (257-258)
    - Color 1 Page or Spread: Campaign   (259-283)
    - Less Than a Page B/W or Color: Single   (284-287)
    - Less Than a Page B/W or Color: Campaign   (288-290)
- OUTDOOR
    - Single   (291-304)
    - Campaign   (305-309)
- TRADE
    - B/W 1 Page or Spread: Single   (310-314)
    - Color 1 Page or Spread: Single   (315-340)
    - Less Than a Page B/W or Color: Single   (341-343)
    - Any Size B/W or Color: Campaign   (344-347)
- COLLATERAL
    - Brochures Other Than By Mail   (348-354)
    - Sales Kits (355-356)
    - Direct Mail: Single   (357-371)
    - Direct Mail: Campaign   (372)
    - Point of Purchase and In-Store   (373-396)
    - Self-Promotion   (397-399)
    - Posters   (400-423)

1995 PUBLIC SERVICE/POLITICAL FINALISTS
- Newspaper or Magazine: Single   (424-429)
- Newspaper or Magazine: Campaign   (430-432)
- Outdoor and Posters   (433-439)
- Radio: Single   (440-441)
- Television: Single   (442-449)

1995 RADIO FINALISTS
- Consumer: Single   (450-465)
- Consumer: Campaign   (466-475)

1995 TELEVISION FINALISTS
- Consumer Over :30 Single   (476-494)
- Consumer :30/:25 Single   (495-544)
- Consumer :30/:25 Campaign   (545-559)
- Consumer :20 and Under: Single   (560-569)
- Consumer :20 and Under: Campaign   (570)
- Consumer Varying Lengths Campaign   (571-575)
- Consumer Under $50,000 Budget   (576-579)
- Non-Broadcast: Cinema   (580-581)
- Non-Broadcast: Out-of-Home   (582-583)
- International Foreign Language Commercial: Television   (584)

1995 COLLEGE FINALISTS   (585-595)

INDEX

THE BOARD OF DIRECTORS

LEE GARFINKEL
Lowe & Partners/SMS
President

TOM THOMAS
Lowe & Partners/SMS
Vice President

EARL CAVANAH
Lowe & Partners/SMS
Treasurer

TONY ANGOTTI
Angotti Thomas Hedge

BOB BARRIE
Fallon McElligott

GARY GOLDSMITH
Goldsmith/Jeffrey

BILL HAMILTON
Ogilvy & Mather

RICHARD KIRSHENBAUM
Kirshenbaum & Bond

ROCHELLE KLEIN
Angotti Thomas Hedge

MIKE LESCARBEAU
Fallon McElligott

TOD SEISSER
Ammirati & Puris/Lintas

DEAN STEFANIDES
Houston Effler Hampel & Stefanides

PRESIDENT'S MESSAGE
LEE GARFINKEL

Every three years, The One Club Board of Directors holds a meeting and chooses one member to be its president. The voting is very discreet. Following tradition, the person elected is usually the one who has just stepped out a moment to go to the bathroom. Or the one drifting off in the corner staring at his watch. Or the last one to show up for the meeting.

Before the unsuspecting victim realizes what has happened, he's being slapped on the back and congratulated on his new appointment. Within moments he is running a meeting he is ill-prepared to lead. The poor soul is now responsible for the most prestigious ad club and award show in the United States. He's not sure if it's a reward for his dedication to the business or some sort of advertising hazing. Like his predecessors, the new president will assume the title as if it's an honor and work tirelessly to preserve the reputation of the Club.

For the last three years, I have attempted to live up to that responsibility. Fortunately, I've had the truly miraculous Mary Warlick and her staff to orchestrate the day-to-day affairs of the Club. Our relationship was not much different than Ronald and Nancy Reagan's. Mary whispered in my ear and I boldly stated our position. During my term, the Club moved to a great new space and held bigger and better events than ever before — everything from Hall of Fame dinners to Portfolio Nights.

Of course, no event is bigger than the One Show. And 1995 was no exception, even if it did contain the usual "whining and dining." Yet after all is said and done, perhaps the single best way to gauge the year in advertising is to go to the One Show or read this book. In an industry overloaded with awards, the One Show is still our most accurate mirror.

I am sure my successor will continue in the tradition of past presidents and keep The One Club and One Show on course. After all, it's a pretty simple task — just listen to Mary.

Judges &
One Club Members

ONE SHOW JUDGES

JIM AITCHISON
Batey Ads/Singapore

DAVID ANGELO
Cliff Freeman & Partners

PAUL BLADE
McKinney & Silver

SIMON BOWDEN
Hill Holliday Connors Cosmopulos

DEAN BUCKHORN
Fallon McElligott

CATHIE CAMPBELL
Ogilvy & Mather

MARTY COOKE
Chiat/Day

TONY DeGREGORIO
TBWA Advertising

SAL DeVITO
DeVito/Verdi

NEIL DROSSMAN
Ryan Drossman & Partners

GEORGE GIER
The Leap Partnership

DEAN HACOHEN
Goldsmith/Jeffrey

DION HUGHES
Hughes Windley

HARRY JACOBS
The Martin Agency

WOODY KAY
Pagano Schenck & Kay

BOB KUPERMAN
Chiat/Day

TOM NELSON
Ammirati & Puris/Toronto

JOE O'NEILL
Hal Riney & Partners

ROBERT REITZFELD
Beaver Reitzfeld

SAM SCALI
Lowe & Partners/SMS

KIRK SOUDER
Ground Zero

HAL TENCH
The Martin Agency

DAVID WECAL
Hill Holliday Connors Cosmopulos

BILL WESTBROOK
Fallon McElligott

TRACY WONG
WongDoody

ONE CLUB MEMBERS

Mike Abadi
Jeffrey Abbott
Fraser Adamson
Michael J. Aimette
Joe Alexander
Wade Alger
Christine Aliferis
Mark Allen
Carl Ally
Pascal Alouidor
Blythe Alpern
David Altschiller
Olivia Altschuler
Patricia Alvey
Ralph Ammirati
Kevin Amter
Jung An
Audrey Anderson
Ron Anderson
Anthony Angotti
Joseph Antonacci
Jill Applebaum
Esti Araten
Stephanie Arculli
Patrizia Arena
Arnold Arlow
Biletzki Armoni
Rachel Armstrong
Stephanie Arnold
Abigail Aron
Lorraine Arroll
Sharilyn Asbahr
Craig Astler
John Athorn
Don Austen
Ted Axelrod
Ruth Ayres
Christian Baffa
Robert Baiocco
Rob Baker
Christophe Bardot
Guy Barnett
Jeanine Barone
Bob Barrie
Lauren Barrocas
Scott Bassen
John Bateman
Tim Bayless
Clifford Beach
Rhonda Beaudette-Lubow
Allan Beaver
Theresa Beck
Wendy Beck
Kris Becker
Wendy Becker
Henry Belfor
Doug Bell
Brian Bellanca
Brian Bellefont
Jacqueline Benitez
Gordon Bennett
Tony Bennett
Danielle Berger
Warren Berger
Steve Berkowitz
Paul Bernasconi
David Bernstein
Wayne Best
Dana Betgilan
Dominique Biger Kahn
Arthur Bijur
Bruce Bildsten
Chris Bingaman
Doug Bixby
Paul Blade
Karen Blanken
Steven Block
Richard Bloom
Alisa Blum
Diana Bosniack
Alix Botwin
Simon Bowden
John Boyle
Eric Bradley
Yvonne Brandt
Scott Brennan
Harvey Briggs
Chris Brignola
Bill Brokaw
Charles Bromley
Stephen Brophy
George Brown
Mark Brown
Timothy Brown
Todd Brunner
Rich Buceta
Kirk Buddy
Gretchen Burckart
Ron Burkhardt
Allison Burton
Jennifer Bushberg
Jaime Butler
Graham Button
Alice Butts
Miguel Caballero
Larry Cadman
Andrew M. Cahill
Dina Calabro
Steve Callen
Jennifer Callery
Cathie Campbell
Ian Caplan
James Caporimo
Paul Cappelli
Rob Carducci
David Carlin
David Carlson
Chris Cater
Emmett Cassell
Angelo Castelli
Hank Champion
Spencer Chan
Wilson Chan
Kevin Cherry
Nelson Cheung
Jay Chiat
Vincent Chieco
Tom Chung
Chris Churchill
Kenny Chuz
Lisa Ciocci
Alexander Clark
Mark Clark
Susan Clark
Matthew Cocco
Henry Cochran
Claudia Coffman
Cindy Cohen
David Cohen
Gary Cohen
Lauren Cohen
Peter Cohen
Gary Colen
Cybill Conklin
Brian Connaughton
Casey Conner
Marty Cooke
Kevin Corfield
David L. Corr
Scott Correll
Colin Costello
Sharla Costello
Ashley Coursey
Ed Cousineau
Jac Coverdale
Court Crandall
Susan Credele
Janna Criscione
Peter Crosby
Kevin Cruickshank
Roderick Cruz
Christine Cucuzza
Greg Curran
Jennifer Currie
Mark Curto
Joanna D'Avanzo
Julie A. Dahlen
Joan Daidone
Trish Daley
Boris Damast
Billy Davaris
Jeffrey Davilla
Jeannine Marie Davis
Stephen Dean
Jay Deegan
Tony DeGregorio
Craig Deitch
Steve Deiters
Ken DeLeon
Laura Dellova
Maria Demartino
Ashley Depp
Allison DeRose
Sal DeVito
Audrey DeVries
Steve Diamond
Christopher Digianni
Steve Dildarian
Gayle Dinerstein
Greg DiNoto
David Dirienz
Brian Dixon
Angela Dominguez
Andrew Donnelly
Steve Doppelt
Tom Doud
Sean Dougherty
Mike Duckworth
Rosalyn Dunham
Laurence Dunst
Jim Durfee
Susan Dwyer
Richard Eber
Roy Edelman
Doron Edut
Shannon Edwards
Arthur Einstein
Aaron Keith Eiseman
Evan Elliot
Stuart Elliot
Alice Elston
Bradford Emmett
Kerey Enderley
Brian English
Wendy Erwin
Camilo Espinel
Eric Essig
Reza Estakhrian
Paul Ewing
Brian Fallon
Peter Farago
Kristi Faulkner
Mark Feigenson
Neil Fein
Judith Fekete
Jeremy Feldman
Sarah Feldman
Mark Fenske
Michael Fetsko
Kerry Feuerman
Michael D. Field
Peggy Fields
Carlo Figueiredo
Luis Figueroa
Michael Fine
Peter Fitz
Maureen Fitzpatrick
Cora Flaster
Mike Flegle
Frank C. Fleizach
James Floersch
Daniel Forman
Cliff Freeman
Robert Fremgen
Jennifer Frost
Eric Fuentecilla
Rosanna Fuentes
Jerry Fury
Frank Fusco
Tom Gabriel
Tom Galati
Andrea Gall
Brendan Gallahue
Michael Gambino
Mark Ganton
Bertrand Garbassi

Thomas Garbellotto
Richard Garcia
Salvador Garcia
Lee Garfinkel
Amil Gargano
Matthew Gargano
Lisa Garrone
Lisa Garza
Dave Gassman
Pamela Gayster
Dean Gemmell
John George
Harold German
Djamila Ghezzar
Steven Gianakouros
George Gier
Carla Gigante
Robert Gilanyi
Frank Ginsberg
Dan Glassman
Tim Godsall
Charles Goldman
Alexandra Goldsmith
Gary Goldsmith
Mark Goldstein
Mia Goldstein
Steven Goldstein
William Goldstein
Sandra Gomes
Mark A. Gonzalez
Geoffrey Goodridge
Beth Goozman
Regina Gormar
Bob Gouveia
Roy Grace
Lorraine Gracey
Stella Grafakos
Jason Graff
Jeff Graybill
Clare Delle Grazie
Jeff Griffith
Bill Groginsky
Brian Gross
Brett Grossman
Philip Growick
Jonathan Grusky
Roland Grybauskas
Eric Guczwa
Zorayma Guevara
Frank Guzzone
Amy Haddad
Paola Hadida-Hassan
Jan Hafer
Jim Hagar
Stephen Haggarty
Matthew Hallock
Trace Hallowell
Bill Hamilton
Dean Hanson
Jon Harcharek
Keith Harmweyer
Yuval Harpaz
Cabell Harris
Jeffrey Harris
Eva Hart
Jim Hayman
Kathleen Hennicke
Roy Herbert
Julissa Herrera

Bill Hillsman
Paul Hirsch
Peter Hirsch
Sigal Hofshi
Barry Holland
Patrick Holland
Dave Holloway
Jenine Holmes
Laurence Horvitz
Ryan Hose
Hugh Hough
Lara Hovanesian
Major Howell
Ginny Howsam
Matthew Hoyt
Ron Huey
Rodney Huff
Dion Hughes
Julie-Anne Hughes
Mark Hughes
Mike Hughes
Neal Hughlett
Amanda Huntzinger
Lisa Hurwitz
Peter Iannerelli
Jessica Iannuzzi
Kim Irelan
Dick Jackson
Ellen Jacobs
Harry M. Jacobs, Jr.
Bruce Jacobson
Holly Jaffe
Paul Jamieson
Joan Jedell
Shawn Jeffrey
Mickey Jenkins
Taline Jessourian
Anthony Johnson
Raymond Johnson
Timothy Joyce
Heward Jue
Joshua Kampta
Charles Kane
Maria Kantlis
Scott Kaplan
Eileen Karakashian
Richard Kaufman
Leslie Kay
Woody Kay
Joseph Kazmierski
Elizabeth Keane
Vincent Keane
Catherine Keating
Katie Keating
Kat Keeley
Yong Keh
Michelle Keller
Kiki Kendrick
Brian Kennedy
Dong-Hyun Kim
Eil Jung Kim
Sae-Won Kim
Jon Michael King
Joe Knezic
T.K. Knowles
Ronni Korn
Renee Korus
Maria Kostyk-Petro
Judy Kozuck

Kurt Kracsun
Gary Krakow
Tamra Kriebel
Helmut Krone
Neal Krouse
Stewart Krull
Paul Krumenacker
Cristy Kruse
Adam Kuhr
Pradeep Kumar
Joseph Kwit
Robert LaBarge
Kevin Labick
Matthew Labul
Diosdado Lagos, Jr.
Timothy Lampkin
Jenny Landey
Steven Landsberg
Barton Landsman
Jeffrey Lang
Andy Langer
Anthony LaPetri
Carole Larson
Gerald LaStarza
Mike Lavigne
Mary Wells Lawrence
Diane Lazarus
Ian Lebowitz
Jennifer Leder
Ann Lee
Hye Sung Lee
Jennie Lee
Patrick Lee
Seam Lee
Sung-Yoon Lee
Taylor Lee
Brian Lefkowitz
Hanne-Zuih Leigh
Neil Leinwohl
Dany Lee Lennon
Jodie Leopold
Grace Lerner
Mike Lescarbeau
Michael Leselrod
Sharon Lesser
Robert Levenson
Ellen Lewis
Jonathan Lewis
John Li
Zhao Wen Li
Ian Li-Pelaez
Tom Lichtenheld
Ann-Marie Light
Darren Lim Chih Yu
Lisa Lipkin
Michael Liss
Wallace Littman
Roger Livingston
Deborah Locke
David Loew
George Lois
Arin Loprete
Joe Lovering
Abby Lovinger
Peter Lubalin
David Lubars
Marc Lucas
Lisa Lurie
Stephen Lynch

Michael Lyons
Tony Macchia
Kevin MacLean
Roz Makarechi
Madhu Malhan
John Malinowski
Karen Mallia
Ellen Mance-Smyth
Sara B. Mandel
Ken Mandelbaum
Bradley Manier
Claudia Manuel
Jennifer Marafiore
David Marino
Louis Marino
Richard Marino
John Mariucci
Kenneth J. Markey
Christopher Markham
Larry Marks
Rhoda Marshall
Caprice Marut
Kimberly Mattig
Michael Maurer
Scott McAfee
Ed McCabe
Nancy McCaleb
Clem McCarthy
Lisa McCarthy
Alex McCausland
Matthew P. McCutchin
Peter McDonald
Kevin McKeon
Paul McKittrick
Rob McPherson
Danielle McVeigh
Lynne Meena
Mark Mendelis
Frank Meo
Mario G. Messina
Lyle Metzdorf
Terri Meyer
Greg Meyers
Marc Meyers
Risa Mickenberg
Michael Migliozzi II
Mark Millar
Don Miller
Gordon Miller
Reid Miller
Stacy Milraney
John Lane Mims
Jonathan L. Mindell
Rebecca Mirkin
Deanna Cohen Mitchell
Gregory Mitchell
Mark Mitchell
Marise Mizrahi
Leonard Monfredo
Ty Montague
Melinda Moore
Rafael Morales
Deborah Morrison
Marco Morsella
Gregory Motylenski
Jim Mountjoy
Christopher Mrozek
William Munch, Jr.
Sibila Munoz

Vinny Muratore
Lexie Murray
Noam Murro
Mark Musto
Narendra Nandoe
Thomas Nathan
Victoria Necea
Robert S. Needleman
Arun K. Nemali
David Newbold
T. Michelle Newman
Steve Nicholas
Raymond Nichols
David Nobay
Jennifer Noble
Susan Nobles
Michael Nwoke
Dick O'Brien
Joe O'Neill
Bill Oberlander
Rip Odell
David Ogilvy
Jin Oh
Vicky Oliver
Peter Oravetz
Seymon Ostilly
Cele Otnes
Tetsuya Otsu
Alvaro Paez
Jack Palancio
Haley Panzer
Steve Papageorge
Joe Paprocki
John Park
Ward Parker
Michael Parrot
Alido Pavan
Michael Pavone
Randall Pelham
Richard Pels
George Perkins
Ellen Perless
Yolanda Petriz
John Petruney
Daniel Pierre
Johan Pihl
Donna Pilch
Marianne Pillsbury
Rosa Pineda
Hether Plansker
Larry Platt
Jonathan Plazonja
Chris Pollock
Shirley Polykoff
Tony Pucca
Nazneen Qazi
Tom Quaglino
Elissa Querze
Keith Quesenberry
Thomas Quitasol
Lisa Quitoni
Dick Raboy
Charles Rachford
Lynda Raihofer
Maria Gabriela Ramos
Suzanne Ramos
Saira Ramoutar
Eldar Rapaport
Ian Reichenthal
Maureen Reilly
David Reinhardt
Robert Reitzfeld
Nancy Rice
Allen Richardson
Carolyn Rie
Terry Rietta
Susannah Rinaldi
Hal Riney
Chris Robb
Gary Robbins
Lori Roberts
Michael Robertson
Phyllis Robinson
Scott Rockwood
Alexis Rodriguez
Manny Rodriguez
Mike Rogers
Gad Romann
Nicholas Romano
Laurie Rosen
Mike Rosen
Ron Rosen
Ron Rosenfeld
Liz Rosenthal
Robert G. Rosenthal
Bernie Rosner
Tom Rost
Mark Rothenberg
Keri Roy
Linda Rudberg-Thibodeau
John Russo
Nat Russo
Mel Rustom
Alan Ruthazer
Kelly Ryan
Nancy Rybczynski
Ted Sabarese
Jennifer Sabolik
Steve Sage
Salomon Sainvil
Carl Sastram
Joanne Scannello
Michael Scarano
Phil Schatz
Glenn Scheuer
Cara Schiavone
Christopher Schifando
Kate Schultz
Joe Sciarotta
Jeff Seide
Tod Seisser
Michael Seymour
Timothy Shaw
Bill Shea
Cally Shea
Theresa Shenberger
Matthew Shepko
Lori Sheppard
Brett Shevack
Edward Shieh
Bob Shiffrar
Albert Shih
Chiun-Kai Shih
Fred Siegel
Kate Silverberg
Daniel Silverstein
Michael Silvia
Sheilini Singh
Leonard Sirowtiz
Steve Skibba
David Skinner
Jonathan Slater
Mike Slosberg
Robert Slosberg
Anne Smith
Colleen Smith
Hillary Smith
Kevin Smith
Marc Smith
Nancy Smith
David Sohn
Richard Solomon
Lee Solon
Jae Son
Vanessa Soto
Cheri Soukop
Andy Spade
Mark Spector
Cody Spinadel
Douglas Spitzer
Helayne Spivak
Andy Srygley
Paige Elizabeth St. John
John Staffen
Joseph Staluppi
Todd Stanley
Scott Stefan
Dean Stefanides
Len Stein
Danielle Stella
Art Stiefel
Bob Stohrer
Chris Stoltz
Kevin Stoohs
Jeffrey Stotsky
Bob Sullivan
James Robert Sullivan, Jr.
Nick Sustana
Heather Swainston
Robert Swartz
Joe Sweet
Leslie Sweet
William Sypher
Norman Tanen
Willie Tang
Abby Terkuhle
Rodolfo Terrada
Mike Tesch
Benny Thomas
Tom Thomas
Benjamin Thompson
Daniel Edward Thompson
Todd Tilford
Adam Torio
Carlos Torres
Robert Torres
Troy Torrison
Mark Townsley
Wendy Tripp
William Troncone
Matthew Trumino
Anastasios Tsiavos
Rebecca Tudor-Foley
Lina Tun Mei Lam
Karl Turkel
Christopher Turner
Ben Urman
Victor Valadez
Jennifer Van Blarcom
Eddie Van Bloem
Peter Van Bloem
Nancy Vecilla
Michael Vella
Paul Venables
Jennifer Venegas
Amy Vensel
Tim Vermillion
Stephen Versandi
Janet Villano
Larry Vine
Michael Vitiello
Joseph Volpicelli
Leila Vuorenmaa
Nina Wachsman
Elaine Wagner
Judy Wald
Marvin Waldman
Alan Washa
Jessica Watts
Steve Wax
Samuel Weber
Lyle Wedemeyer
Jill Weingarten
Eliot Weinstein
Eric Weisberg
Mimi Weisel
Marty Weiss
David Weller
Robert Shaw West
Bill Westbrook
Tobin Wheeler
Steve Whittier
Ronald Scott Wild
Richard Wilde
Tim Williams
Claire Willms
Jennifer Winn
Paul Witt
David Wojdyla
Holly Ann Wojtaszek
Lloyd Wolfe
Alan L. Wolk
David A. Wong
Lai Phun Wong
James Woo
Laura B. Woods
Leslie Wratten
Tobi Wright
Elizabeth Wynn
Seiji Yamaski
Christopher Yates
Richard Yellan
Elaine Yip
Jung Hwan Yoon
Harpaz Yuval
Lynette Zator
Jeffrey Zeldmad
Peter Ziegler
Rainer Zierer

Gold, Silver & Bronze Winners

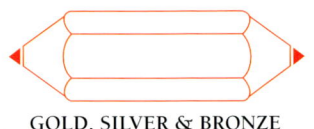

GOLD, SILVER & BRONZE AWARDS

CONSUMER NEWSPAPER OVER 600 LINES: SINGLE

1 GOLD

ART DIRECTOR:
Marc Schattner
WRITER:
Malcolm Pryce
PHOTOGRAPHER:
Marc Schattner
CLIENT:
Simmons
AGENCY:
McCann-Erickson/ Singapore

FOR PRESIDENT ROOSEVELT, A DAY AT THE OFFICE INVOLVED SENDING 750,000 MEN INTO A MINEFIELD. EVER WONDERED HOW HE SLEPT AT NIGHT?

If you've ever had difficulty sleeping because of pressure at work, you should spare a thought for Franklin Roosevelt.

During World War II, memos from his office sent American soldiers onto beaches defended by mines, dive-bombers, even kamikaze death squads.

The D-Day landings.

How on Earth do you sleep with that weight of responsibility on your shoulders? According to Eleanor Roosevelt, the answer was simple. They chose a Simmons bed.

Invented in 1925, it's been sending people to sleep faster than anaesthetic ever since. It's all due to the unique pocket-coil spring system. Instead of being wired together like in ordinary beds, the springs in a Simmons

Another satisfied customer... a Simmons advertisement from the 1930's.

work separately. So the body enjoys the optimum degree of support at every point of contact with the mattress. No bumps or lumps. No sagging.

And no rolling into the middle. Instead both partners lie cocooned in their own cosy niche,

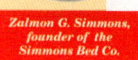
Zalmon G. Simmons, founder of the Simmons Bed Co.

enjoying deep and untroubled slumbers. The sort of sleep in fact which, Doctors now tell us, can have undreamed of implications for our day-to-day health.

Our moods, our powers of concentration, even our ability to fight disease. Dramatic claims for a bed? Maybe. But, don't you owe it to yourself to find out?

You may not have a world war to win. But you could still use our support for the battle in the boardroom.

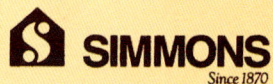
SIMMONS Since 1870

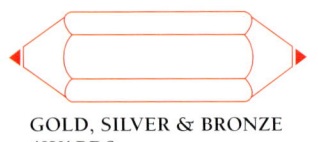

GOLD, SILVER & BRONZE AWARDS

CONSUMER NEWSPAPER
OVER 600 LINES: SINGLE

2 SILVER
ART DIRECTOR:
Paul Hirsch
WRITER:
Mark Waggoner
PHOTOGRAPHER:
Lars Topelmann
CLIENT:
Cycle Oregon
AGENCY:
Cole & Weber/Portland

3 SILVER
ART DIRECTOR:
Marc Schattner
WRITER:
Malcolm Pryce
PHOTOGRAPHER:
Marc Schattner
CLIENT:
Simmons
AGENCY:
McCann-Erickson/Singapore

2 Silver

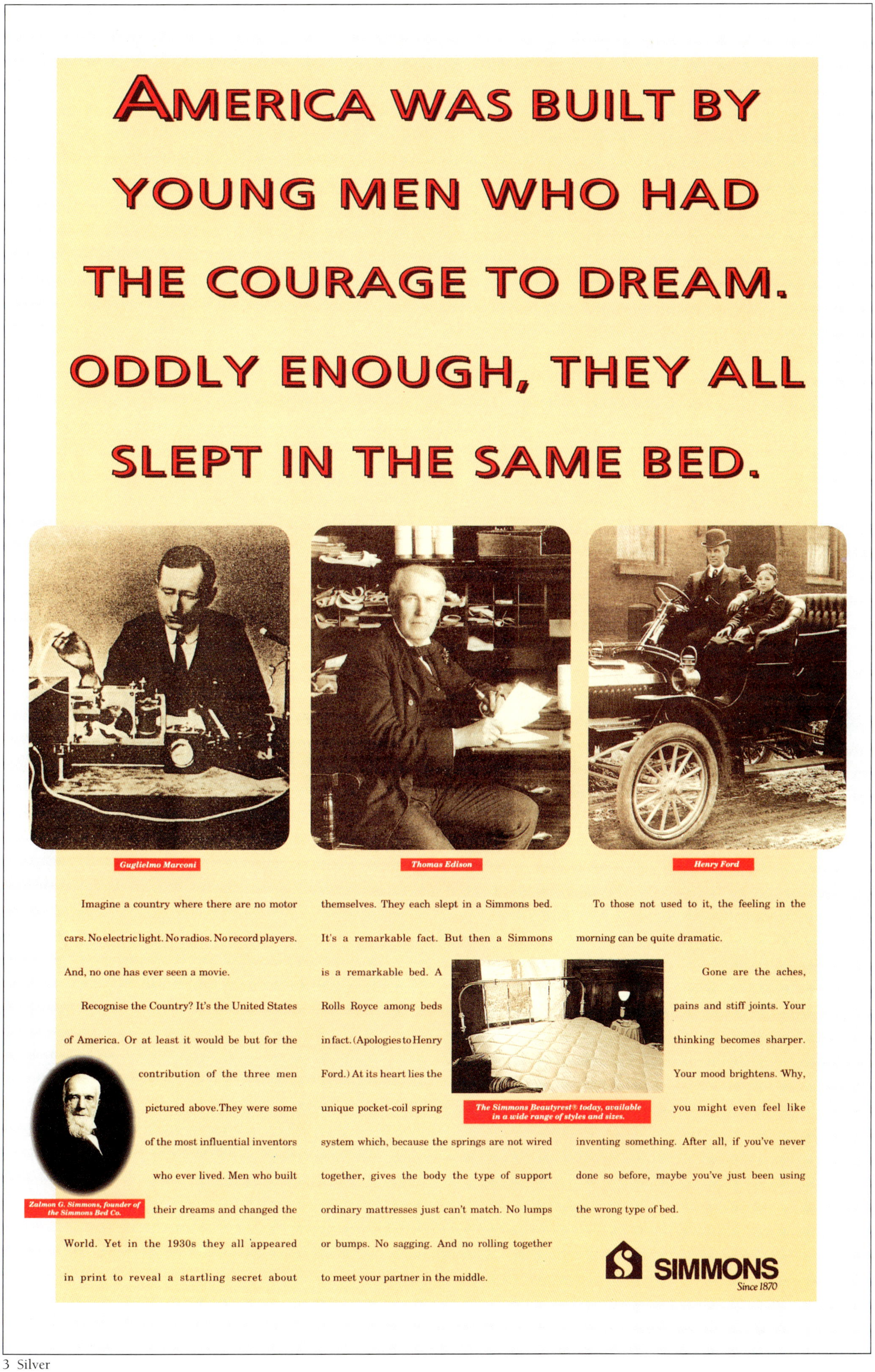

America was built by young men who had the courage to dream. Oddly enough, they all slept in the same bed.

Guglielmo Marconi *Thomas Edison* *Henry Ford*

Imagine a country where there are no motor cars. No electric light. No radios. No record players. And, no one has ever seen a movie.

Recognise the Country? It's the United States of America. Or at least it would be but for the contribution of the three men pictured above. They were some of the most influential inventors who ever lived. Men who built their dreams and changed the World. Yet in the 1930s they all appeared in print to reveal a startling secret about themselves. They each slept in a Simmons bed. It's a remarkable fact. But then a Simmons is a remarkable bed. A Rolls Royce among beds in fact. (Apologies to Henry Ford.) At its heart lies the unique pocket-coil spring system which, because the springs are not wired together, gives the body the type of support ordinary mattresses just can't match. No lumps or bumps. No sagging. And no rolling together to meet your partner in the middle.

Zalmon G. Simmons, founder of the Simmons Bed Co.

The Simmons Beautyrest® today, available in a wide range of styles and sizes.

To those not used to it, the feeling in the morning can be quite dramatic.

Gone are the aches, pains and stiff joints. Your thinking becomes sharper. Your mood brightens. Why, you might even feel like inventing something. After all, if you've never done so before, maybe you've just been using the wrong type of bed.

SIMMONS
Since 1870

GOLD, SILVER & BRONZE AWARDS

CONSUMER NEWSPAPER
OVER 600 LINES: SINGLE

4 BRONZE
ART DIRECTOR:
Stuart Baker
WRITER:
Tony Brignull
PHOTOGRAPHER:
Graham Ford
CLIENT:
Freedom Foods/RSPCA
AGENCY:
Abbott Mead Vickers. BBDO/London

5 BRONZE
ART DIRECTOR:
Allen Richardson
WRITER:
Gary Cohen
PHOTOGRAPHER:
Carl Furuta
CLIENT:
Land Rover North America
AGENCY:
Grace & Rothschild/ New York

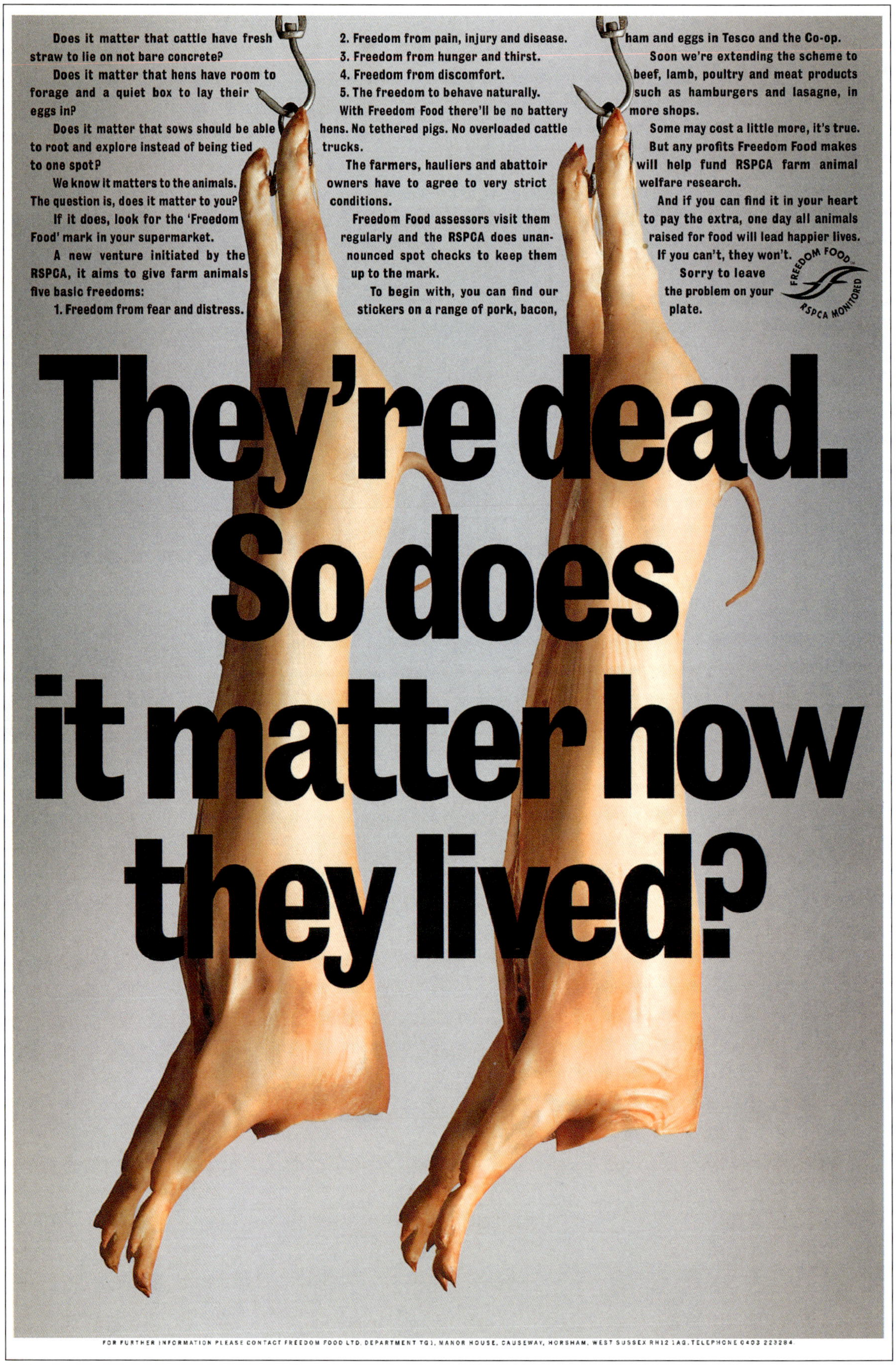

4 Bronze

Our dual airbags deploy in ⅛ of a second. That's approximately six months faster than other 4x4s.

Timing is everything.

The new Discovery from Land Rover is the first 4x4 ever to have dual airbags.

You won't find both driver-side and passenger-side airbags in any other 4x4.

You also won't find the Discovery's atrium-like interior, which seats up to six kids. Or available dual sunroofs to help insure they all tan evenly.

With other features such as ABS, permanent four-wheel drive, a steel inner body cage, and side door beams, it's truly a great place to have children.

So why not call 1-800-FINE 4WD for the nearest dealer? At just under $29,000; the Discovery offers your family a level of security that's unsurpassed.

After all, we believe airbag deployment should be measured with a stopwatch. Not with a calendar.

 DISCOVERY

GOLD, SILVER & BRONZE
AWARDS

CONSUMER NEWSPAPER
OVER 600 LINES:
CAMPAIGN

6 GOLD
ART DIRECTOR:
Marc Schattner
WRITER:
Malcolm Pryce
PHOTOGRAPHER:
Marc Schattner
CLIENT:
Simmons
AGENCY:
McCann-Erickson/
Singapore

America was built by young men who had the courage to dream. Oddly enough, they all slept in the same bed.

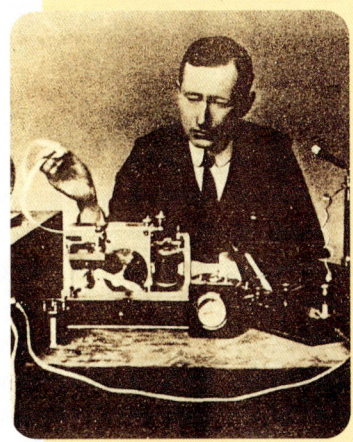

Guglielmo Marconi

Thomas Edison

Henry Ford

Imagine a country where there are no motor cars. No electric light. No radios. No record players. And, no one has ever seen a movie.

Recognise the Country? It's the United States of America. Or at least it would be but for the contribution of the three men pictured above. They were some of the most influential inventors who ever lived. Men who built their dreams and changed the World. Yet in the 1930s they all appeared in print to reveal a startling secret about themselves. They each slept in a Simmons bed. It's a remarkable fact. But then a Simmons is a remarkable bed. A Rolls Royce among beds in fact. (Apologies to Henry Ford.) At its heart lies the unique pocket-coil spring system which, because the springs are not wired together, gives the body the type of support ordinary mattresses just can't match. No lumps or bumps. No sagging. And no rolling together to meet your partner in the middle.

Zalmon G. Simmons, founder of the Simmons Bed Co.

The Simmons Beautyrest® today, available in a wide range of styles and sizes.

To those not used to it, the feeling in the morning can be quite dramatic.

Gone are the aches, pains and stiff joints. Your thinking becomes sharper. Your mood brightens. Why, you might even feel like inventing something. After all, if you've never done so before, maybe you've just been using the wrong type of bed.

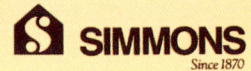

SIMMONS
Since 1870

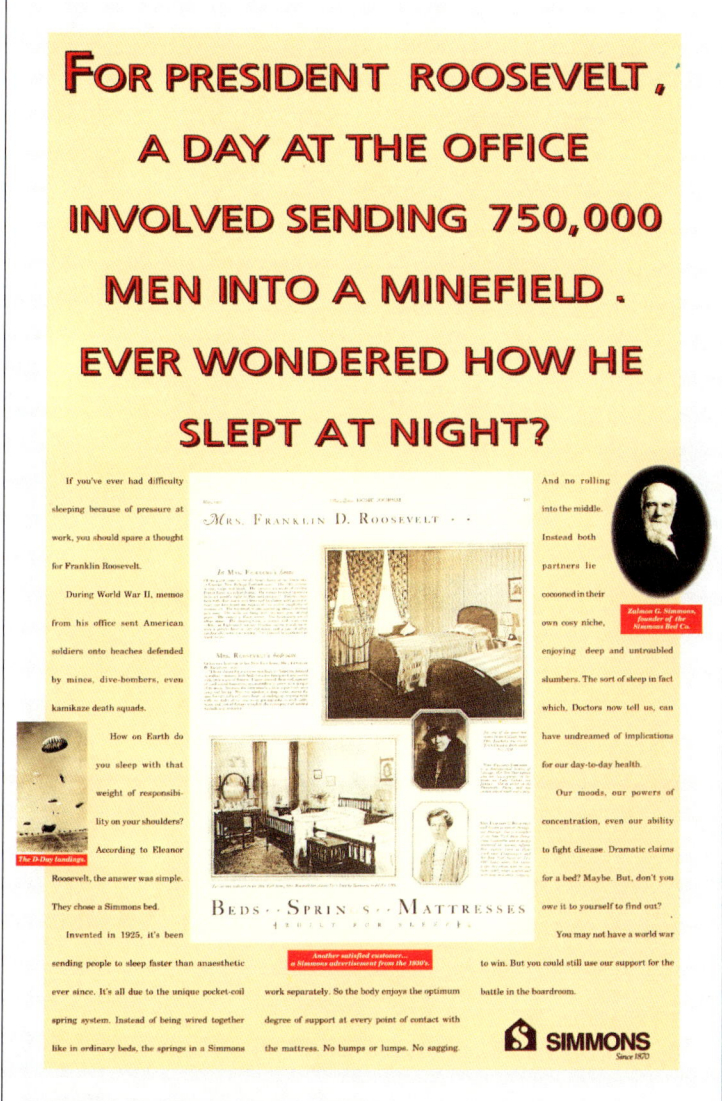
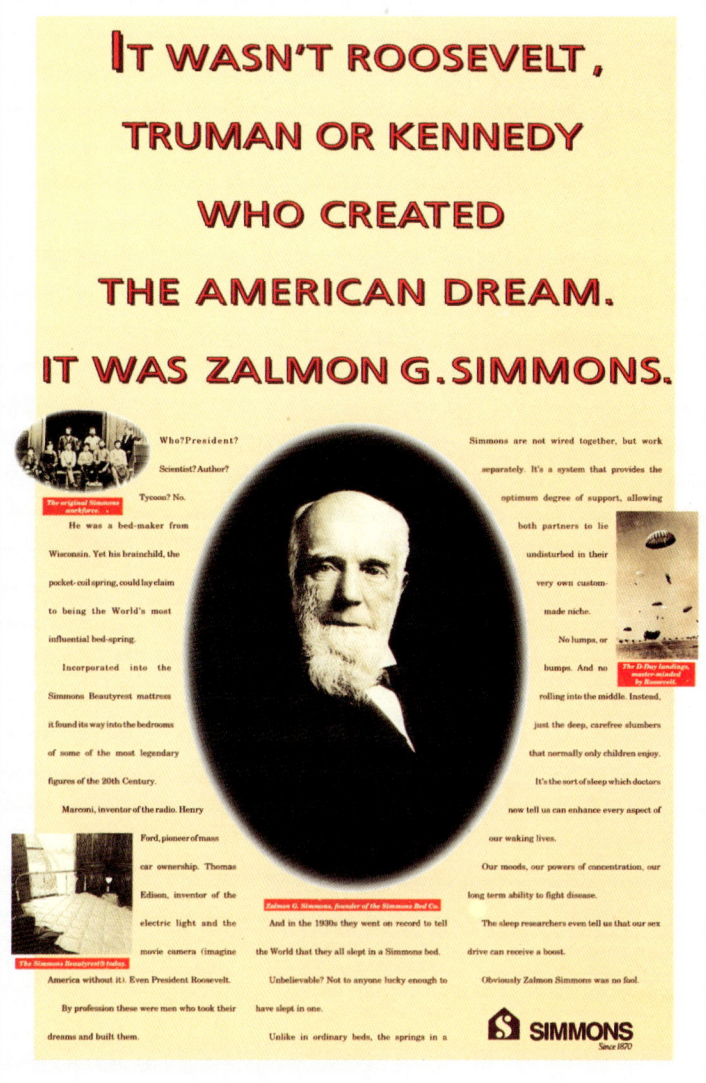

GOLD, SILVER & BRONZE AWARDS

CONSUMER NEWSPAPER
OVER 600 LINES:
CAMPAIGN

7 SILVER
ART DIRECTOR:
Andy Tam
WRITER:
Tony Yeung
ILLUSTRATOR:
Tom Lee
PHOTOGRAPHER:
Ricky Wong
CLIENT:
Whitehall International
AGENCY:
Bates/Hong Kong

GOLD, SILVER & BRONZE AWARDS

CONSUMER NEWSPAPER OVER 600 LINES: CAMPAIGN

8 BRONZE
ART DIRECTOR:
Margaret Johnson
WRITER:
Sally Hogshead
PHOTOGRAPHER:
John Katz
CLIENT:
Body Alarm
AGENCY:
Fallon McElligott/ Minneapolis

SO SIMPLE, YOU CAN USE IT WITH ONE HAND TIED BEHIND YOUR BACK.

Most self-defense products require fancy moves or accurate aim. But just squeeze Body Alarm, and you'll send out a 130 decibel call for help.

BODY ALARM

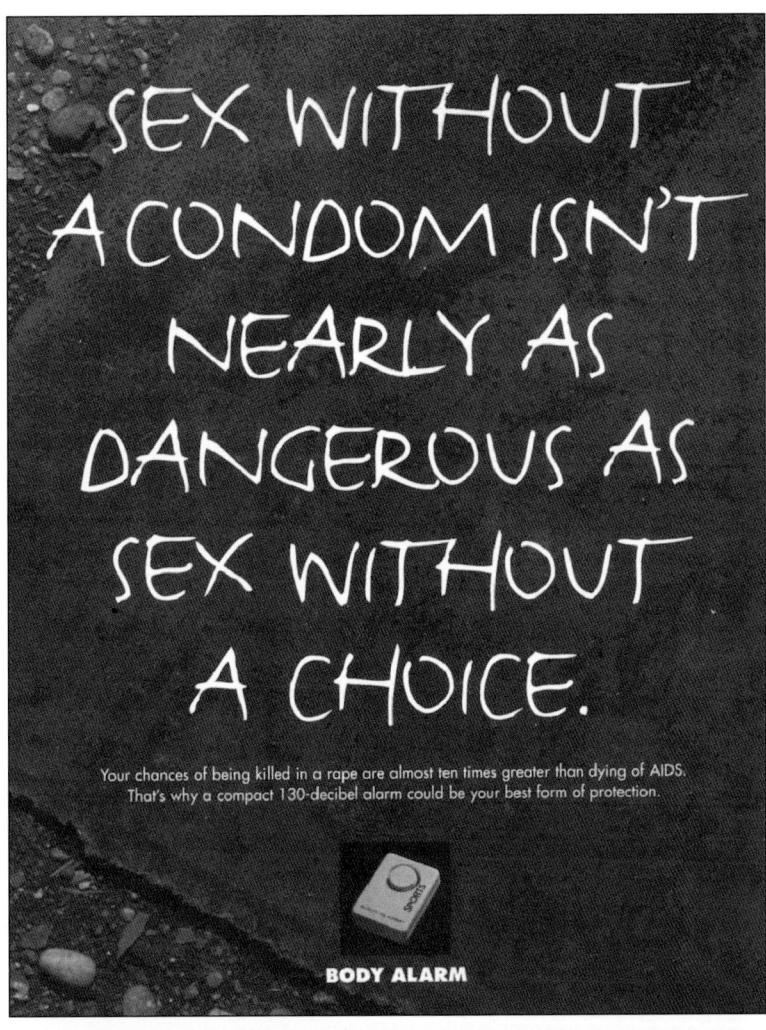

GOLD, SILVER & BRONZE
AWARDS

CONSUMER NEWSPAPER
600 LINES OR LESS:
SINGLE

9 SILVER
ART DIRECTOR:
Phillip Squier
WRITER:
Kim Porter
PHOTOGRAPHER:
Suzanne Opton
CLIENT:
Seattle Post-Intelligencer
AGENCY:
**Elgin Syferd/
DDB Needham, Seattle**

10 BRONZE
ART DIRECTOR:
Paul Hirsch
WRITER:
John Heinsma
PHOTOGRAPHER:
Gary Hush
CLIENT:
Dr. Martens
AGENCY:
Cole & Weber/Portland

for other entertainment possibilities: see "books," "movies" and "art" in the new what's happening. fridays.

9 Silver

Made to last for decades, or until graduation, whichever comes first.

Before you head back to school, pick up a pair of shoes built to last. Dr. Martens Hikers. With their beer-proof leather and pizza-resistant soles, you'll find there's no better shoe for the rigors of college life.

GOLD, SILVER & BRONZE AWARDS

CONSUMER NEWSPAPER
600 LINES OR LESS:
SINGLE

11 BRONZE
ART DIRECTOR:
Paul Hirsch
WRITER:
John Heinsma
PHOTOGRAPHER:
Lars Topelmann
CLIENT:
Dr. Martens
AGENCY:
Cole & Weber/Portland

CONSUMER NEWSPAPER
600 LINES OR LESS:
CAMPAIGN

12 SILVER
ART DIRECTOR:
Paul Hirsch
WRITER:
John Heinsma
PHOTOGRAPHERS:
Lars Topelmann
Gary Hush
CLIENT:
Dr. Martens
AGENCY:
Cole & Weber/Portland

11 Bronze

Fewer British mail carriers go berserk. It must be the shoes.

Spend a few too many days walking around in uncomfortable shoes and it can start to get to you. Perhaps that's why the standard issue shoe for British mail carriers is a pair of Dr. Martens Gibsons. A shoe legendary for its durability, cushioning and fit. After all, it's hard to get disgruntled when you have comfortable feet.

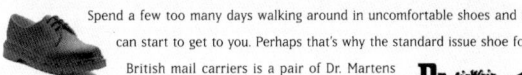

Another leaky, drafty British convertible.

Once again, the British bring us improved ventilation. This time, however, it's in a place you can appreciate it. Your feet. The Dr. Martens sandal. If you've ever owned an MG, you'll feel right at home.

Careful boy, you could hurt your teeth.

If your dog has a thing for chewing shoes, just toss him a pair of Dr. Martens classic 1460 boots. With their bullet-proof construction, practically indestructible soles and tough-as-nails leather, they should be all that's needed to make him break the habit. Along with a few teeth.

GOLD, SILVER & BRONZE AWARDS

CONSUMER NEWSPAPER
600 LINES OR LESS:
CAMPAIGN

13 BRONZE
ART DIRECTORS:
David Ayriss
Paul Hirsch
WRITERS:
John Heinsma
Mark Waggoner
PHOTOGRAPHER:
Gary Hush
CLIENT:
Dr. Martens
AGENCY:
Cole & Weber/Portland

The best shoes your parents' money can buy.

It's back-to-school time, and while you're out spending someone else's money, you might as well stock up on some decent shoes. After all, your parents worked hard for their money. Spend it wisely.

Guaranteed to make three out of four senior classmen think twice about kicking your butt.

Realizing that high school isn't nearly traumatic enough already, upper classmen have invented a multitude of ways to torture freshmen. We, on the other hand, invented the classic 1460 boot. It's tough. It's comfortable. And it looks great whether you're kicking and screaming or merely running away.

Made to last for decades, or until graduation, whichever comes first.

Before you head back to school, pick up a pair of shoes built to last. Dr. Martens Hikers. With their beer-proof leather and pizza-resistant soles, you'll find there's no better shoe for the rigors of college life.

GOLD, SILVER & BRONZE AWARDS

CONSUMER MAGAZINE
COLOR 1 PAGE OR
SPREAD: SINGLE

14 GOLD
ART DIRECTOR:
Steve Luker
WRITER:
Steve Simpson
PHOTOGRAPHERS:
Herb Ritts
Pete Seaward
CLIENT:
Norwegian Cruise Line
AGENCY:
Goodby Silverstein & Partners/San Francisco

15 SILVER
ART DIRECTOR:
Steve Luker
WRITER:
Steve Simpson
PHOTOGRAPHERS:
Herb Ritts
Pete Seaward
Doug Perrine
CLIENT:
Norwegian Cruise Line
AGENCY:
Goodby Silverstein & Partners/San Francisco

16 BRONZE
ART DIRECTOR:
Michael Mazza
WRITER:
Dave O'Hare
ILLUSTRATOR:
Alan Daniels
PHOTOGRAPHER:
Graham Westmoreland
CLIENT:
American Isuzu Motors
AGENCY:
Goodby Silverstein & Partners/San Francisco

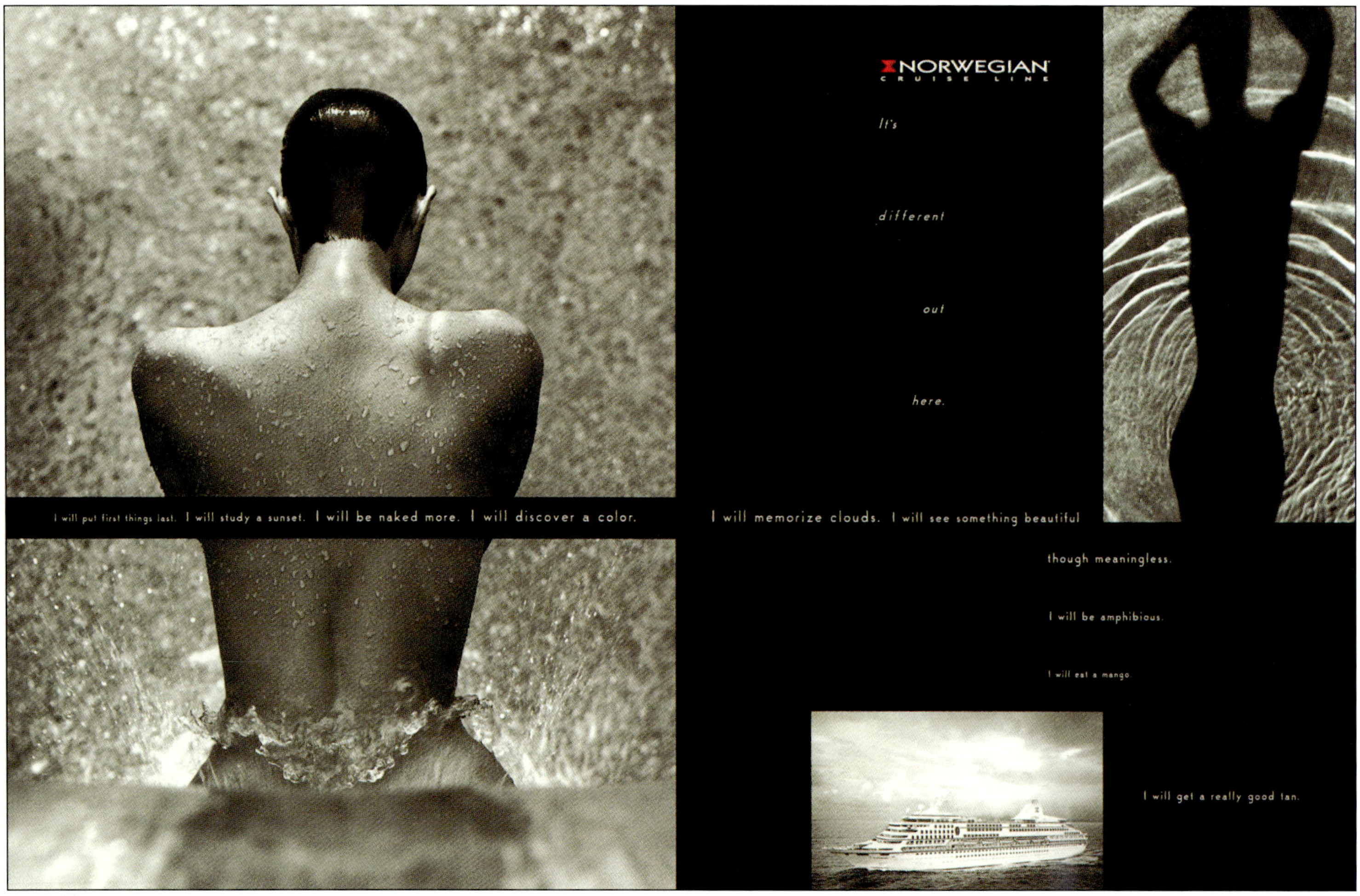

14 Gold

There is no law that says you
can't make love at 4 in the afternoon on a Tuesday
shall not study a sunset or train butterflies   must pay tax on itemized moments of pleasure
may not have extra mushrooms with your steak   can't disembark in Tortola and stay there
must pack worry along with your luggage   can't learn about life from a turtle
must contribute to the GNP every single solitary day of your life
absolutely must act your chronological age not your shoesize   shall maintain strict economies of emotion
can't make love again at 5 in the afternoon on the Tuesday we spoke of earlier
because the laws of the land do not apply the laws are different out here

It's

different

out

here.

NORWEGIAN CRUISE LINE

15 Silver

THE 19TH UNWRITTEN LAW OF DRIVING

THE SHORTEST DISTANCE BETWEEN TWO POINTS
IS ALWAYS UNDER CONSTRUCTION.

THE TROOPER'S REAR MULTI-LINK/COIL SUSPENSION CAN COMFORTABLY HANDLE ALMOST ANYTHING MOTHER NATURE, OR THE DEPT. OF HIGHWAYS, THROW YOUR WAY.

Short of investing heavily in road cone futures, the best way to benefit from the fact that our streets are in a constant state of "improvement," is to buy a Trooper. Besides its obvious height advantage, it possesses a remarkably rugged yet amazingly agile suspension, making for a comfortable, quiet, confident ride—no matter what type of road surface you find yourself coming across. Even a smooth one. Remember those? The Isuzu Trooper. Life's an adventure. Be prepared. (800) 726-2700

ISUZU Practically/Amazing

16 Bronze

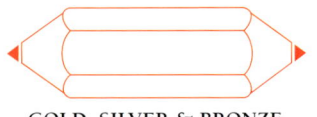

GOLD, SILVER & BRONZE AWARDS

CONSUMER MAGAZINE
COLOR 1 PAGE OR
SPREAD: CAMPAIGN

17 GOLD
ART DIRECTOR:
Steve Luker
WRITER:
Steve Simpson
PHOTOGRAPHERS:
Herb Ritts
Pete Seaward
Doug Perrine
Jim Erickson
CLIENT:
Norwegian Cruise Line
AGENCY:
Goodby Silverstein & Partners/San Francisco

There is no law that says you can't make love at 4 in the afternoon on a Tuesday shall not study a sunset or train butterflies   must pay tax on itemized moments of pleasure may not have extra mushrooms with your steak   can't disembark in Tortola and stay there must pack worry along with your luggage   **can't learn about life from a turtle** must contribute to the GNP every single solitary day of your life absolutely must act your chronological age not your shoesize   shall maintain strict economies of emotion can't make love again at 5 in the afternoon on the Tuesday we spoke of earlier **because the laws of the land do not apply** the laws are different out here

It's different out here.

✕ NORWEGIAN CRUISE LINE

✕ NORWEGIAN CRUISE LINE

It's different out here.

I will put first things last. I will study a sunset. I will be naked more. I will discover a color.   I will memorize clouds. I will see something beautiful though meaningless.

I will be amphibious.

I will eat a mango.

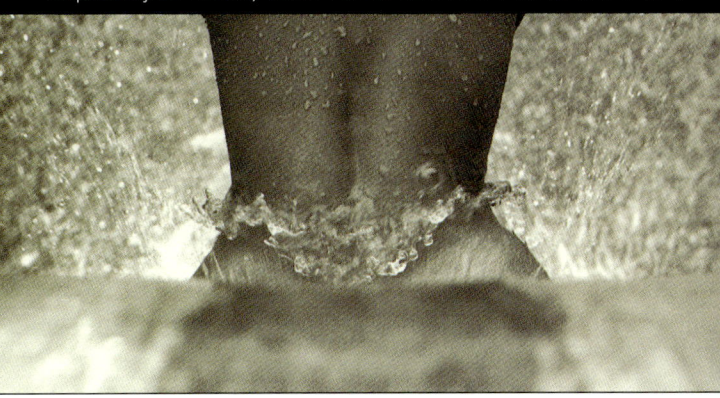

I will get a really good tan.

GOLD, SILVER & BRONZE AWARDS

CONSUMER MAGAZINE
COLOR 1 PAGE OR
SPREAD: CAMPAIGN

18 SILVER
ART DIRECTOR:
Craig Tanimoto
WRITER:
Eric Grunbaum
ILLUSTRATOR:
Charles Anderson Design
PHOTOGRAPHER:
Shawn Michienzi
CLIENT:
Nissan Motor Corporation
AGENCY:
Chiat/Day, Venice

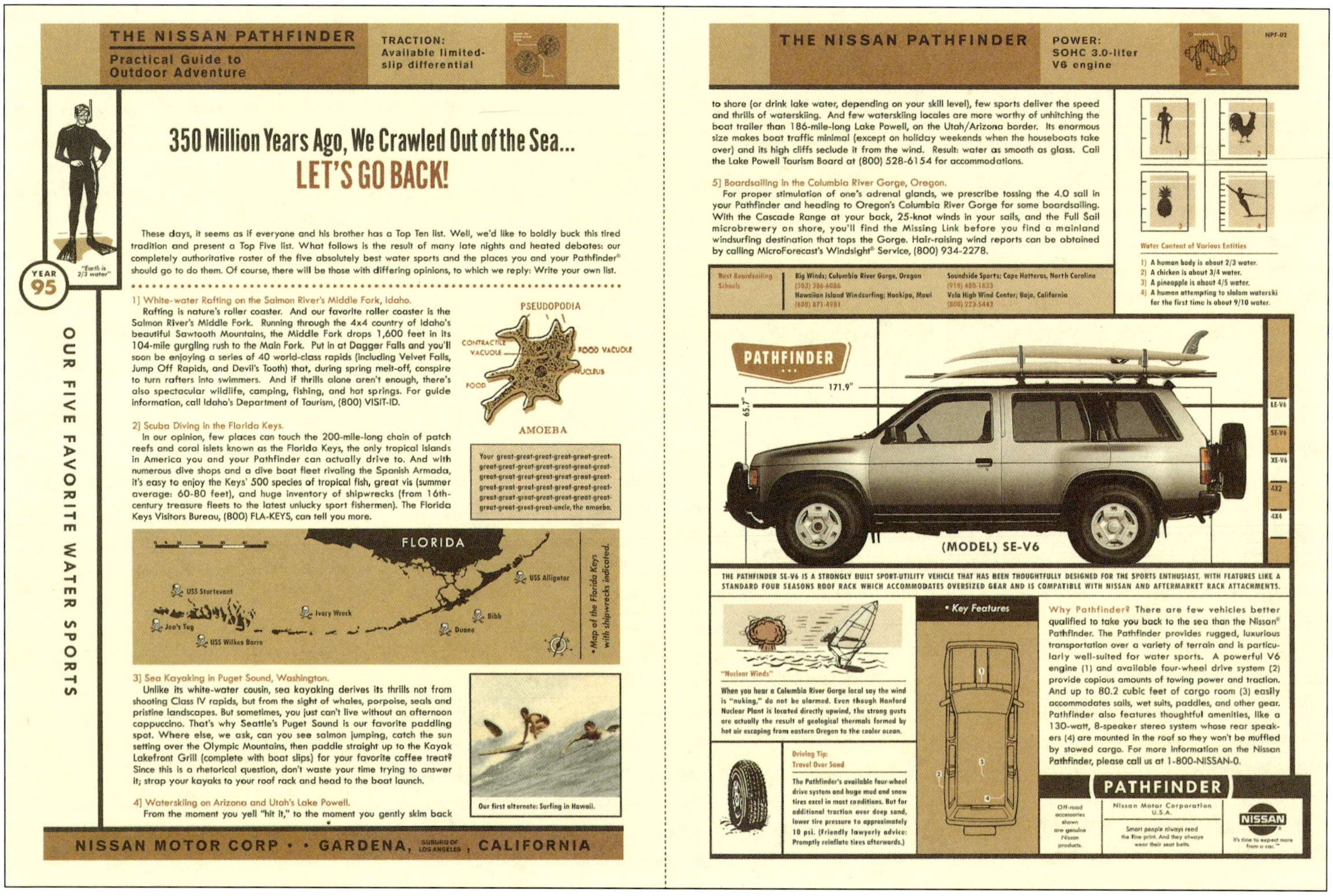

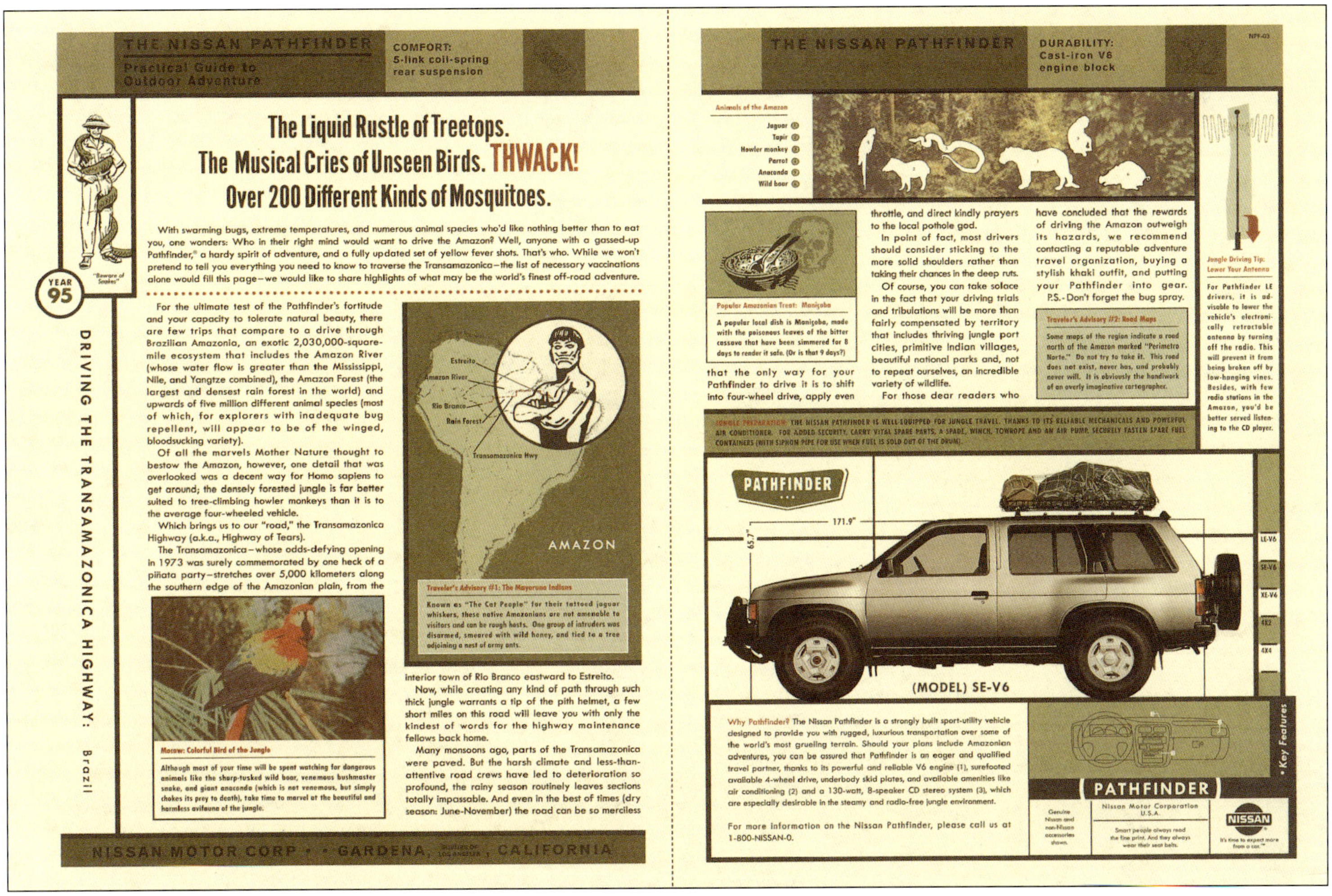
THE NISSAN PATHFINDER
Practical Guide to Outdoor Adventure
COMFORT: 5-link coil-spring rear suspension
"Beware of Snakes"
YEAR 95
DRIVING THE TRANSAMAZONICA HIGHWAY: Brazil
The Liquid Rustle of Treetops.
The Musical Cries of Unseen Birds. THWACK!
Over 200 Different Kinds of Mosquitoes.
With swarming bugs, extreme temperatures, and numerous animal species who'd like nothing better than to eat you, one wonders: Who in their right mind would want to drive the Amazon? Well, anyone with a gassed-up Pathfinder,® a hardy spirit of adventure, and a fully updated set of yellow fever shots. That's who. While we won't pretend to tell you everything you need to know to traverse the Transamazonica—the list of necessary vaccinations alone would fill this page—we would like to share highlights of what may be the world's finest off-road adventure.
For the ultimate test of the Pathfinder's fortitude and your capacity to tolerate natural beauty, there are few trips that compare to a drive through Brazilian Amazonia, an exotic 2,030,000-square-mile ecosystem that includes the Amazon River (whose water flow is greater than the Mississippi, Nile, and Yangtze combined), the Amazon Forest (the largest and densest rain forest in the world) and upwards of five million different animal species (most of which, for explorers with inadequate bug repellent, will appear to be of the winged, bloodsucking variety).
Of all the marvels Mother Nature thought to bestow the Amazon, however, one detail that was overlooked was a decent way for Homo sapiens to get around; the densely forested jungle is far better suited to tree-climbing howler monkeys than it is to the average four-wheeled vehicle.
Which brings us to our "road," the Transamazonica Highway (a.k.a., Highway of Tears).
The Transamazonica—whose odds-defying opening in 1973 was surely commemorated by one heck of a piñata party—stretches over 5,000 kilometers along the southern edge of the Amazonian plain, from the interior town of Rio Branco eastward to Estreito.
Now, while creating any kind of path through such thick jungle warrants a tip of the pith helmet, a few short miles on this road will leave you with only the kindest of words for the highway maintenance fellows back home.
Many monsoons ago, parts of the Transamazonica were paved. But the harsh climate and less-than-attentive road crews have led to deterioration so profound, the rainy season routinely leaves sections totally impassable. And even in the best of times (dry season: June-November) the road can be so merciless
Estreito
Amazon River
Rio Branco
Rain Forest
Transamazonica Hwy
AMAZON
Traveler's Advisory #1: The Mayoruna Indians
Known as "The Cat People" for their tattoed jaguar whiskers, these native Amazonians are not amenable to visitors and can be rough hosts. One group of intruders was disarmed, smeared with wild honey, and tied to a tree adjoining a nest of army ants.
Macaw: Colorful Bird of the Jungle
Although most of your time will be spent watching for dangerous animals like the sharp-tusked wild boar, venemous bushmaster snake, and giant anaconda (which is not venemous, but simply chokes its prey to death), take time to marvel at the beautiful and harmless avifauna of the jungle.
NISSAN MOTOR CORP • • GARDENA, SUBURB OF LOS ANGELES, CALIFORNIA
THE NISSAN PATHFINDER
DURABILITY: Cast-iron V6 engine block
NPF-03
Animals of the Amazon
Jaguar 1
Tapir 2
Howler monkey 3
Parrot 4
Anaconda 5
Wild boar 6
Popular Amazonian Treat: Maniçoba
A popular local dish is Maniçoba, made with the poisonous leaves of the bitter cassava that have been simmered for 8 days to render it safe. (Or is that 9 days?)
that the only way for your Pathfinder to drive it is to shift into four-wheel drive, apply even throttle, and direct kindly prayers to the local pothole god.
In point of fact, most drivers should consider sticking to the more solid shoulders rather than taking their chances in the deep ruts.
Of course, you can take solace in the fact that your driving trials and tribulations will be more than fairly compensated by territory that includes thriving jungle port cities, primitive Indian villages, beautiful national parks and, not to repeat ourselves, an incredible variety of wildlife.
For those dear readers who have concluded that the rewards of driving the Amazon outweigh its hazards, we recommend contacting a reputable adventure travel organization, buying a stylish khaki outfit, and putting your Pathfinder into gear.
P.S.-Don't forget the bug spray.
Traveler's Advisory #2: Road Maps
Some maps of the region indicate a road north of the Amazon marked "Perimetro Norte." Do not try to take it. This road does not exist, never has, and probably never will. It is obviously the handiwork of an overly imaginative cartographer.
Jungle Driving Tip: Lower Your Antenna
For Pathfinder LE drivers, it is advisable to lower the vehicle's electronically retractable antenna by turning off the radio. This will prevent it from being broken off by low-hanging vines. Besides, with few radio stations in the Amazon, you'd be better served listening to the CD player.
JUNGLE PREPARATION: THE NISSAN PATHFINDER IS WELL-EQUIPPED FOR JUNGLE TRAVEL, THANKS TO ITS RELIABLE MECHANICALS AND POWERFUL AIR CONDITIONER. FOR ADDED SECURITY, CARRY VITAL SPARE PARTS, A SPADE, WINCH, TOWROPE AND AN AIR PUMP. SECURELY FASTEN SPARE FUEL CONTAINERS (WITH SIPHON PIPE FOR USE WHEN FUEL IS SOLD OUT OF THE DRUM).
PATHFINDER
171.9"
65.7"
LE-V6
SE-V6
XE-V6
4X2
4X4
(MODEL) SE-V6
Why Pathfinder? The Nissan Pathfinder is a strongly built sport-utility vehicle designed to provide you with rugged, luxurious transportation over some of the world's most grueling terrain. Should your plans include Amazonian adventures, you can be assured that Pathfinder is an eager and qualified travel partner, thanks to its powerful and reliable V6 engine (1), surefooted available 4-wheel drive, underbody skid plates, and available amenities like air conditioning (2) and a 130-watt, 8-speaker CD stereo system (3), which are especially desirable in the steamy and radio-free jungle environment.
For more information on the Nissan Pathfinder, please call us at 1-800-NISSAN-0.
• Key Features
PATHFINDER
Genuine Nissan and non-Nissan accessories shown.
Nissan Motor Corporation U.S.A.
Smart people always read the fine print. And they always wear their seat belts.
NISSAN
It's time to expect more from a car.™

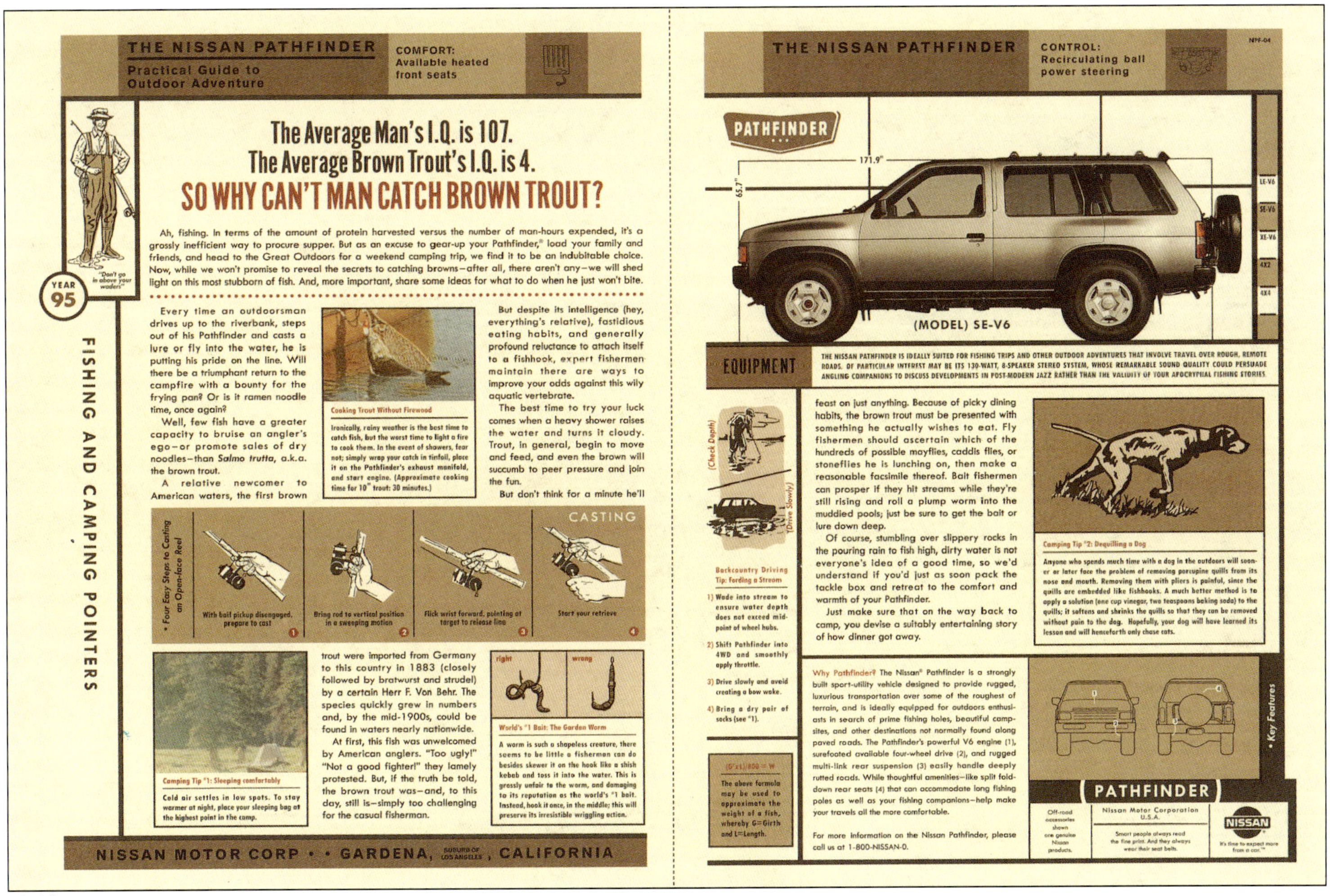
THE NISSAN PATHFINDER
Practical Guide to Outdoor Adventure
COMFORT: Available heated front seats
"Don't go in above your waders"
YEAR 95
FISHING AND CAMPING POINTERS
The Average Man's I.Q. is 107.
The Average Brown Trout's I.Q. is 4.
SO WHY CAN'T MAN CATCH BROWN TROUT?
Ah, fishing. In terms of the amount of protein harvested versus the number of man-hours expended, it's a grossly inefficient way to procure supper. But as an excuse to gear-up your Pathfinder,® load your family and friends, and head to the Great Outdoors for a weekend camping trip, we find it to be an indubitable choice. Now, while we won't promise to reveal the secrets to catching browns—after all, there aren't any—we will shed light on this most stubborn of fish. And, more important, share some ideas for what to do when he just won't bite.
Every time an outdoorsman drives up to the riverbank, steps out of his Pathfinder and casts a lure or fly into the water, he is putting his pride on the line. Will there be a triumphant return to the campfire with a bounty for the frying pan? Or is it ramen noodle time, once again?
Well, few fish have a greater capacity to bruise an angler's ego—or promote sales of dry noodles—than Salmo trutta, a.k.a. the brown trout.
A relative newcomer to American waters, the first brown trout were imported from Germany to this country in 1883 (closely followed by bratwurst and strudel) by a certain Herr F. Von Behr. The species quickly grew in numbers and, by the mid-1900s, could be found in waters nearly nationwide.
At first, this fish was unwelcomed by American anglers. "Too ugly!" "Not a good fighter!" they lamely protested. But, if the truth be told, the brown trout was—and, to this day, still is—simply too challenging for the casual fisherman.
Cooking Trout Without Firewood
Ironically, rainy weather is the best time to catch fish, but the worst time to light a fire to cook them. In the event of showers, fear not; simply wrap your catch in tinfoil, place it on the Pathfinder's exhaust manifold, and start engine. (Approximate cooking time for 10" trout: 30 minutes.)
But despite its intelligence (hey, everything's relative), fastidious eating habits, and generally profound reluctance to attach itself to a fishhook, expert fishermen maintain there are ways to improve your odds against this wily aquatic vertebrate.
The best time to try your luck comes when a heavy shower raises the water and turns it cloudy. Trout, in general, begin to move and feed, and even the brown will succumb to peer pressure and join the fun.
But don't think for a minute he'll feast on just anything. Because of picky dining habits, the brown trout must be presented with something he actually wishes to eat. Fly fishermen should ascertain which of the hundreds of possible mayflies, caddis flies, or stoneflies he is lunching on, then make a reasonable facsimile thereof. Bait fishermen can prosper if they hit streams while they're still rising and roll a plump worm into the muddied pools; just be sure to get the bait or lure down deep.
Of course, stumbling over slippery rocks in the pouring rain to fish high, dirty water is not everyone's idea of a good time, so we'd understand if you'd just as soon pack the tackle box and retreat to the comfort and warmth of your Pathfinder.
Just make sure that on the way back to camp, you devise a suitably entertaining story of how dinner got away.
• Four Easy Steps to Casting an Open-face Reel
CASTING
With bail pickup disengaged, prepare to cast 1
Bring rod to vertical position in a sweeping motion 2
Flick wrist forward, pointing at target to release line 3
Start your retrieve 4
Camping Tip #1: Sleeping comfortably
Cold air settles in low spots. To stay warmer at night, place your sleeping bag at the highest point in the camp.
right
wrong
World's #1 Bait: The Garden Worm
A worm is such a shapeless creature, there seems to be little a fisherman can do besides skewer it on the hook like a shish kebab and toss it into the water. This is grossly unfair to the worm, and damaging to its reputation as the world's #1 bait. Instead, hook it once, in the middle; this will preserve its irresistible wriggling action.
NISSAN MOTOR CORP • • GARDENA, SUBURB OF LOS ANGELES, CALIFORNIA
THE NISSAN PATHFINDER
CONTROL: Recirculating ball power steering
NPF-04
PATHFINDER
171.9"
65.7"
LE-V6
SE-V6
XE-V6
4X2
4X4
(MODEL) SE-V6
EQUIPMENT
THE NISSAN PATHFINDER IS IDEALLY SUITED FOR FISHING TRIPS AND OTHER OUTDOOR ADVENTURES THAT INVOLVE TRAVEL OVER ROUGH, REMOTE ROADS. OF PARTICULAR INTEREST MAY BE ITS 130-WATT, 8-SPEAKER STEREO SYSTEM, WHOSE REMARKABLE SOUND QUALITY COULD PERSUADE ANGLING COMPANIONS TO DISCUSS DEVELOPMENTS IN POST-MODERN JAZZ RATHER THAN THE VALIDITY OF YOUR APOCRYPHAL FISHING STORIES
(Check Depth)
(Drive Slowly)
Backcountry Driving Tip: Fording a Stream
1) Wade into stream to ensure water depth does not exceed midpoint of wheel hubs.
2) Shift Pathfinder into 4WD and smoothly apply throttle.
3) Drive slowly and avoid creating a bow wake.
4) Bring a dry pair of socks (see #1).
Camping Tip #2: Dequilling a Dog
Anyone who spends much time with a dog in the outdoors will sooner or later face the problem of removing porcupine quills from its nose and mouth. Removing them with pliers is painful, since the quills are embedded like fishhooks. A much better method is to apply a solution (one cup vinegar, two teaspoons baking soda) to the quills; it softens and shrinks the quills so that they can be removed without pain to the dog. Hopefully, your dog will have learned its lesson and will henceforth only chase cats.
(G²xL)/800 = W
The above formula may be used to approximate the weight of a fish, whereby G=Girth and L=Length.
Why Pathfinder? The Nissan® Pathfinder is a strongly built sport-utility vehicle designed to provide rugged, luxurious transportation over some of the roughest of terrain, and is ideally equipped for outdoors enthusiasts in search of prime fishing holes, beautiful campsites, and other destinations not normally found along paved roads. The Pathfinder's powerful V6 engine (1), surefooted available four-wheel drive (2), and rugged multi-link rear suspension (3) easily handle deeply rutted roads. While thoughtful amenities—like split fold-down rear seats (4) that can accommodate long fishing poles as well as your fishing companions—help make your travels all the more comfortable.
For more information on the Nissan Pathfinder, please call us at 1-800-NISSAN-0.
• Key Features
PATHFINDER
Off-road accessories shown are genuine Nissan products.
Nissan Motor Corporation U.S.A.
Smart people always read the fine print. And they always wear their seat belts.
NISSAN
It's time to expect more from a car.™

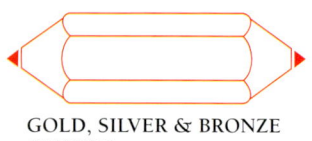

GOLD, SILVER & BRONZE AWARDS

CONSUMER MAGAZINE
COLOR 1 PAGE OR
SPREAD: CAMPAIGN

19 SILVER
ART DIRECTOR:
Michael Mazza
WRITER:
Dave O'Hare
ILLUSTRATOR:
Alan Daniels
PHOTOGRAPHER:
Graham Westmoreland
CLIENT:
American Isuzu Motors
AGENCY:
Goodby Silverstein & Partners/San Francisco

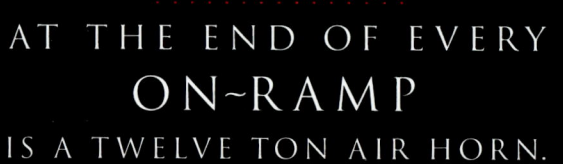

THE 19TH UNWRITTEN LAW OF DRIVING

THE SHORTEST DISTANCE
BETWEEN TWO POINTS
IS ALWAYS UNDER CONSTRUCTION.

THE TROOPER'S REAR MULTI-LINK/COIL SUSPENSION CAN COMFORTABLY HANDLE ALMOST ANYTHING MOTHER NATURE, OR THE DEPT. OF HIGHWAYS, THROW YOUR WAY.

Short of investing heavily in road cone futures, the best way to benefit from the fact that our streets are in a constant state of "improvement," is to buy a Trooper. Besides its obvious height advantage, it possesses a remarkably rugged yet amazingly agile suspension, making for a comfortable, quiet, confident ride—no matter what type of road surface you find yourself coming across. Even a smooth one. Remember those? The Isuzu Trooper. Life's an adventure. Be prepared. (800) 726-2700

ISUZU
Practically/*Amazing*

THE 10TH UNWRITTEN LAW OF DRIVING

THE GUY WHO SETS TIMERS
ON STOPLIGHTS
HAS A SICK SENSE OF HUMOR.

YOU ARE DRIVING ALONG WHEN SUDDENLY YOU ARE REMINDED THAT THE TROOPER COMES WITH 4-WHEEL ANTI-LOCK BRAKES.

Perhaps it's a deep-seated need for attention. Or maybe he's just got a thing for taillights. Whatever the reason, the Trooper comes with power assisted, four-wheel, ventilated disc, anti-lock brakes.* In fact, it is the only sport utility to come standard with such a confident level of stopping power. Don't worry if you don't remember this. Count on Mr. Stop-And-Go to refresh your memory. The Isuzu Trooper. Life's an adventure. Be prepared. (800) 726-2700

ISUZU
Practically/*Amazing*

19 Silver

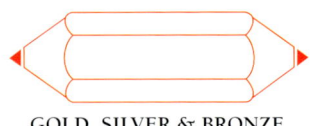

GOLD, SILVER & BRONZE
AWARDS

CONSUMER MAGAZINE
COLOR 1 PAGE OR
SPREAD: CAMPAIGN

20 BRONZE
ART DIRECTOR:
John Doyle
WRITER:
Ernie Schenck
ILLUSTRATOR:
Peter Hall
PHOTOGRAPHERS:
**Sigurgeir Sigurjonsson
Jamey Stillings
Pall Stefansson
Hashi
Geoffrey Stein**
CLIENT:
Akva Spring Water
AGENCY:
**Berlin Cameron
Doyle/New York**

We're told an oasis is a place in the desert where water springs from the earth in abundance. Odd, we don't see any palm trees.

It could not be any more desolate if it were but a frozen boulder adrift in the asteroid belt. It is as barren a stretch of snow and ice as any in this or any other universe. In the winter, the nights are of a cold so intense it immobilizes both thought and flesh. It is a clean cold. A cleansing, purifying cold. A cold that reaches down into the farthest extremities of this wondrous outpost of environmental sanity the Vikings called Iceland. What more fitting place, then, for what may well be the planet's last great reservoir of water in its purest and most undefiled form. In Iceland, we call it Akva.

And there is, in the collective opinion of the people who live here, not another spring water on earth that is quite like it. Untainted. Untouched. Unspoiled. The natural bounty of a country lying happily on the rim of civilization, Akva comes from a place so deep we can only begin to imagine what it must be like there. Untold miles below the glaciers and snowfields, the eternal strata of hardened lava, through which it must travel on an unimaginable 14,000 year journey to the surface.

Fourteen millennia in which to shed itself of sodium and other impurities of every description. Fourteen millennia to work its way through a dizzying maze of cracks and crevices, fourteen millennium of constantly being scrubbed and scraped and cleansed all the way down to its most fundamental elemental molecular structure.

The result of which is a water that is breathtakingly pristine. An ambrosia of primordial origins. A water that's as clear as the Arctic stars on a coal black Icelandic night.

And, as we shouldn't need to tell you, so very cold. We wouldn't have it any other way.

The taste of Akva, as you may be starting to get the impression, is quite unlike any other. Indeed, it has a surprisingly soft quality about it. Delicate, even. One which you will find to be deeply refreshing and quite remarkably bereft of imperfections.

Perhaps you might consider visiting us here in Iceland, in which case may we extend our warmest invitation to sample some Akva for yourself. Of course, it's equally as simple to try our spring water simply by paying a visit to your favorite corner store or delicatessen. (Ask for it by name, if you're having trouble finding it.) We do hope you'll pour yourself a glass of Akva soon and taste for yourself what can happen when a spring water comes from a country known for its glaciers and its ice caverns. If not for its camels.

Akva spring water. The pure soul of Iceland.

Just thinking about how pure our water is sends chills down our spines. (Granted, being within a whisper of the Arctic Circle might have something to do with it.)

When your country lies within a mere thousand miles of the North Pole, life is no ordinary thing. The Northern Lights dance in the polar darkness like a thousand shimmering ribbons. The stars flashing like a billion shards of glass. Your breath all but freezes in the morning air. The sun, what little there is of it, hangs in the winter sky like a ball of ice. A frozen circle of silver fire. And the water, how do we begin to tell you about it?

That it comes from a place buried deep within some impossibly cold subterranean reservoir, untold fathoms beneath our glaciers? That it is the natural bounty of a country that is blessedly isolated, mercifully cut off from civilization by thousands upon thousands of miles of raging ocean? For Iceland, you see, is a most extraordinary place. And the water that comes from here is unlike any other on this, and very possibly any other, planet in the known universe. We have a word for it. Akva. And yet to describe it. Ah, now that is no easy thing. It is, we can tell you, of a remarkable clarity. The word diamond tends to come to mind. There is a purity that borders on the virginal. And the taste. We must tell you all about the taste. But, of course, we're getting ahead of ourselves.

Did we mention that our spring water is the final result of a 14,000 year process of geophysical purification? A natural, if somewhat painfully slow, filtration system in which endless layers of ice, rock, and petrified lava slowly strip away one impurity after the other. Until the purest water known to humankind finally forces its way to the surface well in excess of a thousand centuries later. Untouched. Untainted. Unspoiled by contaminants of any sort.

We would expect that once you've tried a bottle of our spring water for yourself, of course, you will be every bit as taken with its crisp, fresh, Arctic pure taste as those of us here in Iceland who have enjoyed it for centuries. What you will discover, we don't mind telling you, is a spring water that is crisp. Refreshing. Free of sodium. Free of impurities of every description.

In brief, you are going to love Akva as you have not loved any spring water you have ever experienced. So much so, we fervently believe, that once you have tried it, it's most unlikely you will ever again feel compelled to drink any other. And to think you won't even have to visit us here in Iceland to find a bottle. Because Akva is now available at your favorite corner market or deli. Of course, you'll want to ask for it by name, if you're having trouble finding it. A single sip and you will feel like you're on top of the world. Then again, considering where it comes from, what else could you expect?

Akva spring water. The pure soul of Iceland.

GOLD, SILVER & BRONZE
AWARDS

CONSUMER MAGAZINE
LESS THAN A PAGE
B/W OR COLOR: SINGLE

21 SILVER
ART DIRECTOR:
Jim Mountjoy
WRITER:
Ed Jones
CLIENT:
**North Carolina
Travel & Tourism**
AGENCY:
**Loeffler Ketchum
Mountjoy/Charlotte**

CONSUMER MAGAZINE
LESS THAN A PAGE
B/W OR COLOR:
CAMPAIGN

22 GOLD
ART DIRECTOR:
Jim Mountjoy
WRITER:
Ed Jones
CLIENT:
**North Carolina
Travel & Tourism**
AGENCY:
**Loeffler Ketchum
Mountjoy/Charlotte**

Nobody will ever know it wasn't the water that made your pants wet.

WHITEWATER IN
NORTH CAROLINA.
1-800-VISIT-NC

21 Silver

Nobody will ever know it wasn't the water that made your pants wet.

WHITEWATER IN
NORTH CAROLINA.
1-800-VISIT-NC

Row, Row, Row your boat pathetically whimpering like a little weenie down the stream.

WHITEWATER IN
NORTH CAROLINA.
1-800-VISIT-NC

Getting on. Repeatedly screaming out the name of the Supreme Being. Then, weak-kneed, getting off. Kinda like sex, huh?

WHITEWATER IN
NORTH CAROLINA.
1-800-VISIT-NC

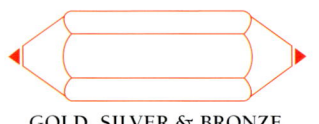

GOLD, SILVER & BRONZE AWARDS

OUTDOOR: SINGLE

23 GOLD
ART DIRECTOR:
Kurt Reifschneider
ILLUSTRATOR:
Bradford Bottonus
CLIENT:
Pacific Science Center
AGENCY:
CF2GS/Seattle

24 SILVER
ART DIRECTORS:
Lara Gilmore
Steve Miller
WRITER:
Paul Spencer
PHOTOGRAPHER:
Howard Berman
CLIENT:
New York State Lottery
AGENCY:
DDB Needham Worldwide/New York

23 Gold

GOLD, SILVER & BRONZE AWARDS

OUTDOOR: SINGLE

25 SILVER
ART DIRECTOR:
Sean Ehringer
WRITER:
Harry Cocciolo
PHOTOGRAPHER:
Dan Escobar
CLIENT:
California Fluid Milk Processor Advisory Board
AGENCY:
Goodby Silverstein & Partners/San Francisco

26 BRONZE
ART DIRECTOR:
Paul Briginshaw
WRITER:
Malcolm Duffy
TYPOGRAPHER:
Joe Hoza
CLIENT:
The Economist
AGENCY:
Abbott Mead Vickers. BBDO/London

25 Silver

26 Bronze

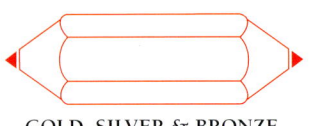

GOLD, SILVER & BRONZE AWARDS

OUTDOOR: CAMPAIGN

27 BRONZE
ART DIRECTOR:
Dante Lombardi
WRITERS:
Paul Venables
Neil Leinwohl
CLIENT:
Comedy Central
AGENCY:
Korey Kay & Partners/ New York

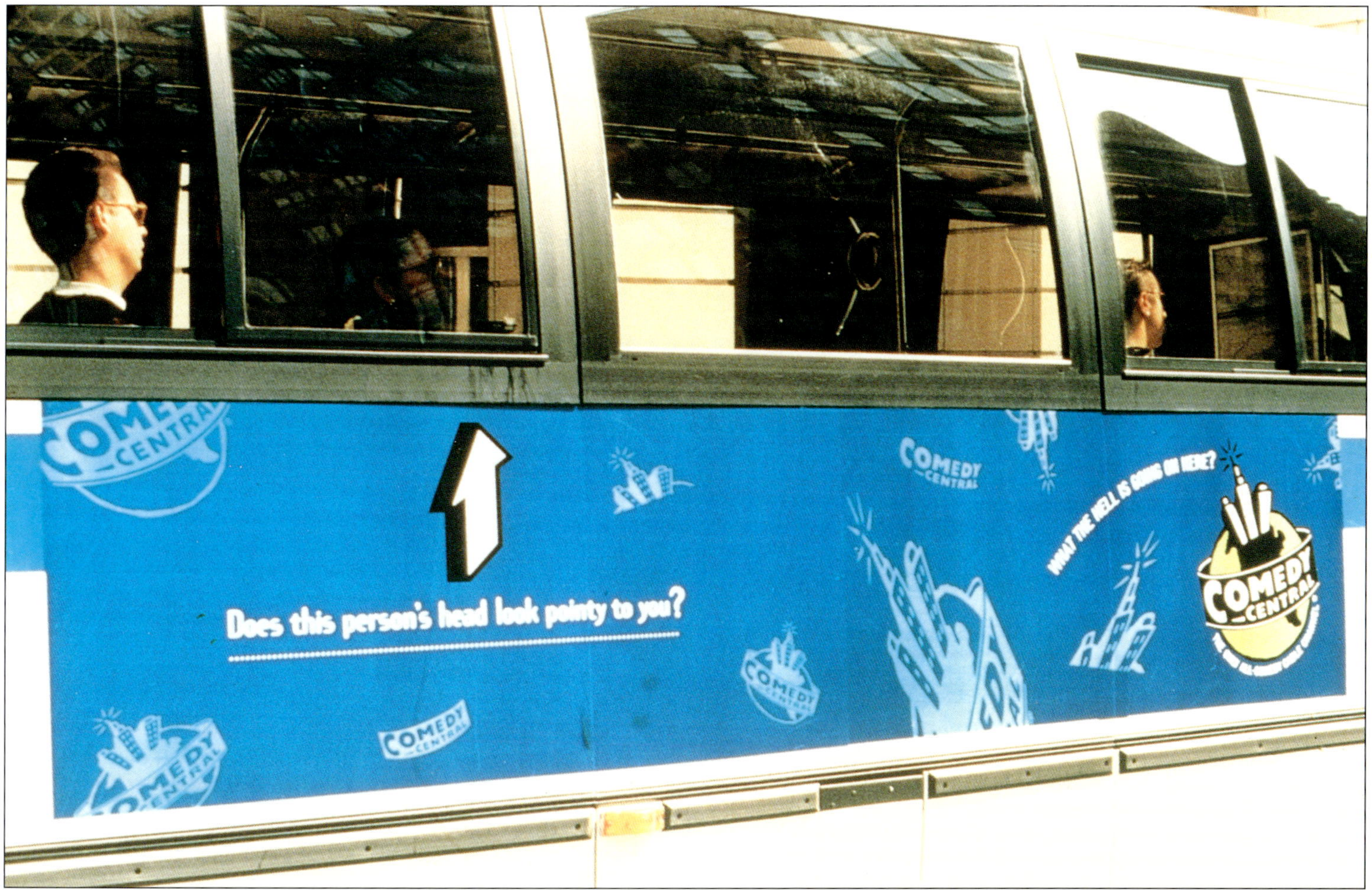
Does this person's head look pointy to you?
WHAT THE HELL IS GOING ON HERE?
COMEDY CENTRAL

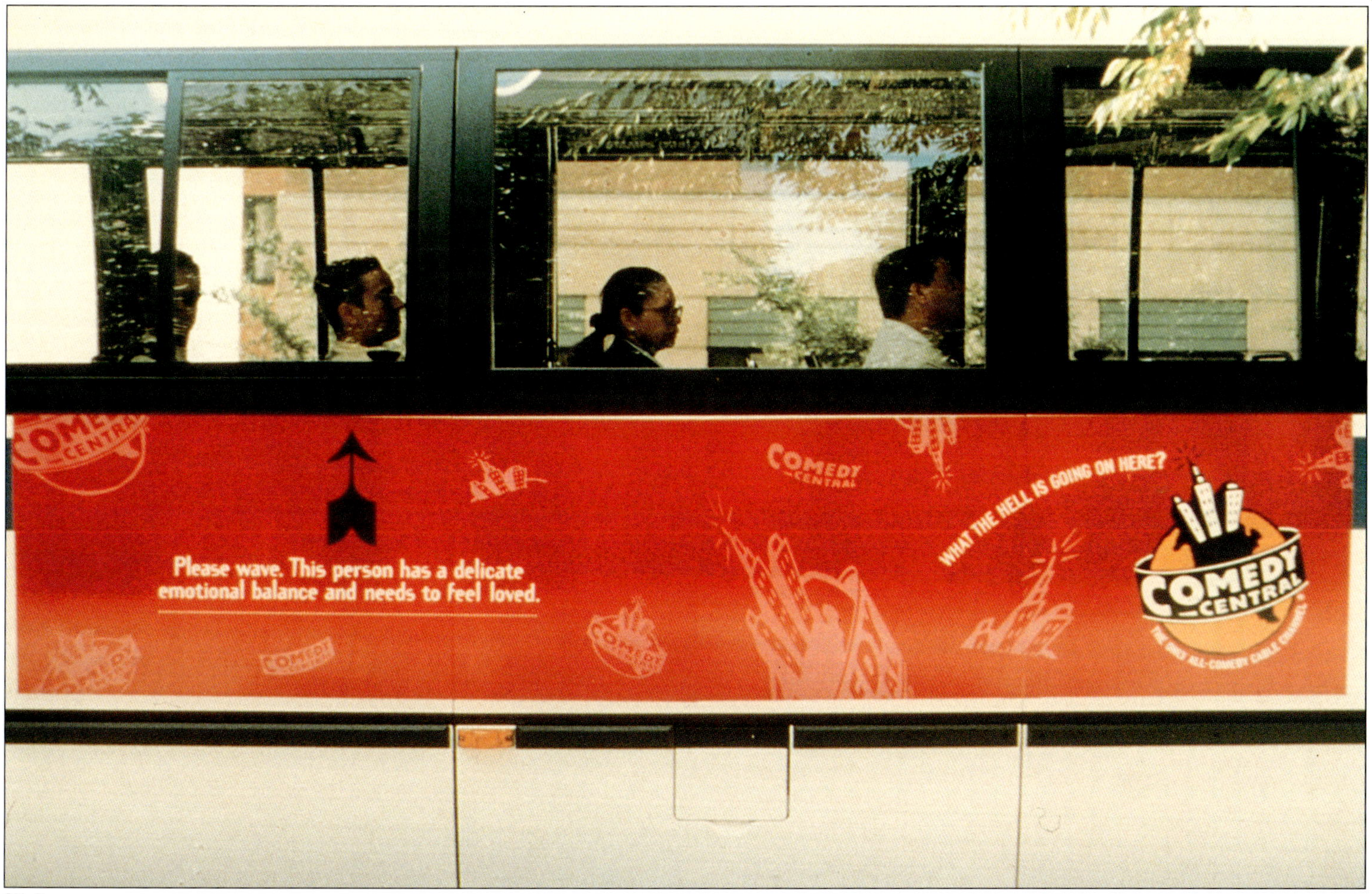
Please wave. This person has a delicate
emotional balance and needs to feel loved.
WHAT THE HELL IS GOING ON HERE?
COMEDY CENTRAL
THE ONLY ALL-COMEDY CABLE CHANNEL

GOLD, SILVER & BRONZE AWARDS

**TRADE
B/W 1 PAGE OR SPREAD: SINGLE**

28 SILVER
ART DIRECTOR:
Henriette Lienke
WRITER:
Tom Miller
PHOTOGRAPHER:
Steve Hellerstein
CLIENT:
Crain's New York Business
AGENCY:
Goldsmith/Jeffrey, New York

**TRADE
COLOR 1 PAGE OR SPREAD: SINGLE**

29 SILVER
ART DIRECTOR:
Joe Paprocki
WRITER:
Luke Sullivan
CLIENT:
Family Life
AGENCY:
Fallon McElligott/ Minneapolis

**TRADE
LESS THAN A PAGE
B/W OR COLOR: SINGLE**

30 SILVER
ART DIRECTOR:
Robert Hamilton
WRITER:
Bob Shiffrar
CLIENT:
Pagano Schenck & Kay
AGENCY:
Pagano Schenck & Kay/ Boston

28 Silver

Life is short. Childhood is shorter.

The years from age 3 to 12 go by so fast. Only one magazine helps parents make the most of them.

WANTED: ONE BRAIN WITH THE BACKBONE STILL ATTACHED.

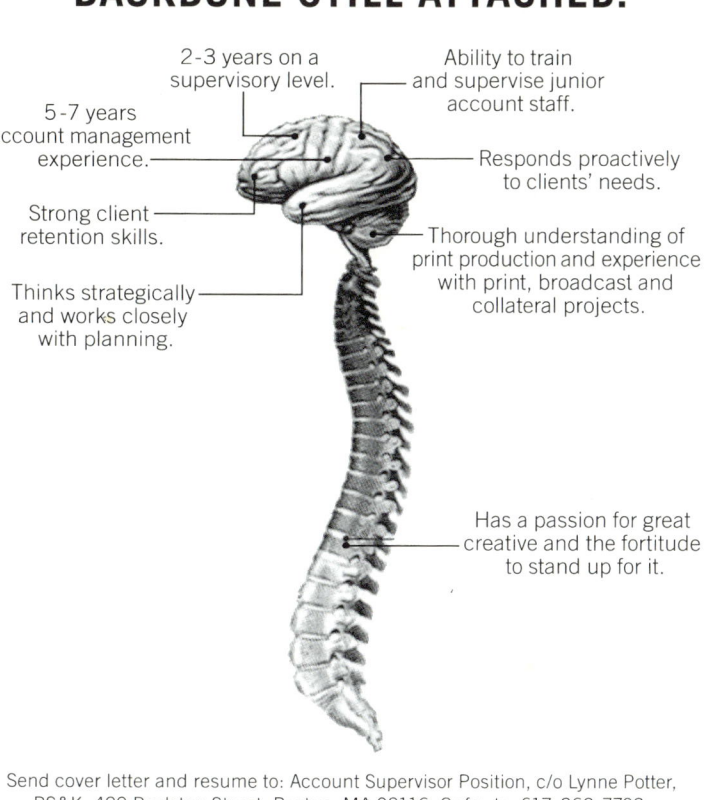

- 5-7 years account management experience.
- 2-3 years on a supervisory level.
- Ability to train and supervise junior account staff.
- Strong client retention skills.
- Responds proactively to clients' needs.
- Thinks strategically and works closely with planning.
- Thorough understanding of print production and experience with print, broadcast and collateral projects.
- Has a passion for great creative and the fortitude to stand up for it.

Send cover letter and resume to: Account Supervisor Position, c/o Lynne Potter, PS&K, 420 Boylston Street, Boston, MA 02116. Or fax to: 617-262-7703.

PAGANO SCHENCK & KAY

GOLD, SILVER & BRONZE AWARDS

TRADE ANY SIZE B/W OR COLOR: CAMPAIGN

31 GOLD
ART DIRECTOR:
Henriette Lienke
WRITER:
Tom Miller
PHOTOGRAPHER:
Steve Hellerstein
CLIENT:
Crain's New York Business
AGENCY:
Goldsmith/Jeffrey, New York

Recent surveys indicate that the majority of New York burglars prefer Crain's subscribers by a margin of 10 to 1.

With readers reporting an average household income of $245,000, that's not surprising.

CRAIN'S NEW YORK BUSINESS
To advertise, call (212) 210-0259.

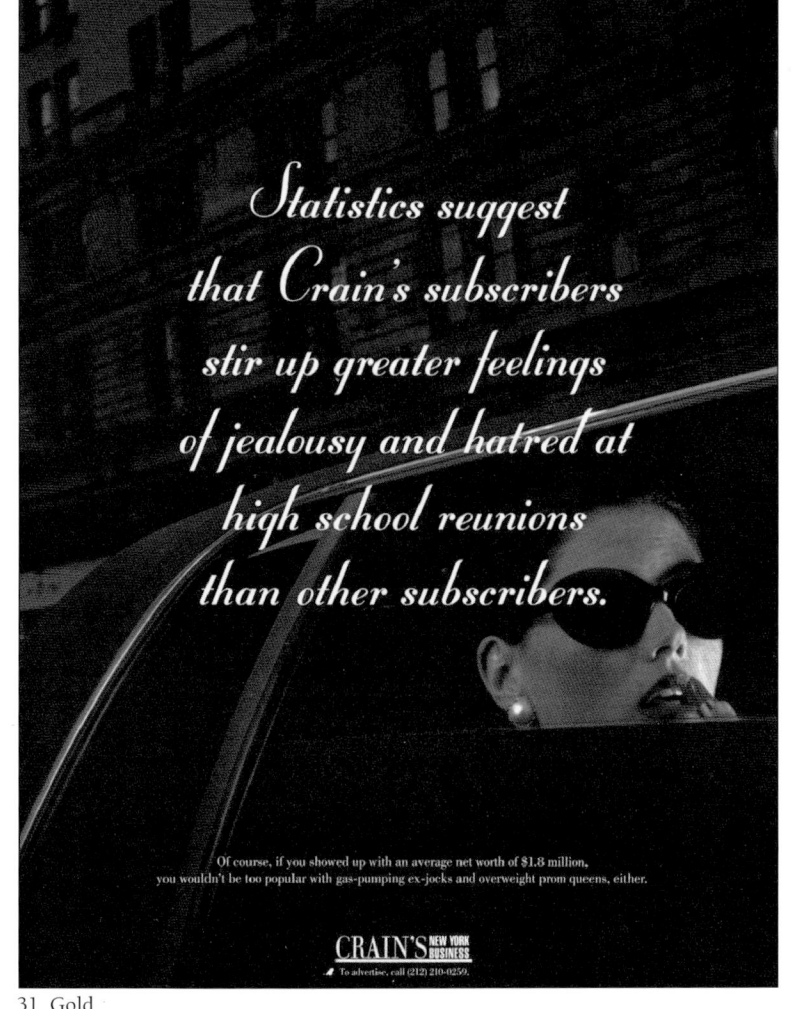

GOLD, SILVER & BRONZE AWARDS

TRADE ANY SIZE B/W OR COLOR: CAMPAIGN

32 SILVER
ART DIRECTOR:
Bob Barrie
WRITER:
Dean Buckhorn
PHOTOGRAPHERS:
David Burnett
Mark Shaw
Alon Reininger
CLIENT:
Time Magazine
AGENCY:
Fallon McElligott/ Minneapolis

It was centuries of hatred.

It was years of bloodshed.

It was less than a minute on the evening news.

Understanding comes with TIME.

In an era of tabloid journalism,
we believe the truth to be
sensational enough.

Understanding comes with TIME.

Two sides to the story.
Two compelling arguments.
Too bad TV news doesn't
have time to explain.

Understanding comes with TIME.

GOLD, SILVER & BRONZE
AWARDS

TRADE ANY SIZE
B/W OR COLOR:
CAMPAIGN

33 BRONZE
ART DIRECTOR:
Steve Mitchell
WRITER:
Doug Adkins
CLIENT:
Dublin Productions
AGENCY:
Hunt Murray/Minneapolis

THE RECIPROCAL ACTION OF THE OPTIC THALAMUS AND THE CEREBRAL CORTEX IN STIMULATING AN EMOTIONAL RESPONSE

or

HOW TO GET A LAUGH.

The elusive laugh. It is common knowledge that the elicitation of this autogenous response involves complex neural activity originating in the thalamus and progressing to the autonomic nervous system *(See Figure 1)*. But through years of intensive research,

Jarl Olsen   Rick Dublin   Jerry Pope

The three stooges could have learned much from these, the pioneers of mirth. Their meticulous, indefatigable research has revolutionized the science of laughter. Plus they can make that really neat fart sound with their armpits.

the directors at Dublin Productions have developed a less simplistic look at the science of evoking spleen-wrenching laughter.

Fig. A

THE ANATOMY OF A JOKE

Question: Why did the chicken cross the road?
Answer: To get to the other side.

The emotional and physical response you are now experiencing is both overwhelming and undeniable. Yet from whence comes this autoneural explosion? The chicken, in its introrse, Piaget-esque existential conundrum, considers the pathway before which it lies. The absurdity which follows creates a reciprocal action in the optic thalamus which in turn excites the internal idio-muscular sense organs and is subsequently externalized; hence, hilarity ensues. (Or, more precisely: $H = <chicken> / xr \wedge 3i - 4y$ (asphalt + Winnebago ÷ roadkill) (wacky factor) $= 1$, according to the Theory of Hilaritivity developed in conjunction with the infamous Chicken Baron of Liechtenstein, A.K.A. "The Chicken Dude.")

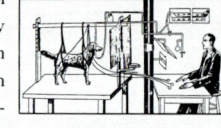

Fig. Q3-14y (Doggy)

Fig. 14u-4 xr-3i

THE DUBLIN CANUS LUPUS EXPERIMENTS

And yet, is this need for mirth unique to humankind? Perhaps no study has shed more light on animal laughter than the now famous Dublin Canus Lupus experiments *(See Figure Q3-14Y)*. Thanks to a multi-million dollar grant from the federal government, we can now say with absolute certainty that dogs are incapable of laughter. Could the same be true of goats, ducks, squid, llamas and the South American yellow-bellied mastodon? Only time, and your valuable tax dollars, will tell.

MEASURING LAUGHTER

Precise laughter measurements can be obtained only through use of the Galvanic skin reflex as related to overt emotional expression. Not surprisingly, the highest Galvanic measurement ever obtained (473,000 GV's) occurred during a 1964 experiment in which researchers measured the systolic pressure increases of subjects viewing a Jerry Lewis film marathon (unsubstantiated reports of 500,000 GV's have been claimed by researchers viewing episodes of "Sinbad").

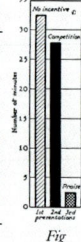

Fig Newton

If you'd like to be the first on your block to surpass the 500,000 GV laugh barrier, call 612-332-8864 for a copy of our reel. And always remember: laughter is a privilege, not a right. If you do not laugh at the appropriate moments during our reel, you will never laugh again.

DUBLIN
PRODUCTIONS

THE ART OF SARCASM
or
WHAT YOU, THE WORLD'S GREATEST LIVING COMIC GENIUS, ALREADY KNOW.

Sarcasm is, without a doubt, the simplest, most accessible form of humor. Indeed, anyone can master this elementary art with but a few moments of instruction. In fact, studies indicate that monkeys often exhibit primitive, yet surprisingly insightful forms of sarcasm before the age of two. Some have even been given their own television sitcoms.

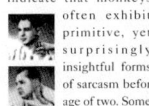
The sarcasm glands regulate the flow of humor to the brain.

Jarl, he of the petite eyebrows and winning smile, is admired by men and adored by women. Rick, a veritable temple of honesty, pours over bids to eliminate every unnecessary nickel. Jerry's habit of dressing up as the Queen of England makes him a wonderful role model for children.

If you thought that the preceding paragraph was not an example of sarcasm, we commend you on your vast intellectual powers. You need not read on for further instruction.

O MELODIOUS DUCK

Consider for a moment the noble duck. This glorious, majestic beast of gossamer wing and singularly angelic voice has inspired many a poet to compose works of mythic proportions. In the words of Wordsworth: "Verily, God did breathe and there was Duck." This example of candid, unexaggerated praise is known as the "Duck Factor" among sarcasmologists. Words spoken without a hint of sarcastic intent, such as everything that you're reading here, have a Duck Factor rating of 1. Sarcasm measuring a DF of more than 100 has been known to sear flesh and melt eyeballs. Obviously, extreme caution is in order when sarcasonating. A true master of sarcasm never uses his art without just provocation.

A state-of-the-art, fully digital, virtual-reality, TFX surround-sound MACH IV sarcasm emulator.

A ricocheting, mesmerizing, comically significant graph.

SARCASMIC GLANDULAR DYSFUNCTION

Sadly, not everyone is born with sarcasm glands. And still others have glands that just never fully developed due to lack of essential sarcasmic stimuli. Fortunately, we've developed a system to assist the sarcastically challenged. To delineate the sarcastic phrase, use quotations. For example: Gosh, you are certainly looking "magnificently Godlike" this morning, Rick. Alternatively, you may follow the sarcastic locution with a ⓢ. For example: I say, Jarl, your slightly upturned chin lends a sassy air to any room.ⓢ

MY, YOU'RE A FAST READER

As much as we enjoy sarcasm, it has no place in an advertisement's call to action. So please call us at 612-332-8864, or simply send your television boards to us. And when we tell you that we are positively entranced and enraptured by your concept and that it's the purest form of inspired genius we have ever witnessed, you can trust that here at Dublin, we speak only the truth.

Sarcasm can be seen resonating smartly from the skull with the use of a sarcasonometer.

DUBLIN PRODUCTIONS

DEATH, MUTILATION, TORTURE
and other
HUMOROUS DIVERSIONS.

A small, frail woman shuffles slowly across a street. She spies a nickel at her feet. Thinking of the medicine she can now afford to buy for her ailing son Joey, she reaches a shaking hand toward her find. She is instantly struck and killed by a speeding manure truck.

Skulls are physically unable to frown.

To the uninitiated few, this quaint little anecdote is simply not funny (small, frail women in particular seem to find this somewhat less than amusing). But to those skilled in the art of dark humor, few things are more hilarious than random, meaningless death.

Jarl Olsen   Rick Dublin   Jerry Pope
Jarl and Jerry, always the wacky pranksters, enjoy a laugh at Rick's expense (local paramedics would later join in the mirth).

THE DARK AGES: OOH LA LA

The origins of dark humor can be traced to that delightful historic period affectionately known as The Dark Ages. A time when millions died in the most shockingly gruesome, uproariously funny ways. Tragically, modern medicine has stripped us of much of this Faustian comicality. But you can relive this age of levity by instituting the following mirth-provocational experiment: First, drug your best friend so that he slips into a deep, albeit temporary, coma. Then simply place him into a coffin and bury him, deep in the earth. Two days later, after you have exhumed said friend, the two of you will be beside yourselves with laughter.[1]

A fluffy, carefree poodle.

YOU SAY TOMATO, I SAY BLOOD-SPURTING ARTERIAL WOUND

Let us now revisit the opening anecdote for a moment. The story of the "Manure Woman" contains elements of dark, sarcastic and ironic humor, making it an unusual "Triple Lutz" of dark humor.

Take this dark humor quiz: A capricious French poodle, frolicking happily, is hideously mangled by some farm equipment. Humorous or not humorous? If you answered "humorous," congratulations. You have the gift.

ETHICAL SHMETHICAL

We would be remiss if we did not address a few ethical concerns. Make no mistake, funerals are definitely not an acceptable place to make jokes about the deceased. We must insist you wait an hour or two. Furthermore, due to some unusual local superstitions and primitive legal constraints, exhumation of dead bodies is not considered funny in Tanzania (thankfully, it remains a hilarious diversion in the rest of the world).

Some common party favors.

Thus enlightened in the ways of dark humor, go forth into the world and cause pain. And if ever you should require further guidance, or if you hear any good dismemberment jokes, call us at 612-332-8864. Together we shall all enjoy a merry laugh, indeed.

[1] Be sure to note the damage he has done to himself in his panic to escape (see also chapter 4: Blood, Sinew and the Occasional Massive Brain Hemorrhage). Self-inflicted wounds are one of the most powerfully visceral forms of humor we have at our disposal.

DUBLIN PRODUCTIONS

GOLD, SILVER & BRONZE AWARDS

COLLATERAL
BROCHURES OTHER
THAN BY MAIL

34 GOLD
ART DIRECTORS:
**Stacy Drummond
Tracy Boychuk
Jeffrey Keyton
David Felton
Johan Vipper**
CLIENT:
MTV
AGENCY:
**MTV Off-Air Creative/
New York**

COLLATERAL
DIRECT MAIL: SINGLE

35 SILVER
ART DIRECTORS:
**Wade Koniakowsky
Sakol Mongkolkasetarin**
WRITERS:
**Jim Real
Kirt Gentry
Brian West
Wade Koniakowsky**
CLIENT:
Orange County Ad Club
AGENCY:
dGWB/Irvine

34 Gold

HOW TO WIN AWARDS WITHOUT DOING GOOD WORK.

If you secretly despise people who win ungodly amounts of advertising awards, you are not alone.

Because for every Tracy Wong or Neil French in the world, there are hundreds of grumbling malcontents who would like nothing more than to see these talented lads, as well as the entire creative department from Goodby, get hit by a bullet train.

But what if we offered you something to help tip the cruel hands of fate in your favor? That's right. A way to give your work, as wretched as it may be, an edge on the judging table.

Well, that's exactly what we're proposing. For as you will soon learn, this 2,840-word circular is literally teeming with tips that you can start using right away. But first, a few words about this sickness we call award shows.

1. THIS SICKNESS WE CALL AWARD SHOWS.

As we're all painfully aware, ad people don't get to sign their ads.

For creative people, this is intolerable. So intolerable, in fact, that in the old days, a bunch of these people banded together to form the first advertising award show. God bless them.

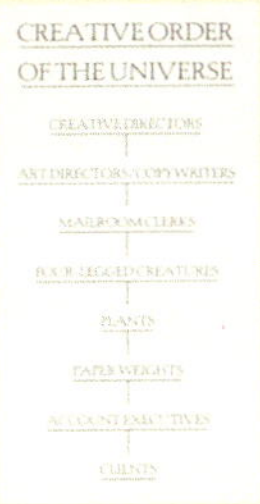
CREATIVE ORDER
OF THE UNIVERSE
CREATIVE DIRECTORS
ART DIRECTORS/COPYWRITERS
MAILROOM CLERKS
FOUR LEGGED CREATURES
PLANTS
PAPER WEIGHTS
ACCOUNT EXECUTIVES
CLIENTS

But, without knowing it, what started out as a nice little forum for ego-gratification has snowballed into a full-blown addiction for thousands. Perhaps you are one of them.

Who can blame you? Simply put, win a major award and people will start recognizing your work. Which will bring calls from headhunters. Who in turn can get you more money. Better assignments. Leading to more awards. Still even more money. A better office. A bigger house... (It's enough to make you want to join a 12-Step Program, isn't it?)

2. THE EFFIES, THE ADDYS, THE NUBBIES & THE WUBBIES.

Given the fact that award shows are an addiction, it should come as no surprise that there are countless unscrupulous piranhas out there willing to feed your habit (and take your money) by offering meaningless shows.

You can avoid all this nonsense by taking heed of our handy little show guide:

7, 8, 9, 12, 15, 17, 20, 22, 24, 25, 32, 33, 37, 42, 45, 48, 51, 56, 69, 72, 76, 77, 78, 84, 89, 90, 91, 98, 100, 102, 105, 107, 112, 118, 126, 127, 134, 139, 140, 142, 148, 153, 167

If you can't fathom the significance of having your name followed by all these numbers, you obviously have no business reading this poster

CA — No medals. No statuettes. No splashy dinner ceremony. And yet, CA is probably the most prestigious show in the country. Why? Well, as Tom Monahan so deftly put it, "It's the thinnest show book around."

The One Show — This is a big one. "Pencils" are awarded to gold, silver and bronze winners. This is the show that made Fallon McElligott famous. Perhaps, it will do the same for you.

The New York Art Directors Annual — A prestigious show, but for some reason, not as prestigious as the other two shows. Writers typically have a gripe with this show. If you'll notice in the credits, they're always listed fifth; after art director, creative director, designer and photographer. Hmmm.

The Clios — Hah!

The Cannes Film Festival — Typically, funky TV spots from Sao Paulo, Brazil and Milan, Italy do well in this show. Occasionally, though, a few Yanks manage to sneak in.

Tellys, Addys, Effies... — What is it about shows ending with the suffix "ies"? With exception to Portland's "Rosies", these shows carry about as much weight as Twiggy. In other words, save your money.

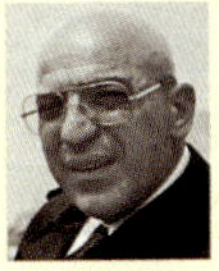

"Who loves ya baby."

3. WHAT? HAVEN'T DONE SQUAT ALL YEAR?

Let's say a call for entries shows up, and you haven't got anything decent to enter. Obviously, time is short. Here are a few hasty field-expedient strategies that might help.

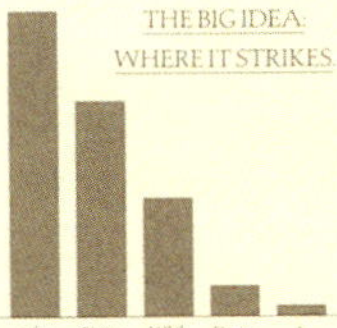
THE BIG IDEA:
WHERE IT STRIKES.
After three beers
Sitting on the John
While watching Oprah
During sex
At work

First off, you have to find a client.

Birth announcements always make for good ads. Heck, you don't even need to have the brat yourself. (Note: Due to the high success rate among cut-rate hacks in this category, many shows have banned these type of entries, so check the fine print.)

In the '80s condom ads were a hit. Nowadays, offbeat clients are still a safe bet. Good ones include tattoo parlors, casket manufacturers, gynecologists and dog psychiatrists.

But if you can't find any clients, we heartily recommend you just start concepting some ads in one of these funky categories, then look for clients to fit your concepts. This is called Minneapolizing.

4. HOW TO CATCH A JUDGE'S EYE.

Judges are a tough lot to peg. What works for a particular group of Cannes judges might not necessarily cut it for One Show judges. It's a bit of a subjective crap shoot.

But not to worry. After sifting through dozens of award show annuals, we have compiled an air-tight list of tricks and hints that have worked in the past. Good luck.

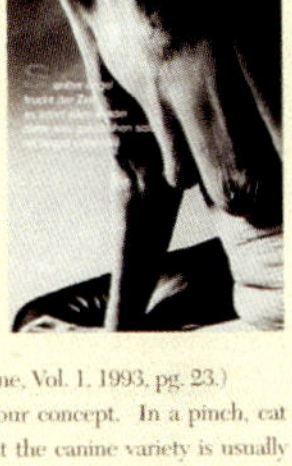

Nudity is hot right now. Especially for the Europeans. Full-frontal shots of male and female genitalia are quite the rage at the moment. As are ads including naked, wrinkled-up, saggy old women. (See Archive magazine, Vol. 1, 1993, pg. 23.)

Whenever possible, work dog poop into your concept. In a pinch, cat poop will serve as an acceptable substitute, but the canine variety is usually preferable. (See the '88 CA, pg. 20. Or the '91 One Show, #44.)

Cutting down Jerry Della Femina has proven quite successful. He's bald, fat, funny looking and surprisingly available for photo shoots. (See the '86 One Show, #358. Or the '92 CA, pg. 116.)

Here's an oldie-but-goodie. Account executives and clients are the ideal targets. You can capitalize on this by creating house ads or promo pieces that poke fun at them. If you can work both into the same piece, all the better.

Or how about this? Try and get project work (e.g. matchbooks, napkins, flyers) for neat accounts like Nike, Porsche or maybe Harley Davidson. Judges will invariably assume that the work came from equally neat agencies.

5. TIPS FOR WRITERS.

Long copy ads have proven to be a gold mine for writers over the past few years.

Will this continue?

We can't be sure, but if you hurry, you might just be able to ride on the coattails of this trend.

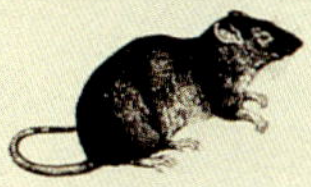

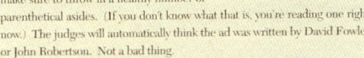

Ever wonder why CA put these silly illustrations in their radio section? It's to get art directors to read the scripts.

And while you're writing long copy, make sure to throw in a healthy number of parenthetical asides. (If you don't know what that is, you're reading one right now.) The judges will automatically think the ad was written by David Fowler or John Robertson. Not a bad thing.

With regards to radio. Whenever possible, try hiring a British voice-over talent. Coupled with a dry-witted English-style script, you might just sucker the judges into thinking the spot actually came from Britain.

Have you ever considered teaming up with an art director who's into all visual solutions? If he or she is any good, you could win scads of awards without even breaking a sweat.

And finally, for print, if you're really desperate, try reusing old award-winning headlines. Two years ago, we wouldn't have endorsed this, but during the past 12 months a surprising number of old headlines have resurfaced. It might be worth a shot.

6. TIPS FOR ART DIRECTORS.

We're sorry to report that the trend of setting type from bigger to smaller has run its course. However, hand-written type is staging a strong comeback. (The harder you make it to read, the better.)

2"

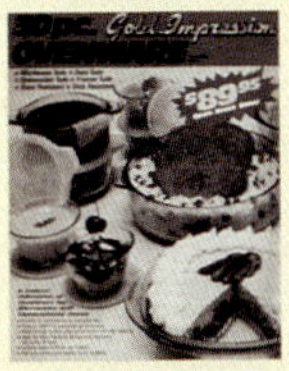
Gold Impression
$89.95

3"

Reduce your ads to this size to see how they'll look in the show books.

If you're fresh out of ideas, try a process called "blending." It works something like this. Look through a few award show annuals, and pick the three or four looks you like best. Then simply mix and match the varying styles to suit your needs.

Here's a curious observation.

Have you noticed that some of the best art directors around have weird names? It's true. Guys named Houman, Jelly and Cabell have all been wildly successful in the shows. Coincidence? Perhaps. But if you're stuck with a boring name like Bob or Ned, try changing it to something strange. Names like Brule, Niamh or Sakol should do nicely. ◄ - - - - - - - - - - - - - *(This is a widow. Definite points off on the judging table.)*

7. GETTING YOUR ADS TO RUN.

Once you've amassed a slew of concepts, you'll need a quick way to run your ads. A cheap way to do this is to convince your clients to start their own magazine. If they won't go for it, start your own.

If you've got outdoor, try this tip: Build a scale model of a billboard with your ad on it, and shoot a photograph from ground level alongside a real freeway. After a while the judges may figure it out, but by then you'll probably already be in the show book.

If worse comes to worse, and you can't find a way to run your ads, at least make it look like they ran. This can be accomplished by doctoring up phony insertion orders on your Mac. (Hey, we're not endorsing this practice, just stating something that desperate people actually do.)

8. ENTRY DEADLINES. HOW TO DELAY THE INEVITABLE.

Are entry deadlines a reality, or simply a myth created by the various award shows to stir up panic at agencies across the nation?

We lean toward the latter. For the most part, it seems, the deadlines aren't really deadlines at all.

To see if a show's deadline is for real or not, try this test: A few days before the "deadline", give the show office a ring. Usually you'll find that the deadline has been pushed back anywhere from two to seven days. There is usually no fee for this type of extension, which can occur two or three times before the people in charge of the show feel they've gotten enough entries to balance their budget. Then, and only then, the actual deadline is set in stone.

The bottom line? Don't sweat it, you have plenty of time.

9. FUNDING YOUR AWARD SHOW HABIT.

There's an art to prying more money from your agency's purse string holders for award shows. It all starts with the check request. (Note: Before submitting the check request, make sure it's padded with an extra few thousand dollars in entry fees. More on this later.)

Be ready to revive your agency president after presenting the check request.

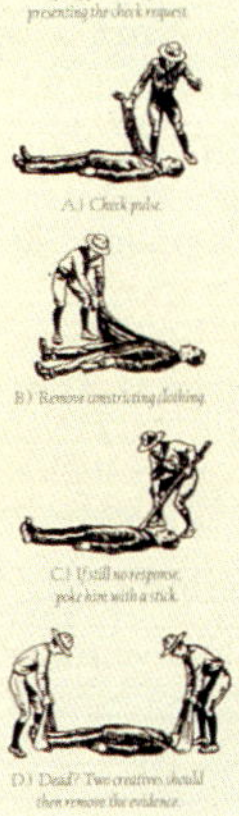

A.) Check pulse.

B.) Remove constricting clothing.

C.) If still no response, poke him with a stick.

D.) Dead? Two creatives should then remove the evidence.

Soon after your agency's president gets the check request, you will undoubtedly hear various muffled obscenities shouted from behind his door. "What?!! This is eight times that of last year. How did this happen?" Here's where you've got to schmooze him.

First try this line, "Hey, your partner approved this months ago." If that doesn't work try this, "Under your leadership, our work has gotten eight times better than last year."

If he's still got smoke creeping up his shorts, it's time to bring out the big guns. "If we enter any less than this, our competitors will sweep the award shows, word will get out, they'll get more clients, our clients will leave and in six months we'll be out of business."

It'll take a day or so, but he'll come around. Then all you need to do is come up with some sort of compromise. Which brings us back to the padded check request. Just delete the entries you really didn't even want to enter in the first place. (Note: If you are a creative director, do not make the deletions a democratic process within your department.) See how nicely all this is coming together?

10. PRESENTATION. YOUR SECRET WEAPON.

Superior looking reprints can often help a bad concept on the judging table. Or at least that's what many creative people think.

Example. We know of one famous creative director who swears by spot-varnished reprints with a minimum 2" border. He's so anal about this, that he was rumored to have taken a swing at a production manager because she forgot this mandate.

Over at the Ball Partnership (a place that actually does good work), they make it a point to make their reprints as large as possible. "Table presence," they're fond of calling it.

Another good thing to remember is that a quality 3 ml. non-gloss laminant will take away from the fact that you're merely entering high resolution color outputs that you printed in the back office.

11. JUDGING. THE ULTIMATE CRAP SHOOT.

What happens when you lock a smattering of people into a hotel meeting room with 12,000 or so ads to judge?

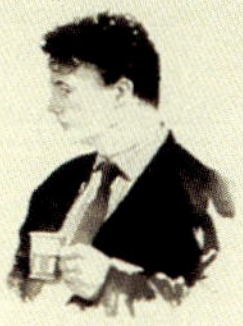

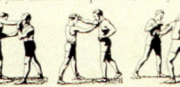

The quintessential British award show judge. Notice the tie and upturned nose.

A lot of people are still trying to figure this one out. Because, what happens behind those closed, hallowed doors is always a mysterious and fascinating process.

Some people, and rightly so, take the whole thing very seriously.

CA for instance. Judges are forbidden from even speaking to each other when they're reviewing work. This is a good thing in our opinion. It is better to have silence than allowing a few loud mouths to spoil the judging.

In England, they take the process even more seriously. If you doubt this fact, look through the photos of the judges in any British D&AD Annual. You'll notice that a high percentage of them are dressed as if they were going to have an audience with the Queen. Maybe that's why they think their advertising is so much more culturally superior and enriching than ours.

Now, should you (or your creative director) ever be asked to judge a national show, your ship has indeed come in. If you doubt this, just reference your favorite national award show annual, pick a judge and cross reference the index to see how they and their agency fared. Enlightening, isn't it?

12. THE NIGHT OF THE SHOW.

This is it. The night you've been waiting for all year. The night you'll get to parade up on stage and thumb your nose at all those who work elsewhere. The night you'll see your salary increase 150%. The night you'll become immortal in the world of advertising.

But more likely, the night you'll walk home empty-handed bitching about how stupid award shows are. If that's the case, don't feel glum. Hundreds of creatives go through this year after year and survive quite well, usually at the big mega-agencies in Detroit.

But if, by chance, you do capture a prize, here are a few tips to help you milk the most out of your winnings:

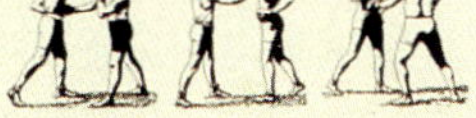

Always make sure you congratulate the winners after the show.

When consoling friends who didn't do so well, say something like, "Hey, your ads should've won!" (Even though they know inside you're secretly saying "Ha, ha. I won! I won! Neener, neener, neener.")

If given the opportunity to make a speech, say something trivial or thank the client for being a genius.

And always carry your award in your left hand. That way your right will be free to shake your future boss' hand after you accept that new job you're bound to be offered within minutes.

13. HOW TO DISPLAY YOUR AWARDS.

If you work in an agency, you should by all means display them in your office. It's best to be nonchalant about it, though. (One Show Pencils make excellent doorstops and Belding Bowls are great spittoons.)

The only time to be overt in displaying awards is salary review time. Just make sure the actual review process takes place in your office.

Now, if your name is on the door, it's best to display your biggest, most magnificent looking awards in a prominent place. Like the lobby. Clients will be impressed. Even if they have no idea what the hell you won them for.

Which brings up an age-old question. Do clients even care about awards? Is the Pope Mormon? Clients live in their own world of frustration, resentment and bureaucracy.

Just be happy you live in your world and not theirs.

14. LAST RESORTS.

What, still no awards? Take heart.

In reality, awards don't really matter. All awards do is allow creatives to bask in a bombastic, self-congratulatory glow. (And if you actually believe that, why are you still reading this?)

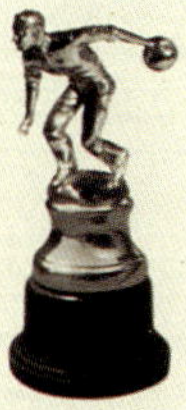

Just because your work isn't winning awards, doesn't mean you can't.

But if you're still looking to soothe that bruised ego of yours, there are a number of things you can do.

Maybe it's time for a career change? Truck driving and bartending schools abound. Check your yellow pages.

Win your agency bowling party trophy. Take home your softball team trophy. Or go down to your neighborhood trophy shop and buy a few of your own.

There must be something you're good at, isn't there?

15. CONCLUSION.

Sorry, but in this business nothing is ever concluded. Like we said, award shows are addicting. It's all a downward spiral. But we hope this will help turn the tide for you.

If you've had a run of bad luck, keep trying and happy hunting.

And if you're already winning heaps of awards, then damn you.

GOLD, SILVER & BRONZE AWARDS

COLLATERAL POINT OF PURCHASE AND IN-STORE

36 GOLD
ART DIRECTOR:
Rob Rich
WRITER:
Kara Goodrich
CLIENT:
Stork's Landing
AGENCY:
Leonard/Monahan, Providence

37 SILVER
ART DIRECTOR:
Carol Henderson
WRITER:
Dean Buckhorn
PHOTOGRAPHER:
Jim Arndt
CLIENT:
Lanzera
AGENCY:
Fallon McElligott/Minneapolis

36 Gold

GOLD, SILVER & BRONZE AWARDS

COLLATERAL
SELF-PROMOTION

38 GOLD
ART DIRECTOR:
Adam Chasnow
WRITER:
Adam Chasnow
CLIENT:
Adam Chasnow
AGENCY:
DDB Needham
Worldwide/New York

COLLATERAL
POSTERS

39 GOLD
ART DIRECTOR:
Ian Barry
WRITER:
Steve Dolbinski
ILLUSTRATOR:
Davidson & Company
PHOTOGRAPHER:
Bryan Morehead
CLIENT:
Invisible Fencing Company
AGENCY:
Arnold Finnegan Martin/Richmond

38 Gold

39 Gold

GOLD, SILVER & BRONZE AWARDS

COLLATERAL
POSTERS

40 SILVER
ART DIRECTOR:
Roger Bentley
WRITER:
Scott Wild
PHOTOGRAPHER:
Ken Anderson
CLIENT:
The Big House
AGENCY:
Dalbey & Denight Advertising/Portland

41 BRONZE
ART DIRECTOR:
Damon Williams
WRITER:
Chris Jacobs
DESIGNER:
Troy King
PHOTOGRAPHER:
Chris Davis
CLIENT:
The Skydiving Center
AGENCY:
Hughes Advertising/Atlanta

40 Silver

GOLD, SILVER & BRONZE AWARDS

PUBLIC SERVICE/
POLITICAL NEWSPAPER
OR MAGAZINE: SINGLE

42 SILVER
ART DIRECTOR:
Sean Thompson
WRITER:
Ros Sinclair
PHOTOGRAPHER:
Terry O'Neill
CLIENT:
Crisis
AGENCY:
SP Lintas/London

43 BRONZE
ART DIRECTOR:
Denise Crandall
WRITER:
Court Crandall
CLIENT:
St. Joseph's
AGENCY:
Ground Zero/Venice

42 Silver

HANCOCK PARK ADJ

3bd/2ba 2000 S.F. Bay windows, hardwood floors, garage parking. 1 Month Free! $500 deposit OAC $1150/mo. 213-381-5443.

HEATING GRATE

With all the homes in this section, it's a shame so many people have to settle for this one. Help the homeless, call the St. Joseph Center at (310)396-6468.

HOLLYWOOD CLASSIC

Courtyard bungalow. Hardwood floors, lots of light, built-in bookcases, dining table, benches. Singles $420/mo. 10-unit building w/ laundry. 1135 N. Lodi Place. (213) 931-8715

GOLD, SILVER & BRONZE AWARDS

PUBLIC SERVICE/
POLITICAL NEWSPAPER
OR MAGAZINE:
CAMPAIGN

44 GOLD
ART DIRECTOR:
Bob Barrie
WRITER:
Luke Sullivan
CLIENT:
People for the Ethical Treatment of Animals
AGENCY:
Fallon McElligott/ Minneapolis

If you still buy Gillette products after reading this ad, you're either a sadist or a major shareholder.

Gillette pays experimenters to pour substances like Liquid Paper into rabbits' eyes.

Gillette pays them to abrade rabbits' skin and pour chemicals directly onto the wounds.

They pay them to force substances like deodorants and shaving cream down the throats of restrained animals.

And later, all the animals are killed, since they are no longer "scientifically viable."

What few people know is that none of these tests is required by law. And none of them makes Gillette's products any safer. Yet they continue to have them done, even though more than 500 other companies have switched to non-animal tests, like computer and *in vitro* tests.

In the infamous force-feeding test, products like shampoo or shaving cream are forced down animals' throats. Proving exactly what?

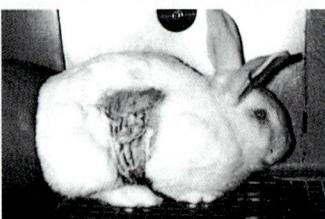

Worse than the "skin irritancy" test is the "eye irritancy" test in which chemicals are dripped into the animals' eyes.

You can help stop this torture. Call Gillette at 1-800-872-7202 and say you won't be buying Silkience, White Rain, Sensor, Soft & Dri, Right Guard, Liquid Paper, or Flair pens until the company permanently bans all tests on animals.

Then send any Gillette products that are still in your cabinets or office to: Mr. Alfred Zeien, CEO of Gillette, addressed to Gillette, Prudential Tower, Boston, MA 02199. Demand a full refund. And tell everyone you know not to buy any Gillette products.

Please join us and help make Gillette a kinder company.

Yes, I want to help stop animal testing. Please send me a Gillette Action Pack. Enclosed is my tax-deductible contribution of:
☐ $15 ☐ $25 ☐ $50 ☐ $100 ☐ other

Name
Address
City   State   Zip

PeTA

People for the Ethical Treatment of Animals, P.O. Box 42516, Washington, D.C. 20015

Can you scream louder than the animals in Gillette's testing labs?

In addition to the "skin irritancy" tests (in which chemicals are poured onto abraded, wounded skin), there is the infamous "eye irritancy" test, in which they pour chemicals into the eyes.

Call Gillette at 1-800-872-7202 and make yourself heard.

Ask them why they're still torturing animals in outdated product tests when 500 other companies have switched to non-animal tests, like computer and *in vitro* tests.

Ask them if they're still pouring Liquid Paper into the eyes of rabbits, when such a test doesn't make this office product any safer for human beings.

Ask them if they're still doing "skin irritancy" tests, in which they abrade rabbits' skin and pour chemicals directly onto the open wounds.

Ask them if they're still doing force-feeding tests, in which groups of animals are force-fed huge amounts of chemicals like shampoo or shaving cream.

Animals are force-fed products like shampoos or deodorants. Proving exactly what?

If you don't get a satisfactory answer, join us. Tell your friends not to buy any Gillette products. Products like Foamy, Right Guard, Silkience, Sensor, White Rain, Liquid Paper, Dry Idea, Soft & Dri, or Flair pens.

And send any Gillette products you still have in your house or office to Mr. Alfred Zeien, CEO of Gillette, addressed to Gillette, Prudential Tower, Boston, MA 02199. Demand a full refund.

Please help us make Gillette a kinder company.

Yes, I want to help stop animal testing. Please send me a Gillette Action Pack. Enclosed is my tax-deductible contribution of:
☐ $15   ☐ $25   ☐ $50   ☐ $100   ☐ other

Name _____
Address _____
City _____ State ____ Zip _____

PeTA

People for the Ethical Treatment of Animals, P.O. Box 42516, Washington, D.C. 20015

If no law requires Gillette to pour Liquid Paper® into the eyes of rabbits, one has to assume they do it for fun.

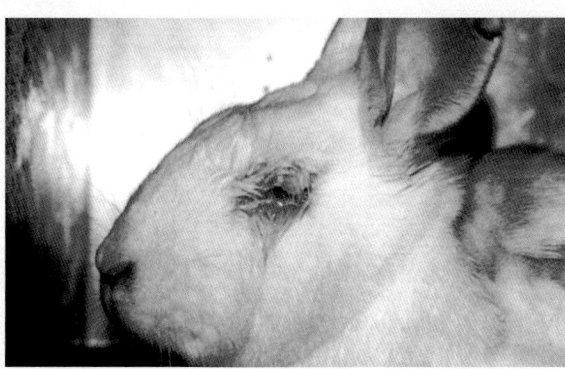

In the infamous "eye irritancy" test (dating from the '40s), chemicals are poured into the eyes of animals, after which they are killed.

Gillette pays experimenters to pour substances like Liquid Paper into rabbits' eyes.

Gillette pays them to abrade rabbits' skin and pour chemicals directly onto the wounds.

They pay them to force substances like deodorants and shaving cream down the throats of restrained animals.

And later, all the animals are killed, since they are no longer "scientifically viable."

None of these tests is required by law. And none of them makes Gillette's products any safer. Yet they continue to have them done, even though more than 500 other companies have switched to non-animal tests, like computer and *in vitro* tests.

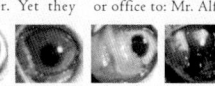

Rabbits produce few tears, so caustic substances aren't washed away.

You can help stop this torture. Call Gillette at 1-800-872-7202 and say you won't be buying Silkience, White Rain, Sensor, Soft & Dri, Dry Idea, Right Guard, Foamy shaving cream, Liquid Paper, or Flair pens until the company permanently bans all tests on animals.

Companies like Avon and Revlon don't torture animals. Why does Gillette?

Then send any Gillette products still in your cabinets or office to: Mr. Alfred Zeien, CEO of Gillette, addressed to Gillette, Prudential Tower, Boston, MA 02199. Demand a full refund. And tell everyone you know not to buy any products Gillette has on the market until the torture stops.

Please join us and help make Gillette a kinder company.

Yes, I want to help stop animal testing. Please send me a Gillette Action Pack. Enclosed is my tax-deductible contribution of:
☐ $15   ☐ $25   ☐ $50   ☐ $100   ☐ other

Name _____
Address _____
City _____ State ____ Zip _____

PeTA

People for the Ethical Treatment of Animals, P.O. Box 42516, Washington, D.C. 20015

GOLD, SILVER & BRONZE AWARDS

PUBLIC SERVICE/
POLITICAL NEWSPAPER
OR MAGAZINE:
CAMPAIGN

45 SILVER
ART DIRECTORS:
David Caballero
Lucho Correa
WRITER:
Toni Segarra
PHOTOGRAPHER:
Fernando Manso
CLIENT:
Amnesty International
AGENCY:
Delvico Bates/Barcelona

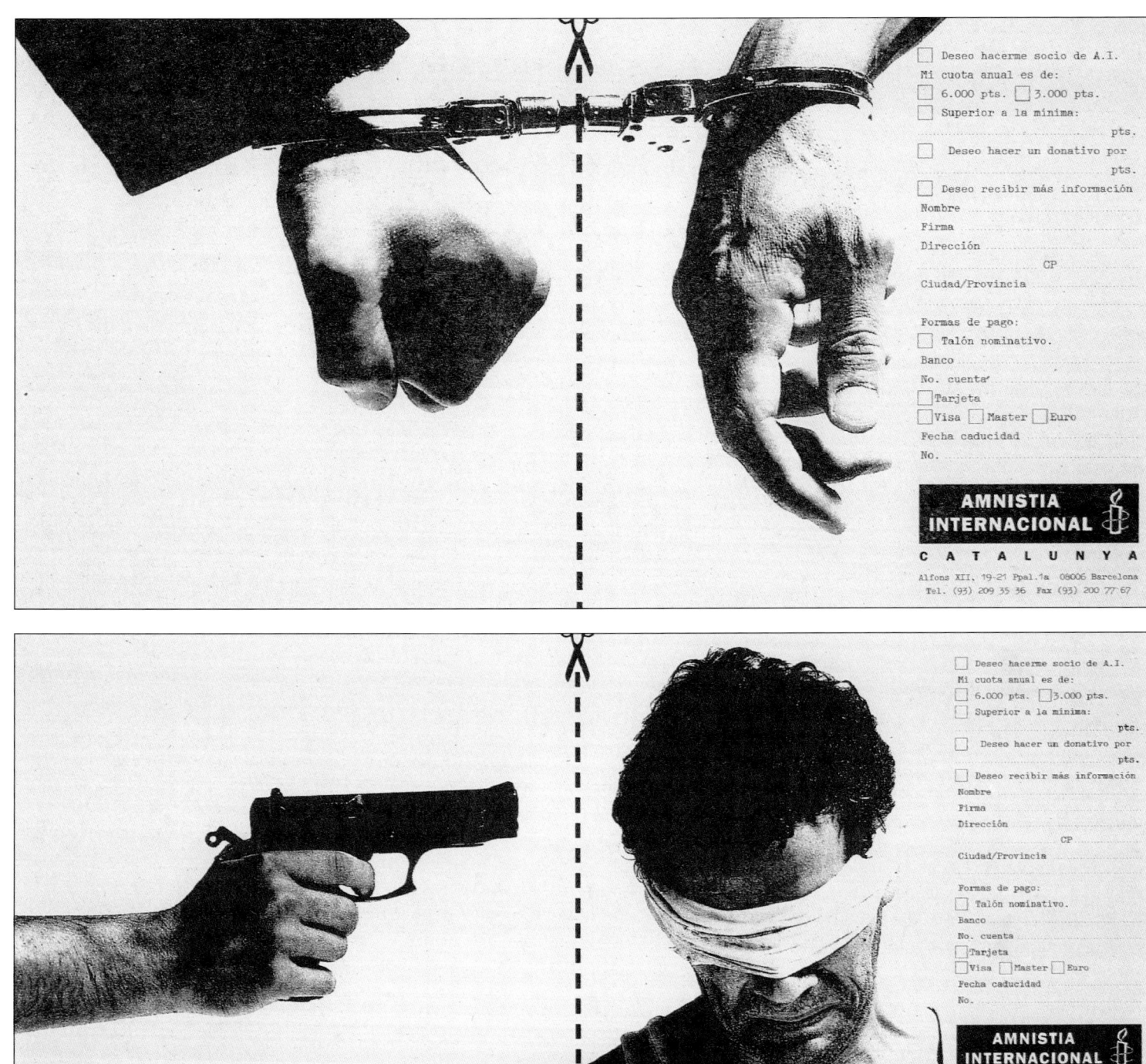

GOLD, SILVER & BRONZE AWARDS

PUBLIC SERVICE/
POLITICAL OUTDOOR
AND POSTERS

46 GOLD
ART DIRECTOR:
Randy Hughes
WRITER:
Bill Johnson
CLIENT:
Mothers Against Drunk Driving
AGENCY:
Clarity Coverdale Fury/ Minneapolis

47 SILVER
ART DIRECTOR:
Ellen Steinberg
WRITER:
Mike Lescarbeau
CLIENT:
Children's Cancer Research Fund
AGENCY:
Fallon McElligott/ Minneapolis

48 BRONZE
ART DIRECTOR:
Taras Wayner
WRITER:
Taras Wayner
CLIENT:
American Lung Association of Maryland
AGENCY:
Earle Palmer Brown/ Bethesda

Tell these people to stop drinking and driving.
(They obviously won't listen to us.)

We didn't want to name names, but if it will make Minnesotans think twice before driving drunk then it will have been worth a little embarrassment.

The 1994 Minnesota DWI Hall of Shame.
Mothers Against Drunk Driving.

46 Gold

S	M	T	W	T	F	S
		1	2	3	4	5
		Children	diagnosed	with	cancer	have
6	7	8	9	10	11	12
to	cherish	every	day.	Please	make	today
13	14	15	16	17	18	19
as	meaningful	to	you	as	it	is
20	21	22	23	24	25	26
to	them.	Send	a	donation	to	the
27	28	29	30	31		
Children's	Cancer	Research	Fund.	(612) 929-5535		

47 Silver

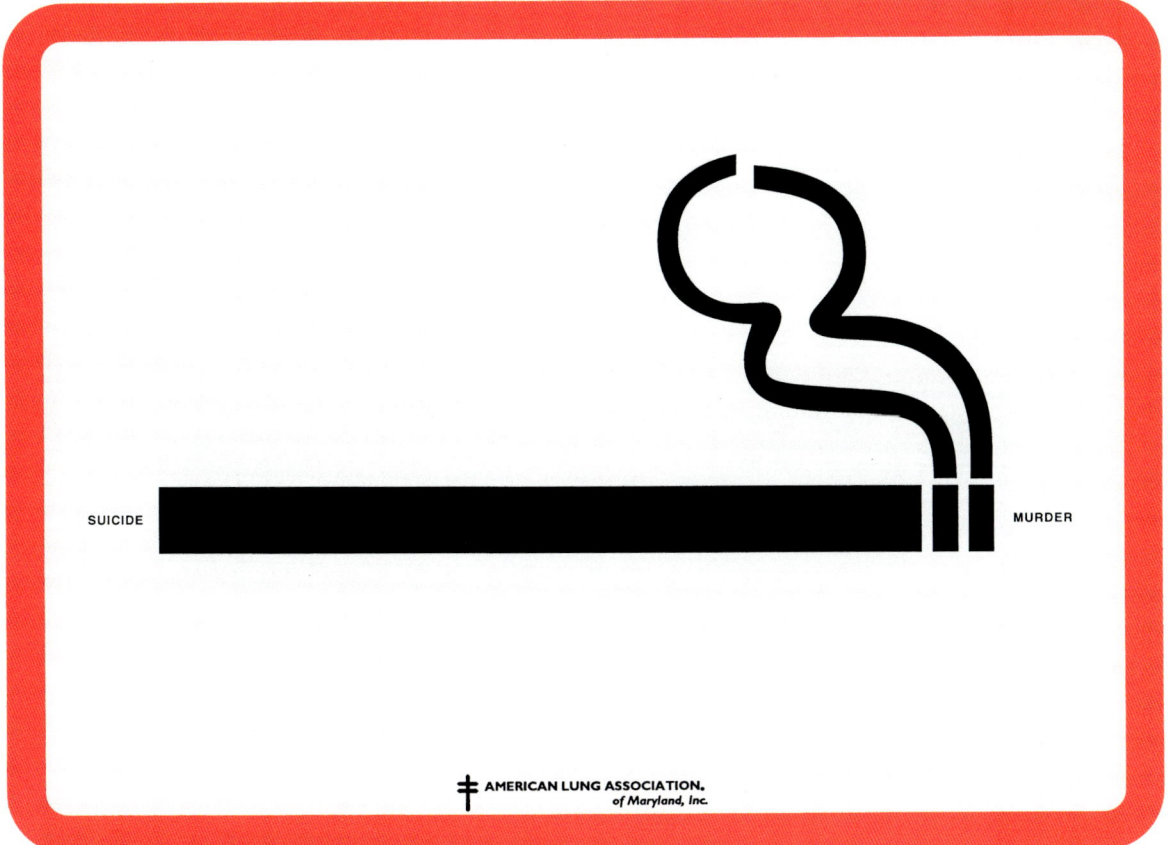

SUICIDE — MURDER

✝ AMERICAN LUNG ASSOCIATION. of Maryland, Inc.

48 Bronze

GOLD, SILVER & BRONZE AWARDS

PUBLIC SERVICE/
POLITICAL RADIO:
SINGLE

49 GOLD
WRITERS:
Ken Lewis
Dave Gardiner
Stu Cooperrider
AGENCY PRODUCERS:
Harry McCoy
Chris Palumbo
CLIENT:
Massachusetts Department of Public Health
AGENCY:
Houston Effler Herstek Favat/Boston

PUBLIC SERVICE/
POLITICAL RADIO:
CAMPAIGN

50 GOLD
WRITERS:
Ken Lewis
Dave Gardiner
Stu Cooperrider
AGENCY PRODUCERS:
Harry McCoy
Chris Palumbo
CLIENT:
Massachusetts Department of Public Health
AGENCY:
Houston Effler Herstek Favat/Boston

49 Gold

JANET SACKMAN: You may get cancer or heart disease. But one thing I doubt you'll ever get from tobacco companies is the truth. They keep saying you can't get hooked on cigarettes. But the truth is nicotine is extremely addictive. In fact, many smokers light up even after they lose their vocal cords to cancer. My name is Janet Sackman. I'm not here because I got hooked and have cancer. I'm here because I was a model in cigarette ads and helped convince a lot of young people to smoke. I hope I can convince you not to.

ANNCR: A message from the Massachusetts Department of Public Health.

50 I Gold

JANET SACKMAN: You may get cancer or heart disease. But one thing I doubt you'll ever get from tobacco companies is the truth. They keep saying you can't get hooked on cigarettes. But the truth is nicotine is extremely addictive. In fact, many smokers light up even after they lose their vocal cords to cancer. My name is Janet Sackman. I'm not here because I got hooked and have cancer. I'm here because I was a model in cigarette ads and helped convince a lot of young people to smoke. I hope I can convince you not to.

ANNCR: A message from the Massachusetts Department of Public Health.

50 II

PATRICK REYNOLDS: Do you know what's in cigarettes? I can tell you right now the answer is no. Because the last thing tobacco companies want is for you to know how many poisonous chemicals there are in cigarettes. And there are plenty. Stuff like formaldehyde, cyanide, in fact, some of the chemicals in cigarettes are so poisonous that it's illegal to dump them into landfills. But apparently, tobacco companies think it's okay to dump them into our lungs. The worst thing is, they do it without telling you. Because you won't find a list of the chemicals anywhere on the pack or in their ads. I'm Patrick Reynolds. My grandfather founded the RJ Reynolds tobacco company. That means my family's name is on the side of more than seven billion cigarette packs a year. Why am I telling you this? I want my family to be on the right side for a change.

ANNCR: A message from the Massachusetts Department of Public Health.

50 III

VICTOR CRAWFORD: Maybe they'll get to your little brother or sister. Or maybe they'll get to the kid down the street. But it's pretty clear to me tobacco companies are after children. Why? Because they know that 90 percent of smokers start before they reach the age of twenty. So they have to hook children who aren't old enough to know better. Unfortunately, they seem to be doing a pretty good job. Take a look around. Tobacco companies sponsor the sporting events that kids' heroes play in. One tobacco company even uses a cartoon character in their advertising. And nearly a million kids start smoking every year. Of course marketing cigarettes to kids would be highly unethical, so tobacco companies just keep denying it. What makes me such an expert in all this? My name is Victor Crawford. I was a lobbyist for the tobacco industry for five years, so I know how tobacco compainies work. I lied. And I'm sorry.

ANNCR: A message from the Massachusetts Department of Public Health.

GOLD, SILVER & BRONZE AWARDS

PUBLIC SERVICE/
POLITICAL TELEVISION:
SINGLE

51 GOLD
ART DIRECTOR:
Paul Brazier
WRITER:
Peter Souter
AGENCY PRODUCER:
Francine Linsey
PRODUCTION COMPANY:
Paul Weiland Film Company
DIRECTOR:
David Garfath
CLIENT:
Queen Elizabeth's Foundation for Disabled People
AGENCY:
Abbott Mead Vickers. BBDO/London

52 SILVER
ART DIRECTOR:
Carol DeMelio
WRITER:
Steven Landsberg
AGENCY PRODUCERS:
Sally Hotchkiss
Neal Bergman
PRODUCTION COMPANY:
Red Car
CLIENT:
The Advertising Council/ Department of Transportation
AGENCY:
Wells Rich Greene BDDP/ New York

53 BRONZE
ART DIRECTOR:
Carol DeMelio
WRITER:
Steven Landsberg
AGENCY PRODUCERS:
Sally Hotchkiss
Neal Bergman
PRODUCTION COMPANY:
Red Car
CLIENT:
The Advertising Council/Department of Transportation
AGENCY:
Wells Rich Greene BDDP/ New York

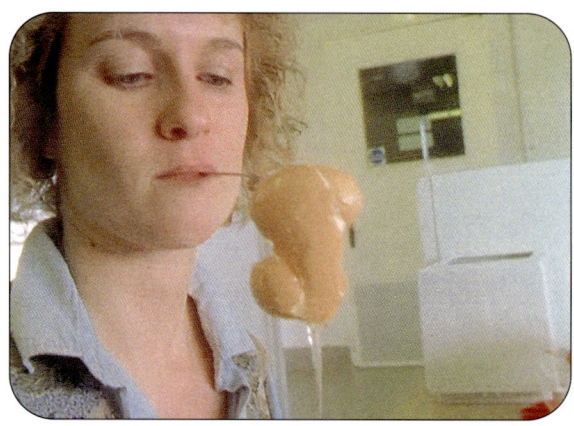

51 Gold

ANNCR: After what you've seen, do you really find it so difficult to write a check?

SUPER: QUEEN ELIZABETH'S FOUNDATION FOR DISABLED PEOPLE.

52 Silver

MOM: Who is that swimming? Get your legs up!

ALEX: Like this?

MOM: That's the way.

FRIEND: What are you doing? Now you're kicking, Al!

ALEX: I'm almost there.

MOM: Okay.

SUPER: ALEX BISHOP. KILLED BY A DRUNK DRIVER ON NOVEMBER 8, 1992 ON KENT-KANGLEY ROAD IN KENT, WASHINGTON.

MOM: Whoa . . . you made it all the way.

ANNCR: If you don't stop your friend from driving drunk, who will?

MOM: Good job!

ANNCR: Do whatever it takes.

MOM: Are you having a good time?

ALEX: Yeah.

SUPER: FRIENDS DON'T LET FRIENDS DRIVE DRUNK.

53 Bronze

PARTY GUESTS (SINGING): *Happy birthday to you, happy birthday to you, happy birthday dear Miranda, happy birthday to you.*

GUESTS: Yeah! What a fun birthday! Wow!

SUPER: MIRANDA FAY STANDIFORD. KILLED BY A DRUNK DRIVER ON MAY 1, 1994 ON HIGHWAY 60 IN BORDEN, INDIANA.

GUESTS: Do you need a scissors or something? Yeah!

ANNCR: If you don't stop your friend from driving drunk, who will? Do whatever it takes.

GUESTS: Yeah! Oh Wow!

SUPER: FRIENDS DON'T LET FRIENDS DRIVE DRUNK.

GOLD, SILVER & BRONZE AWARDS

PUBLIC SERVICE/
POLITICAL TELEVISION:
CAMPAIGN

54 GOLD

ART DIRECTOR:
Dave Gardiner
WRITERS:
Ken Lewis
Stu Cooperrider
AGENCY PRODUCER:
Harry McCoy
PRODUCTION COMPANIES:
Palomar
Picture Park
DIRECTOR:
Neil Abramson
CLIENT:
Massachusetts Department of Public Health
AGENCY:
Houston Effler Herstek Favat/Boston

54 I Gold

SUPER: THE TRUTH

JANET SACKMAN: You may get cancer but I doubt you'll get the truth from tobacco companies. They keep saying you can't get hooked on cigarettes. Even though many smokers who lose their vocal cords can't quit. I'm Janet Sackman. I was a model in cigarette ads and convinced many young people to smoke. I hope I can convince you not to.

SUPER: MASS. DEPT. OF PUBLIC HEALTH.

54 II

SUPER: THE TRUTH

PATRICK REYNOLDS: Do you know what's in cigarettes? No. Because the last thing tobacco companies want is for you to know how many poisonous chemicals there are in cigarettes. So they just don't tell you. Not on the pack, not in their ads. I'm Patrick Reynolds, the grandson of RJ Reynolds. My family's name is printed on the side of seven billion packs a year. Why am I telling you this? I want my family to be on the right side for a change.

SUPER: MASS. DEPT. OF PUBLIC HEALTH.

54 III

SUPER: THE TRUTH

VICTOR CRAWFORD: Maybe they'll get your little brother or sister. Or maybe the kid down the block. But one thing is perfectly clear to me, tobacco companies are after children. Why? Because tobacco companies know that 90 percent of smokers start as children before they know any better. Of course, marketing to kids is unethical, so they just deny it. I'm Victor Crawford. I was a tobacco lobbyist for five years so I know how tobacco companies work. I lied. And I'm sorry.

SUPER: MASS. DEPT. OF PUBLIC HEALTH.

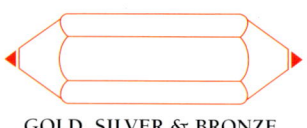

GOLD, SILVER & BRONZE AWARDS

CONSUMER RADIO: SINGLE

55 GOLD
WRITERS:
Dante Lombardi
Rob Slosberg
AGENCY PRODUCER:
Jill Kay
CLIENT:
Comedy Central
AGENCY:
Korey Kay & Partners/ New York

56 SILVER
WRITER:
Ryan Ebner
AGENCY PRODUCER:
Adrienne Cummins
CLIENT:
Millers Outpost
AGENCY:
Butler Shine & Stern/ Sausalito

57 BRONZE
WRITER:
Dean Hacohen
PRODUCTION COMPANY:
Soundtrack Studios
CLIENT:
Crain's New York Business
AGENCY:
Goldsmith/Jeffrey, New York

55 Gold

(SFX: PHONE RINGING, ANSWERING MACHINE PICKS UP)

WOMAN: Hi! You've reached the Suicide Crisis Hotline. Because your call is important to us, a caring, nurturing counselor will be with you as soon as one is available. If you have a touch-tone phone you can access our automated counseling system. Press one if you're on the ledge. Press two if you've got a dry cleaning bag on your head. Press three for double suicides. And make sure your partner is ready on an extension. Those making desperate bids for attention, press four. If you can't wait, we suggest you watch Comedy Central, the only all comedy cable channel. While suicide is never the answer to your problems, some original comedy may be. Comedy so suprising you'll ask, "What the hell is going on here?" Mystery Science Theater 3000, for example, is like watching cheesy movies with three of your funniest friends. That sounds positive, doesn't it?

ANNCR: Comedy Central. Tune in, laugh so hard you fall off the couch, sue us.

WOMAN: Thanks for holding. We'll be with you in just a moment . . .

(SFX: MUZAK)

56 Silver

(MUSIC: SOFT PIANO)

ANNCR: These days, being a teenager can be rough. So many questions, so many changes. And as a parent, it's sometimes difficult to recognize when something's wrong. But there are warning signs you can look for: Does your child frequent second-hand clothing stores, own a higher-than-average amount of polyester or wear concert T-shirts from bands like Sludgemunch, Vomit Tool or Parts Chicken Parts? If so, these may actually be cries for help. Desperate cries for clothing that doesn't suck.

We're Millers Outpost. And we specialize in helping parents recognize the signs before it's too late. Not only do we carry a wide selection of cool tops, jeans and other apparel, we also have counselors on hand in every store. People who know, because they've been there themselves. Like Christa.

CHRISTA: Six months ago I was mixing plaids and stripes. Thanks Millers Outpost.

ANNCR: So this Christmas, remember Millers Outpost. Together we can make it.

Millers Outpost. Why pay the price of shopping somewhere else?

57 Bronze

ANNCR: On any given Saturday night on the Upper West Side of Manhatten, hundreds of meticulously-dressed people file into the Metropolitan Opera. There, in one of New York's most elegant theaters, they take their seats, cross their legs, and for two hours, sometimes three, sit in the dark without a clue as to what's going on. Of course, for those New York executives who are used to walking into meetings without having read the latest *Crain's New York Business,* that feeling is not altogether unfamiliar.

GOLD, SILVER & BRONZE AWARDS

CONSUMER RADIO: CAMPAIGN

58 GOLD
WRITERS:
Trevor Robinson
Alan Young
AGENCY PRODUCER:
Kathleen Rainey
CLIENT:
Britvic
AGENCY:
Howell Henry Chaldecott Lury & Partners/London

59 SILVER
WRITER:
Ryan Ebner
AGENCY PRODUCER:
Adrienne Cummins
CLIENT:
Millers Outpost
AGENCY:
Butler Shine & Stern/Sausalito

58 I Gold

The caller contacts the Black & White Color photo processing lab. He explains that he needs a roll of film developed discreetly.

He then goes on to explain that the film contains pictures of him cavorting naked with a can of apple Tango in his flat. The man in the photo lab is happy to develop the pictures but obviously doesn't want to know the details. The caller insists on telling him everything, including dressing the can up in dolls' clothes: "We're in love and I take her everywhere with me."

58 II

A desperate caller gets in touch with a British Rail lost property office. He explains he's lost a can of apple Tango on a train from London to Glasgow. It was packed with ice, although the ice would have melted since he lost it several weeks ago.

The lost property man goes off to look for the soft drink, but can't find it. Our caller becomes frantic: "What if some skanky Scotsman's got her and he's drinking her out of a plastic cup?" The lost property man hangs up.

The caller rings back and accuses the lost property man of kidnapping the can, "You've got her haven't you, you've drunk my can of apple Tango." The lost property man hangs up again.

58 III

The irate caller rings a lawyer, Mr. Tunney, for legal advice. He says he wants to sue Britvic, the makers of apple Tango.

He explains to the lawyer that a can of apple Tango talks to him, she makes him do things like eating dead dogs and wearing women's clothes. The caller points out that he didn't actually eat dead dogs: "I'm not stupid Mr. Tunney!"

The lawyer tells him he will need medical evidence. The caller says: "I don't need medical evidence, I've got a flat full of dead dogs."

The caller becomes angry with the lawyer, eventually threatening to sue him. The lawyer says go ahead. The caller asks if he knows any good lawyers before hanging up.

59 Silver

(MUSIC: SOFT PIANO)

ANNCR: Adolescence. It's a time when "fitting in" can be the hardest part of all. It's an awkward time. A time of change, confusion. And a time of so many questions.

BOY 1: Who am I?

GIRL: Am I normal?

BOY 2: Do people like me?

ANNCR: But, as a parent, you can help. By giving them love, support, and most importantly, by giving them clothes that don't suck. Clothes that don't scream, "I'm a total dweeb" or "Hey, look, my parents still dress me." Clothes that let a teenager walk confidently down the school hallway, free from the fear of being laughed at, ostracized, or duct-taped to the lockers by the varsity wrestling team.

We're Millers Outpost. And we have counselors standing by in every store to help by providing parents with options. Like cool tops, jeans and other apparel that definitely aren't butt-ugly. So this Christmas, remember Millers Outpost. Together we can help our children to a brighter tommorow. Millers Outpost. Why pay the price of shopping anywhere else?

GOLD, SILVER & BRONZE AWARDS

CONSUMER TELEVISION OVER :30 SINGLE

60 GOLD
ART DIRECTOR:
Warren Eakins
WRITER:
Bob Moore
AGENCY PRODUCER:
Jane Brimblecombe
PRODUCTION COMPANY:
Pytka
DIRECTOR:
Joe Pytka
CLIENT:
Nike International
AGENCY:
Wieden & Kennedy/ Amsterdam

61 SILVER
ART DIRECTORS:
Jason Peterson
Paul Hirsch
Izzy DeBellis
WRITERS:
Izzy DeBellis
Paul Hirsch
Jason Peterson
AGENCY PRODUCER:
Deborah Sullivan
PRODUCTION COMPANY:
Epoch Films
DIRECTOR:
Jeff Priess
CLIENT:
NBA
AGENCY:
Fallon McElligott Berlin/ New York

62 SILVER
ART DIRECTOR:
Steve Luker
WRITER:
Steve Simpson
AGENCY PRODUCER:
Elizabeth O'Toole
PRODUCTION COMPANY:
Ritts/Hayden
DIRECTOR:
Carlton Chase
CLIENT:
Norwegian Cruise Line
AGENCY:
Goodby Silverstein & Partners/San Francisco

60 Gold

(SFX: THUNDER CRASHING)
(SFX: SOUND OF BALL FLYING)
(SFX: CROWD CHEERING, POWER KICK, BRICKS SMASHING)
(SFX: FAST MOVING BALL, CROWD CHEERING)
(SFX: BALL BEING KICKED, BRICKS SMASHING)
(SFX: FAST MOVING BALL, PIGEON WINGS FLAPPING, NOISE OF HEADER, BRICKS SMASHING)
(SFX: SMASHING BRICKS, MOVING BALL, KICKING SOUND, SMASHING BRICKS)
(SFX: MOVING BALL, CRASH OF BROKEN GLASS)
(SFX: SOUND OF SIGN SWINGING)
SUPER: NIKE.

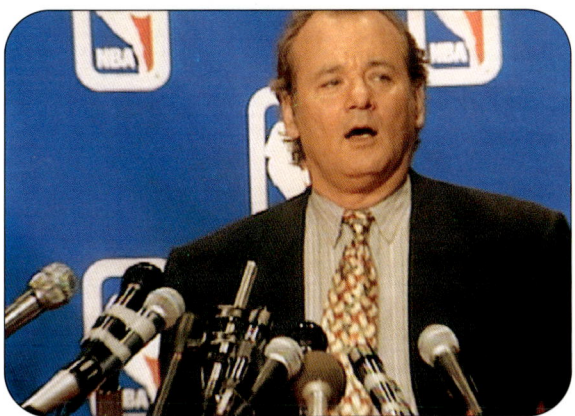

61 Silver

AHMAD RASHAD: We are moments away from the much anticipated press conference. It's about to begin. Let's listen in.

BILL MURRAY: Thank you for coming out. I have an announcement to make that will come as a shock and suprise to some of you. I have decided to retire from the field of entertainment so that I may pursue a dream. I want to play in the NBA. I know that some of you will have questions.

REPORTER: Why are you doing this?

BILL: I have achieved everything possible in my own field. I am at the pinnacle of my industry and I have nothing else to prove.

REPORTER: Have you ever won an oscar?

BILL: No. Not an Oscar.

REPORTER: Were you ever nominated?

BILL: No. I wasn't nominated either, no. But, I have an Emmy for writing.

62 Silver

ANNCR: A new constitution for the world.

(MUSIC: "BLUE MOON" BY THE COWBOY JUNKIES)

ANNCR: Article 1, Section 3.

SUPER: ARTICLE 1, SECTION 3. WE SHALL FORM A MORE PERFECT UNION.

ANNCR: Article 3, Section 2.

SUPER: ARTICLE 3, SECTION 2. WINTER WILL BE EXILED.

ANNCR: Article 4, Section 7.

SUPER: ARTICLE 4, SECTION 7. WORK SHALL BE ABOLISHED.

ANNCR: Article 6, Section 6.

SUPER: ARTICLE 6, SECTION 6. WE SHALL HAVE ADVENTURES.

ANNCR: Article 10, Section 1. There will be peace and hope. And really good food. And beer.

SUPER: IT'S DIFFERENT OUT HERE. NORWEGIAN CRUISE LINE.

GOLD, SILVER & BRONZE AWARDS

CONSUMER TELEVISION OVER :30 SINGLE

63 BRONZE
ART DIRECTORS:
Greg Bell
John Leu
WRITERS:
John Leu
Greg Bell
Cliff Freeman
AGENCY PRODUCER:
MaryEllen Duggan
PRODUCTION COMPANY:
Crossroads Films
DIRECTOR:
Bruce Hurwit
CLIENT:
Little Caesars
AGENCY:
Cliff Freeman & Partners/ New York

64 BRONZE
ART DIRECTOR:
Sean Ehringer
WRITER:
Harry Cocciolo
AGENCY PRODUCER:
Cindy Epps
PRODUCTION COMPANY:
Propaganda Films
DIRECTOR:
Jeffrey Goodby
CLIENT:
California Fluid Milk Processor Advisory Board
AGENCY:
Goodby Silverstein & Partners/San Francisco

63 Bronze

(MUSIC: HEROIC STYLE, BUILDS THROUGHOUT)

MODERATOR: Okay . . . how many of you would like more cheese on your pizza? Okay . . . How many of you would like more toppings on your pizza? Okay . . . more cheese? Okay . . . more toppings? Okay . . . more cheese? . . . more toppings? . . . More? . . . More? . . . More? . . . More toppings? Cheese? . . . Toppings? . . . More?

(MUSIC: REACHES A CRESCENDO)

RESEARCHER: Well . . . that's every man, woman, and child.

ANNCR: By popular demand, it's the new Little Caesars Pleasers Menu. More meat, more cheese, more pepperoni, more toppings. Any two for one low price. Satisfaction guaranteed or your money back.

LITTLE CAESAR: Pizza! Pizza!

64 Bronze

MAN: Tom, can I make a suggestion? You're fired!!!

(SFX: TRUCK HORN WAILING)

MAN: Aaaaaaaaaaah!!!!!

(SFX: CHIMES, FLAPPING BIRD WINGS)

WOMAN: Welcome to eternity.

(MUSIC: PIANO INTRO, THEN SLOW JAZZ)

(SFX: DOOR SHUTTING, TICKING, CAT PURRING)

MAN: Heaven! . . . yes! . . . Hmmm . . . milk! . . . Wait a minute. Where am I ?

ANNCR: Got Milk?

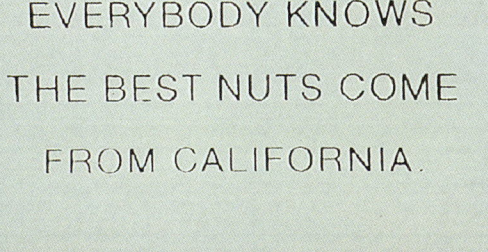

GOLD, SILVER & BRONZE AWARDS

CONSUMER TELEVISION :30/:25 SINGLE

65 GOLD
ART DIRECTOR:
Jerry Gentile
WRITER:
Scott Vincent
AGENCY PRODUCER:
Michelle Burke
PRODUCTION COMPANY:
Johns + Gorman Films
DIRECTOR:
Jeff Gorman
CLIENT:
California Sunkist Pistachios
AGENCY:
Chiat/Day, Venice

66 GOLD
ART DIRECTORS:
Andrew Christou
Eric C. King
WRITERS:
Derek Barnes
James LeMaitre
AGENCY PRODUCER:
Donna Portaro
PRODUCTION COMPANY:
Pytka
DIRECTOR:
Joe Pytka
CLIENT:
Nike
AGENCY:
Wieden & Kennedy/ Portland

65 Gold
INTERVIEWER: So what does sound toning do?
SUPER: AUGUST PRIEST. SOUND TONER.
PRIEST: It opens your heart chakra, so you feel unconditional love just vibrating throughout all of you. Comfortably and easily. You can feel your guardian angel surrounding you. Creating balance and harmony.
(SFX: SOUND TONING)
SUPER: EVERYBODY KNOWS THE BEST NUTS COME FROM CALIFORNIA.
ANNCR: Sunkist California Pistachios. Now that's a nut.
SUPER: CALIFORNIA PISTACHIOS.

66 Gold
SUPER: DAY 21.
(SFX: BEEPING OF RADAR GUN)
(SFX: BEEPING, WINGS FLAPPING)
SUPER: PLAY BALL. PLEASE.
(SFX: BEEPING, WINGS FLAPPING)
SUPER: NIKE.

GOLD, SILVER & BRONZE AWARDS

CONSUMER TELEVISION
:30/:25 SINGLE

67 SILVER
ART DIRECTOR:
Jerry Gentile
WRITER:
Scott Vincent
AGENCY PRODUCER:
Michelle Burke
PRODUCTION COMPANY:
Johns + Gorman Films
DIRECTOR:
Jeff Gorman
CLIENT:
California Sunkist Pistachios
AGENCY:
Chiat/Day, Venice

68 SILVER
ART DIRECTORS:
Jason Peterson
Paul Hirsch
Izzy DeBellis
WRITERS:
Izzy DeBellis
Paul Hirsch
Jason Peterson
AGENCY PRODUCER:
Deborah Sullivan
PRODUCTION COMPANY:
Epoch Films
DIRECTOR:
Jeff Priess
CLIENT:
NBA
AGENCY:
Fallon McElligott Berlin/ New York

69 BRONZE
ART DIRECTOR:
Johan Gulbranson
WRITER:
Oistein Borge
AGENCY PRODUCER:
Knut E. Jensen
PRODUCTION COMPANY:
Leo Film
DIRECTOR:
Johan Gulbranson
CLIENT:
Time Foto
AGENCY:
Leo Burnett/Oslo

67 Silver
(SFX: BIKE BELL RINGING)
(MUSIC: "THREE BLIND MICE")
SUPER: EVERYBODY KNOWS THE BEST NUTS COME FROM CALIFORNIA.
ANNCR: Sunkist California Pistachios. Now that's a nut.
SUPER: CALIFORNIA PISTACHIOS.

68 Silver

BILL MURRAY: Check it. I got a foul.

KID: Foul.

BILL: Right here.

KID: It wouldn't have been a foul if you made the shot.

BILL: It's the first one I've called, man, come on. Still game point. Okay, you ready? What is this, your mother coming to get you here?

KID: Where?

BILL: See that, in the NBA, when some guy starts talking about your momma you don't listen up. You stay right here. My mother, my father, my dog, my brothers and sisters, I'm all about the game. Baby . . .

KID: I got it.

BILL: . . . you better get hungry or you're not going to be there with me.

69 Bronze

SUPER: WE BLOW UP YOUR FAVORITE HOLIDAY PICTURE!

SUPER: TIME PHOTO. 1-HOUR PHOTO.

GOLD, SILVER & BRONZE AWARDS

CONSUMER TELEVISION
:30/:25 CAMPAIGN

70 GOLD

ART DIRECTOR:
Jerry Gentile
WRITER:
Scott Vincent
AGENCY PRODUCER:
Michelle Burke
PRODUCTION COMPANY:
Johns + Gorman Films
DIRECTOR:
Jeff Gorman
CLIENT:
California Sunkist Pistachios
AGENCY:
Chiat/Day, Venice

70 I Gold

INTERVIEWER: So what does sound toning do?

SUPER: AUGUST PRIEST. SOUND TONER.

PRIEST: It opens your heart chakra, so you feel unconditional love just vibrating throughout all of you. Comfortably and easily. You can feel your guardian angel surrounding you. Creating balance and harmony.

(SFX: SOUND TONING)

SUPER: EVERYBODY KNOWS THE BEST NUTS COME FROM CALIFORNIA.

ANNCR: Sunkist California Pistachios. Now that's a nut.

SUPER: CALIFORNIA PISTACHIOS.

70 II

BUDDY: My angel name is Sanfernandinaki. People call me Buddy.

(SFX: BUDDY CHANTING, CHIME SOUND)

(SFX: HEAVY BREATHING SOUNDS FROM BUDDY, MORE CHANTING)

BUDDY: We have spiritual parties at our house about once every other month. If you're at all interested, we'll invite you.

SUPER: EVERYBODY KNOWS THE BEST NUTS COME FROM CALIFORNIA.

ANNCR: Sunkist California Pistachios. Now that's a nut.

SUPER: CALIFORNIA PISTACHIOS.

70 III

(SFX: BIKE-BELL RINGING)

(MUSIC: "THREE BLIND MICE")

SUPER: EVERYBODY KNOWS THE BEST NUTS COME FROM CALIFORNIA.

ANNCR: Sunkist California Pistachios. Now that's a nut.

SUPER: CALIFORNIA PISTACHIOS.

GOLD, SILVER & BRONZE AWARDS

CONSUMER TELEVISION
:30/:25 CAMPAIGN

71 SILVER
ART DIRECTORS:
Jason Peterson
Paul Hirsch
Izzy DeBellis
WRITERS:
Izzy DeBellis
Paul Hirsch
Jason Peterson
AGENCY PRODUCER:
Deborah Sullivan
PRODUCTION COMPANY:
Epoch Films
DIRECTOR:
Jeff Priess
CLIENT:
NBA
AGENCY:
Fallon McElligott Berlin/
New York

72 BRONZE
ART DIRECTOR:
Rohitash Rao
WRITER:
Eric Silver
AGENCY PRODUCER:
Nancy Hacohen
PRODUCTION COMPANY:
HKM Productions
DIRECTOR:
Jesse Dylan
CLIENT:
Good Guys Auto
AGENCY:
Earle Palmer Brown/
Richmond

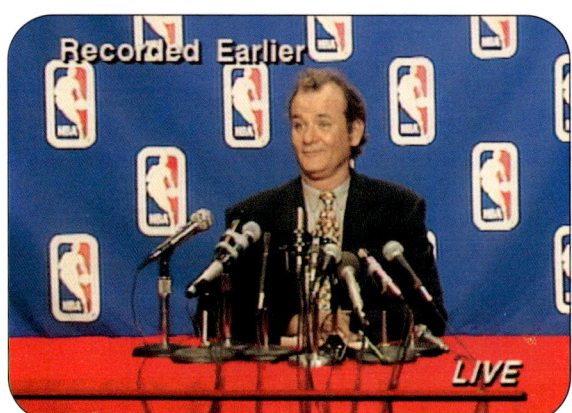

71 Silver

BILL MURRAY: You know, I don't understand why you're being so tough on me Mr. Rashad. You weren't this tough on Michael Jordan or Scottie Pippen. I mean, just because I want to play? Maybe you and I should play sometime, you know?

AHMAD RASHAD: Mr. Murray, I'm not trying to play in the National Basketball Association.

BILL: You can call me Bill, I mean, not Mr. Murray, you know, I know it's . . . think of this as the locker room.

AHMAD: You were calling a press conference saying that you were going to play basketball and we found out here today you never played in college, you never played in high school.

BILL: S-So?

72 Bronze

MECHANIC: It's a Chevy . . . Camaro I believe. . . . Six cylinder . . . and it's blue.

SUPER: GOOD GUYS AUTO. WE KNOW CARS SO WELL, IT'S KINDA CREEPY.

GOLD, SILVER & BRONZE AWARDS

CONSUMER TELEVISION :20 AND UNDER: CAMPAIGN

73 GOLD
ART DIRECTOR:
Tim Hanrahan
WRITER:
Hank Perlman
AGENCY PRODUCER:
Ben Grylewicz
PRODUCTION COMPANY:
Radical Media
DIRECTORS:
Bryan Buckley
Frank Todaro
CLIENT:
ESPN
AGENCY:
Wieden & Kennedy/ Portland

073 I Gold

MAN 1: So Kirk, emotions really run that high during the play-offs?

SUPER: KIRK MULLER. MONTREAL CANADIENS.

KIRK: What'd you say?

MAN 1: Nyuh, nyuh. Excuse me.

MAN 2: Let's get out of here. I told you you shouldn't ask him that question.

MAN 1: Excuse me.

MAN 2: Get out of the way!

MAN 1: Excuse me! Taxi!

SUPER: MONTREAL CANADIENS VS. BOSTON BRUINS. CONFERENCE QUARTERFINALS.

MAN 2: Taxi! Taxi!

SUPER: THE STANLEY CUP PLAYOFFS ESPN. TOMORROW 8:30 PM.

73 II
SUPER: MIKE RICHTER. NEW YORK RANGERS.
(SFX: SLAP SHOTS)
(SFX: SQUEAKING AS PLEXIGLASS IS WIPED CLEAN)
SUPER: NEW YORK ISLANDERS VS. NEW YORK RANGERS.
SUPER: THE STANLEY CUP PLAYOFFS. ESPN.

73 III
SUPER: BRETT HULL. ST. LOUIS BLUES.
CONSTRUCTION WORKER: We're clear.
(SFX: SLAP SHOT)
(SFX: BUILDING BEING DEMOLISHED)
SUPER: DALLAS STARS VS. ST. LOUIS BLUES.
SUPER: THE STANLEY CUP PLAYOFFS. ESPN.

GOLD, SILVER & BRONZE AWARDS

CONSUMER TELEVISION
VARYING LENGTHS
CAMPAIGN

74 GOLD

ART DIRECTORS:
Andrew Christou
Eric C. King
WRITERS:
Derek Barnes
James LeMaitre
AGENCY PRODUCER:
Donna Portaro
PRODUCTION COMPANY:
Pytka
DIRECTOR:
Joe Pytka
CLIENT:
Nike
AGENCY:
**Wieden & Kennedy/
Portland**

74 I Gold
SUPER: PLAY BALL.
SUPER: PLEASE.
SUPER: NIKE.

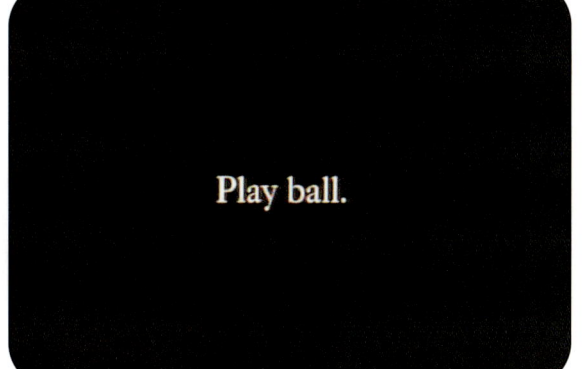

74 II
SUPER: PLAY BALL.
SUPER: PLEASE.
SUPER: NIKE.

74 III
FAN: Get off the field! You're a bum! You don't deserve to be on a baseball field! You! Yeah, You! I'm talking to you! Don't make me come out there!
SUPER: PLAY BALL.
SUPER: PLEASE.
FAN: You know I'm talking to ya!
SUPER: NIKE.

GOLD, SILVER & BRONZE
AWARDS

CONSUMER TELEVISION
VARYING LENGTHS
CAMPAIGN

75 SILVER
ART DIRECTORS:
Greg Bell
Donna Weinheim
John Leu
WRITERS:
Michelle Roufa
Arthur Bijur
Greg Bell
John Leu
Cliff Freeman
AGENCY PRODUCERS:
Anne Kurtzman
MaryEllen Duggan
PRODUCTION COMPANIES:
Crossroads Films
Harmony Pictures
DIRECTORS:
Mark Story
Charles Wittenmaier
Bruce Hurwit
CLIENT:
Little Caesars
AGENCY:
Cliff Freeman & Partners/
New York

CONSUMER TELEVISION
UNDER $50,000 BUDGET

76 GOLD
ART DIRECTOR:
Rohitash Rao
WRITER:
Eric Silver
AGENCY PRODUCER:
Nancy Hacohen
PRODUCTION COMPANY:
HKM Productions
DIRECTOR:
Jesse Dylan
CLIENT:
Good Guys Auto
AGENCY:
Earle Palmer Brown/
Richmond

75 Silver

GRANNY: Have you ever seen anything more amazing than Little Caesars Italian Sausage Pizza?

BABY (SINGING): *Give my regards to Broadway . . .*

FATHER: No.

ANNCR: Italian Sausage Pizza! Loaded with sausage, peppers and onions. The newest from a whole menu of Little Caesars Pleasers. Any two for $9.98.

LITTLE CAESAR: Pizza! Pizza!

ANNCR: Or get one for $5.99!

LITTLE CAESAR: Pizza!

76 Gold

MECHANIC: It's an American car . . . Cadillac. . . . Power windows . . . power steering. . . . And the air conditioning is on the fritz.

SUPER: GOOD GUYS AUTO. WE KNOW CARS SO WELL, IT'S KINDA CREEPY.

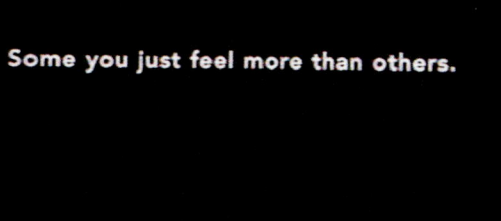

GOLD, SILVER & BRONZE AWARDS

NON-BROADCAST CINEMA

77 BRONZE
ART DIRECTOR:
Heidi Flora
WRITER:
Kevin Jones
AGENCY PRODUCER:
Sam Walsh
PRODUCTION COMPANY:
Straight Cut
EDITOR:
Johnna Turiano
CLIENT:
Seattle International Film Festival
AGENCY:
Cole & Weber/Seattle

INTERNATIONAL FOREIGN LANGUAGE COMMERCIAL: TELEVISION

78 GOLD
ART DIRECTOR:
Elvio Sanchez
WRITERS:
Carlos Bayala
Sandra Schapoff
AGENCY PRODUCERS:
Luis Pompeo
Roberto Carsillo
PRODUCTION COMPANY:
Sorin
DIRECTOR:
Carlos Sorin
CLIENT:
Reckitt & Colman
AGENCY:
Young & Rubicam/Buenos Aires

77 Bronze
SUPER: EVERY DAY WE ARE BOMBARDED BY BILLIONS OF TINY PARTICLES OF LIGHT.
SUPER: SOME YOU JUST FEEL MORE THAN OTHERS.
SUPER: CINEMA SEATTLE PRESENTS THE SEATTLE INTERNATIONAL FILM FESTIVAL XX.
SUPER: SEE WHAT THE WORLD IS COMING TO MAY 20–JUNE 12.

78 Gold
(SFX: DRUM BEAT)
(SFX: INSECT-LIKE CHANTING)
(SFX: SPRAYING OF INSECTICIDE, CHANTING STOPS)
SUPER: SHELLTOX KILLS MOSQUITOS. THE MAXIMUM POWER OF KNOCKING THEM OUT.

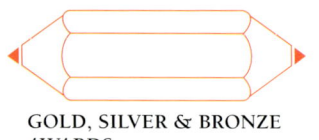

GOLD, SILVER & BRONZE AWARDS

COLLEGE COMPETITION
ASSIGNMENT: BRAND
NAME BAR SOAP

79 GOLD
ART DIRECTOR:
Michael Cohen
WRITER:
Curtis Smith
COLLEGE:
Portfolio Center/Atlanta

80 SILVER
ART DIRECTOR:
Allison Burton
WRITER:
Allison Burton
COLLEGE:
East Texas State University/Commerce, TX

81 BRONZE
ART DIRECTORS:
Jay Russell
Colleen Smith
WRITERS:
Jay Russell
Wade Alger
COLLEGE:
Southern Methodist University/Dallas

79 Gold

> **I'M GOING TO WASH YOUR MOUTH OUT WITH A BAR OF SODIUM TALLOWATE, TRICLOCARBAN AND CARBOLIC ACID.**

In Case You've Forgotten, Ivory is 99 44/100% Pure.

80 Silver

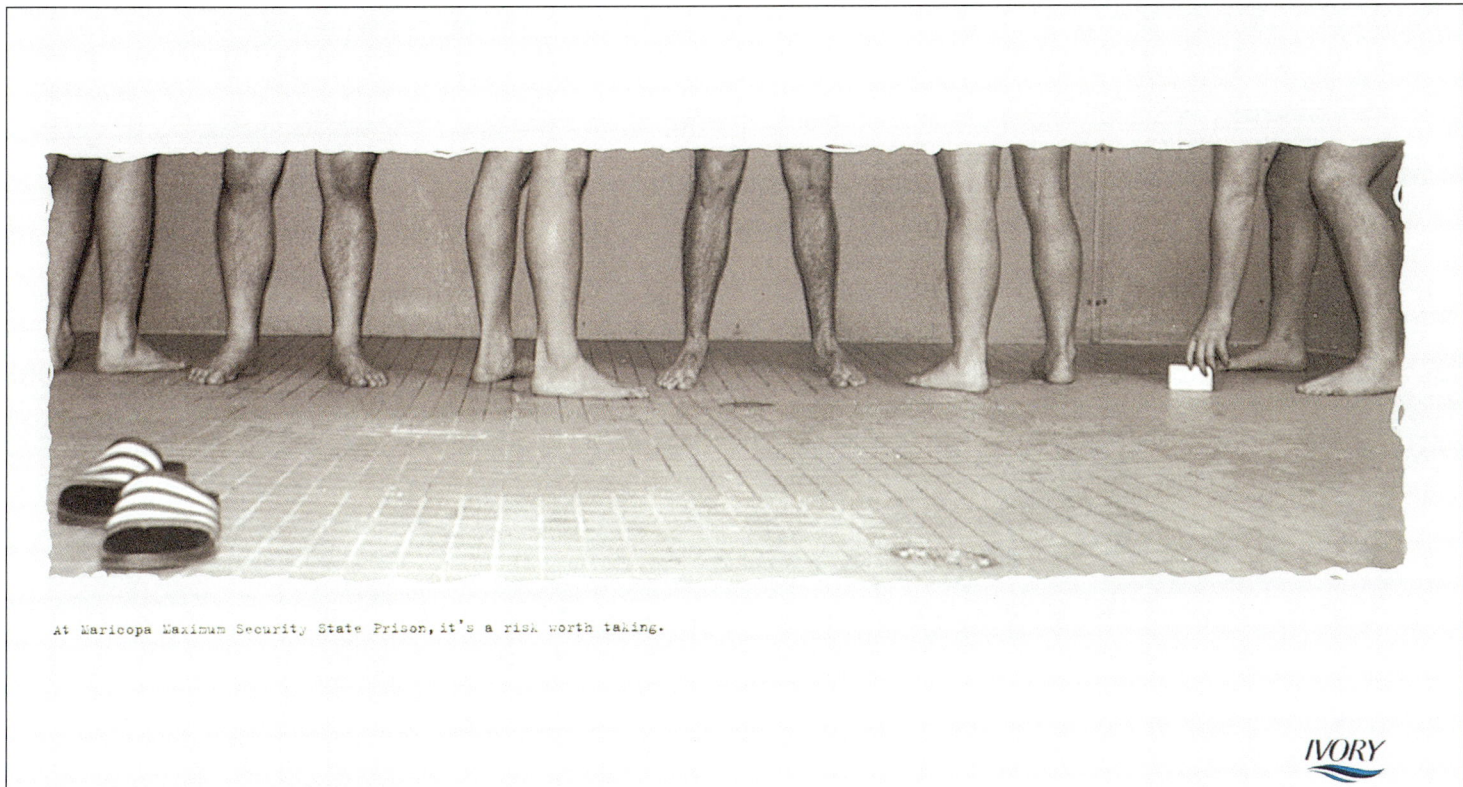

At Maricopa Maximum Security State Prison, it's a risk worth taking.

IVORY

81 Bronze

Best of Show

(SFX: THUNDER CRASHING)

(SFX: SOUND OF BALL FLYING)

(SFX: CROWD CHEERING, POWER KICK, BRICKS SMASHING)

(SFX: FAST MOVING BALL, CROWD CHEERING)

(SFX: BALL BEING KICKED, BRICKS SMASHING)

(SFX: FAST MOVING BALL, PIGEON WINGS FLAPPING, NOISE OF HEADER, BRICKS SMASHING)

(SFX: SMASHING BRICKS, MOVING BALL, KICKING SOUND, SMASHING BRICKS)

(SFX: MOVING BALL, CRASH OF BROKEN GLASS)

(SFX: SOUND OF SIGN SWINGING)

SUPER: NIKE.

Best of Show

ART DIRECTOR:
Warren Eakins
WRITER:
Bob Moore
AGENCY PRODUCER:
Jane Brimblecombe
PRODUCTION COMPANY:
Pytka
DIRECTOR:
Joe Pytka
CLIENT:
Nike International
AGENCY:
Wieden & Kennedy/ Amsterdam

*The
Gold Award Winners
on the
Gold Award Winners*

THE GOLD AWARD
WINNERS ON THE
GOLD AWARD WINNERS

CONSUMER NEWSPAPER
OVER 600 LINES:
SINGLE AND CAMPAIGN

AGENCY
McCann-Erickson/Singapore
CLIENT
Simmons

We started with the more obvious ways to advertise a bed such as wine glasses balancing on the mattress. Then we picked up the corporate brochure and found buried among the facts and figures a reference to a series of ads they'd produced in the 1930s. It was like finding a pile of Rembrandt paintings hidden in the attic. Testimonials by Roosevelt, Edison, Marconi, Henry Ford . . . only God Almighty was missing. It would have been criminal negligence not to bring them to the attention of a wider public. Of course, finding Rembrandts in the attic is a stroke of amazing good fortune. The skill, if there is any, lies in recognizing their value. If we hadn't, we would probably have run the wine glass on the mattress.

MARC SCHATTNER
MALCOLM PRYCE

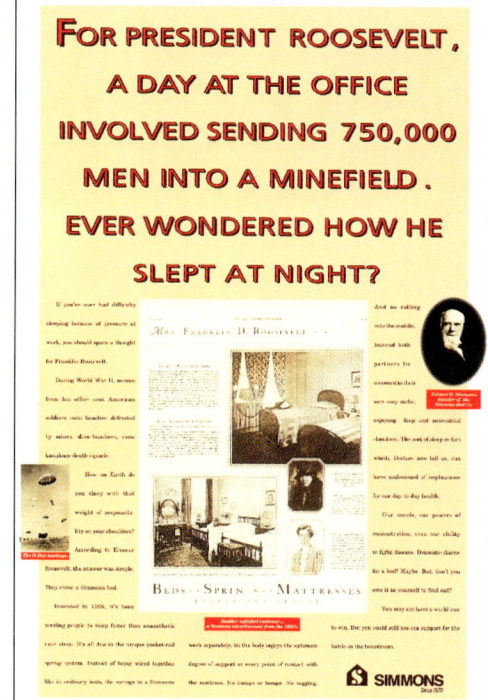

1

34

COLLATERAL
BROCHURES OTHER THAN BY MAIL

AGENCY
MTV Off-Air Creative/New York
CLIENT
MTV

Conceptually, this project is a celebration of all things superficial and decorative in life, thus the title of the book: Fluff. But beyond that, Fluff deals with the fact that so many young adults today have lost the notion of how to have fun. They live in a world where the face of violence is a young one. The prospect of unemployment, the fear of AIDS, the notion that they will not surpass the success of their parents, all contribute to a pervasive sense of anxiety. In an attempt to counter that widespread stress for a brief moment, this project celebrates the world of fun and excess, the joy of watching a sunset, the thrill of making love in a field, the idea that it's okay to waste time, and the fact that wasting time well is an art form. But that doesn't mean we should ever forget those who die at an early age at the barrel of a gun, or from the virus known as HIV. The design, the creative aspects, and the art direction of this project are all secondary to the overall concept. Needless to say, the creatives had loads of fun and we are thankful that we are here to have created this book. We dedicate it to those who could not enjoy its celebration of life.

STACY DRUMMOND
TRACY BOYCHUK
JEFFREY KEYTON
DAVID FELTON
JOHAN VIPPER

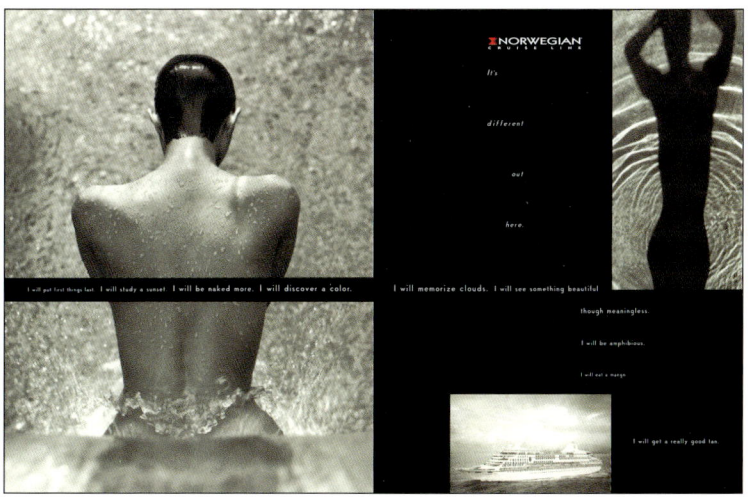

CONSUMER MAGAZINE
COLOR 1 PAGE OR SPREAD: SINGLE AND CAMPAIGN

AGENCY
Goodby Silverstein & Partners/San Francisco
CLIENT
Norwegian Cruise Line

We heard of an experiment, the goal of which was to produce a universally popular painting. Focus groups were conducted, and respondents were asked what kinds of things they liked in paintings. Respondents stated that they liked paintings that contained the following elements: blue skies, dark storm clouds, meadows, mountains, cows, water, twenty-threeish lovers and exotic animals from Asia or preferably Africa. The sponsors of the survey studied the responses well and set to work. They produced the absolutely infallible painting. The painting featured a bright blue sky and black storm clouds. There was a river in it, with a cow, an elephant and a lion insouciantly drinking together. The river bank rioted with simultaneously blooming flowers that in nature bloomed in different seasons. And a semi-nude couple in Greco-Roman robes watched peacefully over the whole damn mess.

We decided to take a less scientific approach.

STEVE SIMPSON
STEVE LUKER

OUTDOOR: SINGLE

AGENCY:
CF2GS/Seattle
CLIENT:
Pacific Science Center

Outdoor is a tough medium. It's like an advertising form stripped naked. Somebody once told me that outdoor is the world's biggest blank canvas for someone to paint a picture on. And that if you think the easel behind that canvas would more clearly communicate your idea, show that. I think the Titanica board works because I tried to follow these non-rules.

Honestly, if I said that concepting this board was a struggle, I would be lying. Taking the visual of the ship and making the whole board sink seemed like a natural to me. It was the first thing I did. Out of a sense of duty, I then did a bunch of other ideas, but none were as clean.

The real heroes of this project are the client and the AE. And in a weird way, a huge chunk of ice.

KURT REIFSCHNEIDER

THE GOLD AWARD WINNERS ON THE GOLD AWARD WINNERS

CONSUMER MAGAZINE
LESS THAN A PAGE
B/W OR COLOR: CAMPAIGN

AGENCY
Loeffler Ketchum Mountjoy/Charlotte
CLIENT
North Carolina Travel & Tourism

If there's one thing our agency has hopefully proven by now, it's that we can do the elegant headline, beautiful photo, meticulously art directed ad thing for North Carolina pretty well.

This was an opportunity to do something decidedly different. Here, in fact, was a chance to do what larger East Coast clients aren't exactly renowned for: ads that actually begged for a push-the-envelope attitude.

The "wet pants" line was the first one out of the box. (It still seems a little obvious to us. Does it to you?) The others came fairly quickly thereafter.

What probably made these ads achieve medaldom, though, is the deceptively simple-looking art direction. About midway through the layout process, we came to a key impasse: On the wall was what we'd call the "West Coast X-er award-winning formula layout"; i.e., one where there's a cool visual engulfed by blaring typefaces (typically done in different point sizes).

We knew it would probably win awards.

We also knew that it just wasn't us.

Many layouts later, we had what you see here.

Enduring lessons: 1. Learn to recognize golden (pardon the pun) opportunities and don't let them pass you by; 2. Remember that once you've done a good concept, you're only halfway home. You've got another concept left to do: fresh, original art direction; 3. If it feels like a formula, flush it; 4. Use words like "wet pants," "weenie" and "sex" in your headlines. Judges eat it up.

Do all these things and you too can be a gold award winner.

ED JONES
JIM MOUNTJOY

Nobody will ever know it wasn't the water that made your pants wet.

WHITEWATER IN NORTH CAROLINA.
1-800-VISIT-NC

**TRADE
ANY SIZE B/W OR COLOR:
CAMPAIGN**

AGENCY
Goldsmith/Jeffrey, New York
CLIENT
Crain's New York Business

"Sixty-seven percent in top management."

"That's a good fact."

"No, that's a lot of big shots in sweet Armanis styling it up in floor-to-ceiling window offices."

"Ninetieth floor Penthouse views."

"Executive washrooms."

"Heated toilet seat."

"Helipads."

"Oak paneled executive-only elevators."

"Yeah, these guys are too good to get in an elevator with us unwashed masses."

"Well, at least when the brakes fail they'll have plenty of time to contemplate their sins."

"Before becoming spatula fodder."

"Right? See your life flash by for 90 agonizing stories Mr. Corner Office!"

"Mr. VIP, meet Mr. Gravity."

"Think of the dry cleaning bill."

"Think if we presented it."

"Think if they bought it."

"Think if it won a gold pencil."

"Yeah, right."

"As if."

TOM MILLER
HENRIETTE LIENKE

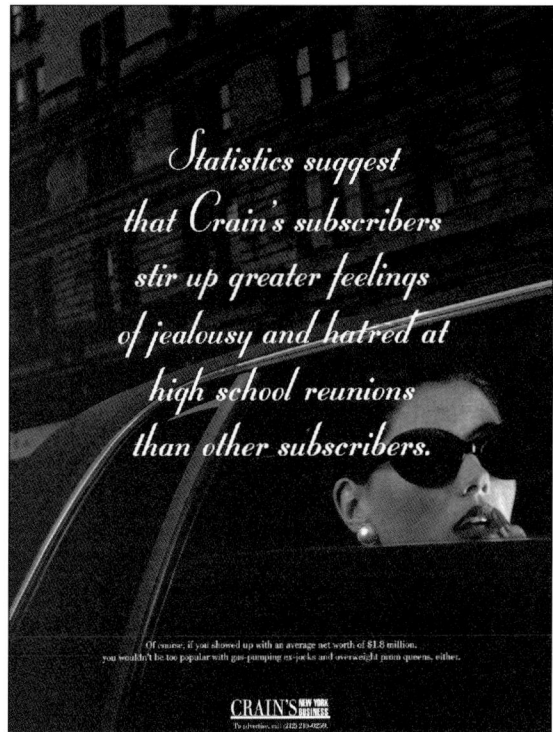

THE GOLD AWARD WINNERS ON THE GOLD AWARD WINNERS

**COLLATERAL
POINT OF PURCHASE AND IN-STORE**

AGENCY
Leonard/Monahan, Providence
CLIENT
Stork's Landing

It was unplanned. But we're happy about it anyway.

ROB RICH
KARA GOODRICH

**COLLATERAL
SELF-PROMOTION**

AGENCY
DDB Needham Worldwide/New York
CLIENT
Adam Chasnow

Looking back on it, maybe taking that job at McCann wasn't so stupid after all.

ADAM CHASNOW

36

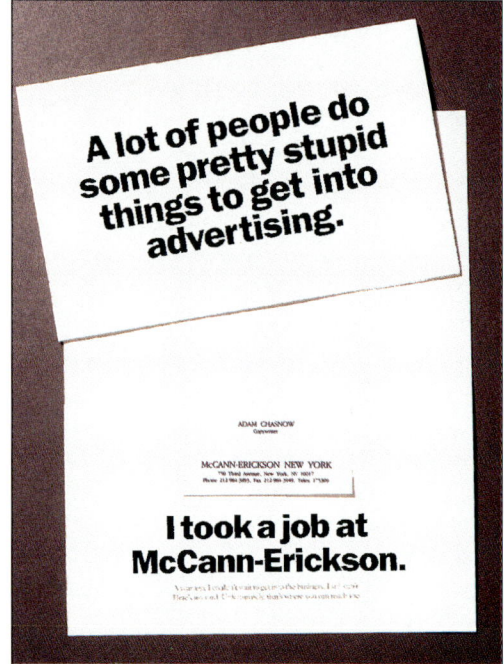

38

39

**COLLATERAL
POSTERS**

AGENCY
Arnold Finnegan Martin/Richmond
CLIENT
Invisible Fencing Company

The dog is resting comfortably.

STEVE DOLBINSKI
IAN BARRY

PUBLIC SERVICE/POLITICAL
OUTDOOR AND POSTERS

AGENCY
Clarity Coverdale Fury/Minneapolis
CLIENT
Mothers Against Drunk Driving

Actually, all we did was borrow an old idea. Like from the 1700s. In those days, people who were found guilty of public drunkenness were put in the stocks and humiliated right out in the public square. Apparently, the theory was people are a lot less likely to commit a crime if they know they're going to be made into a laughing stock in front of their friends and neighbors. As far as we know, it worked back then. We thought it might work now.

So we got a list of multiple DWI offenders and their addresses. We named it the 1994 Minnesota DWI Hall of Shame. We wrote a flat headline. We kept the layout basic and clean. (Originally, we wanted to include the offenders' phone numbers too, so they'd get lots of harassing phone calls, but the lawyers wigged.)

Anyway, the poster got printed. Our client got noticed. The DWI offenders got pissed. And we got gold.

Hmm . . . maybe next year we should revive the idea of the scarlet letter.

BILL JOHNSON
RANDY HUGHES

PUBLIC SERVICE/POLITICAL
NEWSPAPER OR MAGAZINE: CAMPAIGN

AGENCY
Fallon McElligott/Minneapolis
CLIENT
People for the Ethical Treatment of Animals

This is a great client. There is no confusion in the company about their mission statement. From the receptionist on up, every employee knows what the organization is about: "Animals are not ours to eat, wear or experiment on."

They are a radical group, and radical in the '60s meaning of the term. They wave hand-lettered signs, chain themselves to CEO's desks, interfere with stuffy corporate functions, embarrass, enrage, lampoon, and generally make a nuisance of themselves.

The ads they ask us to do are always aggressive, always single-minded, and never watered down by any committee. Virtually every ad we have ever shown them has run as is. And while many clients start by asking for aggressive ads ("Let's really go after them!"), PETA doesn't back off when they finally see the work. They appreciate the hard edges, and they run the ads.

As for doing the ads, it's fairly easy—a shot of an abused animal, a caustic headline, that's about it. There's no great creative leap here. What's different is, again, the client actually runs them.

LUKE SULLIVAN
BOB BARRIE

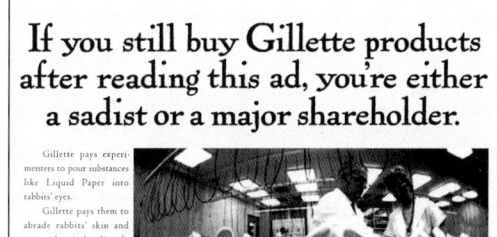

THE GOLD AWARD WINNERS ON THE GOLD AWARD WINNERS

PUBLIC SERVICE/POLITICAL
RADIO: SINGLE

AGENCY
Houston Effler Herstek Favat/Boston
CLIENT
Massachusetts Department of Public Health

As hard as Mrs. Sackman is working to speak, what she's saying must be pretty damned important. And her sincerity makes you want to work just as hard to listen. That's how it was in person, that's how we put it on the radio. It's harsh and simple, but it's honest. Apparently, a lot of people can't take the full sixty seconds. In which case the spot has really made its point.

KEN LEWIS
DAVE GARDINER
STU COOPERRIDER

PUBLIC SERVICE/POLITICAL
RADIO: CAMPAIGN

AGENCY
Houston Effler Herstek Favat/Boston
CLIENT
Massachusetts Department of Public Health

The tobacco companies try to hide the truth because they understand its power. We had the truth working for us, so what we had to do was find people to give it credibility. Who better than people who had been a part of the deceit?

KEN LEWIS
DAVE GARDINER
STU COOPERRIDER

PUBLIC SERVICE/POLITICAL
TELEVISION: CAMPAIGN

AGENCY
Houston Effler Herstek Favat/Boston
CLIENT
Massachusetts Department of Public Health

A study in persistence and luck. All along the way, everything had to fall into place to make this campaign good. A smart strategic direction, tons of input, a daring client, people with the guts to come forward, a director who desperately wanted these spots and then showed why. Production problems actually worked to our benefit. We even had to replace one of the spokespersons at the last minute. The replacement: Janet Sackman.

You have to start with a good idea, but it's only an idea without follow-through.

KEN LEWIS
DAVE GARDINER
STU COOPERRIDER

PUBLIC SERVICE/POLITICAL TELEVISION: SINGLE

AGENCY
Abbott Mead Vickers. BBDO/London
CLIENT
Queen Elizabeth's Foundation for Disabled People

QEFDP train severely disabled people to do useful, fulfilling work and to live their lives independently. We were asked to help them raise money to build a new training centre. The inspiration for the ad came from what we saw at their old building. We met a girl with no arms or legs who performed seemingly impossible physical tasks with dignity and determination. It made what we do for a living seem shamefully easy. And it also made writing a cheque seem easy. We did a shorter version but it didn't communicate the repetitiousness, tedium and danger involved in making a meal with your mouth as well as this three minute cut. The film helped to raise 800,000 pounds. If you see it and it moves you maybe we can raise some dollars too.

PAUL BRAZIER
PETER SOUTER

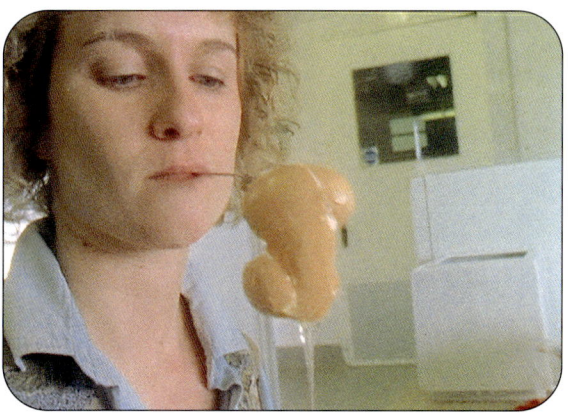

CONSUMER RADIO: SINGLE

AGENCY
Korey Kay & Partners/New York
CLIENT
Comedy Central

When you're trying to write any sort of comedy, you quickly realize there are only three truly funny topics: 1. The Bathroom (which includes toilets, enemas, adult diapers, fecal matter, etc.); 2. Sex (which includes fornication, masturbation, beastiality, genitalia, etc.), and of course; 3. Death (which, by the way, includes serious bodily injury). When coming up with the Suicide Hotline spot, we went with tried and true category number three.

This radio spot was written not as a mockery of suicide, but as a statement against those annoying electronic voices that answer phones. We figured the upbeat woman you always hear on these things, along with the utter impersonality of it all, was a nice contrast to the very serious topic.

Also, a lot of credit has to go to Art and Mark, the clients. To buy a spot like this, you gotta have nice-sized cojones. (See category number two.)

DANTE LOMBARDI
ROB SLOSBERG

THE GOLD AWARD WINNERS ON THE GOLD AWARD WINNERS

CONSUMER RADIO: CAMPAIGN

AGENCY
Howell Henry Chaldecott Lury & Partners/London

CLIENT
Britvic

A couple of years ago we heard this album by two guys called the Jerky Boyz. Basically, these guys phone unsuspecting members of the public and wind them up. Great idea, we thought. Great idea. Very funny.

Then we forgot about it. A year and a half went by. One Friday afternoon we got this panic brief to do a radio campaign for Apple Tango to back up the TV work we'd done earlier. So we wrote a few ideas. The client bought some and it was sort of okay. The kind of scripts that you aren't embarrassed about but aren't particularly proud of either.

We got a bit honest with each other, admitting the scripts weren't great which was quite depressing. Then something brilliant happened. We remembered the Jerky Boyz.

We ran the idea by the account team. We asked them to try unselling the idea they had already sold and sell this new idea to the client. The only problem was we wanted to do it live and unscripted. So the client would have to buy a rough idea with nothing tangible to get a hold on.

The client agreed. Nice geezer.

So we spent a couple of days in a studio with four London phone directories, three actors/friends, a producer, and just started calling people. We called undertakers, Croation Orthodox priests, fruit merchants, Chinese restaurants . . . we must have made 60 or 70 calls in all.

After each good call we had to call the people back and get their permission to use them in an ad. Some people loved the idea. Some people yelled very unpleasant names at us down the phone.

We'd like to thank everyone who helped. And our apologies to the Croation Orthodox priest. We're sorry . . . we won't do it again.

TREVOR ROBINSON
ALAN YOUNG

CONSUMER TELEVISION
OVER :30 SINGLE

AGENCY
Wieden & Kennedy/Amsterdam
CLIENT
Nike International

The making of "The Wall" was a long journey. From the time we started working on it until the time it was finished the spot took ten months and over 80,000 miles of travel to complete.

It was a worldwide project in every respect: As a World Cup spot it was to be watched by billions all over the world; the athletes played for teams in Europe, North and South America; the shoot locations were on several continents. Those involved in the production were truly an international group of talented individuals and everyone that touched it plussed it, especially director Joe Pytka, Editel special effects artist Christin Johnson, Sony Music sound designer Albert Ibbitson, and agency producer Jane Brimblecombe.

The spot had to be universal—visual and not language-oriented. There was nothing culture-specific about it. Soccer cuts across national borders and mind-sets. Yet the physical settings needed to be recognizable: Paris, Milan, Berlin, London, New York, Rio, and Mexico City.

When we first got the idea in a hotel room in Rio we thought it would be too wildly expensive to pull off. But we were so excited about it we dashed off some thumbnails to Bill Davenport, Head of Broadcast Production at Wieden & Kennedy/Portland. He immediately saw the possibilities and quickly determined it could be done for less than we'd imagined. Creative directors Dan Wieden and Susan Hoffman embraced it and enthusiasm for the idea was contagious. Before we knew it Nike signed off and we were on our way.

As arduous as it was all those months shooting players and locations all over the world, sometimes in the lousiest of weather, the toughest part of the project lay ahead of us when all the film came together in L.A. for post-production. It wasn't just a matter of editing film—it became virtually frame-by-frame animation. Buildings were altered in shape and size, day was made into night, structures were created digitally, new skies were dropped in—we even placed new heads on bodies.

Creating the illusion that each player really was a painting on the side of a building was an amazing artistic and technical triumph and took hundreds of hours to accomplish.

The soundtrack was the crowning touch.

At the end of those ten months, when we all sat down in Sony's big surround-sound theater and watched the finished spot, we were truly thrilled. Then seeing it on the air, giving Nike credibility in a sport with which they'd previously been unassociated, was ultimately and completely gratifying.

WARREN EAKINS
BOB MOORE

THE GOLD AWARD
WINNERS ON THE
GOLD AWARD WINNERS

CONSUMER TELEVISION
:30/:25 SINGLE

AGENCY
Chiat/Day, Venice
CLIENT
California Sunkist Pistachios

This campaign is the result of a client having the courage to remember two simple things: it's not brain surgery, it's advertising. And when all is said and done, it's just a nut. Make the spots funny, and people will buy them.

JERRY GENTILE
SCOTT VINCENT

65

CONSUMER TELEVISION
:30/:25 SINGLE

AGENCY
Wieden & Kennedy/Portland
CLIENT
Nike

We spent about three nights trying to come up with an idea, and got nowhere. Then, ten minutes before we had to present to Dan, Andrew pulls out a campaign from his student book for a local lingerie shop. All we did was change the logo.

ANDREW CHRISTOU
ERIC C. KING
DEREK BARNES
JAMES LeMAITRE

66

CONSUMER TELEVISION
:30/:25 CAMPAIGN

AGENCY
Chiat/Day, Venice
CLIENT
California Sunkist Pistachios

The client finally gives us the thumbs up to start looking for some "eccentric" characters. It's California. This is going to be a piece of cake.

About a week goes by, the casting director comes back with a guy who does the "one-man band" type of deal, a guy who can make his voice sound like he's in an echo chamber, and a guy who wears like twenty hats at the same time.

We started to get that hollow feeling. That "if all we can find is a guy who juggles chain saws, we're pretty much dead" kind of feeling.

Just as we're coming to terms with the fact that we're about to produce the world's most boring campaign we get a call. "Would you be interested in a guy who claims he can align your internal organs by yelling into your back?" Yes. Yes, we would.

JERRY GENTILE
SCOTT VINCENT

CONSUMER TELEVISION
:20 AND UNDER: CAMPAIGN

AGENCY
Wieden & Kennedy/Portland
CLIENT
ESPN

We've been doing this campaign for the last two hockey seasons and it's always been a lot of fun. We've been lucky to work with each other, a really good client that pretty much lets us do whatever we want, and cool hockey players who are willing to do just about anything if they think it's funny.

One thing we've learned is that there's a direct correlation in the NHL between penalty minutes and comedic ability. The more a player fights, the funnier he is. Which brings up the point that we're for fighting. We think it's a necessary part of the game that helps protect the skilled players, your Gretzky's and your Bures, from flagrant stick work and assorted cheap shots. Hockey is and always will be a game of intimidation. That's one of the things that makes it so interesting and entertaining to watch. If an opposing player takes a liberty with one of your superstars, you have to be able to stick up for him to ensure that it won't happen again. Let's face it, the bench clearing brawls and goon tactics of the '70s are behind us and now the league's blessed with great players like Brendan Shanahan, Rick Tochet, Ken Daneyko, Cam Neely, and Adam Graves—guys who can play the game as well as anybody and, when called upon, can drop the gloves in order to protect their teammates. Plus, the fact is that we enjoy a good, spontaneous, fairly-fought hockey fight. And so do the majority of the fans. Thanks for the award.

TIM HANRAHAN
HANK PERLMAN

THE GOLD AWARD
WINNERS ON THE
GOLD AWARD WINNERS

**CONSUMER TELEVISION
VARYING LENGTHS CAMPAIGN**

AGENCY
Wieden & Kennedy/Portland
CLIENT
Nike

When the baseball commissioner canceled the season after the 34th day of the players strike, it also ended our campaign. Had the season/strike lasted longer, here's what you would've seen:

Day 36:

Close-up of a lonely fan's face. He's pale, he's drooling, his pupils are dilated. He's mumbling and blabbering to himself. He is catatonic. Pull away to reveal him rolling around in the outfield grass, wearing nothing but shoes and a batting glove. Title card: Play ball, please.

Day 57:

Lonely fan sitting in bleachers of empty stadium, picking his ear. Pulls finger out of ear, looks at end of finger. Title card: Play ball, please.

Day 105:

Lonely fan sitting at home on a very comfortable couch. Title card: Play ball, please.

Day 152:

Lonely fan standing outside left field gate looking into the ball park. With hands clenching the chain link fence, he slowly turns to camera as we see a tear gently fall from his eye. Title card: Play ball, please.

Day 223:

Lonely fan running through stadium holding his crotch. He runs into the men's room. Title card: Play ball, please.

Day 310:

The lonely fan acts out both parts of a scene in which an owner and a player bludgeon each other with aluminum fungo bats. Title card: Play ball, please.

Day 323:

Lonely fan finally gets fed up, leaves the stadium and attempts to buy a hockey ticket.

ANDREW CHRISTOU
ERIC C. KING
DEREK BARNES
JAMES LeMAITRE

**CONSUMER TELEVISION
UNDER $50,000 BUDGET**

AGENCY
Earle Palmer Brown/Richmond
CLIENT
Good Guys Auto

A One Show gold pencil is good. . . . You can't write with it . . . but it's still good. . . . And it's not real gold . . . but it's still good. . . . In fact as far as imitation gold pencils go, this is probably one of the best.

ERIC SILVER
ROHITASH RAO

78

INTERNATIONAL FOREIGN LANGUAGE COMMERCIAL: TELEVISION

AGENCY
Young & Rubicam/Buenos Aires
CLIENT
Reckitt & Colman

For those who've only seen the spot in the Annual's synthesis, it's about a man who faces the tremendously hard task of educating his six children all by himself.

Suffering from a cancer that's killing him day after day, the man struggles against the early '50s textile industry monopoly, gathering his co-workers in a victorious trade union.

Tragedy takes place when Bonny, the family horse, stumbles and falls while the six little kids are riding him. The little kids learn a hard lesson as they have to sacrifice Bonny's life because of his broken leg.

After years of court battle, the father is rewarded with the custody of his children and marries his teenage love Brenda (a wonderful Jessica Lange).

Life, death and other surprises blend, building a story cocktail that looks like a big basketball that keeps bouncing back and forth. The memory of Bonny tortures Jack, the youngest brother, who desperately runs away to Asia Minor, looking for a similar specimen. Finally, the father, dressed as a marrochy, sits down on a small cushion to pray all day and kills a mosquito.

ELVIO SANCHEZ
CARLOS BAYALA
SANDRA SCHAPOFF

79

COLLEGE COMPETITION

SCHOOL:
Portfolio Center/Atlanta
ASSIGNMENT:
Brand Name Bar Soap

After beating our heads against a wall for about two weeks, we still hadn't come up with the big idea. Hoping for some inspiration, we decided to concept in a nearby church. While throwing change into the basin of holy water, we suddenly had an Epiphany.

We immediately raced to our computer and comped-up our vision. After submitting it to the One Show, we then prayed for victory, as well as forgiveness.

(Crack!)

Hey, was that thunder?

MICHAEL COHEN
CURTIS SMITH

Print Finalists

CONSUMER NEWSPAPER
OVER 600 LINES:
SINGLE

82
ART DIRECTOR:
Peter Gausis
WRITER:
Alfredo Marcantonio
TYPOGRAPHER:
Joe Hoza
CLIENT:
The Economist
AGENCY:
Abbott Mead Vickers.
BBDO/London

83
ART DIRECTOR:
Ron Brown
WRITER:
David Abbott
TYPOGRAPHER:
Joe Hoza
CLIENT:
The Economist
AGENCY:
Abbott Mead Vickers.
BBDO/London

84
ART DIRECTOR:
Andy Arghyrou
WRITER:
Pat Doherty
TYPOGRAPHER:
Joe Hoza
CLIENT:
The Economist
AGENCY:
Abbott Mead Vickers.
BBDO/London

85
ART DIRECTOR:
Doug Robinson
WRITER:
Tom Nelson
PHOTOGRAPHER:
Ron Fehling
CLIENT:
Labatt Breweries
of Canada
AGENCY:
Ammirati & Puris/
Toronto

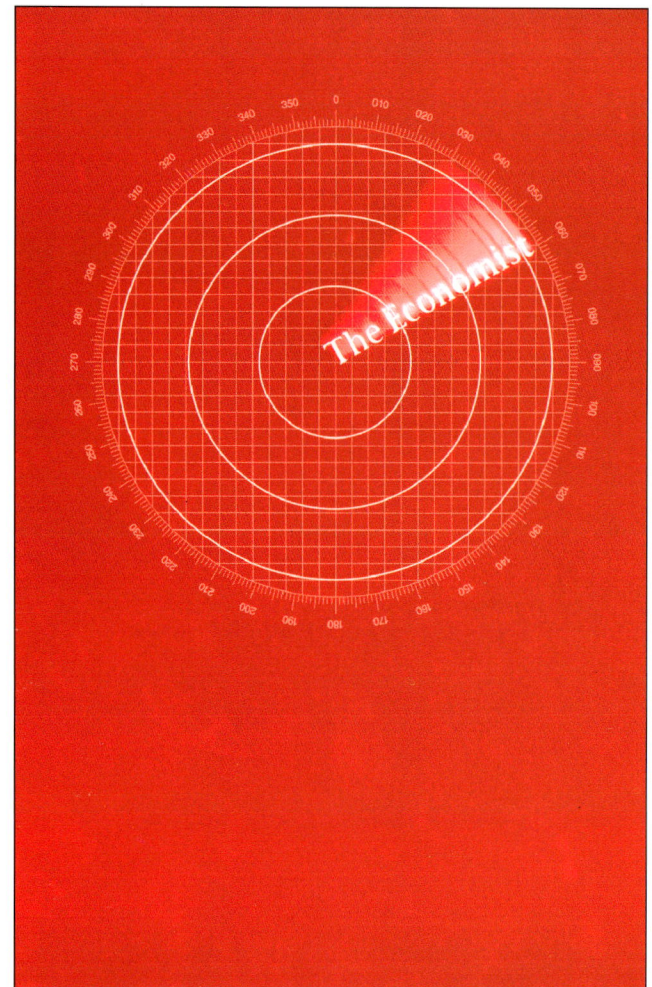
82

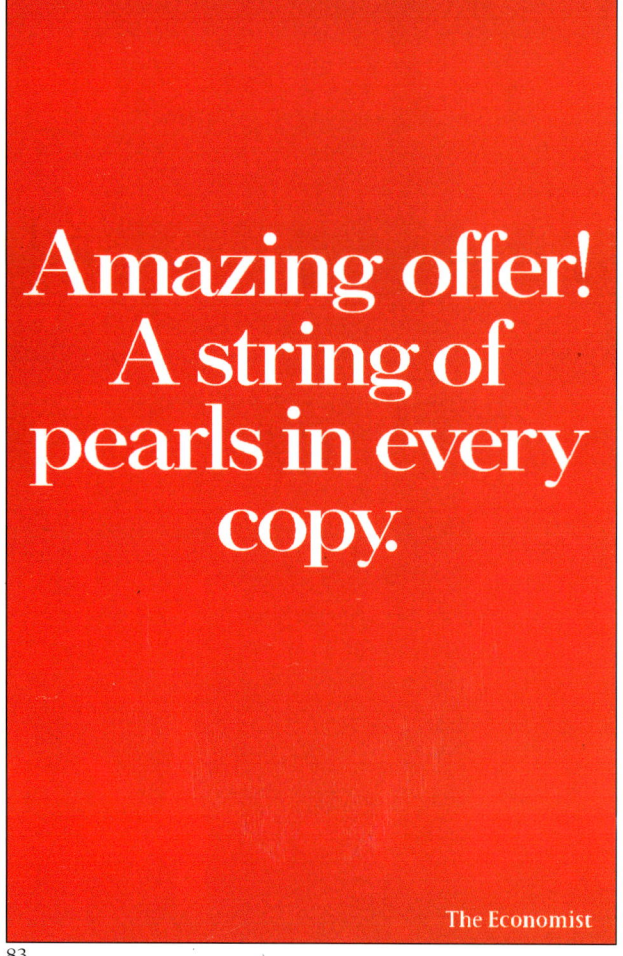
83

CONSUMER NEWSPAPER
OVER 600 LINES:
SINGLE

86
ART DIRECTOR:
Doug Robinson
WRITER:
Tom Nelson
PHOTOGRAPHERS:
Rich McKechnie
Nancy Jackson
CLIENT:
Labatt Breweries of Canada
AGENCY:
Ammirati & Puris/ Toronto

87
ART DIRECTOR:
Doug Robinson
WRITER:
Tom Nelson
PHOTOGRAPHER:
Rick McKechnie
CLIENT:
Labatt Breweries of Canada
AGENCY:
Ammirati & Puris/ Toronto

88
ART DIRECTOR:
Doug Robinson
WRITER:
Tom Goudie
PHOTOGRAPHER:
Rick McKechnie
CLIENT:
Labatt Breweries of Canada
AGENCY:
Ammirati & Puris/ Toronto

89
ART DIRECTOR:
Kathryn Windley
WRITER:
Dion Hughes
PHOTOGRAPHER:
Lamb & Hall
CLIENT:
Saab Cars USA
AGENCY:
Angotti Thomas Hedge/ New York

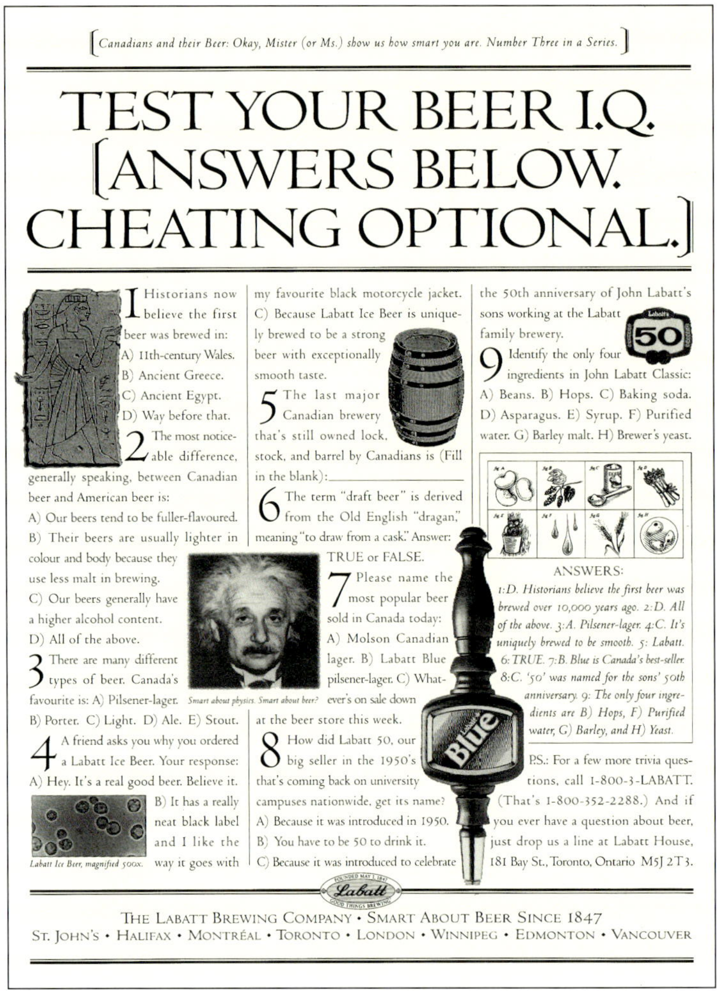

[*Canadians and their Beer: It's time for another round of beer trivia. Number Fourteen in a Series.*]

"I'LL TAKE BEER TRIVIA FOR TWO HUNDRED, ALEX."

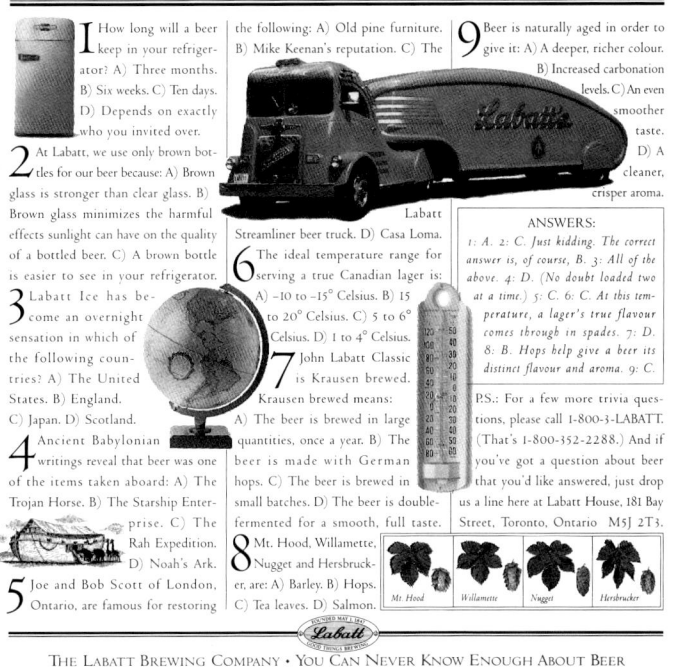

1. How long will a beer keep in your refrigerator? A) Three months. B) Six weeks. C) Ten days. D) Depends on exactly who you invited over.

2. At Labatt, we use only brown bottles for our beer because: A) Brown glass is stronger than clear glass. B) Brown glass minimizes the harmful effects sunlight can have on the quality of a bottled beer. C) A brown bottle is easier to see in your refrigerator.

3. Labatt Ice has become an overnight sensation in which of the following countries? A) The United States. B) England. C) Japan. D) Scotland.

4. Ancient Babylonian writings reveal that beer was one of the items taken aboard: A) The Trojan Horse. B) The Starship Enterprise. C) The Rah Expedition. D) Noah's Ark.

5. Joe and Bob Scott of London, Ontario, are famous for restoring the following: A) Old pine furniture. B) Mike Keenan's reputation. C) The Labatt Streamliner beer truck. D) Casa Loma.

6. The ideal temperature range for serving a true Canadian lager is: A) −10 to −15° Celsius. B) 15 to 20° Celsius. C) 5 to 6° Celsius. D) 1 to 4° Celsius.

7. John Labatt Classic is Krausen brewed. Krausen brewed means: A) The beer is brewed in large quantities, once a year. B) The beer is made with German hops. C) The beer is brewed in small batches. D) The beer is double-fermented for a smooth, full taste.

8. Mt. Hood, Willamette, Nugget and Hersbrucker, are: A) Barley. B) Hops. C) Tea leaves. D) Salmon.

9. Beer is naturally aged in order to give it: A) A deeper, richer colour. B) Increased carbonation levels. C) An even smoother taste. D) A cleaner, crisper aroma.

ANSWERS:
1: A. 2: C. Just kidding. The correct answer is, of course, B. 3: All of the above. 4: D. (No doubt loaded two at a time.) 5: C. 6: C. At this temperature, a lager's true flavour comes through in spades. 7: D. 8: B. Hops help give a beer its distinct flavour and aroma. 9: C.

P.S.: For a few more trivia questions, please call 1-800-3-LABATT. (That's 1-800-352-2288.) And if you've got a question about beer that you'd like answered, just drop us a line here at Labatt House, 181 Bay Street, Toronto, Ontario M5J 2T3.

Mt. Hood Willamette Nugget Hersbrucker

Labatt

THE LABATT BREWING COMPANY • YOU CAN NEVER KNOW ENOUGH ABOUT BEER
ST. JOHN'S • HALIFAX • MONTRÉAL • TORONTO • LONDON • WINNIPEG • EDMONTON • VANCOUVER

THE NEW SAAB 900 CONVERTIBLE. SAAB

CONSUMER NEWSPAPER
OVER 600 LINES:
SINGLE

90
ART DIRECTORS:
Grover Tham
Tham Khai Meng
WRITERS:
Jim Aitchison
Kash Sree
Tham Khai Meng
CLIENT:
Raffles Hotel, Singapore
AGENCY:
Batey Ads/Singapore

91
ART DIRECTOR:
John Doyle
WRITER:
Ernie Schenck
PHOTOGRAPHER:
Geoffrey Stein
CLIENT:
Shreve Crump & Low
AGENCY:
Berlin Cameron Doyle/
New York

92
ART DIRECTOR:
Sybi Rossouw
WRITER:
Errol Denman
CLIENT:
Combined Motor
Holdings
AGENCY:
Berry Bush De Villiers Di
Bella Bellamy/Cape Town

93
ART DIRECTOR:
John Butler
WRITER:
Mike Shine
CLIENT:
Virtual World
AGENCY:
Butler Shine & Stern/
Sausalito

THE NEW VOLVO 850 T5, SEEN HERE WITH ITS 3 CLOSEST GERMAN RIVALS.

In both its class and price range, the new Volvo 850 T5 is surprisingly quick. Beneath its sedate exterior, a 2,3litre, 20 valve, 5 cylinder, turbocharged engine will safely propel you from 0-100km/h in 7,4 seconds (British Car, Jan 1994). And to an enviable top speed of 240km/h.

Even its fourth gear acceleration rivals those of several supercars (let alone, its more spirited luxury German counterparts). More surprising, is how reassured this performance makes you feel. With power, we believe, must come responsibility.

At top speed the 850 T5 remains rock steady. It responds quickly and crisply to your demands, with award winning safety features and roadholding abilities Volvo is renowned for.

Helping you avoid a collision long before it even becomes a reality. So whilst it accelerates "quicker than any Volvo has the right to" (British Esquire, Dec 1993) it does so as safely as only Volvo knows how to.

VOLVO
A CAR YOU CAN BELIEVE IN

FOR FURTHER DETAILS CALL 0800 334 457 TOLL FREE FROM ANYWHERE IN THE COUNTRY. THE VOLVO 850 RANGE COMPRISES THE GLT 2,5ℓ, 20 VALVE AND THE TURBO 2,3ℓ, 20 VALVE IN BOTH SEDAN AND SPORTWAGON, IN MANUAL OR AUTOMATIC.

HE'S YOUR boyfriend and he's got a cute butt and he buys you flowers and he says funny stuff and yesterday he gazed a little too long at one of the Laker's Cheerleaders and he's three pods down and you're about to blow that cute little butt straight to kingdom come.

VIRTUAL WORLD
Adventure. Exploration. Pulverization.
7510 Hazard Center Drive #211, San Diego, 619-294-9200

CONSUMER NEWSPAPER
OVER 600 LINES:
SINGLE

94
ART DIRECTOR:
Marc Gallucci
WRITER:
Michael Sheehan
ILLUSTRATOR:
Kent Barton
TYPOGRAPHER:
Leslie Bistrowitz
CLIENT:
Abigail Adams Historical Society
AGENCY:
Clarke Goward/Boston

95
ART DIRECTOR:
Marc Gallucci
WRITER:
Michael Sheehan
ILLUSTRATOR:
Chris Gall
CLIENT:
American Hard Cider Company
AGENCY:
Clarke Goward/Boston

96
ART DIRECTOR:
Paul Hirsch
WRITER:
Mark Waggoner
PHOTOGRAPHER:
Lars Topelmann
CLIENT:
Cycle Oregon
AGENCY:
Cole & Weber/Portland

97
ART DIRECTOR:
Bill Karow
WRITER:
David Baldwin
PHOTOGRAPHER:
Morgan Henry
CLIENT:
The Oregonian
AGENCY:
Cole & Weber/Portland

CONSUMER NEWSPAPER
OVER 600 LINES:
SINGLE

98
ART DIRECTOR:
Bill Karow
WRITER:
David Baldwin
PHOTOGRAPHER:
Morgan Henry
CLIENT:
The Oregonian
AGENCY:
Cole & Weber/Portland

99
ART DIRECTOR:
Roger Bentley
WRITER:
Scott Wild
PHOTOGRAPHER:
Ken Anderson
CLIENT:
The Big House
AGENCY:
Dalbey & Denight Advertising/Portland

100
ART DIRECTOR:
Roger Bentley
WRITER:
Scott Wild
PHOTOGRAPHER:
Ken Anderson
CLIENT:
The Big House
AGENCY:
Dalbey & Denight Advertising/Portland

101
ART DIRECTOR:
Patrick Low
WRITERS:
Mark Fong
Patrick Low
PHOTOGRAPHER:
Mun's Studio
CLIENT:
Borneo Motors/ Lexus Division
AGENCY:
Dentsu Young & Rubicam/Singapore

98

99

Your car wears prison made products. Now you can too.

For a free catalog of clothing made by inmates in rehabilitation, call 1-800-597-7472.

True, a Lexus won't be your first car. Then again, running a company probably wasn't your first job.

CONSUMER NEWSPAPER
OVER 600 LINES:
SINGLE

102
ART DIRECTOR:
Rohitash Rao
WRITER:
Eric Silver
PHOTOGRAPHER:
Karl Steinbrenner
CLIENT:
India House
AGENCY:
Earle Palmer Brown/
Richmond

103
ART DIRECTOR:
Ellen Steinberg
WRITER:
Mike Gibbs
PHOTOGRAPHER:
Kerry Peterson
CLIENT:
Nikon
AGENCY:
Fallon McElligott/
Minneapolis

104
ART DIRECTOR:
Joe Paprocki
WRITER:
Mike Gibbs
PHOTOGRAPHER:
Joe Lampi
CLIENT:
Star Tribune
AGENCY:
Fallon McElligott/
Minneapolis

105
ART DIRECTOR:
Dean Hanson
WRITER:
Bruce Bildsten
PHOTOGRAPHER:
Joe Paczkowski
CLIENT:
Timex Corporation
AGENCY:
Fallon McElligott/
Minneapolis

102

103

Since March 19, 1944, the Minnesota Poll has been maintained by the Star Tribune in order to keep the public informed about a variety of opinions residents hold on a number of topics ranging from pre-election thoughts to family and social issues to favorite desserts.

APPARENTLY, IN MINNESOTA, EVEN OPINIONS CAN FREEZE.

WE'VE BEEN taking the temperature in Minnesota for 50 years. Not with a thermometer, mind you, but with the Minnesota Poll.

As you might guess, there's been a wide range of readings. Some hot. Some, as you would surely guess, cold.

For example, one poll in 1950 showed that 86 percent of Minnesotans were pretty hot on the idea of granting Alaska and Hawaii statehood. While another taken in 1963 revealed that a majority of Minnesotans were cool on the idea of racing to the moon.

Moreover, these two instances point out very clearly that the Minnesota Poll is also an excellent barometer of change. Today, Alaska and Hawaii are well-known states, and parts of the moon are covered with footprints. So, what's the big deal? Things change, right?

Well, not always. Because some of the results of the Minnesota Poll over the past 50 years seem to be saying that the more things change, the more they do indeed stay the same.

Just like the two polls pictured on this page. Far apart in years. Extremely close in results. There are others, too. Skeptical Twins fans from 30 years ago. A 40-year-old desire for improved health care. Serious concerns about what the future holds. Over time, the poll results on these topics have changed very little. For all intents, some do appear to be frozen.

A fact that makes the Minnesota Poll all the more compelling. Is there perpetual Minnesotan in all of us, who thinks the same thing year after year after year? Or are these nearly identical findings just a quirk? A happenstance of facts and figures.

Well, you decide. Keep your eyes open for upcoming polls in this, our 50th anniversary year – and many, many years to come.

After all, we've recently partnered with WCCO television, and as far as we're all concerned, the last busy 50 years were really just a long warm-up. StarTribune ❹Four News

THE MINNESOTA POLL. 50 YEARS OF UNIQUELY MINNESOTAN THOUGHT.

★ ★ ★ ★

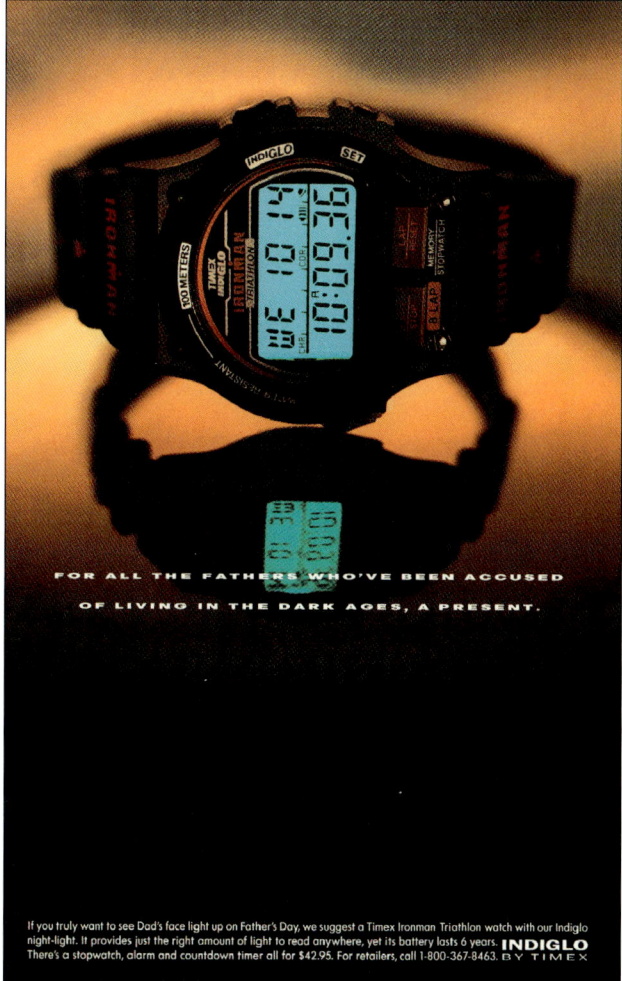

CONSUMER NEWSPAPER
OVER 600 LINES:
SINGLE

106
ART DIRECTOR:
Mike Fetrow
WRITER:
Doug Adkins
ILLUSTRATOR:
Kate Thomssen
CLIENT:
Moose Hockey
AGENCY:
Hunt Murray/Minneapolis

107
ART DIRECTOR:
Ed Parks
WRITER:
Steve Connelly
PHOTOGRAPHER:
Nathanial Butler
CLIENT:
The Boston Globe
AGENCY:
Ingalls Quinn & Johnson/Boston

108
ART DIRECTOR:
Gary Marshall
WRITER:
Paul Marshall
CLIENT:
By Invitation Only
AGENCY:
Leagas Delaney/London

109
ART DIRECTOR:
Dave Beverley
WRITER:
Rob Burleigh
CLIENT:
The Guardian
AGENCY:
Leagas Delaney/London

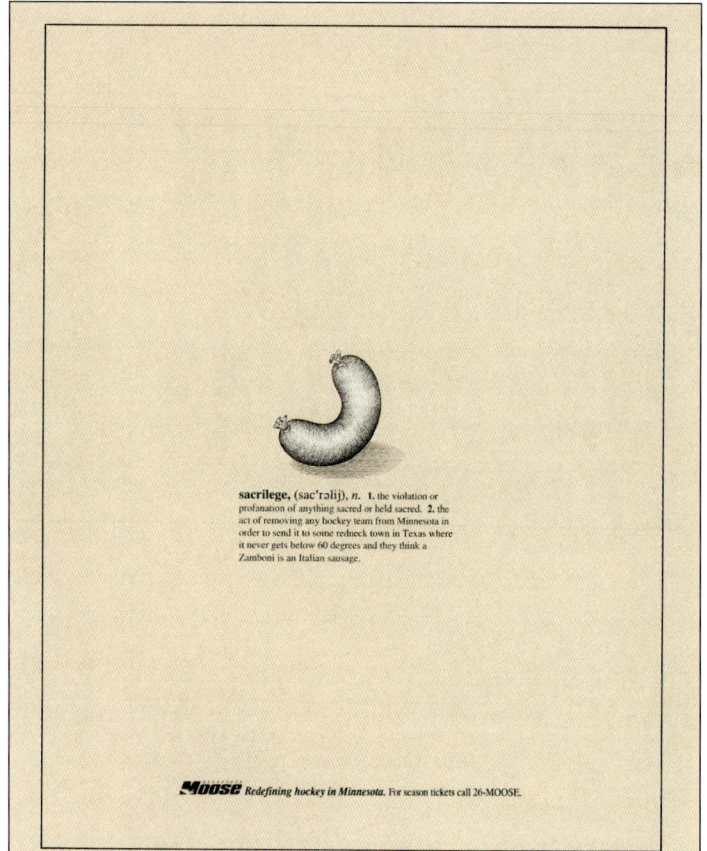
106

107

CONSUMER NEWSPAPER
OVER 600 LINES:
SINGLE

110
ART DIRECTOR:
Gary Marshall
WRITER:
Paul Marshall
CLIENT:
The Natural History Museum
AGENCY:
Leagas Delaney/London

111
ART DIRECTOR:
Gary Marshall
WRITER:
Paul Marshall
CLIENT:
The Natural History Museum
AGENCY:
Leagas Delaney/London

112
ART DIRECTOR:
Martin Galton
WRITERS:
Tony Barry
Dave Hieatt
CLIENT:
Porsche
AGENCY:
Leagas Delaney/London

113
ART DIRECTOR:
Cliff Sorah
WRITER:
Raymond McKinney
CLIENT:
The Poe Museum
AGENCY:
The Martin Agency/Richmond

110

111

Catalytic converters, recyclable parts, reduced emissions.
There's no point owning a 911 without a planet to drive it on.

The awesome new Porsche 911 is a performance car everyone can aspire to. The alloy Boxer engine saves weight and therefore fuel. Yet powers from 0 to 60 in 5.6 seconds. It also features a hydraulic valve adjustment system, whereby exhaust valves open and close more efficiently to reduce emissions.

Meanwhile the twin metal catalysers treat the remaining gases more effectively than conventional ceramic converters. Combine this with the fact that all plastics over 50g are earmarked for recycling, that 67% of all the cars we've ever built are still on the road and you'll understand why people think the world of Porsche. And vice versa.

For more details, write or send your recyclable business card to Julian Ormerod, Porsche Information, PO Box 300, Crawley, West Sussex, RH10 2YW. Or telephone 0622 722212.

PORSCHE

POE FANTASIZED ABOUT A WOMAN WHO WAS JUST LIKE HIS MOTHER: DEAD.

Poe, like every red-blooded man, aspired towards beauty. He compared this yearning to "the desire of the moth for the star."

But, Poe's concept of beauty, was, how shall we say this, tilted a bit toward the morbid. To put things in a modern perspective, the supermodels in the Sports Illustrated Swimsuit Issue would not have been his cup of tea.

He was obsessed with the beauty outside of this world. The "Beauty above...the glories beyond the grave." In other words, Poe pictured Cupid not as a good-natured, chubby cherub, but as a dark-cloaked Grim Reaper. To him, nothing was more poetical than the death of a beautiful woman.

Here, take a look at his poem "Annabel Lee." The narrator's girlfriend dies one cloudy night, chilled by a wind supposedly sent down by jealous angels. The narrator goes on to say that even death cannot kill the love the two feel for each other: "And so, all the night-tide, I lay down by the side/ Of my darling - my darling - my life and my bride. In her tomb by the sounding sea."

And don't think this behavior was isolated to characters in his stories. Poe himself even went so far as to propose marriage to a woman in a cemetery. (Relax, she was alive at the time.)

What triggered this obsession? The death of his mother when he was a child? The loss of his young wife to tuberculosis? Or was it a culmination of many incidents? The death or loss of the women he loved was one of the most constant factors that Poe faced in his life. No one knows for sure. Stop by the Poe Museum at 1914 East Main Street right here in Richmond. Or give us a call at 648-5523 to learn about other of Poe's strange obsessions. We have letters, manuscripts and other assorted oddities. And don't worry. All of the women who work here are alive and well.

THE POE MUSEUM

CONSUMER NEWSPAPER
OVER 600 LINES:
SINGLE

114
ART DIRECTOR:
Bob Meagher
WRITER:
John Mahoney
ILLUSTRATOR:
Bob Meagher
CLIENT:
Residence Inn
AGENCY:
The Martin Agency/ Richmond

115
ART DIRECTOR:
Steve Davis
WRITER:
Liz Paradise
PHOTOGRAPHERS:
Alex Bee
Robert Stevens
CLIENT:
Audi
AGENCY:
McKinney & Silver/ Raleigh

116
ART DIRECTOR:
Keith Weinman
WRITERS:
Stephen P. Gill
Ben Resnikoff
PHOTOGRAPHER:
Michael Furman
CLIENT:
BMW of North America
AGENCY:
Mullen Advertising/ Wenham, MA

117
ART DIRECTOR:
Bruce Matchett
WRITERS:
Ian Brown
Stuart Fermor
PHOTOGRAPHER:
Bruce Hamilton
CLIENT:
Lane Walker Rudkin
AGENCY:
Ogilvy & Mather/ Auckland

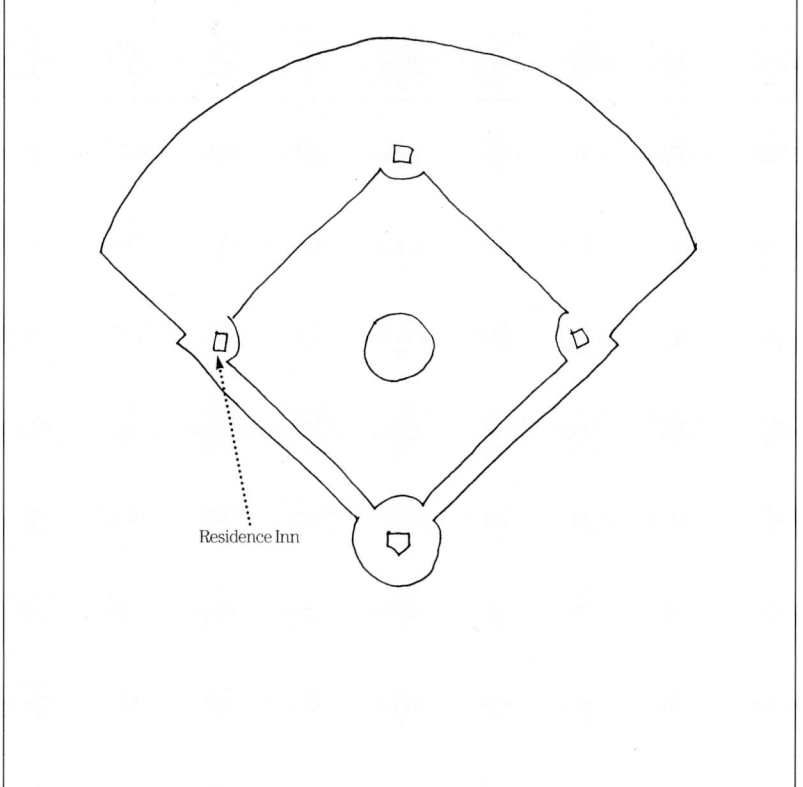

THE NEW 7-SERIES

How the army keep their privates warm.

Few people have felt the bite of a Burnham winter. They say that if you leave a plum out overnight, by morning it's a prune.

It's this kind of extreme cold that had these rugged individuals reaching for their ThermaTech underwear.

Made from hard wearing polypropolene, ThermaTech will serve you with distinction. It's extra light, supremely washable and quick drying - ideal when you're out in the field on manoeuvres. And a unique weave pattern draws moisture away from the skin for increased comfort and warmth.

Of course, you don't have to undergo six weeks of basic training to pull on a set of ThermaTech underwear. As a civilian, you'll find a complete range at your favourite store.

So whether it's your privates or your Sergeant Majors, there's no better way to keep them warm than ThermaTech.

ThermaTech
Unisex Polypropylene Thermal Underwear/Actionwear

CONSUMER NEWSPAPER
OVER 600 LINES:
SINGLE

118
ART DIRECTOR:
Neil French
WRITER:
Neil French
ILLUSTRATOR:
Warren Madill
PHOTOGRAPHER:
Alex Kaikeong
CLIENT:
Seagram/Martell
AGENCY:
Ogilvy & Mather/
Singapore

119
ART DIRECTOR:
Maria Kostyk-Petro
WRITERS:
Lisa Rettig-Falcone
Alan Levine
PHOTOGRAPHER:
Steve Bronstein
CLIENT:
V&S Vin & Sprit AB
AGENCY:
TBWA Advertising/
New York

120
ART DIRECTOR:
John Vitro
WRITER:
John Robertson
PHOTOGRAPHER:
Carl Vandershuit
CLIENT:
Los Angeles Times
AGENCY:
VitroRobertson/San Diego

121
ART DIRECTOR:
John Vitro
WRITER:
John Robertson
PHOTOGRAPHER:
Carl Vandershuit
CLIENT:
Los Angeles Times
AGENCY:
VitroRobertson/San Diego

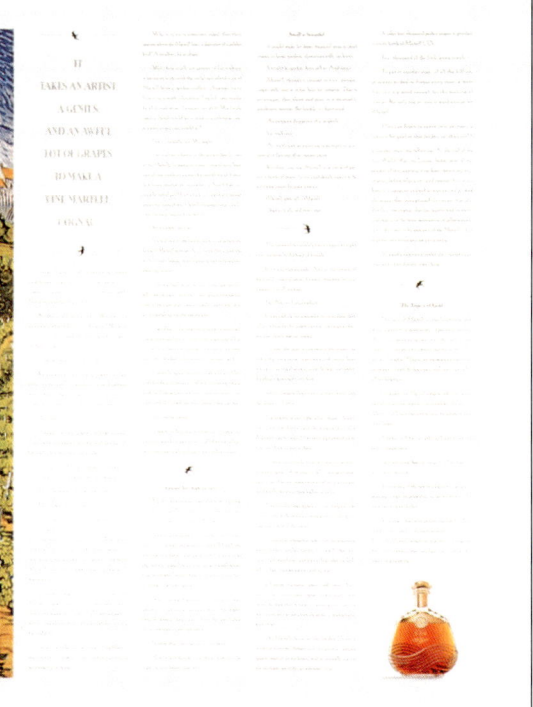

118

119

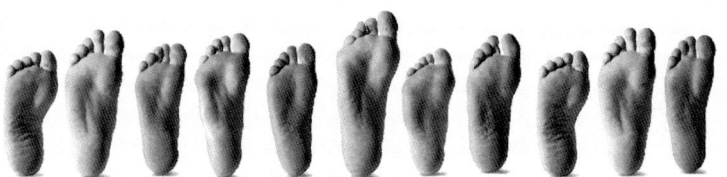

The country of India was very excited about sending its soccer team to the World Cup, for the first time, in 1950. They were told, though, that their players would not be allowed to play barefoot. Rather than put on shoes, they withdrew from the tournament, and India has never qualified for the World Cup finals since then.

This is just one of the facts your kids can learn about the World Cup by reading the "Soccer Times" insert in Sunday's paper. It has games, puzzles and stats about the World Cup. Look for it. And your kids can even learn some important things. Like, for instance, life did exist before million-dollar shoe contracts. **Los Angeles Times** SOCCER TIMES

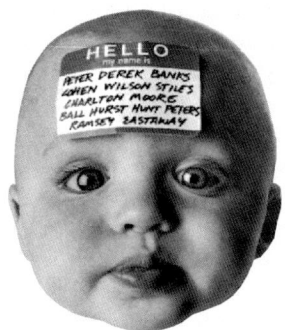

When England won the World Cup Soccer Championship in 1966, one fan was very, very happy. He was so happy he named his son after the entire 11-person team and their coach. The boy's name was Peter Derek Banks Cohen Wilson Stiles Charlton Moore Ball Hurst Hunt Peters Ramsey Eastaway. This is just one of the amazing facts your kids can read about in the special "Soccer Times" insert in Sunday's paper. It has games, puzzles and fun trivia for your kids. So look for it. And hopefully, your kids already have a name, so they don't need to be concerned. **Los Angeles Times** SOCCER TIMES

CONSUMER NEWSPAPER OVER 600 LINES: SINGLE

122
ART DIRECTOR:
Todd Gallentine
WRITER:
Mark Mendelis
CLIENT:
Shin's Restaurant
AGENCY:
Weiss Whitten Stagliano/New York

CONSUMER NEWSPAPER OVER 600 LINES: CAMPAIGN

123
ART DIRECTORS:
Andy Arghyrou
Ron Brown
Mike Harris
WRITERS:
David Abbott
Pat Doherty
David Newton
PHOTOGRAPHER:
Nigel Haynes
TYPOGRAPHER:
Joe Hoza
CLIENT:
The Economist
AGENCY:
Abbott Mead Vickers. BBDO/London

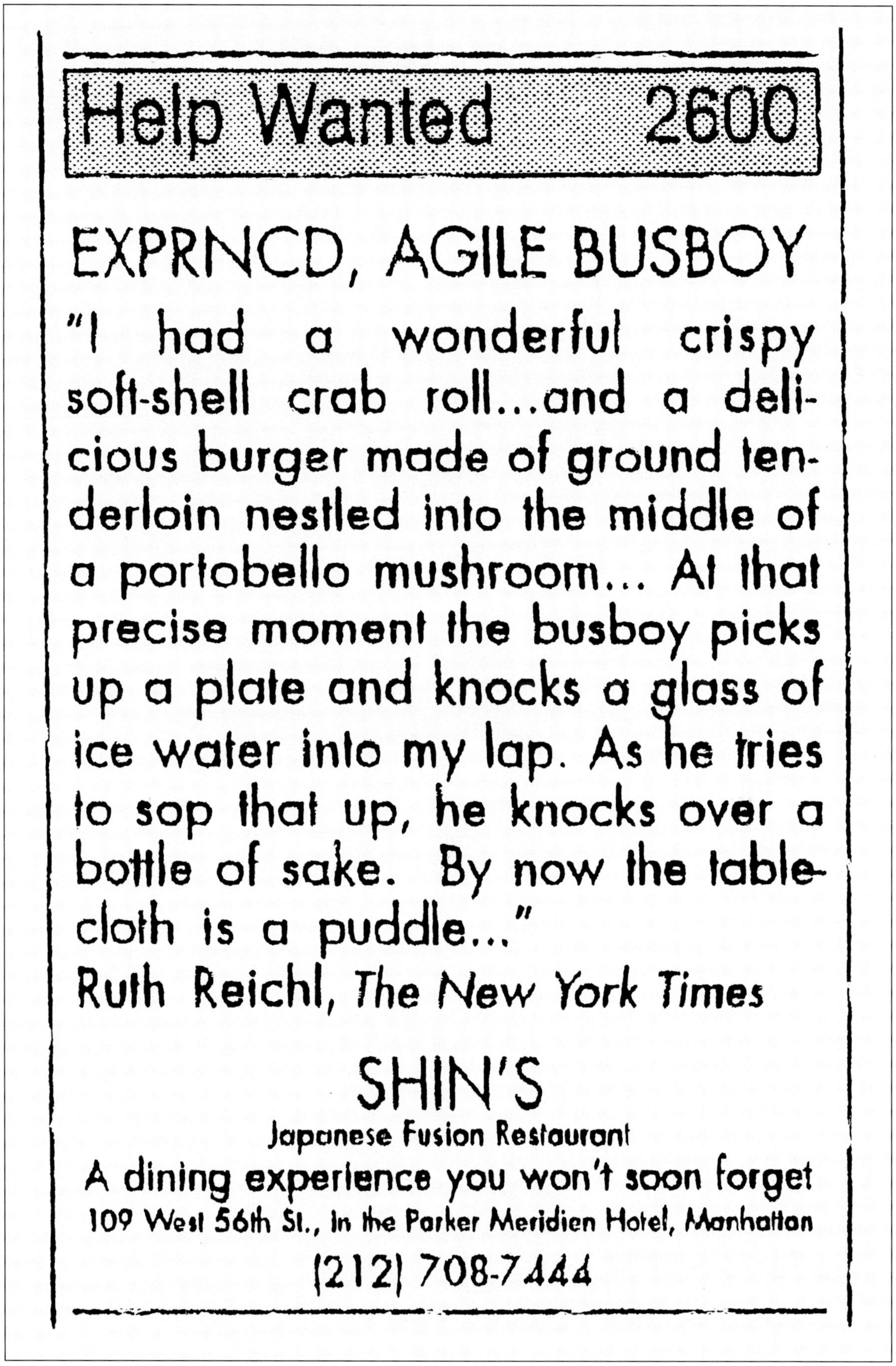

Help Wanted 2600

EXPRNCD, AGILE BUSBOY

"I had a wonderful crispy soft-shell crab roll...and a delicious burger made of ground tenderloin nestled into the middle of a portobello mushroom... At that precise moment the busboy picks up a plate and knocks a glass of ice water into my lap. As he tries to sop that up, he knocks over a bottle of sake. By now the tablecloth is a puddle..."
Ruth Reichl, *The New York Times*

SHIN'S
Japanese Fusion Restaurant
A dining experience you won't soon forget
109 West 56th St., In the Parker Meridien Hotel, Manhattan
(212) 708-7444

Amazing offer! A string of pearls in every copy.

The Economist

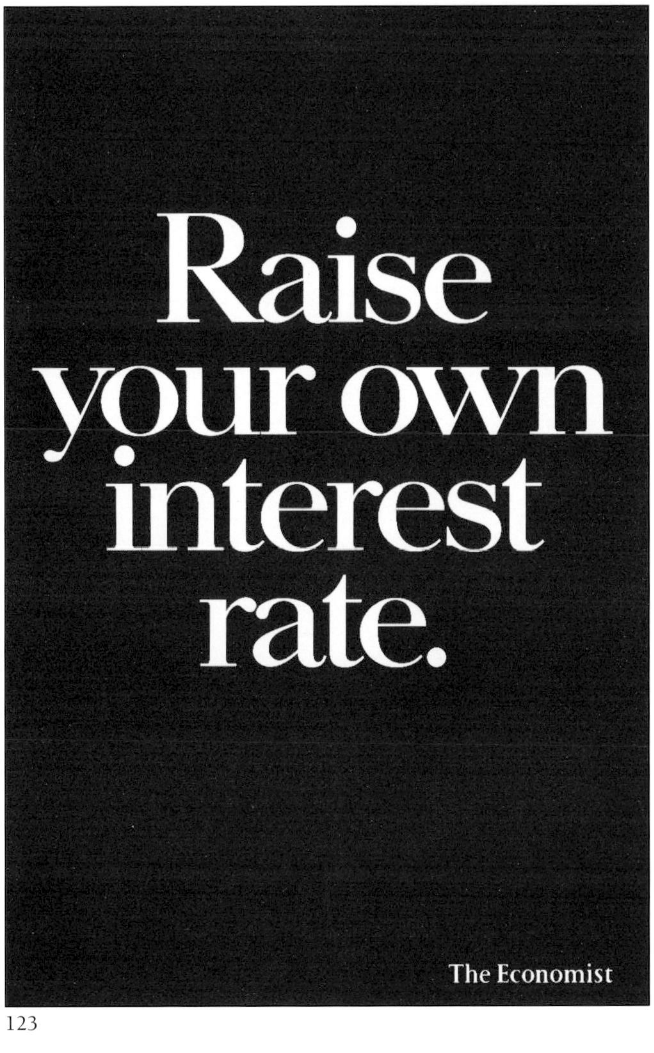

Raise your own interest rate.

The Economist

20 8 5   5 3 15 14 15 13 9 19 20

CONSUMER NEWSPAPER
OVER 600 LINES:
CAMPAIGN

124
ART DIRECTOR:
Stuart Baker
WRITER:
Tony Brignull
PHOTOGRAPHERS:
Graham Ford
Jack Bankhead
Ken Griffiths
CLIENT:
Freedom Foods/RSPCA
AGENCY:
Abbott Mead Vickers.
BBDO/London

125
ART DIRECTOR:
Greg Martin
WRITER:
Nick Bell
PHOTOGRAPHER:
Mike Russell
CLIENT:
IKEA
AGENCY:
Abbott Mead Vickers.
BBDO/London

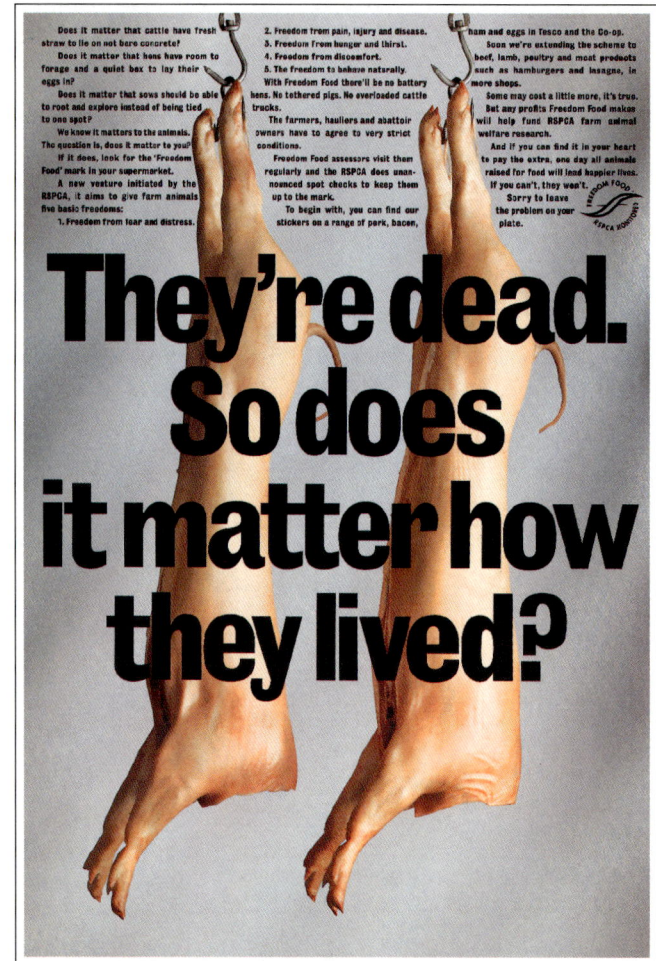

CONSUMER NEWSPAPER
OVER 600 LINES:
CAMPAIGN

126
ART DIRECTOR:
Doug Robinson
WRITER:
Tom Nelson
PHOTOGRAPHERS:
Chris Gordaneer
Rick McKechnie
Orville Fisher
CLIENT:
Labatt Breweries of Canada
AGENCY:
Ammirati & Puris/ Toronto

127
ART DIRECTOR:
Doug Robinson
WRITER:
Tom Nelson
PHOTOGRAPHERS:
Rick McKechnie
Ron Fehling
Nancy Jackson
CLIENT:
Labatt Breweries of Canada
AGENCY:
Ammirati & Puris/ Toronto

[Canadians and their Beer: A toast to our D-Day veterans. Number Four in a Series.]

"IT WAS A BEAUTIFUL JUNE MORNING. AND I WAS TERRIFIED."

Fifty years ago this morning, a few brave Canadians landed on a beach called Juno to take Europe back from a man named Hitler.

It seems so long ago. Unless you were actually there.

"The waves were high and the assault craft was tossing around like a cork," writes Charlie Martin in *Battle Diary*. "The moment the ramp came down, heavy machine-gun fire broke out from behind the seawall."

Eddie Goodman's tank blew up in a minefield on the beach. So he simply climbed out and found another one.

"None of us knew what we were going into," recalls former paratrooper George Green. "And anybody who tells you they weren't scared is a plain liar."

After the war, Charlie went to work for the Department of Agriculture. Eddie enrolled in law school. And George? He spent more than 32 years here at Labatt. He retired in 1979.

Today, like hundreds of Labatt men and women who served in the Canadian armed forces during the war, he'll probably remember what it was like to be young and at war.

And we happen to think it's important for those of us who weren't there to remember those who were.

Which is why Labatt is making a contribution to raise a Canadian D-Day monument in Caen, France, as a memorial to Canadian POWs.

Why we're helping to send D-Day veterans to ceremonies in Normandy this summer.

Why we're mailing a commemorative poster to Canadian veterans associations nationwide.

And why we're offering a handsome large-scale print of Captain Orville Fisher's historic painting of the Canadian D-Day landing (pictured below), with proceeds going to support vets and their families.

For your copy, send a $15 cheque or money order to: D-Day Poster, P.O. Box 275, Station A, Mississauga, Ontario L5A 3A1. Please allow six to eight weeks for delivery.

For over 147 years, our employees, our customers, our friends, and our families have played their part whenever our country needed them.

And it only seems fitting to remember the ones who rose to the challenge fifty years ago this morning.

THE LABATT BREWING COMPANY • WE REMEMBER
ST. JOHN'S • HALIFAX • MONTRÉAL • TORONTO • LONDON • WINNIPEG • EDMONTON • VANCOUVER

[Canadians and their Beer: This Canada Day, a toast to these fine Canadians. Number Six in a Series.]

DON'T YOU GET THIRSTY JUST LOOKING AT 'EM?

Ever wonder how this country earned its international reputation for brewing so many great beers?

Pictured here are just a few of the reasons.

In the world of beer, these are some of the most impressive names on the planet.

That's why, as Canada Day approaches and you consider which of Canada's great beers to celebrate with, it only seems right to recall the great Canadians responsible for so many great choices.

Please notice that not all of these individuals are named Labatt.

After all, as much as we'd like to think that Canada's envied reputation for brewing is the sole result of our heroic efforts here at Labatt, it isn't.

What if an Englishman named John Molson had gotten cold feet and had never sailed over to Montreal back in 1782?

What if Alexander Keith of Nova Scotia had decided to make buttermilk instead of beer?

Or if Susannah Oland hadn't taught her three boys the recipe for her brown October ale?

And what if Thomas Carling and Eugene O'Keefe had poured their energies into the restaurant business?

Frankly, we find it difficult to imagine a Canada without all of them.

Each, in their own way, was fanatical about quality. They and their talented successors have done much to elevate Canadian brew to the lofty status it enjoys among discerning beer drinkers all around the globe.

In 1846, one year before starting a small Ontario brewery, a farmer named John Kinder Labatt wrote to his wife: "I fancy I should like brewing better than anything else."

And we like to think that John K. would be the first to raise a toast to his many talented competitors.

Perhaps this weekend, you will, too.

P.S.: For a handy list of activities this Canada Day weekend, from parades to picnics to fireworks, all you have to do is call us at 1-800-3-LABATT. (That's 1-800-352-2288.)

With the assistance of Canada Day Committees in 20 cities, we've put together a short list of what's going on this weekend in your neck of the woods.

THE LABATT BREWING COMPANY • HAVE A SAFE CANADA DAY, EH?
ST. JOHN'S • HALIFAX • MONTRÉAL • TORONTO • LONDON • WINNIPEG • EDMONTON • VANCOUVER

[Canadians and their Beer: What happens to that beer bottle when you're finished? Number Nine in a Series.]

IT ISN'T JUST OUR BEER THAT GETS RECYCLED.

They say that cats have nine lives. But a Labatt beer bottle does way better than that.

When you're finished with it, we clean, sterilize, and re-use that beer bottle anywhere from 15 to 20 more times.

All you have to do is bring 'em back. We'll do the rest.

It's all part of an industry-wide effort that makes the brewing business in Canada one of the most environmentally responsible businesses there is.

Does Labatt's commitment to your environment make you feel a little happier about your choice in beer? Consider these facts.

It makes cows happy. Because the grains and yeasts left over at the end of the Labatt brewing process are never thrown away. They make some of the most nutritious cattle feeds around.

It makes trees happy. Because virtually every scrap of cardboard and paper waste in our breweries is gathered and recycled.

It even makes rivers and streams happy. Because even the inks to print our labels and the glues to stick them on with are evaluated on their environmental impact.

If you worked at any Labatt brewery, you'd see the program at work every day. Special bins are strategically located to make it a habit to recycle everything from the plastic straps that bind pallets to the cardboard we use to make cases. Worn-out bottles are recycled to make new bottles.

We're currently testing a new biodegradable lubricant for our conveyor belts.

Even the rubber work-gloves we wear down on the brewery floor are recycled when they wear out. (Rubber boots are next.)

No wonder Labatt has already surpassed 1996 industry goals for reducing our landfill waste.

If you'd like to support these efforts, keep buying our beer. And keep returning your bottles and cans.

If you'd like to give us your thoughts on recycling, call 1-800-3-LABATT. (That's 1-800-352-2288.) Or write to us here at Labatt House, 181 Bay Street, Toronto, Ontario M5J 2T3.

We're not perfect. But we're doing better every day.

THE LABATT BREWING COMPANY • HEY, WE LIVE HERE TOO.
ST. JOHN'S • HALIFAX • MONTRÉAL • TORONTO • LONDON • WINNIPEG • EDMONTON • VANCOUVER

[Canadians and their Beer: Okay, Mister (or Ms.) show us how smart you are. Number Three in a Series.]

TEST YOUR BEER I.Q. [ANSWERS BELOW. CHEATING OPTIONAL.]

1. Historians now believe the first beer was brewed in:
A) 11th-century Wales.
B) Ancient Greece.
C) Ancient Egypt.
D) Way before that.

2. The most noticeable difference, generally speaking, between Canadian beer and American beer is:
A) Our beers tend to be fuller-flavoured.
B) Their beers are usually lighter in colour and body because they use less malt in brewing.
C) Our beers generally have a higher alcohol content.
D) All of the above.

3. There are many different types of beer. Canada's favourite is: A) Pilsener-lager. B) Porter. C) Light. D) Ale. E) Stout.

4. A friend asks you why you ordered a Labatt Ice Beer. Your response:
A) Hey. It's a real good beer. Believe it.
B) It has a really neat black label and I like the way it goes with my favourite black motorcycle jacket.
C) Because Labatt Ice Beer is uniquely brewed to be a strong beer with exceptionally smooth taste.

Labatt Ice Beer, magnified 500x.

5. The last major Canadian brewery that's still owned lock, stock, and barrel by Canadians is (Fill in the blank):

6. The term "draft beer" is derived from the Old English "dragan," meaning "to draw from a cask." Answer: TRUE or FALSE.

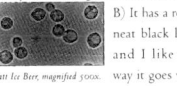
Smart about physics. Smart about beer?

7. Please name the most popular beer sold in Canada today:
A) Molson Canadian lager. B) Labatt Blue pilsener-lager. C) Whatever's on sale down at the beer store this week.

8. How did Labatt 50, our big seller in the 1950's that's coming back on university campuses nationwide, get its name?
A) Because it was introduced in 1950.
B) You have to be 50 to drink it.
C) Because it was introduced to celebrate the 50th anniversary of John Labatt's sons working at the Labatt family brewery.

9. Identify the only four ingredients in John Labatt Classic:
A) Beans. B) Hops. C) Baking soda. D) Asparagus. E) Syrup. F) Purified water. G) Barley malt. H) Brewer's yeast.

ANSWERS:
1: D. Historians believe the first beer was brewed over 10,000 years ago. 2: D. All of the above. 3: A. Pilsener-lager. 4: C. It's uniquely brewed to be smooth. 5: Labatt. 6: TRUE. 7: B. Blue is Canada's best-seller. 8: C. '50' was named for the sons' 50th anniversary. 9: The only four ingredients are B) Hops, F) Purified water, G) Barley, and H) Yeast.

P.S.: For a few more trivia questions, call 1-800-3-LABATT. (That's 1-800-352-2288.) And if you ever have a question about beer, just drop us a line at Labatt House, 181 Bay St., Toronto, Ontario M5J 2T3.

THE LABATT BREWING COMPANY • SMART ABOUT BEER SINCE 1847
ST. JOHN'S • HALIFAX • MONTRÉAL • TORONTO • LONDON • WINNIPEG • EDMONTON • VANCOUVER

[Canadians and their Beer: And now, a few words about coming attractions. Number Five in a Series.]

YOU'RE NOT THE ONLY ONE THINKING ABOUT YOUR NEXT BEER.

You'd like Cam Murray's job. When he isn't checking the hop harvest in Bavaria or hunting for the best barley on the Canadian Prairies, he's inventing new beers at our experimental brewery in London, Ontario.

Of course, to get a job this fun, you'd need some pretty serious scientific credentials.

Fact is, Cam and his eight-person team of brewing experts may well have more degrees and initials after their names than some university faculties.

So what's a bunch of future Nobel Prize winners doing working for the last major Canadian brewery owned lock, stock, and barrel by Canadians?

Well, these are the beer geniuses who brought you the real draft smoothness of our cold-filtered Labatt Genuine Draft.

The people who discovered the way to put real beer taste into our low-alcohol Labatt .5.

Labatt Brewmaster Cam Murray checks out the barley harvest. Hey, our field trips really are field trips.

The team behind Labatt's patented method for Ice Brewing?

Just to listen to these guys talk makes you want to reach for a cold one.

"Today, the new and interesting beers are new twists on old ideas," says brewmaster Alan Griffiths. "English stouts. Belgian ales. German lagers. Bocks. Weiss beers. The history of beer is so rich and varied. And we're re-discovering and re-inventing it every day."

At any given moment, they have half a dozen or more recipes brewing. Constantly searching for minor improvements and major breakthroughs.

"When we hit on something really neat, we'll all get together and give it a try," says brewmaster Bill Van der Meer. "This might be the only place on the planet where people actually look forward to meetings."

Would you like to give Cam and his team a little input into the delicious problem of what beer we should brew next?

Give us a ring at 1-800-3-LABATT (that's 1-800-352-2288) and let us know what kind of beers you think we should be looking into. Or just drop us a line at Labatt House, 181 Bay St., Toronto, Ontario M5J 2T3.

Hey, who knows? It's possible you could wind up helping us to make Canadian beer history.

Just like Cam.

1865 • 1950 • 1951 • 1977 • 1983 • 1992 • 1993 • 1993 • 1994

THE LABATT BREWING COMPANY • NEW IDEAS BREWING SINCE 1847
ST. JOHN'S • HALIFAX • MONTRÉAL • TORONTO • LONDON • WINNIPEG • EDMONTON • VANCOUVER

[Canadians and their Beer: Let's play ball! Number Eight in a Series.]

WHY BATTING AVERAGES ARE RARELY DISCUSSED OVER A FINE CHARDONNAY.

What is it about baseball and beer besides the fact that both begin with B? When it's two down in the bottom of the ninth, name one fan who heads to the fridge for a tarty zinfandel.

Want more evidence? Consider the 28 top baseball parks across North America. Last year, 2,268 games were played, and an estimated 69,700,311.5 beers were consumed. Yet not a single frozen lemon daiquiri was ordered.

So there must be something about beer and baseball. What is it?

Baseball is a game of patience and skill. Not unlike brewing a great beer. You can't rush good baseball. And only a fool would rush a good beer.

Are you a righty or lefty?

There are more spooky parallels: The world of baseball is one of infinite variety. Same for the world of beer. (Over 100 different beers are served at the 28 ballparks.) It takes all kinds.

And you can talk baseball till you're blue in the face. You can talk beer almost as long.

A lot of it comes down to individual preference. Day or night games? Shortstop or centrefield? Lefty or righty? Hey, it's up to you. (Lager or ale? Bottles or cans?)

Maybe it's simply that both baseball and beer are at their best in the summer. And since everybody seems to love summer most of all, maybe beer and baseball are just along for the ride.

But we doubt it. Part of us thinks it's the other way around. That baseball is a key reason for summer's continued popularity. (We can't even begin to speculate about beer.)

In any event, we will continue our quest for answers. And as we happen to own both a brewery and a baseball team, we will get back to you at once if we discover a definitive link.

Of course, if you think of something first, write us at Labatt House, 181 Bay St., Toronto, Ontario M5J 2T3. Or call 1-800-3-LABATT. (That's 1-800-352-2288.)

Meanwhile, we will leave you with our latest hypothesis:

Ever wonder why ballplayers toast each other with expensive champagne after winning a big championship?

We suspect they're saving their beer.

P.S.: Beer fans and ball fans alike will be glad to know our Blue Big Inning is back for its sophomore season. Tune-in to Blue Jay games on TSN for complete details.

In 1924, who set the record for a single-season batting average, with an unsurpassed .424? (Answer: Rogers Hornsby)

THE LABATT BREWING COMPANY • WHO PUT THE "BAT" IN LABATT?
ST. JOHN'S • HALIFAX • MONTRÉAL • TORONTO • LONDON • WINNIPEG • EDMONTON • VANCOUVER

CONSUMER NEWSPAPER
OVER 600 LINES:
CAMPAIGN

128
ART DIRECTOR:
John Doyle
WRITERS:
Ernie Schenck
Dylan Lee
PHOTOGRAPHER:
Geoffrey Stein
CLIENT:
Shreve Crump & Low
AGENCY:
Berlin Cameron Doyle/
New York

129
ART DIRECTORS:
Anjana Kacker
John Butler
WRITERS:
Marianne Shine
Mike Shine
CLIENT:
The Northgate Mall
AGENCY:
Butler Shine & Stern/
Sausalito

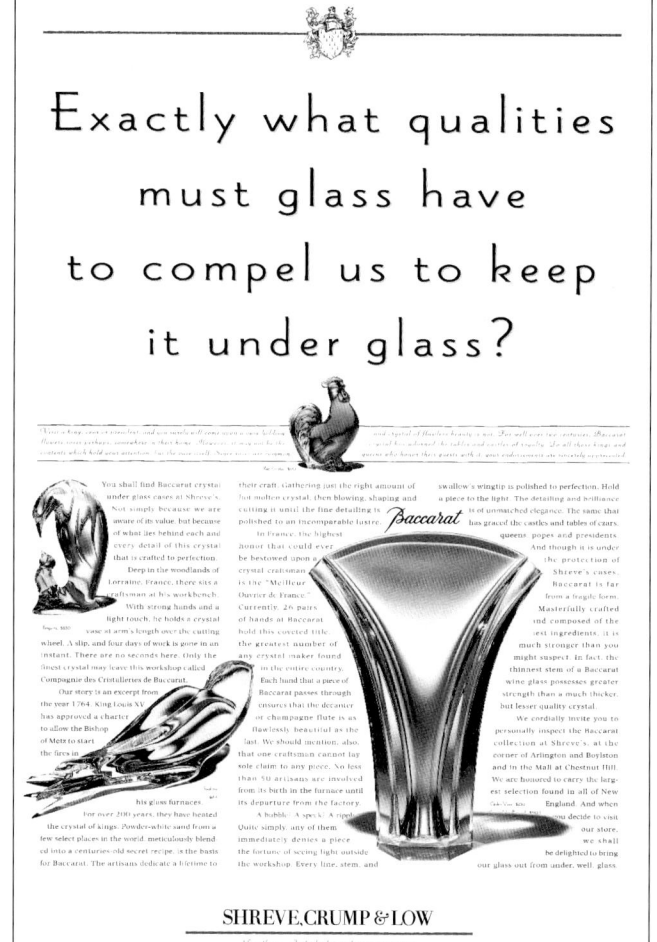

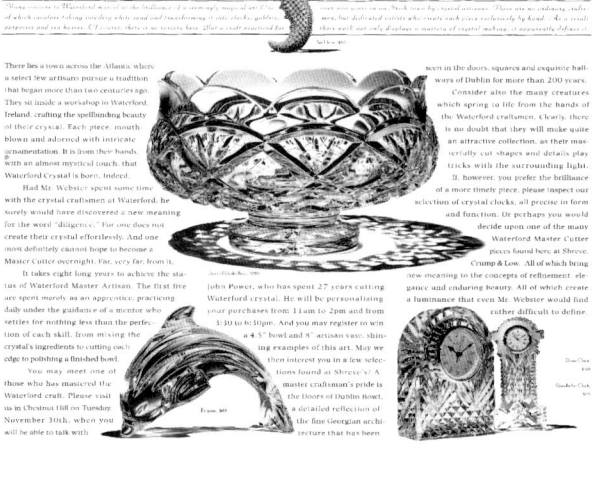

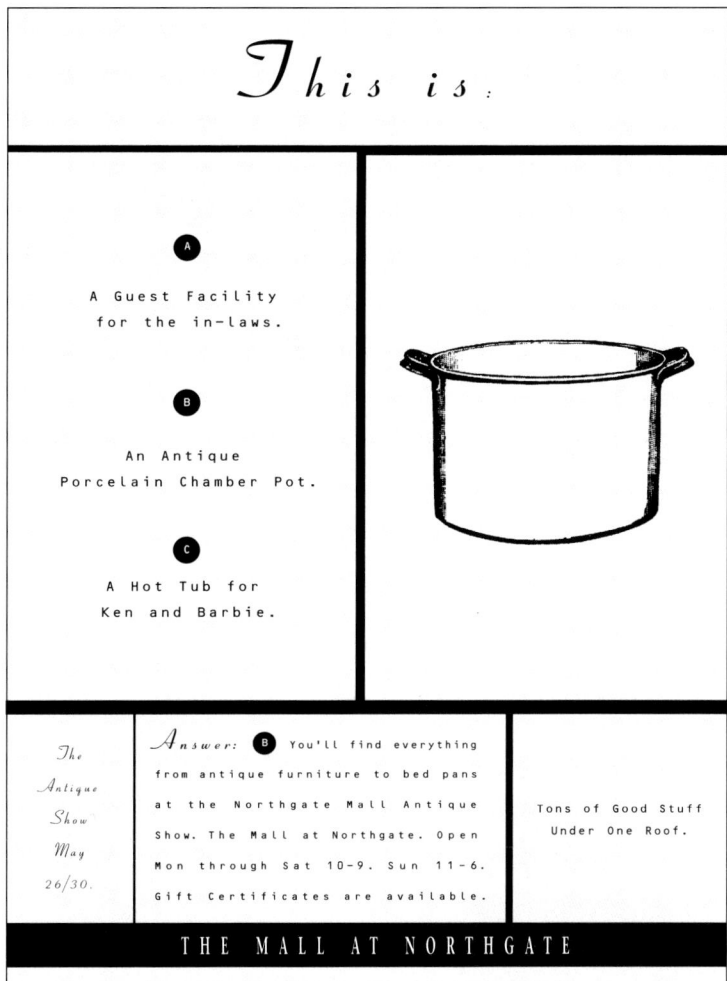

This is:

A A Guest Facility for the in-laws.

B An Antique Porcelain Chamber Pot.

C A Hot Tub for Ken and Barbie.

The Antique Show May 26/30.

Answer: **B** You'll find everything from antique furniture to bed pans at the Northgate Mall Antique Show. The Mall at Northgate. Open Mon through Sat 10-9. Sun 11-6. Gift Certificates are available.

Tons of Good Stuff Under One Roof.

THE MALL AT NORTHGATE

In Marin   Highway 101   Terra Linda Exit

This is:

A Instant argument ending device.

B Ceramic Vase.

C Fishbowl for ugly fish.

Sidewalk Clearance Sale January 14, 15 & 16th

Answer: **B** You'll find this and all kinds of other stuff at greatly reduced prices at the Northgate Mall January Sidewalk Clearance Sale. Open Monday – Saturday 10-9. Sunday 11-6. Gift Certificates are always available.

Tons of Good Stuff Under One Roof.

THE MALL AT NORTHGATE

In Marin   Highway 101   Terra Linda Exit

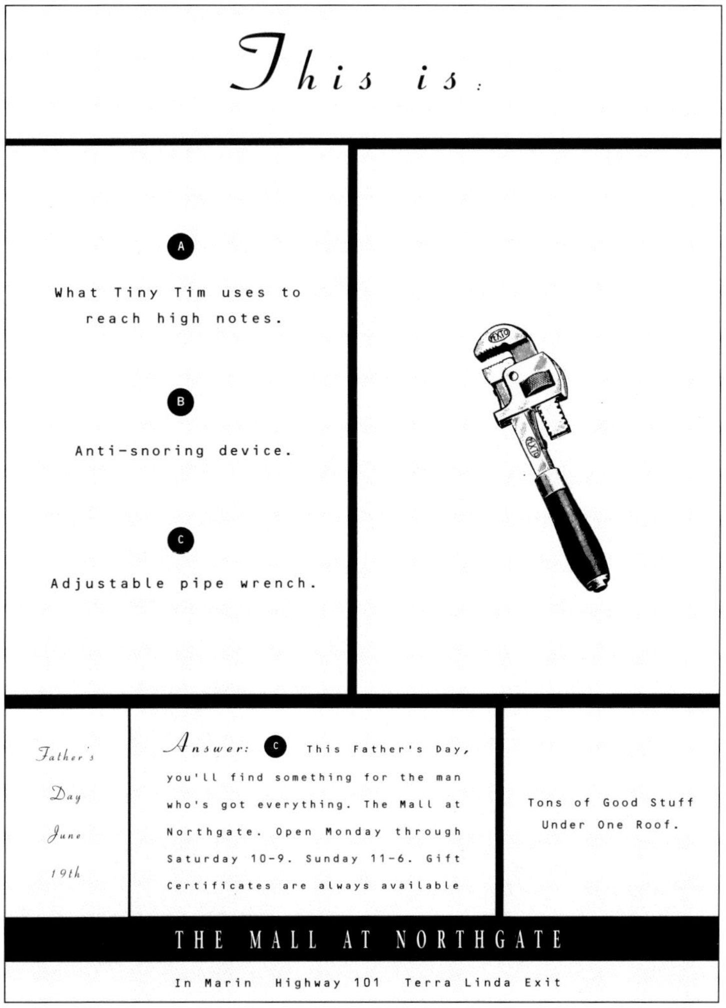

This is:

A What Tiny Tim uses to reach high notes.

B Anti-snoring device.

C Adjustable pipe wrench.

Father's Day June 19th

Answer: **C** This Father's Day, you'll find something for the man who's got everything. The Mall at Northgate. Open Monday through Saturday 10-9. Sunday 11-6. Gift Certificates are always available

Tons of Good Stuff Under One Roof.

THE MALL AT NORTHGATE

In Marin   Highway 101   Terra Linda Exit

CONSUMER NEWSPAPER
OVER 600 LINES:
CAMPAIGN

130
ART DIRECTOR:
Paul Hirsch
WRITER:
Mark Waggoner
PHOTOGRAPHER:
Lars Topelmann
CLIENT:
Cycle Oregon
AGENCY:
Cole & Weber/Portland

131
ART DIRECTOR:
Roger Bentley
WRITER:
Scott Wild
PHOTOGRAPHER:
Ken Anderson
CLIENT:
The Big House
AGENCY:
Dalbey & Denight Advertising/Portland

CONSUMER NEWSPAPER
OVER 600 LINES:
CAMPAIGN

132
ART DIRECTOR:
Joe Paprocki
WRITER:
Mike Gibbs
PHOTOGRAPHER:
Joe Lampi
CLIENT:
Star Tribune
AGENCY:
Fallon McElligott/
Minneapolis

133
ART DIRECTOR:
Dean Hanson
WRITER:
Bruce Bildsten
PHOTOGRAPHER:
Joe Paczkowski
CLIENT:
Timex Corporation
AGENCY:
Fallon McElligott/
Minneapolis

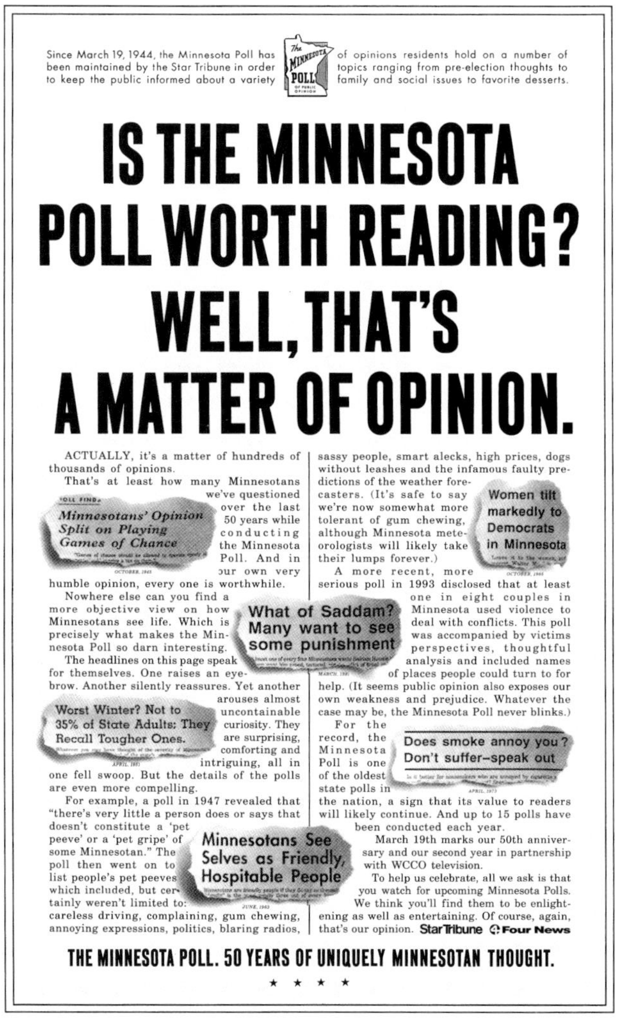

CONSUMER NEWSPAPER
OVER 600 LINES:
CAMPAIGN

134
ART DIRECTORS:
Steve Luker
Grant Richards
WRITERS:
Steve Simpson
Albert Kelly
ILLUSTRATORS:
Mark Rurka
Shui Wong
CLIENT:
Pacific Bell
AGENCY:
Goodby Silverstein & Partners/San Francisco

135
ART DIRECTORS:
Tan Shen Guan
Polly Chu
WRITERS:
Raymond Chau
Gideon Todes
CLIENT:
South China Morning Post
AGENCY:
J. Walter Thompson/Hong Kong

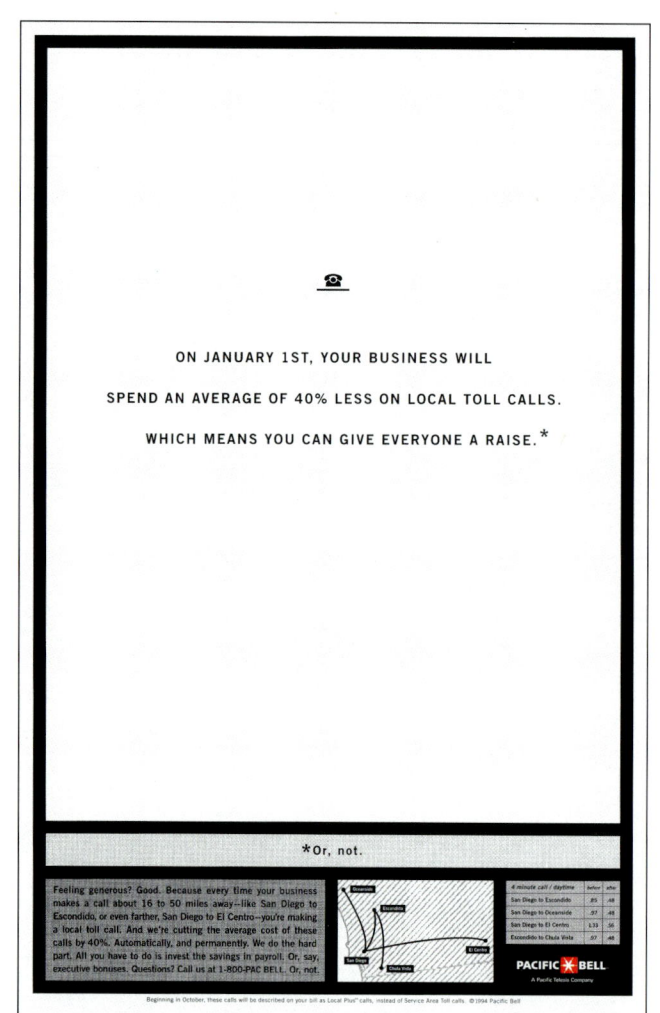
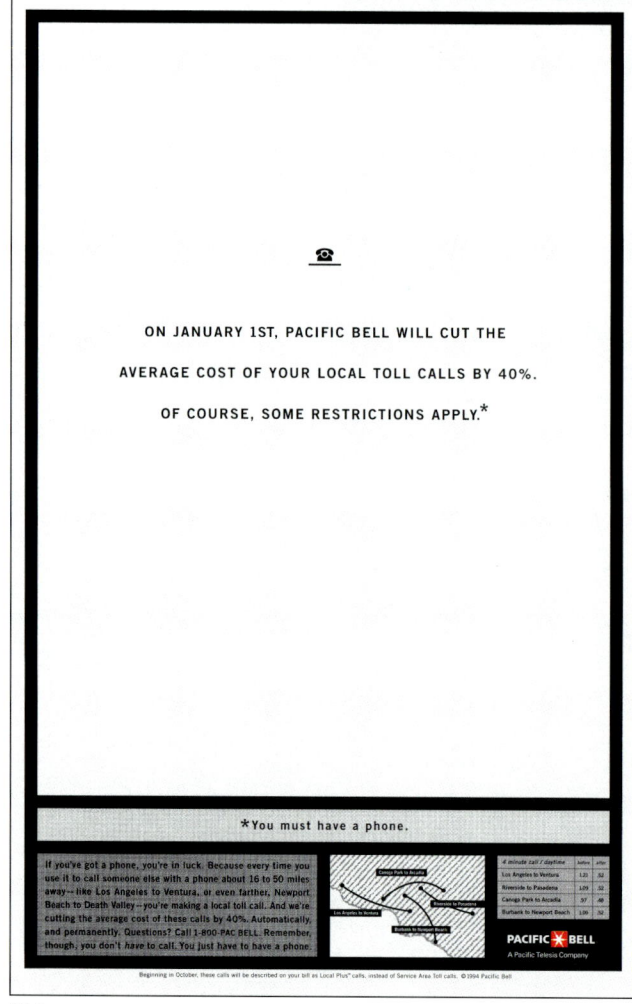
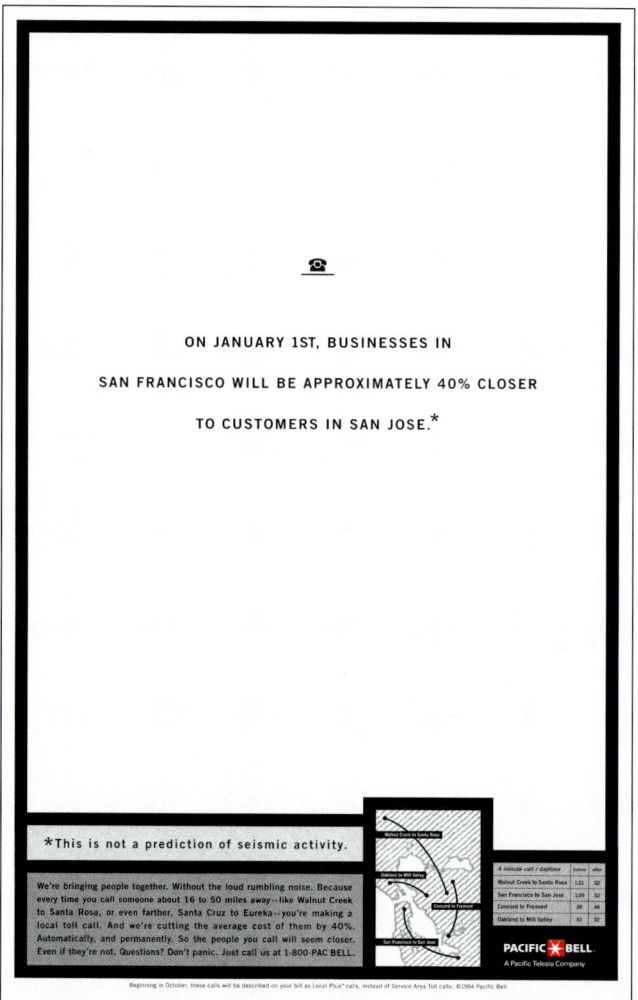

CONSUMER NEWSPAPER
OVER 600 LINES:
CAMPAIGN

136
ART DIRECTORS:
Dave Beverley
Martin Galton
Dave Dye
WRITERS:
Rob Burleigh
Tony Barry
Dave Hieatt
PHOTOGRAPHERS:
Earl Smith
Laurie Haskell
CLIENT:
Porsche
AGENCY:
Leagas Delaney/London

137
ART DIRECTORS:
Mark Fuller
Cathy Oliver
Sean Riley
WRITERS:
Ron Huey
Tripp Westbrook
PHOTOGRAPHERS:
Brad Miller
John Konkal
CLIENT:
Mercedes-Benz
of North America
AGENCY:
The Martin Agency/
Richmond

EVERY GEAR IS PASSING GEAR.

IT BEGAN AS A TINY DOT IN YOUR REARVIEW MIRROR.

DUST THY NEIGHBOR.

CONSUMER NEWSPAPER
OVER 600 LINES:
CAMPAIGN

138
ART DIRECTOR:
Cliff Sorah
WRITER:
Raymond McKinney
CLIENT:
The Poe Museum
AGENCY:
The Martin Agency/
Richmond

139
ART DIRECTOR:
Stephen Blair
WRITER:
Jeff Lewis
PHOTOGRAPHER:
Phil Marco
ILLUSTRATOR:
Sharpshooter Studios
CLIENT:
Coca-Cola Foods Canada
AGENCY:
McCann-Erickson/
Toronto

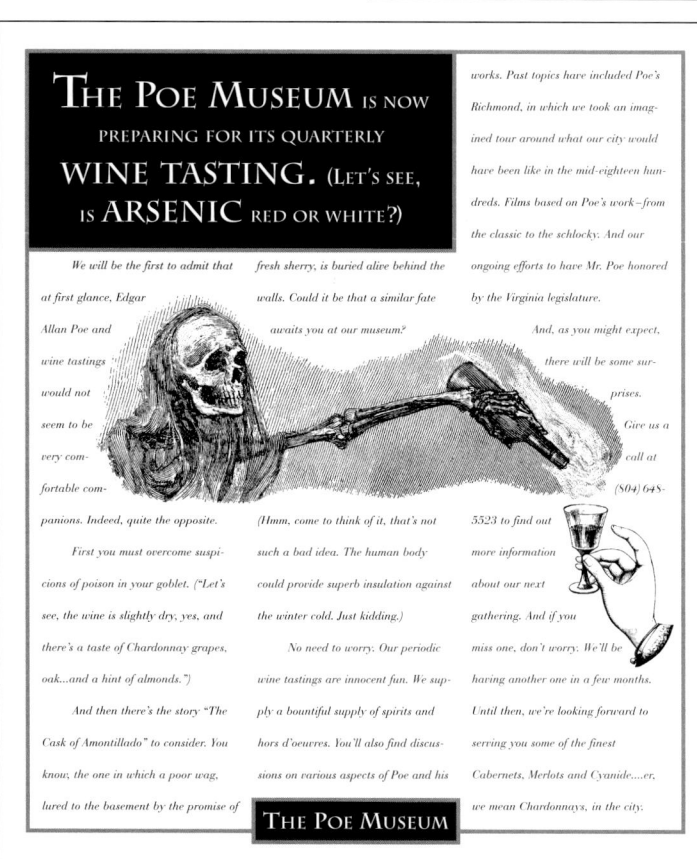

CONSUMER NEWSPAPER
OVER 600 LINES:
CAMPAIGN

140
ART DIRECTOR:
Greg Huff
WRITER:
Tim Wallis
ILLUSTRATORS:
Antar Dayal
Karel Havlicek
PHOTOGRAPHER:
Tom Casalini
CLIENT:
Meijer
AGENCY:
**Meyer & Wallis/
Milwaukee**

141
ART DIRECTOR:
Ron Wilcox
WRITER:
Steve Saari
PHOTOGRAPHER:
Russ Quackenbush
CLIENT:
Bill Hallman Shoes
AGENCY:
**Underdog Advertising/
Boston**

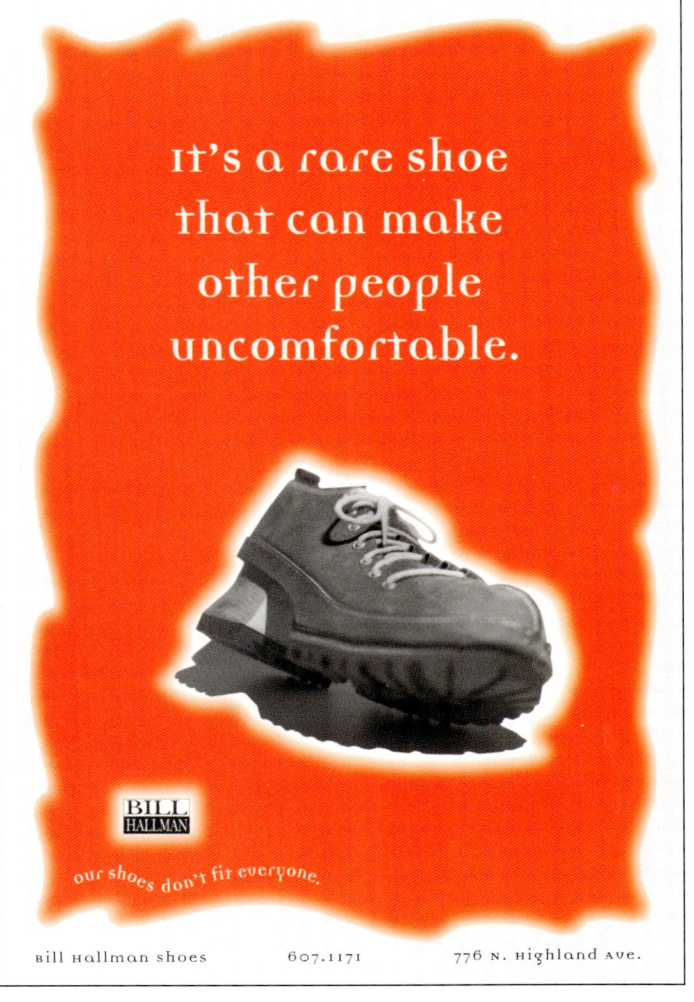

CONSUMER NEWSPAPER
OVER 600 LINES:
CAMPAIGN

142
ART DIRECTOR:
John Vitro
WRITER:
John Robertson
PHOTOGRAPHER:
Carl Vandershuit
CLIENT:
Los Angeles Times
AGENCY:
VitroRobertson/San Diego

143
ART DIRECTOR:
John Vitro
WRITER:
John Robertson
ILLUSTRATORS:
Brian Cairns
Greg Hally
Frank Viva
CLIENT:
Gray Cary Ware & Freidenrich
AGENCY:
VitroRobertson/San Diego

When the World Cup Soccer Championship was played in 1966, some thieves broke in and stole the golden trophy, which was worth tens of thousands of dollars. The police searched for days, but couldn't find it. Then, when everyone was about to give up, a small black and white dog named Pickles found the trophy buried behind some bushes in a London garden. Pickles became an instant hero. This is just one of the fun facts that your kids can read about in our "Soccer Times" insert in Sunday's paper. It has games, puzzles and trivia about the World Cup. Look for it. It's in the paper. And if you have trouble finding it, maybe you can ask your dog to help. Los Angeles Times

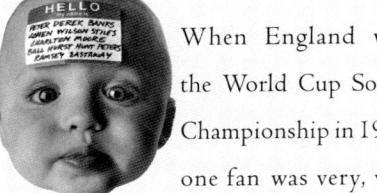

When England won the World Cup Soccer Championship in 1966, one fan was very, very happy. He was so happy he named his son after the entire 11-person team and their coach. The boy's name was Peter Derek Banks Cohen Wilson Stiles Charlton Moore Ball Hurst Hunt Peters Ramsey Eastaway. This is just one of the amazing facts your kids can read about in the special "Soccer Times" insert in Sunday's paper. It has games, puzzles and fun trivia for your kids. So look for it. And hopefully, your kids already have a name, so they don't need to be concerned. Los Angeles Times

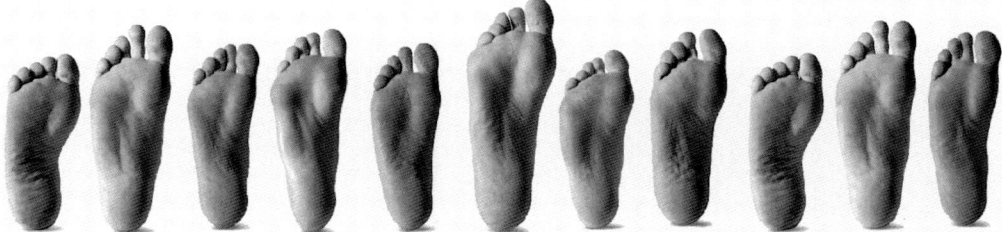

The country of India was very excited about sending its soccer team to the World Cup, for the first time, in 1950. They were told, though, that their players would not be allowed to play barefoot. Rather than put on shoes, they withdrew from the tournament, and India has never qualified for the World Cup finals since then.

This is just one of the facts your kids can learn about the World Cup by reading the "Soccer Times" insert in Sunday's paper. It has games, puzzles and stats about the World Cup. Look for it. And your kids can even learn some important things. Like, for instance, life did exist before million-dollar shoe contracts. Los Angeles Times

The idea that one person can solve your problems is a myth perpetuated by some attorneys and an occasional superhero from the planet Krypton.

A blue bodysuit with a big letter "S" on the front doesn't go very far these days in solving some of the challenges facing a business.

Business issues, especially those encountered by companies in California, have become very complex. And if your company is in the international arena, we don't need to tell you how complicated things can become.

That's why we've approached this increasingly complex and confusing environment with a very simple idea.

You need a team. Not a superhero.

Because one attorney, one person, cannot necessarily solve all your problems or provide all the expertise you need.

One attorney can, however, assemble a core group of people with the exact specialties your situation requires. So you're never in a position of paying for help you don't need. Or needing help but unable to get it.

And, we should stress, we consider you a member of this team. Which is why we strongly believe in regular, personal contact with key executives at our clients' businesses, and in attending many of the same trade conferences as our clients. We find we can anticipate clients' needs by staying fully aware of the latest developments affecting their industry.

Our approach is really very simple. But with the world getting more complex every day, it's our opinion that there's really only one way to solve problems. And that's to solve them together.

To start the solution, call Greg Gallo in Palo Alto at (415) 328-6561 or ask for Jay Jeffcoat in San Diego at (619) 699-2807.

GRAY CARY WARE ♦ FREIDENRICH

This may be the first time that 260 lawyers helped write an ad and there's no small print in it.

When you hire our law firm, it's our belief that you should get exactly that.

Our entire law firm.

You are a Gray Cary Ware & Freidenrich client. Which means you have the total resources of our statewide firm, both in Southern and Northern California, completely at your disposal.

Resources, of course, is another word for people. So what makes our people so different?

To begin with, we talk to each other. We work together as a team, with a strong belief in collaboration and open communication.

The better we understand the state of your business, the better we can counsel you, from a legal perspective, on options, considerations, issues.

This is not a promise that will go away shortly after the honeymoon period.

It is the way we do business; the way we have structured our entire firm.

If you need help or advice in a particular area—say, in technology licensing, venture capital financing, an IPO, litigation, employment law, product liability or environmental law—we will assemble a group of people with the exact experience you need.

You'll find that we have vast experience with companies at all stages of development. If you're a family-owned business, or a limited partnership, we can meet your special needs.

We also have a great deal of expertise with international companies, and the unique opportunities they present.

If you'd like to find out more about how we can work together, call us. And we'll put together the team. In San Diego, please call Jay Jeffcoat at (619) 699-2807. Or Paul Kreutz in Palo Alto at (415) 328-6561.

GRAY CARY WARE ♦ FREIDENRICH

When the word "partnership" is mentioned in a law office, it usually means a career move, not a way of thinking.

When we talk about partnership, we mean something much more important than a career path.

Our most important partnership is with our clients. We sit down and solve a client's problems together as a team.

This is not just a hollow claim. It is, simply, good business. Because, these days, business issues and legal issues are becoming increasingly inter-connected.

What's likely to happen to your company in the next quarter?

Will there be new hirings, or will there be layoffs? Will you be in search of venture financing? Is an IPO in the works?

Will you be pursuing technology licensing agreements?

In our view, it is our responsibility as your law firm to understand the complete picture, and not just the legal issues.

If your company is biotech or biomedical, you may find yourself talking to one of our attorneys who also has an advanced degree in life sciences.

Or perhaps you're a high technology or start-up company in search of capital. We can provide access to our extensive ties in the venture capital, investment banking and commercial banking communities.

Simply put, we believe every legal issue is also a business issue.

The fact that there is so little separating us from our clients is the biggest thing that separates us from other law firms.

To start the dialogue, please call Jay Jeffcoat in San Diego at (619) 699-2807, or Paul Kreutz in Palo Alto at (415) 328-6561.

GRAY CARY WARE ♦ FREIDENRICH

CONSUMER NEWSPAPER
OVER 600 LINES:
CAMPAIGN

144
ART DIRECTOR:
Danielle Lanz
WRITER:
Andre Benker
PHOTOGRAPHER:
Adrian Fritschi
CLIENT:
Triumph International
AGENCY:
Wirz Werbeberatung AG/
Zurich

CONSUMER NEWSPAPER
600 LINES OR LESS:
SINGLE

145
ART DIRECTOR:
John Doyle
WRITERS:
Ernie Schenck
Dylan Lee
PHOTOGRAPHER:
Hashi
CLIENT:
Akva Spring Water
AGENCY:
Berlin Cameron Doyle/
New York

146
ART DIRECTOR:
John Doyle
WRITER:
Ed Crayton
PHOTOGRAPHER:
Hashi
CLIENT:
Akva Spring Water
AGENCY:
Berlin Cameron Doyle/
New York

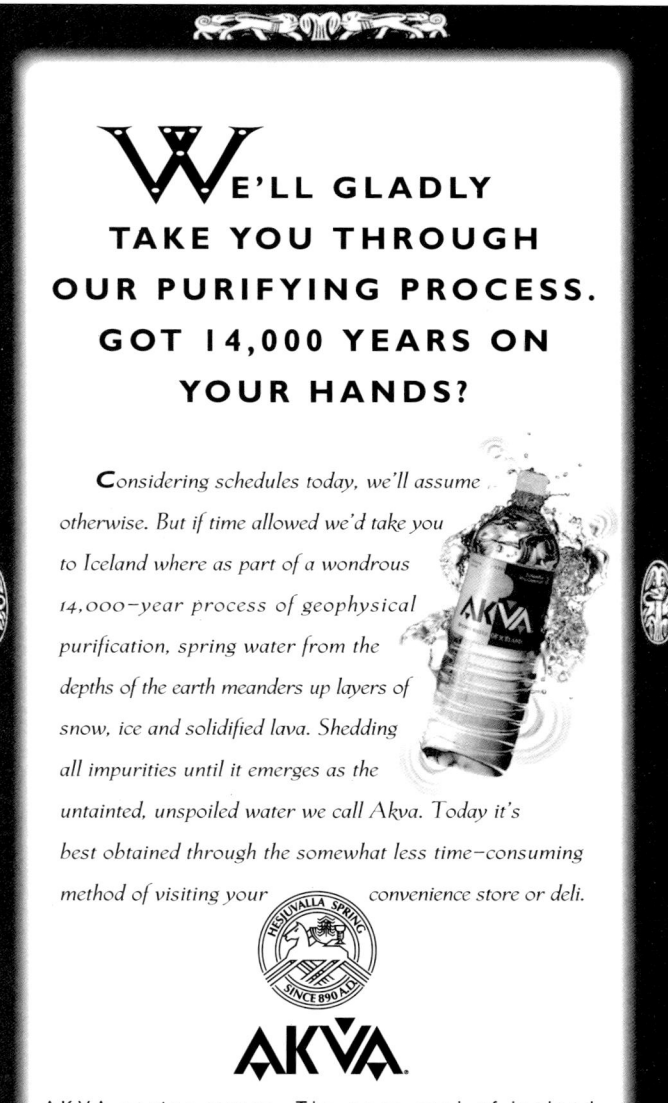

CONSUMER NEWSPAPER
600 LINES OR LESS:
SINGLE

147
ART DIRECTOR:
Steve Evans
WRITER:
Richard Overall
ILLUSTRATOR:
Frankie Ey
CLIENT:
Clemenger Adelaide
AGENCY:
Clemenger Adelaide/
Eastwood, Australia

148
ART DIRECTOR:
David Ayriss
WRITER:
Mark Waggoner
PHOTOGRAPHER:
Gary Hush
CLIENT:
Dr. Martens
AGENCY:
Cole & Weber/Portland

149
ART DIRECTOR:
Paul Hirsch
WRITER:
John Heinsma
PHOTOGRAPHER:
Gary Hush
CLIENT:
Dr. Martens
AGENCY:
Cole & Weber/Portland

150
ART DIRECTOR:
Paul Hirsch
WRITER:
John Heinsma
PHOTOGRAPHER:
Gary Hush
CLIENT:
Dr. Martens
AGENCY:
Cole & Weber/Portland

And she says she's not coming back until we find her a junior assistant. One with design and Macintosh skills, at least 2 years experience with Photoshop, QuarkXPress and Freehand and who would like to work for an ad agency. Please send your written application to the Production Manager, P.O. Box 265 Eastwood, South Australia 5063.

Our Mac operator has unexpectedly quit.

Six trillion rooftops in one night. What did you think he'd wear, penny loafers?

Your elves are bickering, the reindeer are cranky, and Mrs. Claus told you to be home two hours ago. How do you circle the globe in one night and still remain jolly? Simple. With a pair of comfy, air-cushioned Dr. Martens on your feet. And 51 solid weeks of vacation time.

Dr. Martens AirWair

Black leather, low-cut and revealing. Perfect for high school.

It's back-to-school time. And as any girl will tell you, the most important thing in life is shoes, more shoes, and did we mention shoes? Mary Janes, air-cushioned comfort from Dr. Martens.

The best shoes your parents' money can buy.

It's back-to-school time, and while you're out spending someone else's money, you might as well stock up on some decent shoes. After all, your parents worked hard for their money. Spend it wisely.

CONSUMER NEWSPAPER
600 LINES OR LESS:
SINGLE

151
ART DIRECTOR:
David Ayriss
WRITER:
Mark Waggoner
PHOTOGRAPHER:
Gary Hush
CLIENT:
Dr. Martens
AGENCY:
Cole & Weber/Portland

152
ART DIRECTOR:
David Ayriss
WRITER:
Mark Waggoner
PHOTOGRAPHER:
Gary Hush
CLIENT:
Dr. Martens
AGENCY:
Cole & Weber/Portland

153
ART DIRECTORS:
Shane Gibson
Matt Eastwood
WRITERS:
Shane Gibson
Matt Eastwood
PHOTOGRAPHER:
Bernie Gibson
CLIENT:
Liaison Condoms
AGENCY:
DDB Needham
Worldwide/North Sydney

154
ART DIRECTOR:
Dean Hanson
WRITER:
Dean Buckhorn
CLIENT:
Ameritech Corporate
AGENCY:
Fallon McElligott/
Minneapolis

In the spirit of the holidays, we offer a shoe even more durable than fruitcake.

Our classic 1460 boot is so well built, it can withstand oil, fat, acid, petrol and alkali. To say nothing of tree sap, eggnog, cranberry sauce and your Auntie Golda's rock-like fruitcake.

151

They won't just impress your friends. As an added bonus, they'll aggravate your parents.

Dr. Martens' classic 1460 boots. They're comfortable, they're durable, and you can even get your parents to pay for them. Just tell them you're getting a mohawk. Then settle for the shoes.

152

To a golfer, this is Woodstock.

It's not often you can see this many legendary performers in one place. Don't miss the Ameritech Senior Open as the stars of the Senior PGA Tour take on the incredible course at Stonebridge Country Club. To order your tickets, call 1-800-SENIOR-1. It should be an unforgettable show. **The Ameritech Senior Open. July 11-17.**

CONSUMER NEWSPAPER
600 LINES OR LESS:
SINGLE

155
ART DIRECTOR:
Ellen Steinberg
WRITER:
Luke Sullivan
PHOTOGRAPHERS:
Kerry Peterson
Shawn Michienzi
CLIENT:
Jim Beam Brands
AGENCY:
Fallon McElligott/
Minneapolis

156
ART DIRECTOR:
Bob Barrie
WRITER:
Sally Hogshead
PHOTOGRAPHER:
Kerry Peterson
CLIENT:
Nikon
AGENCY:
Fallon McElligott/
Minneapolis

157
ART DIRECTOR:
Bob Barrie
WRITER:
Sally Hogshead
PHOTOGRAPHER:
Kerry Peterson
CLIENT:
Nikon
AGENCY:
Fallon McElligott/
Minneapolis

158
ART DIRECTOR:
Debbie Klonk
WRITER:
Lane Strauss
CLIENT:
Edison's Birthplace
Museum
AGENCY:
Griswold-Eshleman/
Cleveland

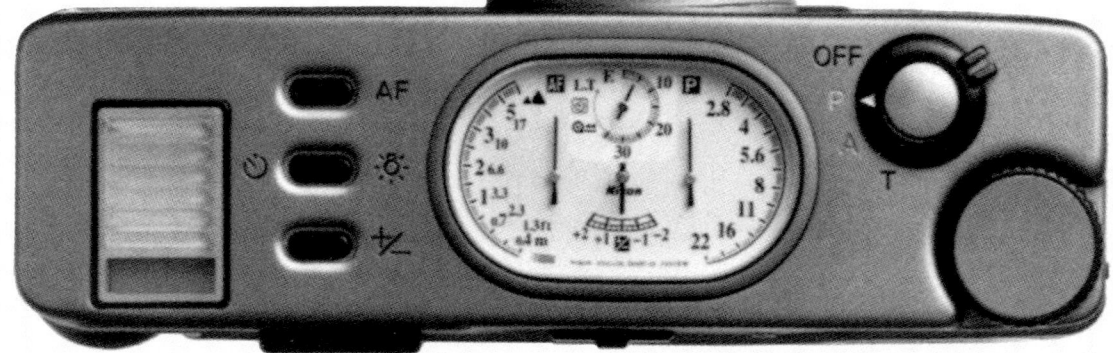

Because those Austin Healey glove compartments are so tiny.

The 35Ti has superior autofocus, a meticulous analog display, and the finest 35mm Nikkor f/2.8 lens we've ever made. All that, and you'll still have room for gloves.

Nikon
We take the world's greatest pictures.
Yours.

In 1847, Thomas Edison discovered breast milk.

EDISON'S BIRTHPLACE
MILAN, OHIO 419-499-2135

CONSUMER NEWSPAPER
600 LINES OR LESS:
SINGLE

159
ART DIRECTOR:
Gerard Vaglio
WRITER:
Neal Hughlett
PHOTOGRAPHER:
Carl Furuta
CLIENT:
Land Rover
North America
AGENCY:
Grace & Rothschild/
New York

160
ART DIRECTOR:
Jeff Griffith
WRITER:
Joe Lovering
PHOTOGRAPHER:
Jim Salzano
CLIENT:
Miss Vera's Finishing
School
AGENCY:
Griffith/Lovering,
New York

161
ART DIRECTOR:
Jeff Griffith
WRITER:
Joe Lovering
PHOTOGRAPHER:
Jim Salzano
CLIENT:
Miss Vera's Finishing
School
AGENCY:
Griffith/Lovering,
New York

162
ART DIRECTOR:
Timothy Delaney
WRITER:
Timothy Delaney
CLIENT:
Guitar Works
AGENCY:
Hal Riney & Partners/
Chicago

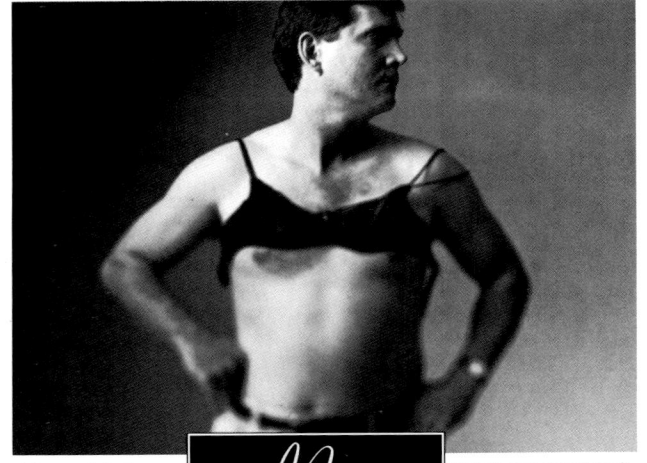

Everyone who cross dresses has something to hide.

Not to worry.

You simply need "cheater's panties." Now you see it. Now you don't.

At Miss Vera's Finishing School, we'll teach you all the basics of cross dressing. In fact, we'll teach you every trick in the book. That's what makes us America's foremost cross dressing academy.

Our experienced faculty will work with you in one-on-one classes at our Manhattan campus. From courses in dressing to depilation to diction, we'll make sure you know how to bring out your best.

Even THE SIMPLEST EVENING GOWN CAN BE RUINED BY A PENIS.

And conceal the rest.

You can enroll for a day, a weekend or a week. You may even feel ready for us to take you out on the town. Because at Miss Vera's, you'll always look outstanding.

But you won't stand out.

MISS VERA'S
FINISHING SCHOOL
For Boys Who Want To Be Girls.
2 1 2 - 2 4 2 - 6 4 4 9

PHONE CLASSES ALSO AVAILABLE IN A VARIETY OF CROSS DRESSING SUBJECTS. CALL 1-900-884-VERA. $2.99/MIN. ADULTS ONLY.   ©1994 MVA

Our amps come in small, medium and eviction notice.

See our wide selection of amps in all makes and sizes.
You may even find one the neighbors will approve of.
739 MAIN STREET, EVANSTON IL (708) 475-0855

The Guitar Works ltd.

CONSUMER NEWSPAPER
600 LINES OR LESS:
SINGLE

163
ART DIRECTOR:
Robert Prins
WRITER:
Jeff Spiegel
CLIENT:
Bornstein Memory School
AGENCY:
Ketchum Advertising/
Los Angeles

164
ART DIRECTOR:
Jeff DiFiore
WRITER:
Matt Peterson
CLIENT:
The Pet Shed
AGENCY:
Last Call Advertising/
New York

165
ART DIRECTOR:
Rob Rich
WRITER:
Kara Goodrich
CLIENT:
Stork's Landing
AGENCY:
Leonard/Monahan
Providence

166
ART DIRECTOR:
Jonathan Mackler
WRITER:
Matt Ashworth
PHOTOGRAPHER:
Steve Barbour
CLIENT:
Beads and Rocks
AGENCY:
The Martin Agency/
Richmond

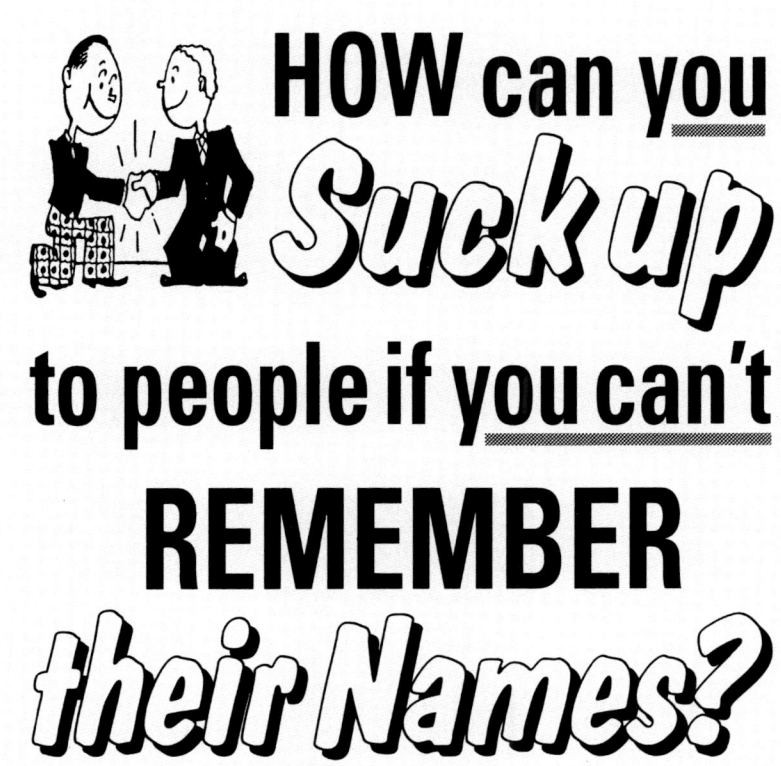

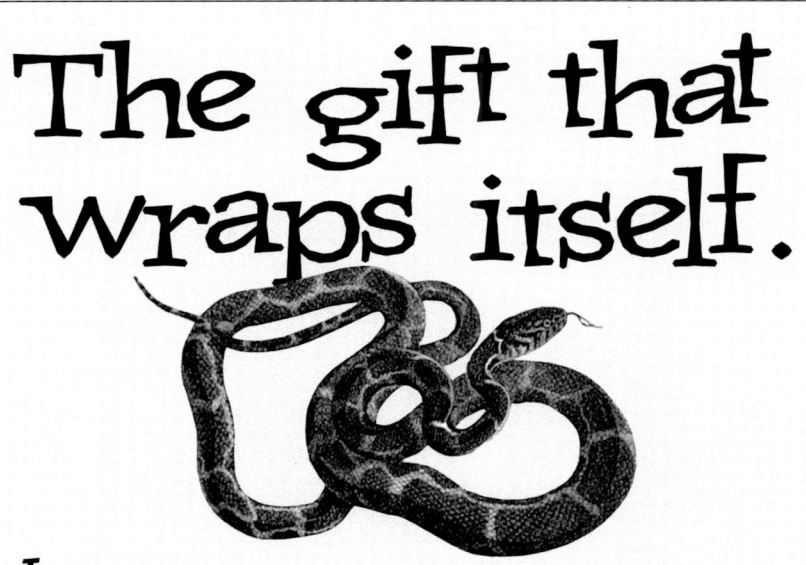

Come see our collection of truly stylish maternity clothes. Because as beautiful as a pregnant woman is, she doesn't need her clothes saying otherwise. Visit our only store at 170 Wayland Square in Providence, 331-4860.

Stork's Landing

Women radiate a special beauty when they're pregnant. No doubt to compensate for the clothes they have to wear.

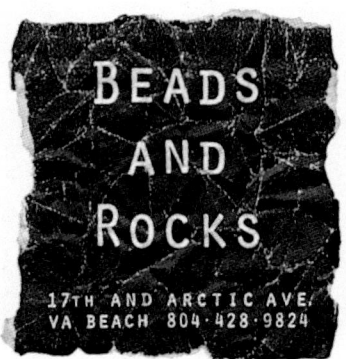

SOMETHING FOR EVERYONE.
(WHO'S LOOKING FOR BEADS OR ROCKS.)

CONSUMER NEWSPAPER
600 LINES OR LESS:
SINGLE

167
ART DIRECTOR:
Jonathan Mackler
WRITER:
Matt Ashworth
PHOTOGRAPHER:
Steve Barbour
CLIENT:
Beads and Rocks
AGENCY:
The Martin Agency/
Richmond

168
ART DIRECTOR:
Pat Wittich
WRITER:
Jonathan Kaler
CLIENT:
National Railway
Historical Society
AGENCY:
The Martin Agency/
Richmond

169
ART DIRECTOR:
Shari Hindman
WRITER:
Steve Bassett
CLIENT:
The Richmond Symphony
AGENCY:
The Martin Agency/
Richmond

170
ART DIRECTOR:
Barney Goldberg
WRITER:
Ron Huey
CLIENT:
The Richmond Symphony
AGENCY:
The Martin Agency/
Richmond

NOT THE PLACE TO GO IF YOU'RE LOOKING FOR STRING.

"THE GREAT YUGO ROBBERY"

"I HEAR THAT WINNEBAGO A COMIN'"

"MIDNIGHT MOPED TO GEORGIA"

There's just no substitute for a train.

THE AUTUMN LEAF EXCURSION • OCTOBER 1-2

To order tickets or for more information, call 231-4324. Outside Richmond, call 1-800-451-6318.

Hear a performer whose career spans more years than you'd like to admit.

"Breaking Up is Hard to Do," "Calendar Girl," "Love Will Keep Us Together." Unlike some things, Neil Sedaka's hits are ageless. Hear him April 23 at 8 p.m. at the Mosque. For tickets, call 262-8100.

The Richmond Symphony presents Neil Sedaka.

Sponsored by Coopers & Lybrand and Oldies 96.5.

In Canada, every kid grows up with a stick in his hands. The tough ones play hockey.

Canada's premier percussion ensemble Nexus performs September 17th and 19th. For tickets, call 262-8100.

The Richmond Symphony

CONSUMER NEWSPAPER
600 LINES OR LESS:
SINGLE

171
ART DIRECTOR:
Shari Hindman
WRITER:
Steve Bassett
CLIENT:
The Richmond Symphony
AGENCY:
The Martin Agency/
Richmond

172
ART DIRECTOR:
Shari Hindman
WRITER:
Ron Huey
CLIENT:
The Richmond Symphony
AGENCY:
The Martin Agency/
Richmond

173
ART DIRECTOR:
Noel Ritter
WRITER:
Joe Alexander
CLIENT:
Riverside Tennis Clinic
AGENCY:
The Martin Agency/
Richmond

174
ART DIRECTOR:
Noel Ritter
WRITER:
Joe Alexander
CLIENT:
Riverside Tennis Clinic
AGENCY:
The Martin Agency/
Richmond

175
ART DIRECTOR:
Chris Harrison
WRITER:
Glen Hunt
PHOTOGRAPHER:
Gary White
CLIENT:
Toronto Star
AGENCY:
Roche Macaulay &
Partners/Toronto

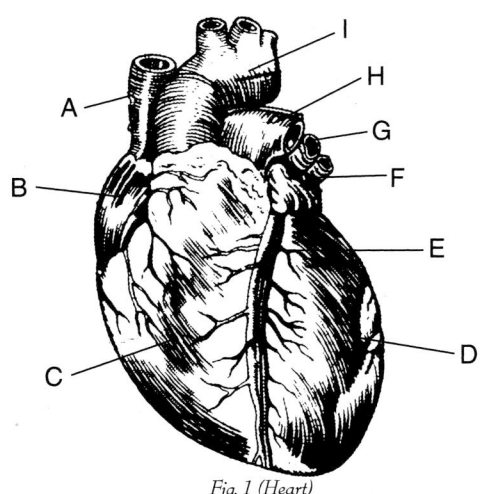

Last seen in San Francisco.

Fig. 1 (Heart)

He's the singer Frank Sinatra called the best in the business. Now a whole new generation has discovered Tony Bennett. See him in concert May 14 at 8 p.m. at the Mosque. For tickets, call 262-8100.

The Richmond Symphony presents Tony Bennett.

Sponsored by Mays & Valentine.

artificial snow
artificial candle
artificial tree
artificial mistletoe

At least you can still have live music.

Hear your favorite carols performed live at the Carpenter Center, December 2 at 8 p.m. and December 4 at 3 p.m. It's the perfect way to get yourself and your family in the holiday spirit. For tickets, call 782-3900.

The Richmond Symphony Holiday Concerts

Sponsored by NationsBank.

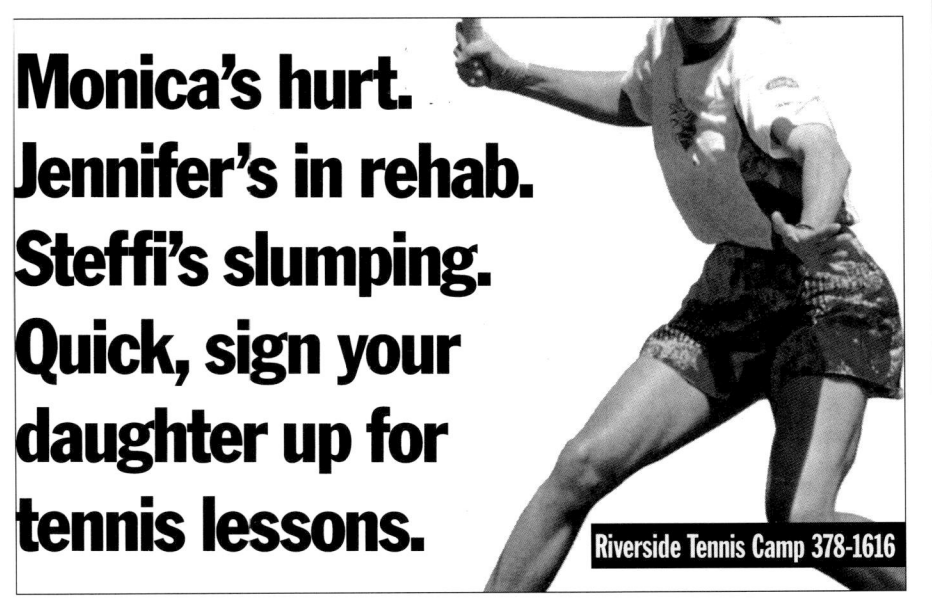

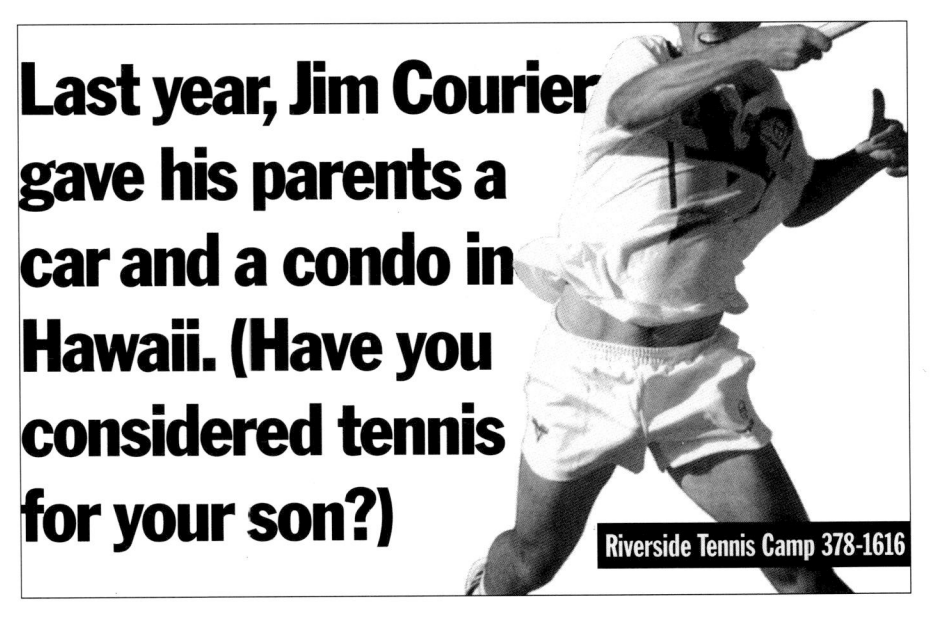

CONSUMER NEWSPAPER
600 LINES OR LESS:
CAMPAIGN

176
ART DIRECTOR:
Penny Duerr
WRITER:
Jim Nelson
PHOTOGRAPHER:
Shawn Michienzi
CLIENT:
Normark
AGENCY:
Carmichael Lynch/
Minneapolis

177
ART DIRECTOR:
Bryan Burlison
WRITER:
Josh Gold
PHOTOGRAPHER:
Imagen Retouching
CLIENT:
Fightertown
AGENCY:
Chiat/Day, Venice

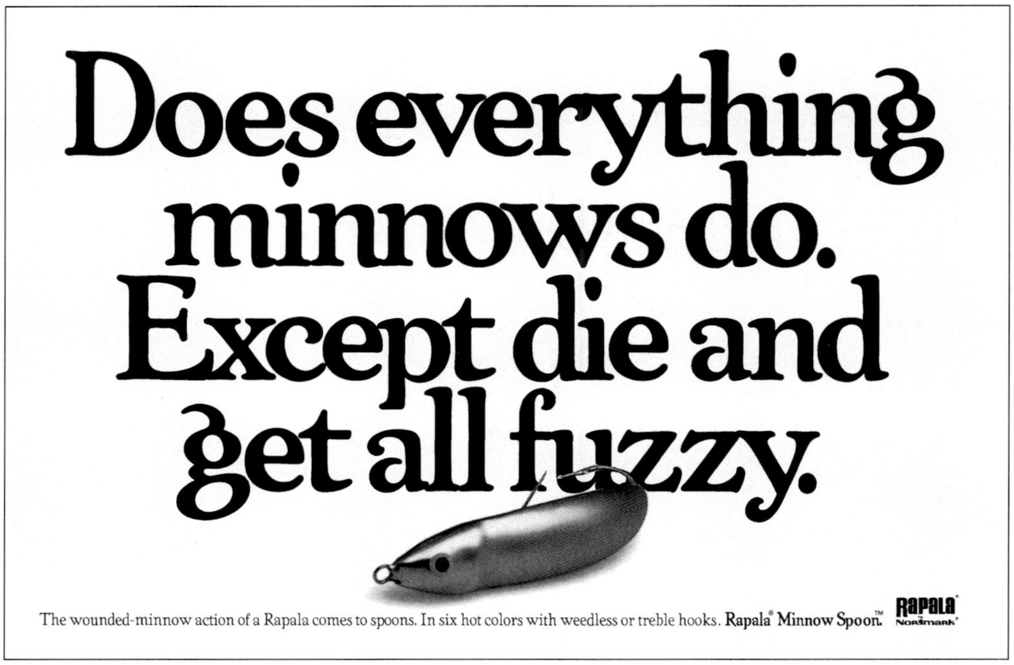

Does everything minnows do. Except die and get all fuzzy.
The wounded-minnow action of a Rapala comes to spoons. In six hot colors with weedless or treble hooks. Rapala® Minnow Spoon.™
Rapala
Normark

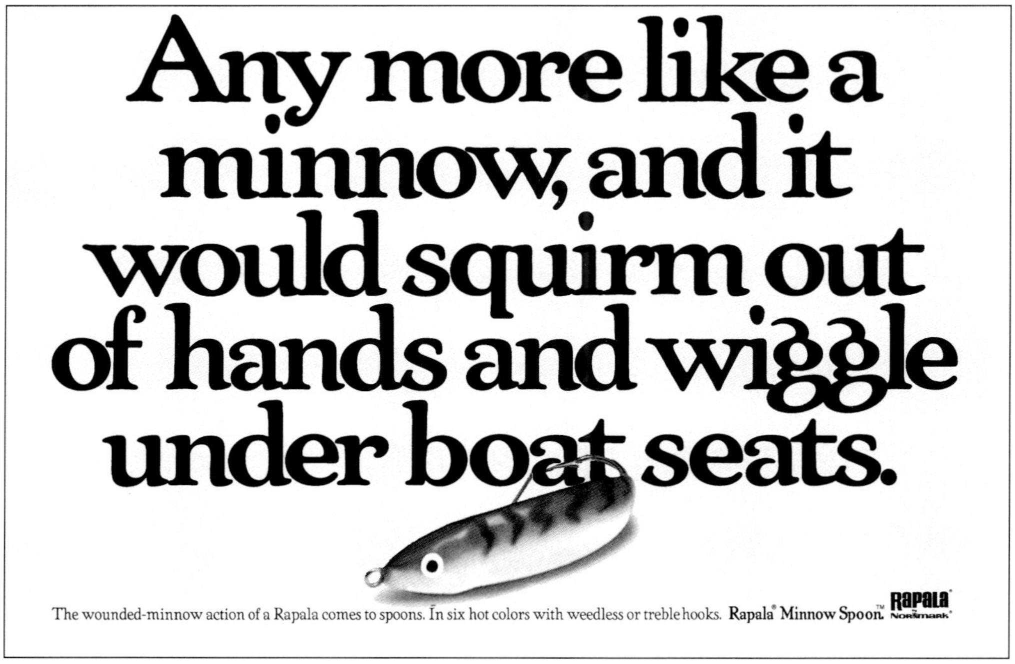

Any more like a minnow, and it would squirm out of hands and wiggle under boat seats.
The wounded-minnow action of a Rapala comes to spoons. In six hot colors with weedless or treble hooks. Rapala® Minnow Spoon.™
Rapala
Normark

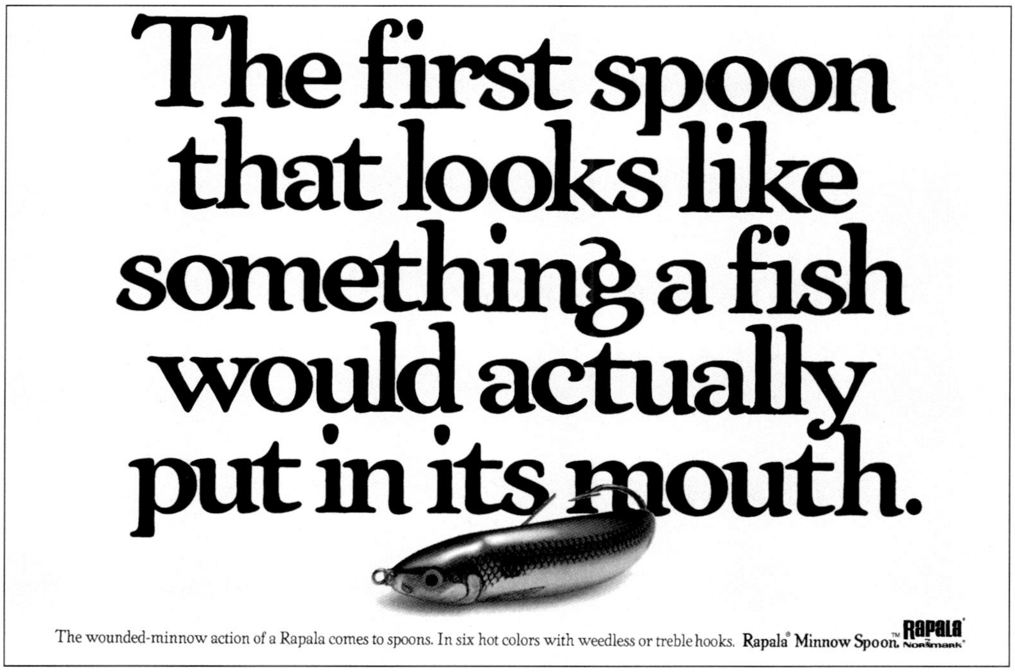

The first spoon that looks like something a fish would actually put in its mouth.
The wounded-minnow action of a Rapala comes to spoons. In six hot colors with weedless or treble hooks. Rapala® Minnow Spoon.™
Rapala
Normark

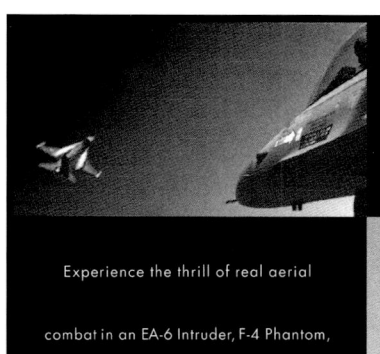

"LADIES AND GENTLEMEN, THE 4PM FLIGHT TO MOSCOW HAS JUST BEEN CANCELED."

Experience the thrill of real aerial combat in an EA-6 Intruder, F-4 Phantom, F-14 Tomcat, F-15 Eagle, or F-16 Falcon flight simulator. For more information please call us at 1-800-9FLY-JET.

FIGHTERTOWN
20521 Teresita, Lake Forest & Regency

WHAT'S THE RUSSIAN WORD FOR BARBECUE?

Experience the thrill of real aerial combat in an EA-6 Intruder, F-4 Phantom, F-14 Tomcat, F-15 Eagle, or F-16 Falcon flight simulator. For more information call 1-800-9FLY-JET.

FIGHTERTOWN
20521 Teresita, Lake Forest & Regency

HUH HUH HUH, UH HUH HUH. HE SAID COCKPIT.

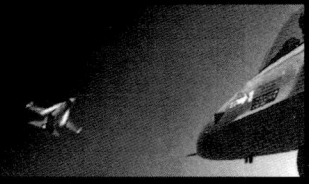

Experience the thrill of real aerial combat in an EA-6 Intruder, F-4 Phantom, F-14 Tomcat, F-15 Eagle, or F-16 Falcon flight simulator. For more information please call us at 1-800-9FLY-JET.

FIGHTERTOWN
20521 Teresita, Lake Forest & Regency

CONSUMER NEWSPAPER
600 LINES OR LESS:
CAMPAIGN

178
ART DIRECTOR:
Steve Evans
WRITER:
Richard Overall
ILLUSTRATOR:
Frankie Ey
CLIENT:
Clemenger Adelaide
AGENCY:
Clemenger Adelaide/
Eastwood, Australia

179
ART DIRECTORS:
David Ayriss
Paul Hirsch
WRITERS:
John Heinsma
Mark Waggoner
PHOTOGRAPHER:
Gary Hush
CLIENT:
Dr. Martens
AGENCY:
Cole & Weber/Portland

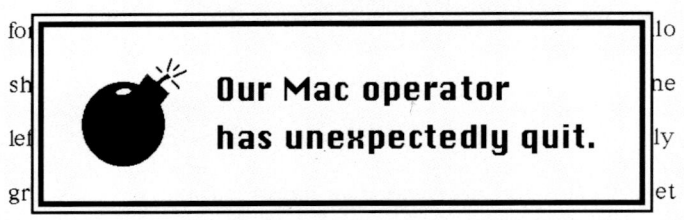

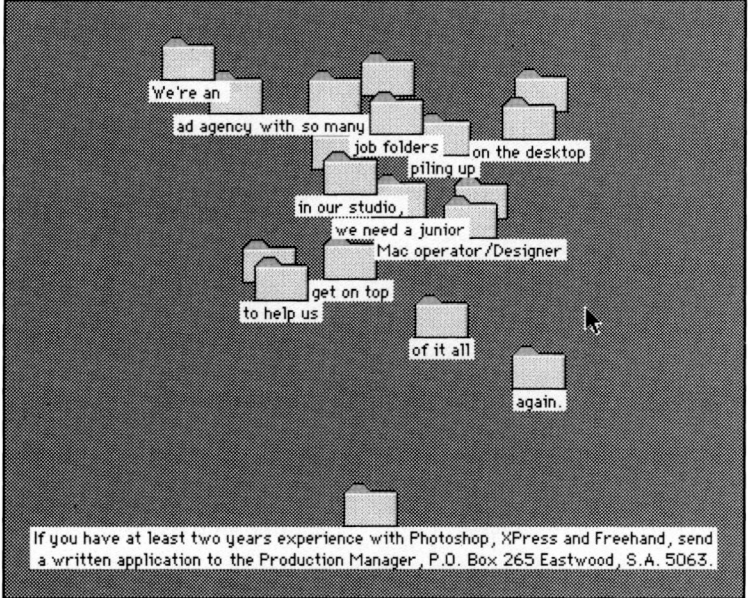

Conservative, in a liberal sort of way.

It doesn't matter whether you lean to the left, the right, backwards or forwards. Either way, you'll find that nothing fits you better than the air-cushioned comfort of a pair of Dr. Martens Gibsons.

They won't just impress your friends. As an added bonus, they'll aggravate your parents.

Dr. Martens' classic 1460 boots. They're comfortable, they're durable, and you can even get your parents to pay for them. Just tell them you're getting a mohawk. Then settle for the shoes.

Black leather, low-cut and revealing. Perfect for high school.

It's back-to-school time. And as any girl will tell you, the most important thing in life is shoes, more shoes, and did we mention shoes? Mary Janes, air-cushioned comfort from Dr. Martens.

CONSUMER NEWSPAPER
600 LINES OR LESS:
CAMPAIGN

180
ART DIRECTOR:
Ellen Steinberg
WRITER:
Luke Sullivan
PHOTOGRAPHERS:
Kerry Peterson
Shawn Michienzi
CLIENT:
Jim Beam Brands
AGENCY:
Fallon McElligott/
Minneapolis

181
ART DIRECTOR:
Bob Barrie
WRITER:
Sally Hogshead
PHOTOGRAPHER:
Kerry Peterson
CLIENT:
Nikon
AGENCY:
Fallon McElligott/
Minneapolis

For the man who has everything, the perfect camera to take pictures of it all.

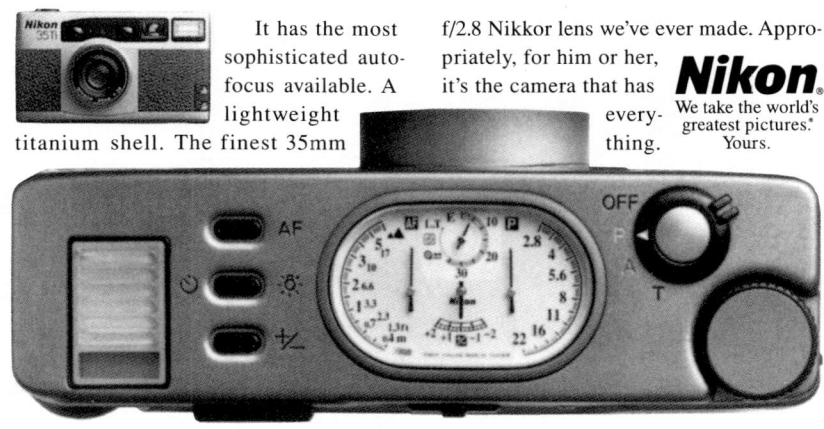

It has the most sophisticated auto-focus available. A lightweight titanium shell. The finest 35mm f/2.8 Nikkor lens we've ever made. Appropriately, for him or her, it's the camera that has everything.

Nikon
We take the world's greatest pictures. Yours.

Your accountant has four months to figure out a way to write it off.

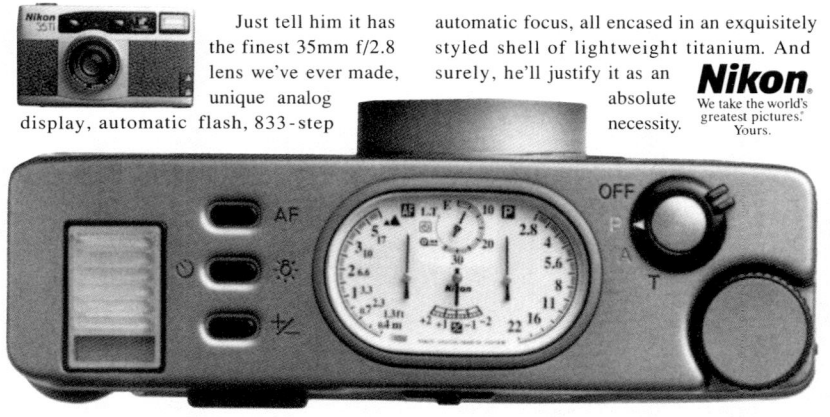

Just tell him it has the finest 35mm f/2.8 lens we've ever made, unique analog display, automatic flash, 833-step automatic focus, all encased in an exquisitely styled shell of lightweight titanium. And surely, he'll justify it as an absolute necessity.

Nikon
We take the world's greatest pictures. Yours.

It's a great stocking stuffer. (As long as the stockings are cashmere.)

The 35mm f/2.8 Nikkor lens is the finest we have ever designed. The automatic focus is virtually flawless. The displays are precision analog. And for the holidays, it's all gift-wrapped in titanium.

Nikon
We take the world's greatest pictures. Yours.

CONSUMER NEWSPAPER
600 LINES OR LESS:
CAMPAIGN

182
ART DIRECTOR:
Jeff Griffith
WRITER:
Joe Lovering
PHOTOGRAPHER:
Jim Salzano
CLIENT:
Miss Vera's Finishing School
AGENCY:
Griffith/Lovering, New York

183
ART DIRECTOR:
Rob Rich
WRITER:
Kara Goodrich
CLIENT:
Stork's Landing
AGENCY:
Leonard/Monahan, Providence

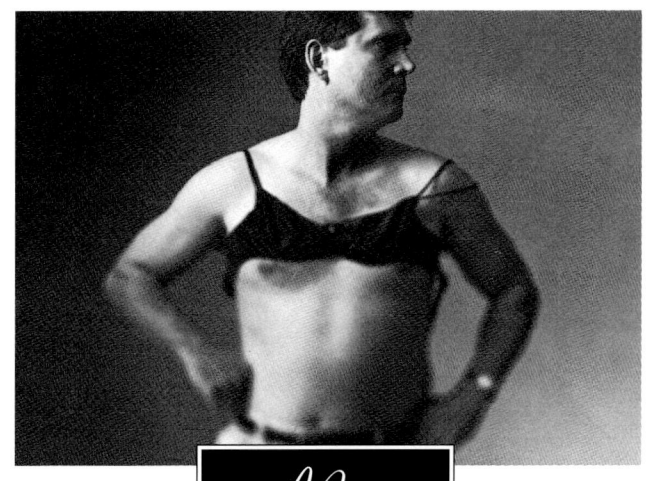

No WONDER YOU FEEL UNCOMFORTABLE CROSS DRESSING. YOUR WIFE'S BRA IS THE WRONG SIZE.

It happens all the time. You need a 42B and all you can get your hands on is a 34C.

At Miss Vera's Finishing School, we have bras (and everything else) in every conceivable size. So when it comes to cross dressing, we're equipped to give you all the support you need.

Our experienced faculty will work with you in one-on-one classes at our Manhattan campus. From courses in make-up and dressing to elocution and walking, we'll help you create a *femmeself* that fits you perfectly.

We even have weekend getaways and excursions around town. Want to dress up and go shopping? To the Metropolitan? The ladies room at The Waldorf? We'll take you every step of the way.

There's a simple reason people from all over the world come to Miss Vera's. No matter what kind of man you are, we can make you a better girl.

Cross our hearts.

MISS VERA'S FINISHING SCHOOL
For Boys Who Want To Be Girls.
2 1 2 - 2 4 2 - 6 4 4 9

PHONE CLASSES ALSO AVAILABLE IN A VARIETY OF CROSS DRESSING SUBJECTS. CALL 1-900-884-VERA. $2.99/MIN. ADULTS ONLY. ©1994 MVA

After A LONG DAY IN WINGTIPS, IT'S NICE TO SLIP INTO A PAIR OF SPIKED HEELS.

From our point of view, there's no better way to unwind. Give us pink chiffon over grey flannel any day.

Miss Vera's is America's only cross dressing academy. So when it comes to turning ordinary men into voluptuous girls, we're all business. Small wonder that hundreds of doctors, lawyers, bankers, and construction workers find their way to our Manhattan campus every year. We've even taught a famous nuclear physicist. (He's now a real bombshell.)

Our experienced faculty will work with you in one-on-one classes for a day, a weekend, or a week. We'll provide everything you need. Tutus. Cocktail dresses. Evening gowns. Maids' uniforms. You name it, we've got it.

So relax. The only wing tips you'll find around here are on our Tinkerbell costume.

MISS VERA'S FINISHING SCHOOL
For Boys Who Want To Be Girls.
2 1 2 - 2 4 2 - 6 4 4 9

PHONE CLASSES ALSO AVAILABLE IN A VARIETY OF CROSS DRESSING SUBJECTS. CALL 1-900-884-VERA. $2.99/MIN. ADULTS ONLY. ©1994 MVA

Be THE SISTER YOU NEVER HAD.

It's a scientific fact. Every man has female genes.

So, it's perfectly logical that he'd want a gingham pinafore to go with them.

At Miss Vera's Finishing School, we can help you become the girl of your dreams.

Our experienced faculty will work with you in one-on-one classes at our Manhattan campus. From courses in make-up and dress-up to elocution and walking, we'll create a female persona that fits you perfectly.

We also have weekend getaways and excursions around town. Want to go shopping for a new nightie? Get your nails done at a salon? Have tea at The Plaza? We'll take you every step of the way.

You could even meet your mother for lunch. And she'll discover something she never knew she had.

A daughter.

MISS VERA'S FINISHING SCHOOL
For Boys Who Want To Be Girls.
2 1 2 - 2 4 2 - 6 4 4 9

PHONE CLASSES ALSO AVAILABLE IN A VARIETY OF CROSS DRESSING SUBJECTS. CALL 1-900-884-VERA. $2.99/MIN. ADULTS ONLY. ©1994 MVA

Come see our collection of truly stylish maternity clothes. Because as beautiful as a pregnant woman is, she doesn't need her clothes saying otherwise. Visit our only store at 170 Wayland Square in Providence, 331-4860.

Stork's Landing

Women radiate a special beauty when they're pregnant. No doubt to compensate for the clothes they have to wear.

You want clothes. Beautiful, stylish, flattering clothes that happen to be maternity wear. Hey, if you wanted camping gear, you'd go to a sporting goods store. Come visit our only store at 170 Wayland Square in Providence, 331-4860.

Stork's Landing

Why do clothes made to accommodate two have to look like they could sleep four?

Nature plays some devious tricks on pregnant women. That's why we have clothes that make pregnancy more fashionable, if not more bearable. Come satisfy one craving at our store at 170 Wayland Square in Providence, 331-4860.

Stork's Landing

Women often experience a heightened sense of taste during pregnancy. Bad timing, considering the clothes.

CONSUMER MAGAZINE
B/W 1 PAGE OR SPREAD:
SINGLE

184
ART DIRECTOR:
Henriette Lienke
WRITER:
Tom Miller
PHOTOGRAPHER:
Kent Kirkley
CLIENT:
Fine Jewelers Guild
AGENCY:
Goldsmith/Jeffrey,
New York

185
ART DIRECTOR:
Jon Soto
WRITER:
Tina Hall
PHOTOGRAPHER:
Alexander Ruas
CLIENT:
Shelter
AGENCY:
Mad Dogs & Englishmen/
New York

CONSUMER MAGAZINE
COLOR 1 PAGE OR
SPREAD: SINGLE

186
ART DIRECTOR:
John Horton
WRITER:
Richard Roster
PHOTOGRAPHER:
Graham Ford
CLIENT:
Sainsbury's
AGENCY:
Abbott Mead Vickers.
BBDO/London

187
ART DIRECTOR:
Frank Guzzone
WRITER:
Paul Hartzell
PHOTOGRAPHER:
Fred Kolhoff
CLIENT:
Austin Nichols & Company/
Wild Turkey
AGENCY:
Angotti Thomas Hedge/
New York

184

185

SAINSBURY'S OLIVES

Would you like a martini with your olive?

SAINSBURY'S Where good food costs less.

Other distilleries add up to
twice as much water
to their bourbon as we do.

Are they more proud
of their water? Or
less proud of their bourbon?

WILD TURKEY
101 proof, real Kentucky.

CONSUMER MAGAZINE
COLOR 1 PAGE OR
SPREAD: SINGLE

188
ART DIRECTOR:
Frank Guzzone
WRITER:
Paul Hartzell
PHOTOGRAPHER:
Fred Kolhoff
CLIENT:
Austin Nichols & Company/
Wild Turkey
AGENCY:
Angotti Thomas Hedge/
New York

189
ART DIRECTOR:
Frank Guzzone
WRITER:
Paul Hartzell
PHOTOGRAPHER:
Jim Hall
CLIENT:
Saab Cars USA
AGENCY:
Angotti Thomas Hedge/
New York

190
ART DIRECTOR:
Rosie Arnold
WRITER:
Charles Hendley
PHOTOGRAPHER:
Mary Ellen Mark
CLIENT:
Levi Strauss & Company/
Europe SA
AGENCY:
Bartle Bogle Hegarty/
London

191
ART DIRECTOR:
Rosie Arnold
WRITER:
Charles Hendley
PHOTOGRAPHER:
Mary Ellen Mark
CLIENT:
Levi Strauss & Company/
Europe SA
AGENCY:
Bartle Bogle Hegarty/
London

Our Master Distiller meticulously samples every batch of bourbon 11 times before it's bottled.

We have a very low turnover in Master Distillers.

WILD TURKEY
101 proof, real Kentucky.

IT GETS ITS AGGRESSIVE STREAK FROM ITS WILD UNCLE.

Its great-grandmother was a tour bus. Its father a safe, practical 900. But the new Saab 900 SE Turbo Coupe shows definite signs of a Type-A personality. Sleeker aerodynamics. 16-inch alloy wheels. A stiffened sports suspension. A 185-horsepower intercooled turbo engine. Switched at birth? No. Just a case of a car company with jet fuel in its bloodlines. **THE NEW 900 SE TURBO COUPE.**

SAAB

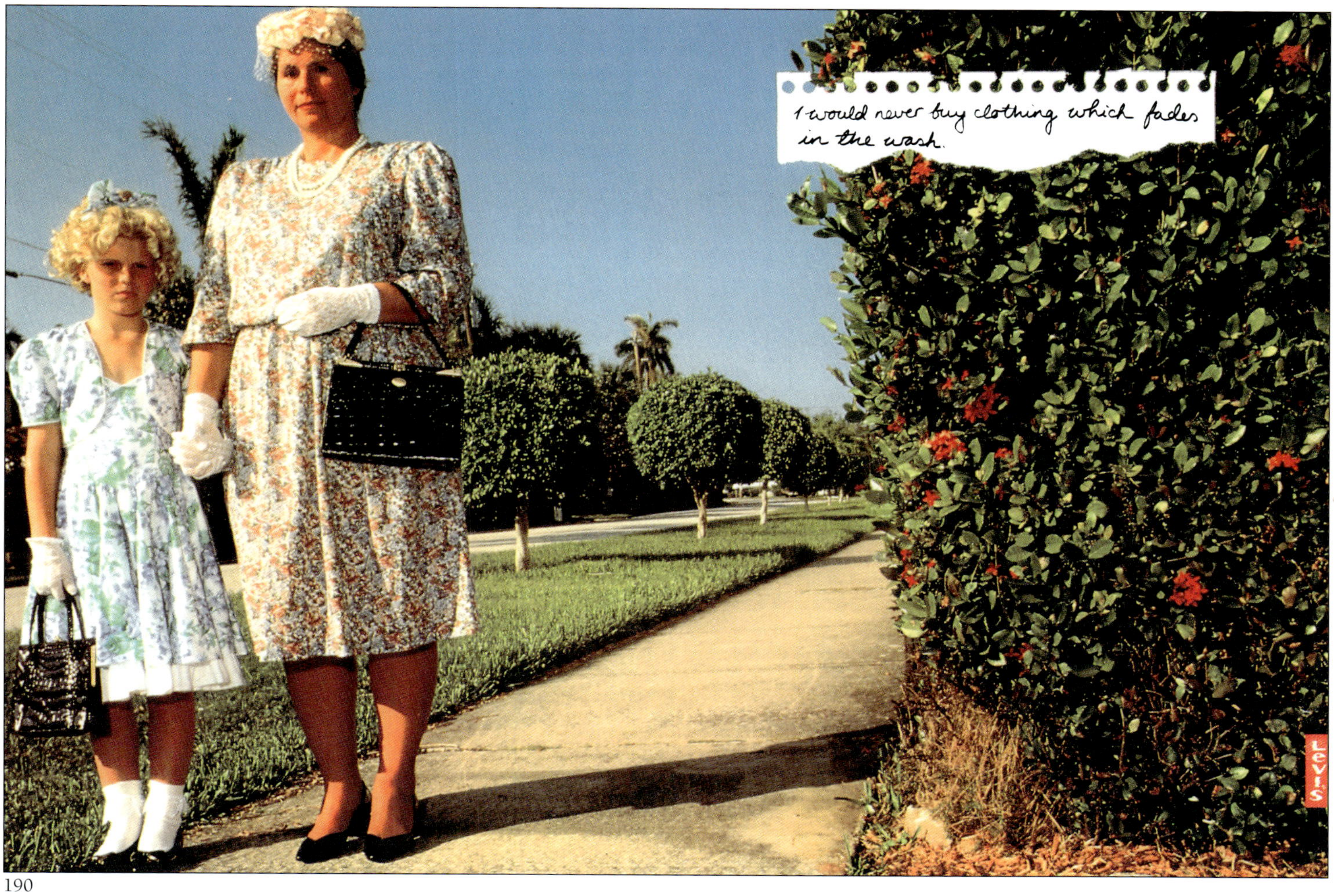
I would never buy clothing which fades in the wash.
LEVI'S

190

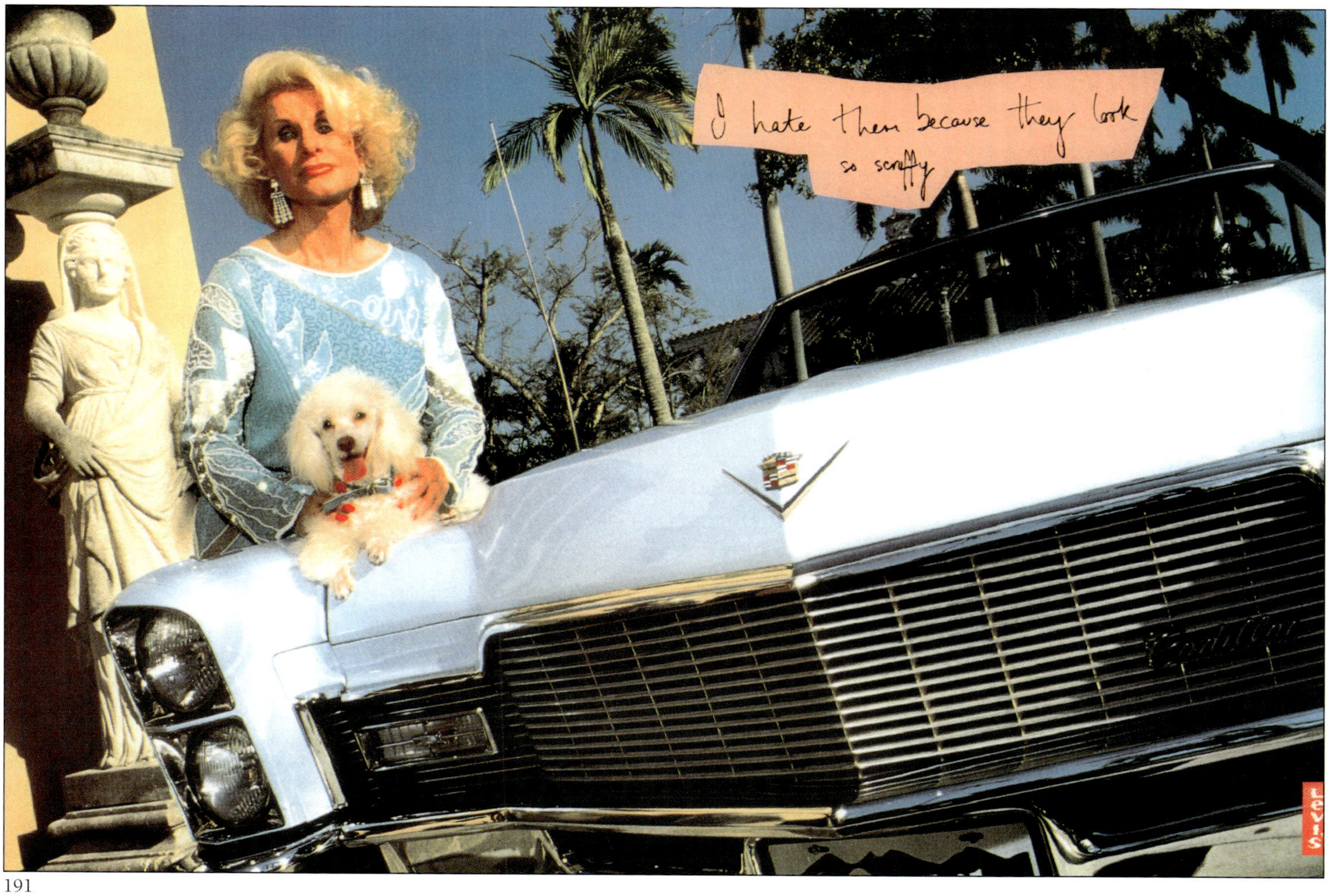
I hate them because they look so scruffy
LEVI'S

191

CONSUMER MAGAZINE
COLOR 1 PAGE OR
SPREAD: SINGLE

192
ART DIRECTOR:
Lye Kok Hong
WRITER:
Jim Aitchison
PHOTOGRAPHER:
Alex Kaikeong
CLIENT:
Mercedes-Benz Asia
AGENCY:
Batey Ads/Singapore

193
ART DIRECTOR:
Susan Westre
WRITER:
Chris Wall
PHOTOGRAPHER:
Michael O'Brien
CLIENT:
Apple Computer
AGENCY:
BBDO/Los Angeles

194
ART DIRECTORS:
Susan Westre
Maggie Choo
WRITERS:
Chris Wall
John Dullaghan
PHOTOGRAPHER:
Michael O'Brien
CLIENT:
Apple Computer
AGENCY:
BBDO/Los Angeles

195
ART DIRECTOR:
Steve Kimura
WRITER:
Steve Skibba
PHOTOGRAPHER:
Rocki Pederson
CLIENT:
Pioneer Electronics USA
AGENCY:
BBDO/Los Angeles

What's on your PowerBook?

Terry Ellis
President of Imago Records

Notes for speeches
Notes to my assistant
Notes regarding a charity dinner I'm organizing
My children's sports schedules
Company marketing plans
Company budgets
A calculator
One of my daughter's poems
America Online
Now Up-to-Date
Microsoft Word
A HyperCard stack cataloguing my wine collection
A fax modem
A personal organizer
A detailed record of my wife's dinner parties
Racehorse breeding records
A calendar of my artists' concerts
PTA meeting notes
Itinerary for the Ellis family vacation
A dictionary
A thesaurus
Archive files of correspondence
A recipe for Yorkshire pudding

Henry Rollins
Musician/Spoken Word Performer

My show log
My workout log
Eye Scream, a book in progress
Get in the Van, a book in progress
Other people's books I'm proofreading
A fax modem
My journal
An article for *Details*
An article for *Elle*
An article for *Purr*
DateBook Pro
Microsoft Word
Virex
PSI Fax
The release schedule for Infinite Zero Records
My tour schedule
The preface to a friend's book
Phone numbers and addresses
Lots of letters
Lots of faxes
A lyric book
Liner notes for Hubert Selby's spoken word CD
Transcripts from recent interviews
Notes for my next video
A list of things that are true

WITH HEARING FIVE TIMES BETTER THAN OURS, THE REASON THEY'RE ALWAYS DOING THIS PROBABLY HAS TO DO WITH THE STEREO.

Man's best friend may also be his toughest stereo critic. But then you don't have to be able to hear a cat at a hundred yards to tell if your car stereo needs help. If it does, why not put in one of Pioneer's six or twelve disc CD changers. They let you play compact discs through your car's FM radio and give you hours of music in perfect digital sound. So if the stereo in your car hasn't exactly been making your ears perk up, give us a call at 1-800-Pioneer, ext. 101, for a dealer. And get the system that won't just sit in your dash and play dead.

PIONEER
The Art of Entertainment

CONSUMER MAGAZINE
COLOR 1 PAGE OR
SPREAD: SINGLE

196
ART DIRECTOR:
John Doyle
WRITER:
Ernie Schenck
ILLUSTRATOR:
Peter Hall
PHOTOGRAPHERS:
**Sigurgeir Sigurjonsson
Hashi, Geoffrey Stein**
CLIENT:
Akva Spring Water
AGENCY:
**Berlin Cameron Doyle/
New York**

197
ART DIRECTOR:
John Doyle
WRITER:
Ernie Schenck
ILLUSTRATOR:
Peter Hall
PHOTOGRAPHERS:
**Pall Stefansson
Sigurgeir Sigurjonsson
Hashi, Geoffrey Stein**
CLIENT:
Akva Spring Water
AGENCY:
**Berlin Cameron Doyle/
New York**

198
ART DIRECTOR:
John Doyle
WRITER:
Ernie Schenck
ILLUSTRATOR:
Peter Hall
PHOTOGRAPHERS:
**Sigurgeir Sigurjonsson
Pall Stefansson
Hashi, Geoffrey Stein**
CLIENT:
Akva Spring Water
AGENCY:
**Berlin Cameron Doyle/
New York**

199
ART DIRECTOR:
John Doyle
WRITER:
Ernie Schenck
ILLUSTRATOR:
Peter Hall
PHOTOGRAPHERS:
**Leen Thijsse
Jamey Stillings
Hashi, Geoffrey Stein**
CLIENT:
Akva Spring Water
AGENCY:
**Berlin Cameron Doyle/
New York**

Six months for the sun to rise. Two years for a glacier to move an inch. But then, it takes 14,000 years just to purify the water.

What kind of country is it where, for very nearly half the year, the sun struggles and scrapes and plods its way toward the horizon at a pace that would, quite frankly, make even the most aged of snails seem like a veritable greyhound by comparison?

Or where a blanket of snow and ice the size of a small nation lumbers over the surface of the earth so incredibly slowly, its movement is undetectable even to the most sophisticated of time lapse motion picture cameras?

A very, very patient one, if we might be so presumptuous as to suggest.

Few things move quickly in Iceland, you see. And a rather good thing it is, too. Especially when one stops to consider that, although our AKVA spring water may be among the purest on the planet, it does take a quite painfully long bit of time for it to get that way. About 14,000 years, give or take a millennium. But rather than throwing numbers about willy nilly, we should take a moment to explain.

As the realities of geophysics would have it, the spring water we know as AKVA begins its tortuous journey to the surface in a place so far within the depth of the planet, it virtually defies comprehension. A place so cold and dark, so absolutely and starkly isolated, no human being will ever gaze upon its mysteries.

Slowly upward it meanders. Forcing its way through layer upon infinite layer of snow. Ice. Solidified lava. Indeed, of time itself. Shedding itself of one impurity after another. Until, untold centuries later, it is set free.

Untouched. Untainted. Unspoiled by the rather unfortunate byproducts of a civilization mired in progress. A water with a taste so soft, so utterly devoid of sodium and other uninvited contaminants, so perfect in every way, we are hard pressed to believe that the Viking gods themselves might not have had more than a little to do with it. (Blessed with a country like ours, it's possible.) It is our opinion, of course, that once you've sampled a bit of our AKVA for yourself, once you have discovered its crisp, clear, exquisitely delicate nature, you'll no doubt share our exuberance for this most extraordinary spring water. Something we fervently hope you will do in the not too distant future simply by paying a visit to your favorite delicatesser or corner market. And soon.

Of course in the event that you should run into trouble finding our spring water, we do encourage you to ask for it by name. We're convinced that you will thoroughly enjoy the pure, Arctic clean, ice clear taste of Akva with your very first bottle. So much so, we can predict that while it may take 14,000 years for our water to come up, it won't take nearly as long to go down.

Akva spring water. The pure soul of Iceland.

Just thinking about how pure our water is sends chills down our spines. (Granted, being within a whisper of the Arctic Circle might have something to do with it.)

When your country lies within a mere thousand miles of the North Pole, life is no ordinary thing. The Northern Lights dance in the polar darkness like a thousand shimmering ribbons. The stars flashing like a billion shards of glass. Your breath all but freezes in the morning air. The sun, what little there is of it, hangs in the winter sky like a ball of ice. A frozen circle of silver fire. And the water, how do we begin to tell you about it?

That it comes from a place buried deep within some impossibly cold subterranean reservoir, untold fathoms beneath our glaciers? That it is the natural bounty of a country that is blessedly isolated, mercifully cut off from civilization by thousands upon thousands of miles of raging ocean?

For Iceland, you see, is a most extraordinary place. And the water that comes from here is unlike any other on this, and very possibly any other, planet in the known universe. We have a word for it. Akva. And yet to describe it. Ah, now that is no easy thing. It is, we can tell you, of a remarkable clarity. The word diamond tends to come to mind. There is a purity that borders on the virginal. And the taste. We must tell you all about the taste. But, of course, we're getting ahead of ourselves.

Did we mention that our spring water is the final result of a 14,000 year process of geophysical purification? A natural, if somewhat painfully slow, filtration system in which endless layers of ice, rock, and petrified lava slowly strip away one impurity after the other.

Until the purest water known to humankind finally forces its way to the surface well in excess of a thousand centuries later. Untouched. Untainted. Unspoiled by contaminants of any sort.

We would expect that once you've tried a bottle of our spring water for yourself, of course, you will be every bit as taken with its crisp, fresh, Arctic pure taste as those of us here in Iceland who have enjoyed it for centuries. What you will discover, we don't mind telling you, is a spring water that is crisp. Refreshing. Free of sodium. Free of impurities of every description.

In brief, you are going to love Akva as you have not loved any spring water you have ever experienced. So much so, we fervently believe, that once you have tried it, it's most unlikely you will ever again feel compelled to drink any other. And to think you won't even have to visit us here in Iceland to find a bottle. Because Akva is now available at your favorite corner market or deli.

Of course, you'll want to ask for it by name, if you're having trouble finding it. A single sip and you will feel like you're on top of the world. Then again, considering where it comes from, what else could you expect?

Akva spring water. The pure soul of Iceland.

CONSUMER MAGAZINE
COLOR 1 PAGE OR
SPREAD: SINGLE

200
ART DIRECTOR:
Carie Meier
WRITER:
Ryan Ebner
PHOTOGRAPHER:
Marko Lavrisha
CLIENT:
The 3DO Company
AGENCY:
Butler Shine & Stern/ Sausalito

201
ART DIRECTOR:
Jim Keane
WRITER:
Jim Nelson
PHOTOGRAPHER:
Bruce Wolf
CLIENT:
Harley-Davidson
AGENCY:
Carmichael Lynch/ Minneapolis

202
ART DIRECTORS:
Jim Keane
Jud Smith
WRITER:
Tom Camp
PHOTOGRAPHER:
Jim Arndt
CLIENT:
Schwinn
AGENCY:
Carmichael Lynch/ Minneapolis

203
ART DIRECTOR:
Craig Tanimoto
WRITER:
Eric Grunbaum
ILLUSTRATOR:
Charles Anderson Design
PHOTOGRAPHER:
Shawn Michienzi
CLIENT:
Nissan Motor Corporation
AGENCY:
Chiat/Day, Venice

200

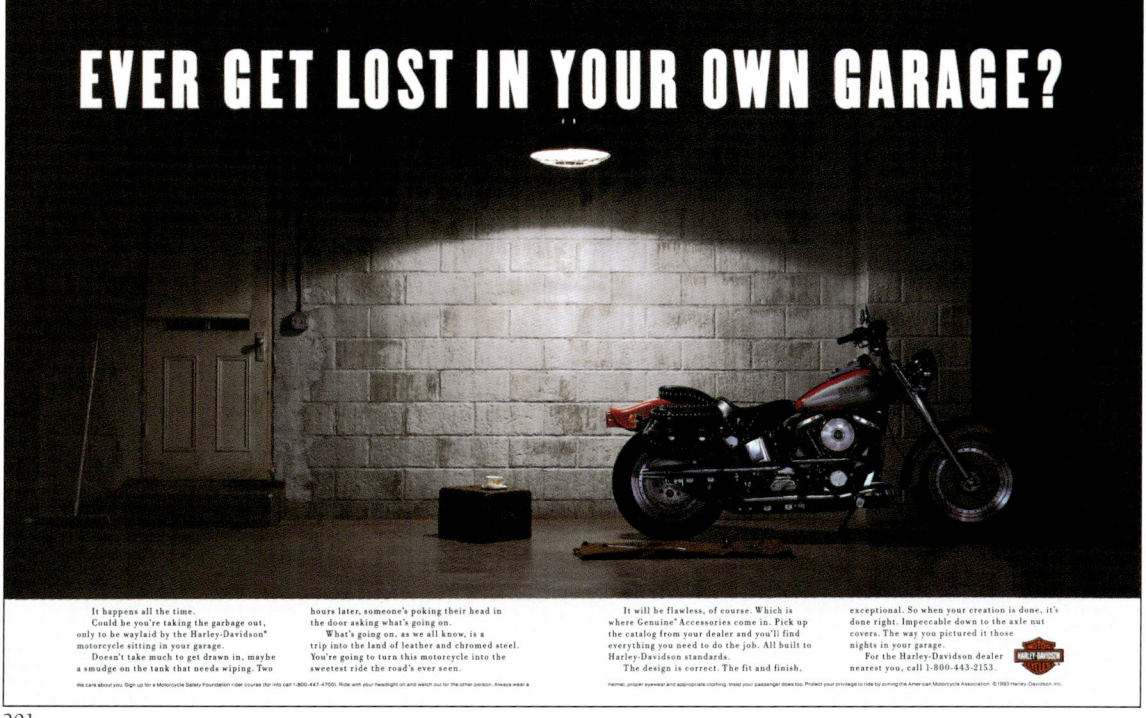
201

CONSUMER MAGAZINE
COLOR 1 PAGE OR
SPREAD: SINGLE

204
ART DIRECTOR:
Craig Tanimoto
WRITER:
Eric Grunbaum
ILLUSTRATOR:
Charles Anderson Design
PHOTOGRAPHER:
Shawn Michienzi
CLIENT:
Nissan Motor Corporation
AGENCY:
Chiat/Day, Venice

205
ART DIRECTOR:
Craig Tanimoto
WRITER:
Eric Grunbaum
ILLUSTRATOR:
Charles Anderson Design
PHOTOGRAPHER:
Shawn Michienzi
CLIENT:
Nissan Motor Corporation
AGENCY:
Chiat/Day, Venice

206
ART DIRECTOR:
Craig Tanimoto
WRITER:
Eric Grunbaum
ILLUSTRATOR:
Charles Anderson Design
PHOTOGRAPHER:
Shawn Michienzi
CLIENT:
Nissan Motor Corporation
AGENCY:
Chiat/Day, Venice

207
ART DIRECTOR:
Craig Tanimoto
WRITER:
Eric Grunbaum
ILLUSTRATOR:
Charles Anderson Design
PHOTOGRAPHER:
Shawn Michienzi
CLIENT:
Nissan Motor Corporation
AGENCY:
Chiat/Day, Venice

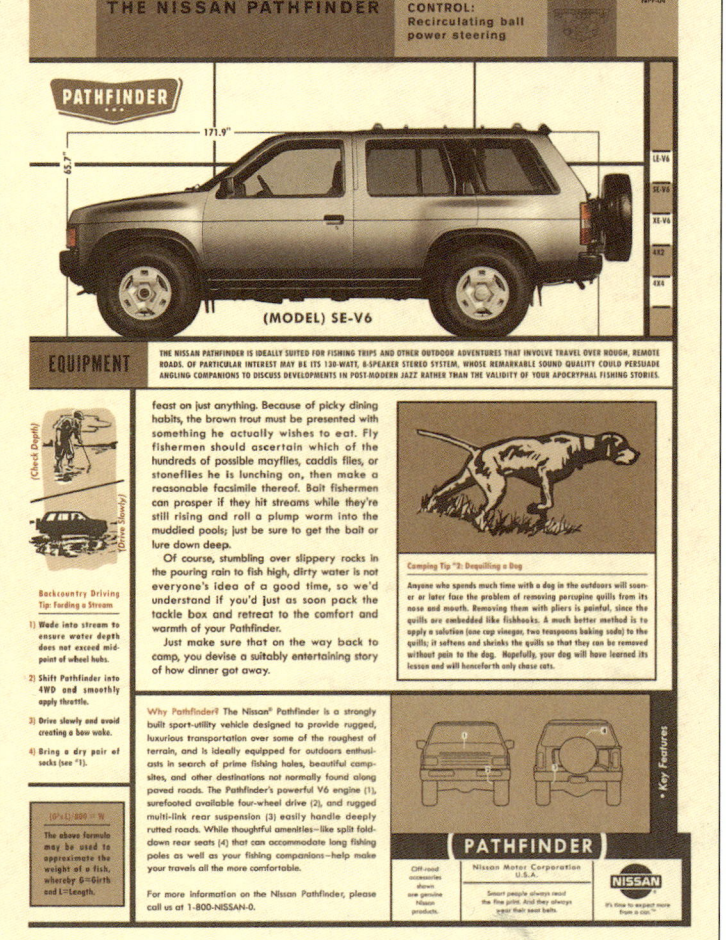

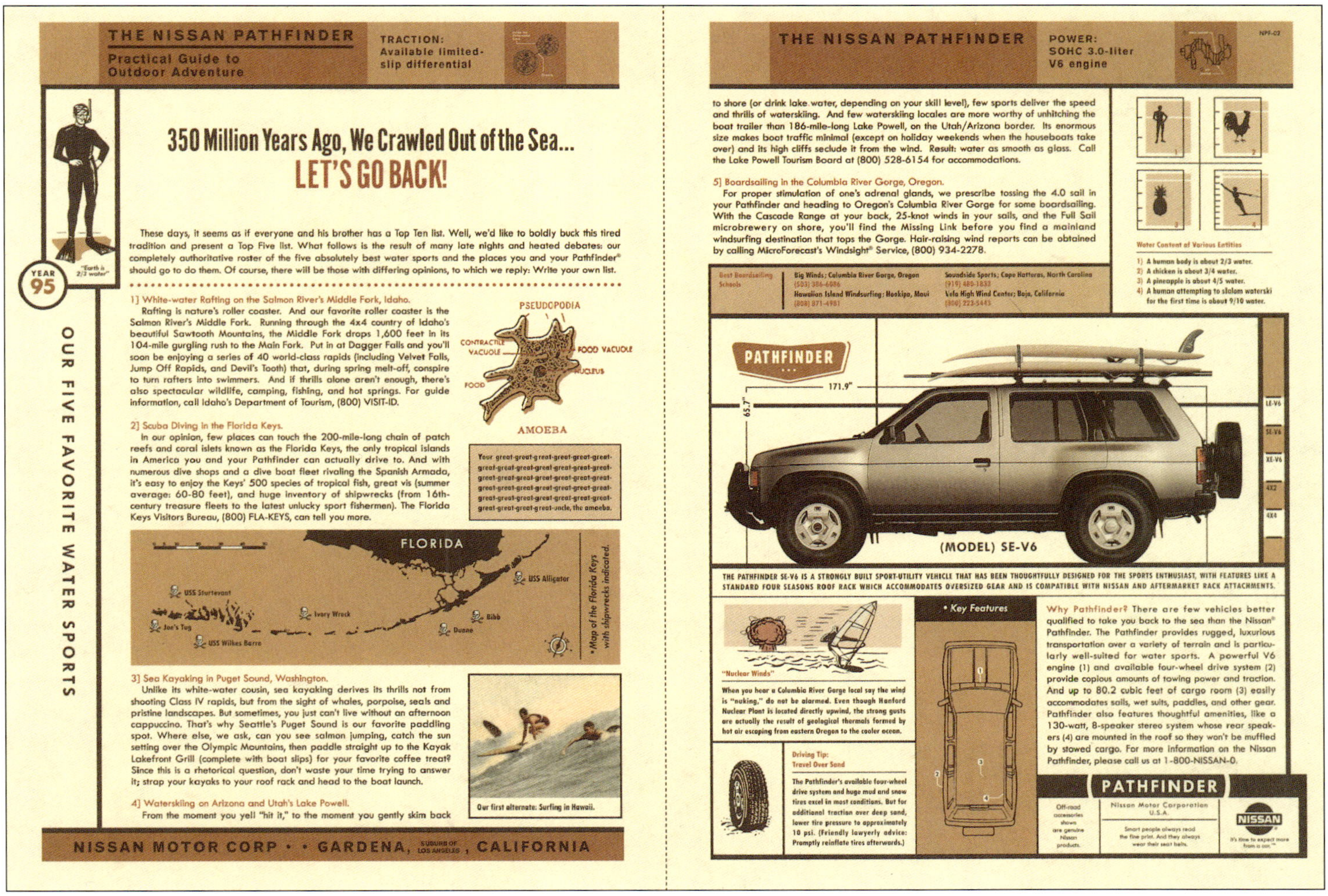
THE NISSAN PATHFINDER
Practical Guide to Outdoor Adventure
TRACTION: Available limited-slip differential
"Earth is 2/3 water"
YEAR 95
OUR FIVE FAVORITE WATER SPORTS
350 Million Years Ago, We Crawled Out of the Sea...
LET'S GO BACK!
These days, it seems as if everyone and his brother has a Top Ten list. Well, we'd like to boldly buck this tired tradition and present a Top Five list. What follows is the result of many late nights and heated debates: our completely authoritative roster of the five absolutely best water sports and the places you and your Pathfinder® should go to do them. Of course, there will be those with differing opinions, to which we reply: Write your own list.
1] White-water Rafting on the Salmon River's Middle Fork, Idaho.
Rafting is nature's roller coaster. And our favorite roller coaster is the Salmon River's Middle Fork. Running through the 4x4 country of Idaho's beautiful Sawtooth Mountains, the Middle Fork drops 1,600 feet in its 104-mile gurgling rush to the Main Fork. Put in at Dagger Falls and you'll soon be enjoying a series of 40 world-class rapids (including Velvet Falls, Jump Off Rapids, and Devil's Tooth) that, during spring melt-off, conspire to turn rafters into swimmers. And if thrills alone aren't enough, there's also spectacular wildlife, camping, fishing, and hot springs. For guide information, call Idaho's Department of Tourism, (800) VISIT-ID.
PSEUDOPODIA
CONTRACTILE VACUOLE
FOOD VACUOLE
NUCLEUS
FOOD
AMOEBA
Your great-uncle, the amoeba.
2] Scuba Diving in the Florida Keys.
In our opinion, few places can touch the 200-mile-long chain of patch reefs and coral islets known as the Florida Keys, the only tropical islands in America you and your Pathfinder can actually drive to. And with numerous dive shops and a dive boat fleet rivaling the Spanish Armada, it's easy to enjoy the Keys' 500 species of tropical fish, great vis (summer average: 60-80 feet), and huge inventory of shipwrecks (from 16th-century treasure fleets to the latest unlucky sport fishermen). The Florida Keys Visitors Bureau, (800) FLA-KEYS, can tell you more.
FLORIDA
USS Sturtevant
Joe's Tug
USS Wilkes Barre
Ivory Wreck
Dunne
Bibb
USS Alligator
• Map of the Florida Keys with shipwrecks indicated.
3] Sea Kayaking in Puget Sound, Washington.
Unlike its white-water cousin, sea kayaking derives its thrills not from shooting Class IV rapids, but from the sight of whales, porpoise, seals and pristine landscapes. But sometimes, you just can't live without an afternoon cappuccino. That's why Seattle's Puget Sound is our favorite paddling spot. Where else, we ask, can you see salmon jumping, catch the sun setting over the Olympic Mountains, then paddle straight up to the Kayak Lakefront Grill (complete with boat slips) for your favorite coffee treat? Since this is a rhetorical question, don't waste your time trying to answer it; strap your kayaks to your roof rack and head to the boat launch.
Our first alternate: Surfing in Hawaii.
4] Waterskiing on Arizona and Utah's Lake Powell.
From the moment you yell "hit it," to the moment you gently skim back
NISSAN MOTOR CORP • • GARDENA, SUBURB OF LOS ANGELES, CALIFORNIA
THE NISSAN PATHFINDER
POWER: SOHC 3.0-liter V6 engine
NPF-02
to shore (or drink lake water, depending on your skill level), few sports deliver the speed and thrills of waterskiing. And few waterskiing locales are more worthy of unhitching the boat trailer than 186-mile-long Lake Powell, on the Utah/Arizona border. Its enormous size makes boat traffic minimal (except on holiday weekends when the houseboats take over) and its high cliffs seclude it from the wind. Result: water as smooth as glass. Call the Lake Powell Tourism Board at (800) 528-6154 for accommodations.
5] Boardsailing in the Columbia River Gorge, Oregon.
For proper stimulation of one's adrenal glands, we prescribe tossing the 4.0 sail in your Pathfinder and heading to Oregon's Columbia River Gorge for some boardsailing. With the Cascade Range at your back, 25-knot winds in your sails, and the Full Sail microbrewery on shore, you'll find the Missing Link before you find a mainland windsurfing destination that tops the Gorge. Hair-raising wind reports can be obtained by calling MicroForecast's Windsight® Service, (800) 934-2278.
Best Boardsailing Schools
Big Winds; Columbia River Gorge, Oregon (503) 386-6086
Hawaiian Island Windsurfing; Hookipa, Maui (808) 871-4981
Soundside Sports; Cape Hatteras, North Carolina (919) 480-1833
Vela High Wind Center; Baja, California (800) 223-5443
Water Content of Various Entities
1) A human body is about 2/3 water.
2) A chicken is about 3/4 water.
3) A pineapple is about 4/5 water.
4) A human attempting to slalom waterski for the first time is about 9/10 water.
PATHFINDER
171.9"
65.7"
LE-V6
SE-V6
XE-V6
4X2
4X4
(MODEL) SE-V6
THE PATHFINDER SE-V6 IS A STRONGLY BUILT SPORT-UTILITY VEHICLE THAT HAS BEEN THOUGHTFULLY DESIGNED FOR THE SPORTS ENTHUSIAST, WITH FEATURES LIKE A STANDARD FOUR SEASONS ROOF RACK WHICH ACCOMMODATES OVERSIZED GEAR AND IS COMPATIBLE WITH NISSAN AND AFTERMARKET RACK ATTACHMENTS.
"Nuclear Winds"
When you hear a Columbia River Gorge local say the wind is "nuking," do not be alarmed. Even though Hanford Nuclear Plant is located directly upwind, the strong gusts are actually the result of geological thermals formed by hot air escaping from eastern Oregon to the cooler ocean.
• Key Features
Driving Tip: Travel Over Sand
The Pathfinder's available four-wheel drive system and huge mud and snow tires excel in most conditions. But for additional traction over deep sand, lower tire pressure to approximately 10 psi. (Friendly lawyerly advice: Promptly reinflate tires afterwards.)
Why Pathfinder? There are few vehicles better qualified to take you back to the sea than the Nissan® Pathfinder. The Pathfinder provides rugged, luxurious transportation over a variety of terrain and is particularly well-suited for water sports. A powerful V6 engine (1) and available four-wheel drive system (2) provide copious amounts of towing power and traction. And up to 80.2 cubic feet of cargo room (3) easily accommodates sails, wet suits, paddles, and other gear. Pathfinder also features thoughtful amenities, like a 130-watt, 8-speaker stereo system whose rear speakers (4) are mounted in the roof so they won't be muffled by stowed cargo. For more information on the Nissan Pathfinder, please call us at 1-800-NISSAN-0.
PATHFINDER
Off-road accessories shown are genuine Nissan products.
Nissan Motor Corporation U.S.A.
Smart people always read the fine print. And they always wear their seat belts.
NISSAN
It's time to expect more from a car.™

THE NISSAN PATHFINDER
Practical Guide to Outdoor Adventure
COMFORT: 5-link coil-spring rear suspension
"Beware of Snakes"
YEAR 95
DRIVING THE TRANSAMAZONICA HIGHWAY: Brazil
The Liquid Rustle of Treetops.
The Musical Cries of Unseen Birds. THWACK!
Over 200 Different Kinds of Mosquitoes.
With swarming bugs, extreme temperatures, and numerous animal species who'd like nothing better than to eat you, one wonders: Who in their right mind would want to drive the Amazon? Well, anyone with a gassed-up Pathfinder,® a hardy spirit of adventure, and a fully updated set of yellow fever shots. That's who. While we won't pretend to tell you everything you need to know to traverse the Transamazonica—the list of necessary vaccinations alone would fill this page—we would like to share highlights of what may be the world's finest off-road adventure.
For the ultimate test of the Pathfinder's fortitude and your capacity to tolerate natural beauty, there are few trips that compare to a drive through Brazilian Amazonia, an exotic 2,030,000-square-mile ecosystem that includes the Amazon River (whose water flow is greater than the Mississippi, Nile, and Yangtze combined), the Amazon Forest (the largest and densest rain forest in the world) and upwards of five million different animal species (most of which, for explorers with inadequate bug repellent, will appear to be of the winged, bloodsucking variety).
Of all the marvels Mother Nature thought to bestow the Amazon, however, one detail that was overlooked was a decent way for Homo sapiens to get around; the densely forested jungle is far better suited to tree-climbing howler monkeys than it is to the average four-wheeled vehicle.
Which brings us to our "road," the Transamazonica Highway (a.k.a., Highway of Tears).
The Transamazonica—whose odds-defying opening in 1973 was surely commemorated by one heck of a piñata party—stretches over 5,000 kilometers along the southern edge of the Amazonian plain, from the interior town of Rio Branco eastward to Estreito.
Now, while creating any kind of path through such thick jungle warrants a tip of the pith helmet, a few short miles on this road will leave you with only the kindest of words for the highway maintenance fellows back home.
Many monsoons ago, parts of the Transamazonica were paved. But the harsh climate and less-than-attentive road crews have led to deterioration so profound, the rainy season routinely leaves sections totally impassable. And even in the best of times (dry season: June-November) the road can be so merciless
Estreito
Amazon River
Rio Branco
Rain Forest
Transamazonica Hwy
AMAZON
Traveler's Advisory #1: The Mayoruna Indians
Known as "The Cat People" for their tattoed jaguar whiskers, these native Amazonians are not amenable to visitors and can be rough hosts. One group of intruders was disarmed, smeared with wild honey, and tied to a tree adjoining a nest of army ants.
Macaw: Colorful Bird of the Jungle
Although most of your time will be spent watching for dangerous animals like the sharp-tusked wild boar, venomous bushmaster snake, and giant anaconda (which is not venemous, but simply chokes its prey to death), take time to marvel at the beautiful and harmless avifauna of the jungle.
NISSAN MOTOR CORP • • GARDENA, CALIFORNIA
THE NISSAN PATHFINDER
DURABILITY: Cast-iron V6 engine block
NPF-03
Animals of the Amazon
Jaguar
Tapir
Howler monkey
Parrot
Anaconda
Wild boar
Popular Amazonian Treat: Maniçoba
A popular local dish is Maniçoba, made with the poisonous leaves of the bitter cassava that have been simmered for 8 days to render it safe. (Or is that 9 days?)
that the only way for your Pathfinder to drive it is to shift into four-wheel drive, apply even throttle, and direct kindly prayers to the local pothole god.
In point of fact, most drivers should consider sticking to the more solid shoulders rather than taking their chances in the deep ruts.
Of course, you can take solace in the fact that your driving trials and tribulations will be more than fairly compensated by territory that includes thriving jungle port cities, primitive Indian villages, beautiful national parks and, not to repeat ourselves, an incredible variety of wildlife.
For those dear readers who have concluded that the rewards of driving the Amazon outweigh its hazards, we recommend contacting a reputable adventure travel organization, buying a stylish khaki outfit, and putting your Pathfinder into gear.
P.S.-Don't forget the bug spray.
Traveler's Advisory #2: Road Maps
Some maps of the region indicate a road north of the Amazon marked "Perimetro Norte." Do not try to take it. This road does not exist, never has, and probably never will. It is obviously the handiwork of an overly imaginative cartographer.
Jungle Driving Tip: Lower Your Antenna
For Pathfinder LE drivers, it is advisable to lower the vehicle's electronically retractable antenna by turning off the radio. This will prevent it from being broken off by low-hanging vines. Besides, with few radio stations in the Amazon, you'd be better served listening to the CD player.
THE NISSAN PATHFINDER IS WELL-EQUIPPED FOR JUNGLE TRAVEL, THANKS TO ITS RELIABLE MECHANICALS AND POWERFUL AIR CONDITIONER. FOR ADDED SECURITY, CARRY VITAL SPARE PARTS, A SPACE, WINCH, TOWROPE AND AN AIR PUMP. SECURELY FASTEN SPARE FUEL CONTAINERS (WITH SIPHON PIPE FOR USE WHEN FUEL IS SOLD OUT OF THE DRUM).
PATHFINDER
171.9"
65.7"
LE-V6
SE-V6
XE-V6
4X2
4X4
(MODEL) SE-V6
Why Pathfinder? The Nissan Pathfinder is a strongly built sport-utility vehicle designed to provide you with rugged, luxurious transportation over some of the world's most grueling terrain. Should your plans include Amazonian adventures, you can be assured that Pathfinder is an eager and qualified travel partner, thanks to its powerful and reliable V6 engine (1), surefooted available 4-wheel drive, underbody skid plates, and available amenities like air conditioning (2) and a 130-watt, 8-speaker CD stereo system (3), which are especially desirable in the steamy and radio-free jungle environment.
For more information on the Nissan Pathfinder, please call us at 1-800-NISSAN-0.
• Key Features
PATHFINDER
Genuine Nissan and non-Nissan accessories shown.
Nissan Motor Corporation U.S.A.
Smart people always read the fine print. And they always wear their seat belts.
NISSAN
It's time to expect more from a car.™

CONSUMER MAGAZINE
COLOR 1 PAGE OR
SPREAD: SINGLE

208
ART DIRECTORS:
Mike Sheen
Joe Shands
WRITER:
David Baldwin
PHOTOGRAPHER:
Gary Hush
CLIENT:
Dr. Martens
AGENCY:
Cole & Weber/Portland

209
ART DIRECTOR:
Mike Sheen
WRITER:
David Baldwin
PHOTOGRAPHER:
Gary Hush
CLIENT:
Dr. Martens
AGENCY:
Cole & Weber/Portland

210
ART DIRECTORS:
Sharon Harms
Steve Mapp
WRITERS:
Pieter Blikslager
Katherine Patterson
ILLUSTRATOR:
Steve Mapp
PHOTOGRAPHER:
Matt Miller
CLIENT:
Gametek
AGENCY:
Crispin & Porter/Miami

211
ART DIRECTORS:
Alex Bogusky
Markham Cronin
WRITER:
Pieter Blikslager
ILLUSTRATOR:
Steve Mapp
PHOTOGRAPHER:
Matt Miller
CLIENT:
Gametek
AGENCY:
Crispin & Porter/Miami

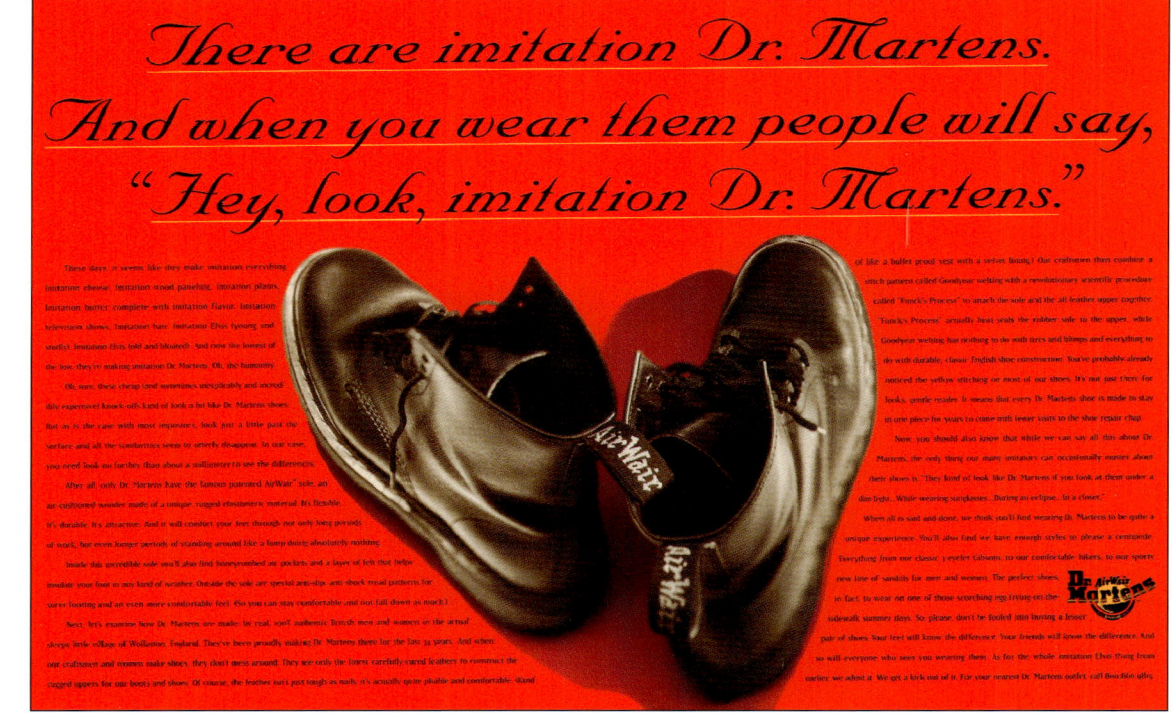
208

209

It's What Happens When Engineers Work In An Ivory Tower
But Have To Drive Over A Few Pedestrians To Get There.
TAXI
NXT VCTM
With a 5-liter V8 and twin 50mm machine guns, the Q-CAB will blow away anything else on the road.
A restraining device in harmony with our overall philosophy: the best defense is a good offense.
You are a 21st Century cabby in a '52 Checker hovercab armed with machine guns. Pick up and drop off fares as you shoot your way through the quarantined city of Kemo. Escape if you can.
To make your journey as peaceful as possible, we've installed a targeting system that can eliminate the inconvenience of busy crosswalks.
A full 180 degrees of unobstructed visibility. Offering the driver complete awareness of the road, making potential accidents easier to pursue.
QUARANTINE™
The relentless pursuit of the pedestrian.
With a revolutionary new titanium bumper, maneuverability simply wasn't a priority.
SLAAB 9000
Q-CAB
It boasts an impressive drag coefficient of 0.60.
GAMETEK
Available for IBM PC's and compatibles on 3.5 disks and PC CD-ROM. Coming soon for 3DO. To test drive a Q-CAB, visit your local QUARANTINE™ retailer or call 1-800-GAMETEK. © 1994 GameTek/Imagexcel. All Rights Reserved.

210

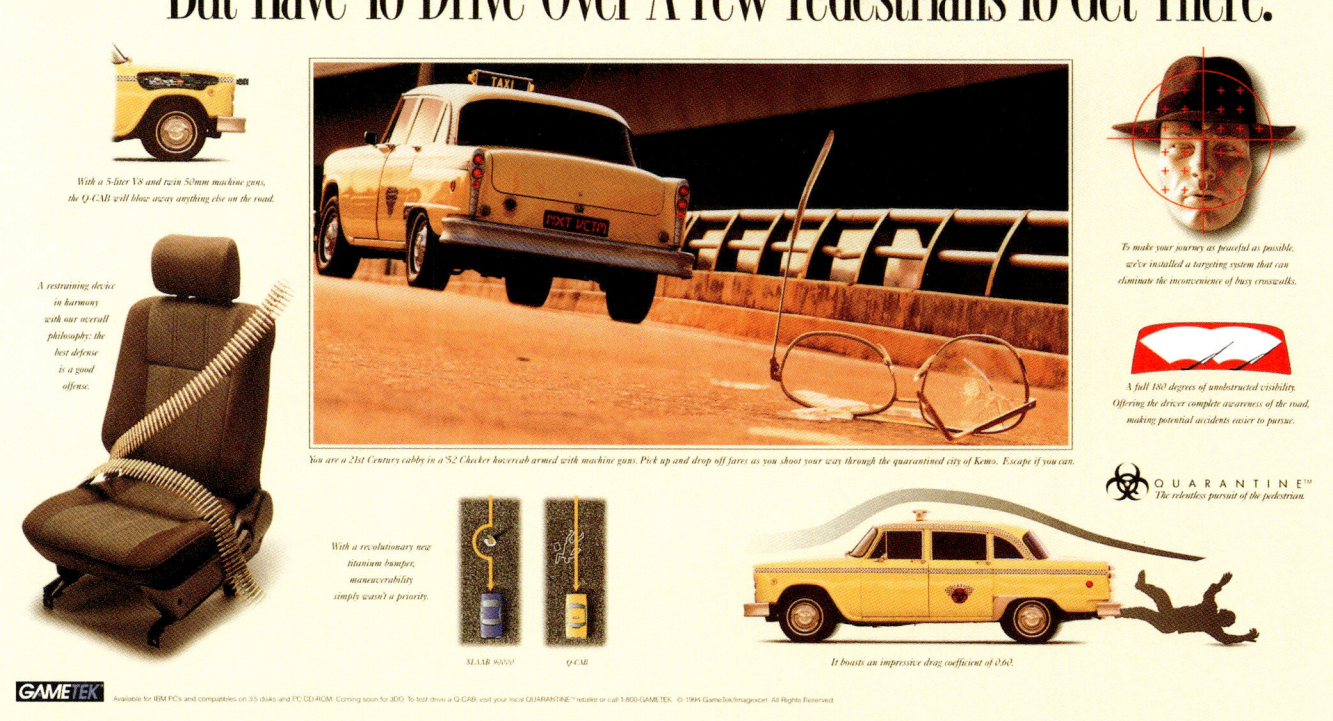

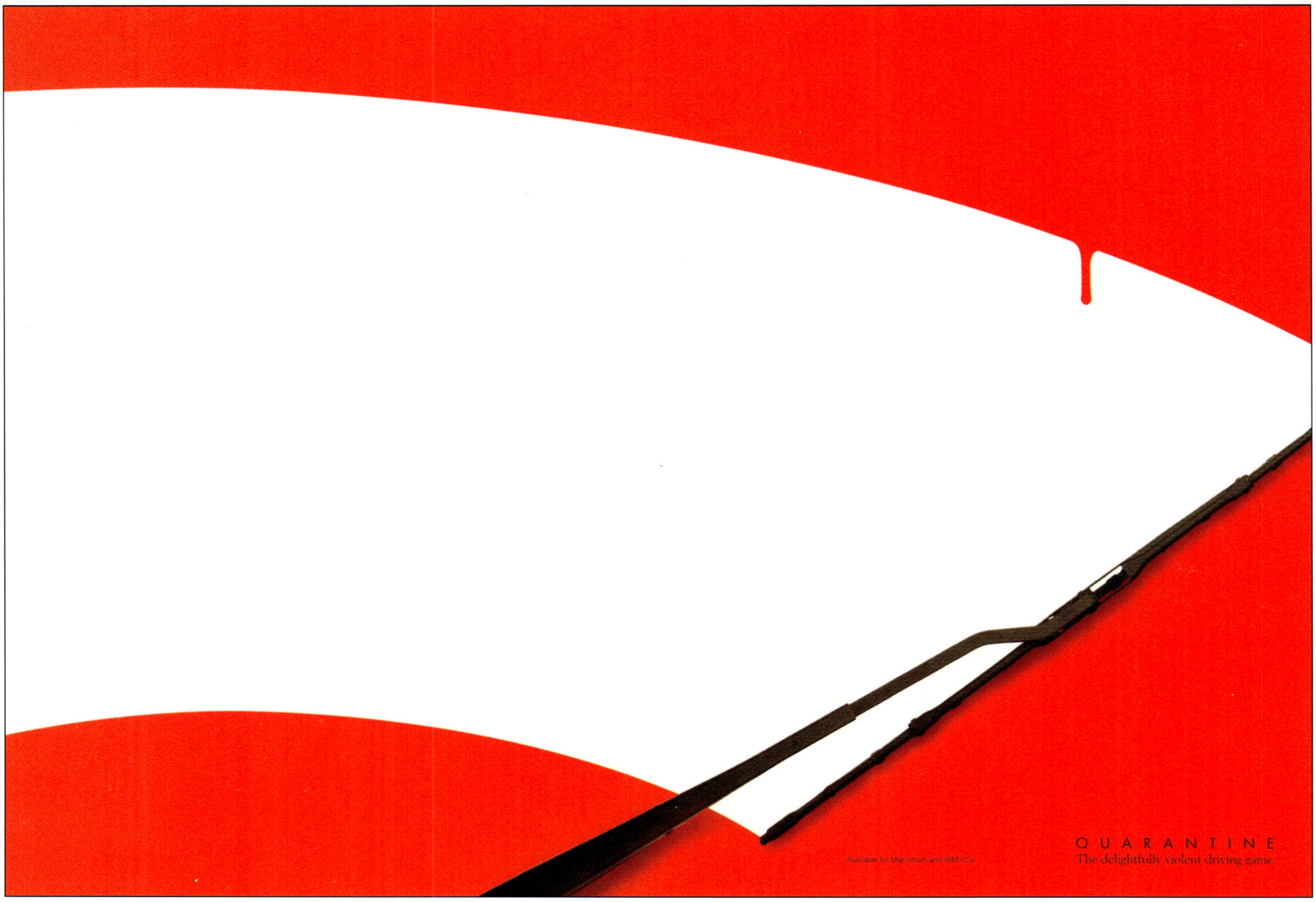
Available for Macintosh and IBM PCs
QUARANTINE
The delightfully violent driving game.

211

CONSUMER MAGAZINE
COLOR 1 PAGE OR
SPREAD: SINGLE

212
ART DIRECTORS:
Stan Block
Sal DeVito
WRITER:
Sal DeVito
PHOTOGRAPHER:
Cailor/Resnick
CLIENT:
Britches
AGENCY:
DeVito/Verdi, New York

213
ART DIRECTORS:
Abi Aron
Rob Carducci
WRITERS:
Rob Carducci
Abi Aron
PHOTOGRAPHER:
Cailor/Resnick
CLIENT:
Shelcore
AGENCY:
DeVito/Verdi, New York

214
ART DIRECTOR:
J. Liegey
WRITER:
Mike Gibbs
PHOTOGRAPHER:
Buck Holzemer
CLIENT:
Nikon
AGENCY:
Fallon McElligott/
Minneapolis

215
ART DIRECTOR:
Joe Paprocki
WRITER:
Doug de Grood
PHOTOGRAPHER:
Carl Furuta
CLIENT:
Ralston Purina Company
AGENCY:
Fallon McElligott/
Minneapolis

212

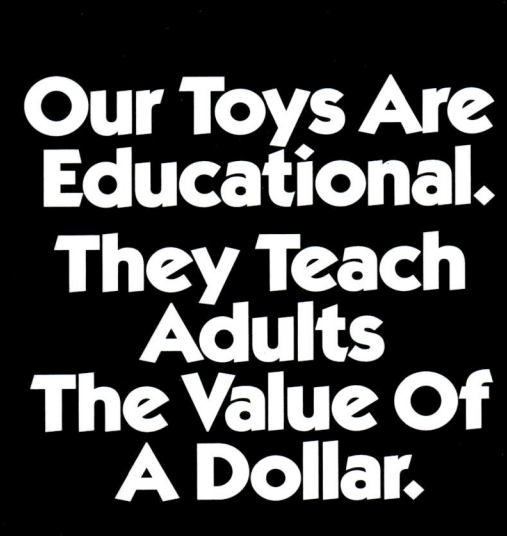

213

From the HOOP Photo File

YOU KNOW THAT FEELING WHEN YOU HEAR THE ROAR OF THE CROWD FROM THE BATHROOM? PHOTOGRAPHERS DON'T.

Nathaniel Butler's night at the game.
Nikon Pro-Sports Photographer

7 out of 10 pro sports photographers use Nikon cameras. For more information call 1-800-NIKON-35

Constantly switching your dog's food can lead to finicky eating.

It's natural to think your dog wants variety. But by constantly switching his food, you could be training him to be a finicky eater. The fact is, a consistent diet of one nutritious food is actually healthier for dogs. That's why you can feel good about feeding your dog Purina® Dog Chow® brand dog food every day. With all the taste and nutrition dogs need. To make those bad eating habits disappear.

Purina® Dog Chow® Every Day.

CONSUMER MAGAZINE
COLOR 1 PAGE OR
SPREAD: SINGLE

216
ART DIRECTOR:
Joe Paprocki
WRITER:
Doug de Grood
PHOTOGRAPHER:
Carl Furuta
CLIENT:
Ralston Purina Company
AGENCY:
Fallon McElligott/
Minneapolis

217
ART DIRECTOR:
Bob Barrie
WRITER:
Mike Lescarbeau
PHOTOGRAPHER:
Timothy White
CLIENT:
Sunset Marquis
Hotel & Villas
AGENCY:
Fallon McElligott/
Minneapolis

218
ART DIRECTOR:
Bob Barrie
WRITER:
Dean Buckhorn
PHOTOGRAPHER:
Michael Metcalf
CLIENT:
Time Magazine
AGENCY:
Fallon McElligott/
Minneapolis

219
ART DIRECTOR:
Dean Hanson
WRITER:
Phil Calvit
PHOTOGRAPHER:
Joe Paczkowski
CLIENT:
Timex Corporation
AGENCY:
Fallon McElligott/
Minneapolis

We covered every moment

of his political career.

Except, of course, for 18 minutes.

Understanding comes with TIME.

A product with one of the highest *"You're kidding me"* scores ever recorded.

The reaction is the same, almost without exception: you tell someone about this new watch that can literally read your personal schedule right off a computer screen, and they look kind of shocked for a moment, then shake their heads. "No, c'mon," they protest, "what does it *really* do?"

But it's the honest truth, every bit of it. All you need is a Timex Data Link watch and the included personal information manager software, a PC loaded with Microsoft® Windows™ 3.1 or later, and a desktop CRT monitor. Now you're ready to start linking.

Just push a few buttons, and hold the watch in front of your computer monitor. The screen will display some flashing bars of light, and in about 20 seconds the watch's little electronic eye will read as many as 70 entries from the Microsoft and Timex Data Link software: appointments, phone numbers, alarms, to-do lists, birthdays and anniversaries. You can also easily import data from Microsoft® Schedule+ for Windows™.

Presto—all that information is now stored right there inside your watch, as portable as the arm you wear it on. You'll never forget another birthday or anniversary. A week before an important date, a little hand with a string around the forefinger appears on the watchface (*Get outta here!*—no, really, it does) as a reminder icon. On the actual

The Timex Data Link watch: it's like science fiction, but without the fiction.

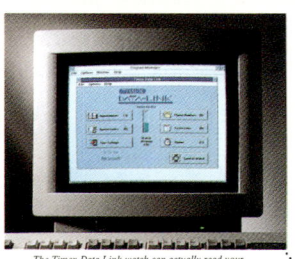

The Timex Data Link watch can actually read your personal information right from your computer screen.

day itself, the icon flashes urgently to let you know that your present- or flower-buying time is rapidly running out.

When an appointment is approaching, the watch beeps to tell you to get going, and tells you who you're supposed to meet, and where.

Oh, and lest we forget, the Timex Data

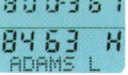

Link is also a watch. It keeps terrific time, displays the second, minute, hour, day, date, month and year, beeps the hour, has multiple alarms, is water resistant to 100 meters, and comes equipped with the Indiglo® night-light.

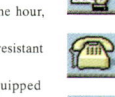

If all this seems like a bit much to believe, we understand.

You're encouraged to examine a Timex Data Link watch with your own eyes, or call 1-800-367-8463 for information. You'll see that everything we've told you is true. Seriously. No lie. Really. Scout's honor.

No kidding.

CONSUMER MAGAZINE
COLOR 1 PAGE OR
SPREAD: SINGLE

220
ART DIRECTOR:
Dean Hanson
WRITER:
Bruce Bildsten
PHOTOGRAPHER:
Joe Paczkowski
CLIENT:
Timex Corporation
AGENCY:
Fallon McElligott/
Minneapolis

221
ART DIRECTOR:
Dean Hanson
WRITER:
Bruce Bildsten
PHOTOGRAPHER:
Joe Paczkowski
CLIENT:
Timex Corporation
AGENCY:
Fallon McElligott/
Minneapolis

222
ART DIRECTOR:
Dean Hanson
WRITER:
Bruce Bildsten
PHOTOGRAPHER:
Joe Paczkowski
CLIENT:
Timex Corporation
AGENCY:
Fallon McElligott/
Minneapolis

223
ART DIRECTOR:
Dean Hanson
WRITER:
Bruce Bildsten
PHOTOGRAPHER:
Joe Paczkowski
CLIENT:
Timex Corporation
AGENCY:
Fallon McElligott/
Minneapolis

222

223

CONSUMER MAGAZINE
COLOR 1 PAGE OR
SPREAD: SINGLE

224
ART DIRECTOR:
Michael Mazza
WRITER:
Dave O'Hare
ILLUSTRATOR:
Alan Daniels
PHOTOGRAPHER:
Graham Westmoreland
CLIENT:
American Isuzu Motors
AGENCY:
Goodby Silverstein & Partners/San Francisco

225
ART DIRECTOR:
Michael Mazza
WRITER:
Dave O'Hare
ILLUSTRATOR:
Alan Daniels
PHOTOGRAPHER:
Graham Westmoreland
CLIENT:
American Isuzu Motors
AGENCY:
Goodby Silverstein & Partners/San Francisco

226
ART DIRECTOR:
Tom Routson
WRITER:
Scott Aal
PHOTOGRAPHER:
Harry DeZitter
CLIENT:
American Isuzu Motors
AGENCY:
Goodby Silverstein & Partners/San Francisco

227
ART DIRECTOR:
Steve Luker
WRITER:
Steve Simpson
PHOTOGRAPHER:
Herb Ritts
Jim Erickson
CLIENT:
Norwegian Cruise Line
AGENCY:
Goodby Silverstein & Partners/San Francisco

224

225

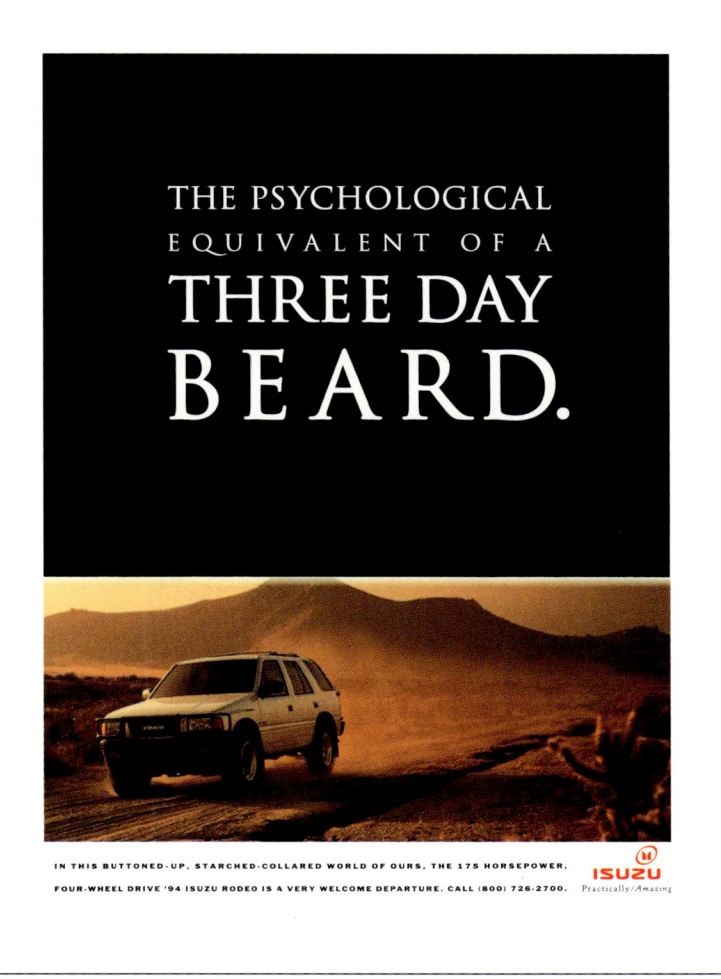

CONSUMER MAGAZINE
COLOR 1 PAGE OR
SPREAD: SINGLE

228
ART DIRECTOR:
Erich Joiner
WRITER:
Bob Kerstetter
PHOTOGRAPHER:
Clint Clemens
CLIENT:
Porsche Cars
North America
AGENCY:
Goodby Silverstein &
Partners/San Francisco

229
ART DIRECTOR:
Roy Grace
WRITER:
Gary Cohen
PHOTOGRAPHER:
Cailor/Resnick
CLIENT:
Land Rover
North America
AGENCY:
Grace & Rothschild/
New York

230
ART DIRECTOR:
Terry Finley
WRITER:
Mark Sweeney
ILLUSTRATOR:
Michael Bull
PHOTOGRAPHER:
Walt Denson
CLIENT:
Crystal Geyser Water
Company
AGENCY:
Hal Riney & Partners/
San Francisco

231
ART DIRECTOR:
Larry Bowdish
WRITER:
Roger Baldacci
ILLUSTRATOR:
Galen Bernard
PHOTOGRAPH:
Sports Illustrated
Picture Sales
CLIENT:
Converse
AGENCY:
Houston Effler Herstek
Favat/Boston

228

229

CONSUMER MAGAZINE
COLOR 1 PAGE OR
SPREAD: SINGLE

232
ART DIRECTORS:
Todd Riddle
Mark Nardi
WRITERS:
Mark Nardi
Todd Riddle
PHOTOGRAPHER:
Jay Maisel
CLIENT:
NEC Computers
AGENCY:
Houston Effler Herstek Favat/Boston

233
ART DIRECTOR:
Paul White
WRITER:
Trevor de Silva
PHOTOGRAPHERS:
Nittin Verdoukal
Paul White
CLIENT:
Royal Air Force
AGENCY:
J. Walter Thompson/London

234
ART DIRECTOR:
Paul White
WRITER:
Trevor de Silva
PHOTOGRAPHERS:
David Gill
CLIENT:
Royal Air Force
AGENCY:
J. Walter Thompson/London

235
ART DIRECTOR:
Dave Dye
WRITER:
Tim Delaney
PHOTOGRAPHER:
The Douglas Brothers
CLIENT:
Adidas
AGENCY:
Leagas Delaney/London

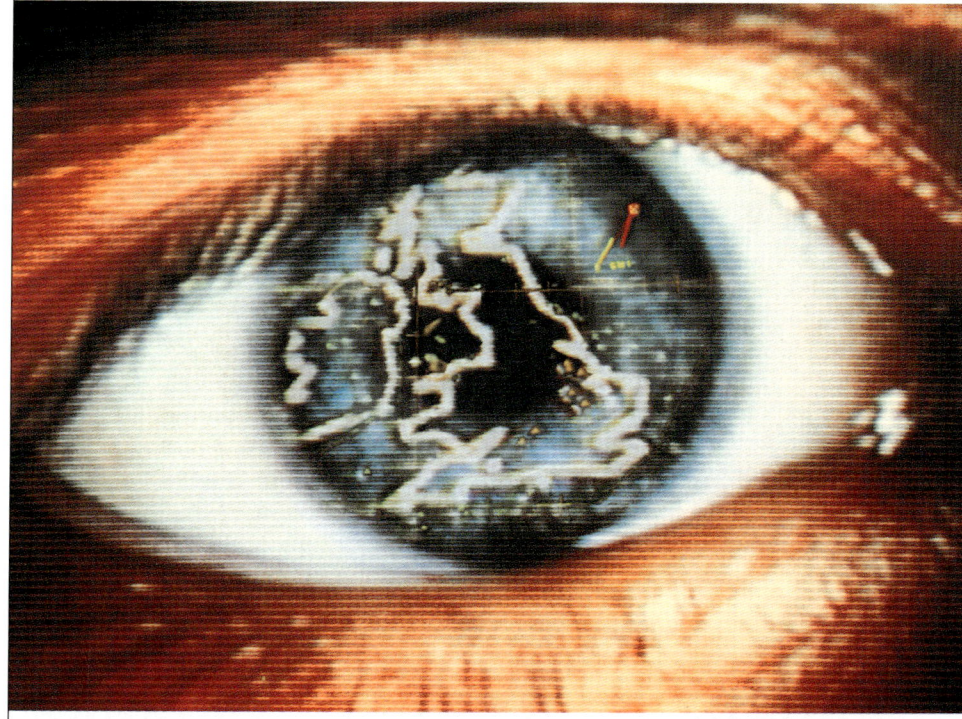

LIKE TO TRY IT FOR REAL?

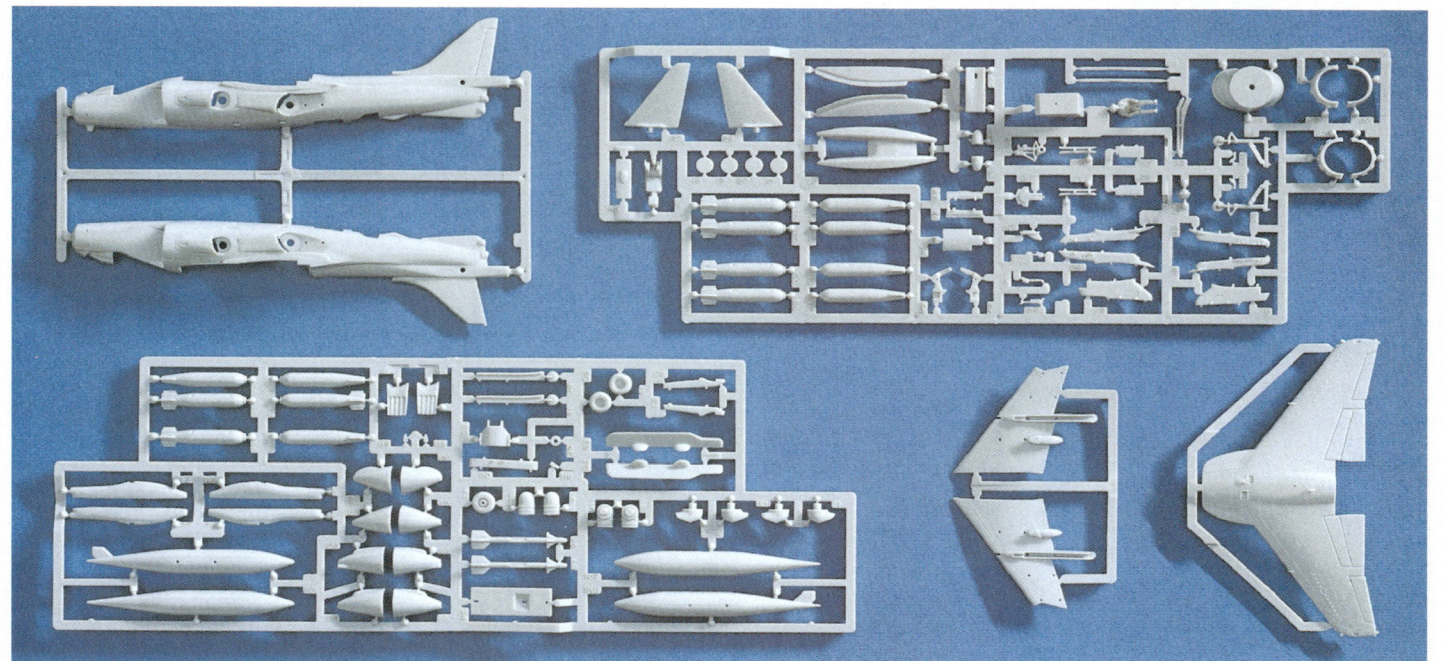

Well, we're able to fix it for you. RAF Ground Trades offer a wide and varied choice of engineering careers.

Perhaps though, engineering just isn't your game. Not to worry, because whatever line of work you're thinking about you can probably do it within the RAF.

Environmental health technician, data analyst, medical assistant, even photographer.

There are some 70 different trades in all. That should give you some idea of the scale we're talking about.

Every single one of them plays a vitally important role within the RAF.

Every one of them helps to keep us operational 24 hours a day, seven days a week. Whichever trade you choose though, you'll receive the best training possible.

So what do you need to get in? Some trades require four GCSEs, some none at all, but it's enthusiasm, energy and commitment that we're really looking for.

It's not just jobs for the boys either, because opportunities exist for both sexes.

Your first posting. It could be anywhere you will have to take a few tests. However, these will help you to determine where your talents really lie.

Once accepted you'll complete seven weeks recruit training. This is followed by intensive training in your specialised trade. Then comes the real thing.

What happens next is up to you. Continue to fulfil your potential and you'll get every opportunity to earn promotion.

If by now you're toying with the idea of in Great Britain. It could even be overseas.

Wherever it is though, you'll be a highly skilled, key component of the RAF, and of the defence of the nation.

a career in the RAF, telephone us on 0345 300 100, and we'll send you further details of exactly where and how you could fit in.

ROYAL AIR FORCE
GROUND TRADES

THERE ARE
PROBLEMS I CAN
ONLY SOLVE
ON A 10 MILE RUN. *Like why I'm not on a 5 mile run. First few miles are spent just unwinding. Removing the baggage you've carried around all day. Miles later you hit a point where you know the only thing that lies ahead is a clear mind. These miles are special. They are worth the pain. This world is quiet and for once you can think without having to. Here you dream while awake. You get insights into the seemingly unsolvable. But your body constantly reminds you these miles aren't easy. Still you keep going. Because there's so much thinking to do. And someone has got to do it.*

adidas

CONSUMER MAGAZINE
COLOR 1 PAGE OR
SPREAD: SINGLE

236
ART DIRECTORS:
Jim Mountjoy
Andy Azula
WRITER:
Ed Jones
PHOTOGRAPHER:
Steve Murray
CLIENT:
North Carolina Travel & Tourism
AGENCY:
Loeffler Ketchum Mountjoy/Charlotte

237
ART DIRECTOR:
Andy Azula
WRITER:
Ed Jones
PHOTOGRAPHER:
Harry DeZitter
CLIENT:
North Carolina Travel & Tourism
AGENCY:
Loeffler Ketchum Mountjoy/Charlotte

238
ART DIRECTOR:
Andy Azula
WRITER:
Ed Jones
PHOTOGRAPHER:
Harry DeZitter
CLIENT:
North Carolina Travel & Tourism
AGENCY:
Loeffler Ketchum Mountjoy/Charlotte

239
ART DIRECTOR:
Andy Azula
WRITER:
Steve Lasch
PHOTOGRAPHER:
Curtis Johnson
CLIENT:
Shakespeare
AGENCY:
Loeffler Ketchum Mountjoy/Charlotte

236

237

SHOW YOUR CHILDREN THAT NOT ALL ENCHANTED FORESTS EXIST IN FAIRY TALES.

NORTH CAROLINA

WHEN WAS THE LAST TIME YOU BRAGGED ABOUT SOMETHING 3 INCHES LONG?

The new Shakespeare Microcast® spincasting reel is actual proof that, in fishing reels at least, size doesn't matter. After all, its hair-trigger sensitivity makes even little 'uns feel like game fish. With ball bearing design, easy castability, 4.1:1 gears and disc drag, Microcast weighs in at a feathery 3.5 oz. Or if underspin's your thing, try the new Microspin™, our identically equipped companion reel. They both take bragging rights to an all-time, er, low.

Shakespeare® SINCE 1897

CONSUMER MAGAZINE
COLOR 1 PAGE OR
SPREAD: SINGLE

240
ART DIRECTOR:
Rob Rich
WRITER:
Kara Goodrich
PHOTOGRAPHERS:
Lee Crum
Susie Cushner
CLIENT:
Keds
AGENCY:
Leonard/Monahan
Providence

241
ART DIRECTOR:
Steve St. Clair
WRITERS:
Andrew Payton
Steve St. Clair
TYPOGRAPHER:
Joseph Pavia
PHOTOGRAPHER:
Chris Kahley
CLIENT:
Pereaux
AGENCY:
Lord Dentsu & Partners/
New York

242
ART DIRECTOR:
Carolyn McGeorge
WRITER:
Joe Alexander
PHOTOGRAPHER:
Dublin Productions
CLIENT:
Healthtex
AGENCY:
The Martin Agency/
Richmond

243
ART DIRECTOR:
Carolyn McGeorge
WRITER:
Joe Alexander
PHOTOGRAPHER:
Dublin Productions
CLIENT:
Healthtex
AGENCY:
The Martin Agency/
Richmond

Why do babies play with their belly buttons when they have $768 worth of toys in the house?

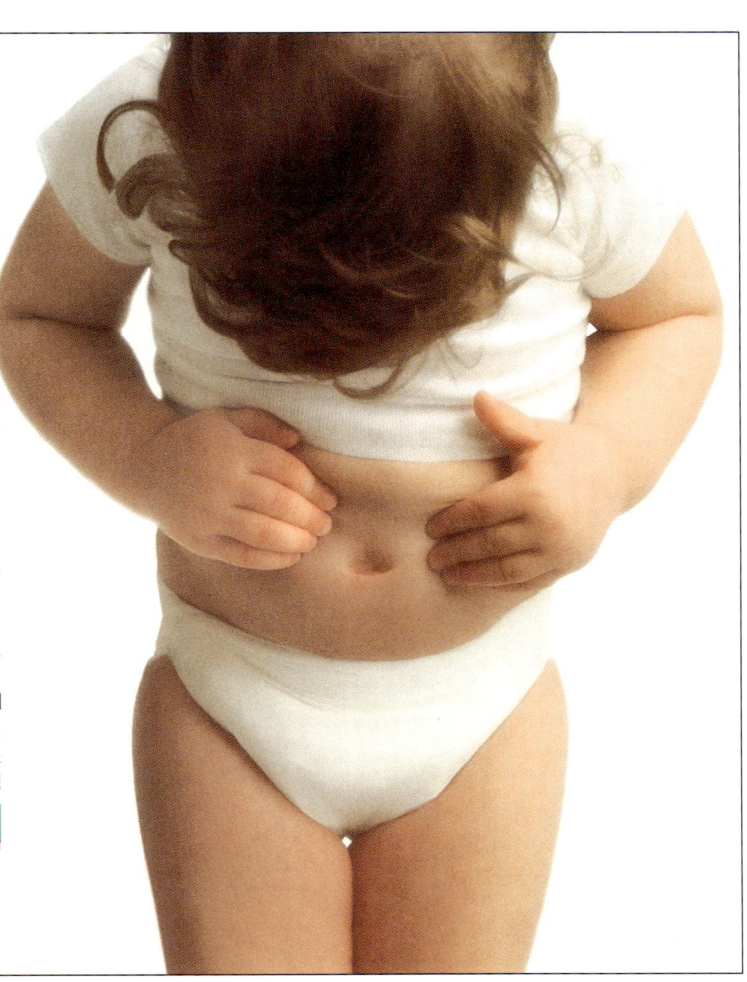

It's round and soft and tickles when you touch it. Your friends squeal and mom turns beet red when you walk around showing it off at the mall. And nobody on earth has one exactly like yours. Gosh, wouldn't you be obsessed with your belly button, too.

Now, moms and dads, we've come up with a great solution. It's called the Healthtex Bodyshirt. A cute little number that acts like a shirt except for three snaps at the crotch that keep it tucked in when your little offspring is springing around the room. Like all our clothing it mixes and matches easily. It's made of a durable cotton blend that holds up wash after wash. And, it's cute. Call us to find out more. You'll be happy you did. And so will that teddy bear she's neglected all these months.

Healthtex
1-800-554-7637

18 months old and already having a fashion crisis.

She let you sleep in an extra 8 minutes. She only spilled half her cereal. She said "moo" when she spotted the dog. So far, so good. Now, what is she going to wear today? No, the colors in that outfit are out. Too trendy. Borrring. Nope, that one, all the kids in day care have. Suddenly, you've got a fashion crisis on your hands. To avoid this, do what mothers have been doing for nearly 75 years. Buy Healthtex. Like our new line of Playwear Denims. You'll never tire of the cute prints and bright colors for boys and girls. They mix and match easily. And, of course, they're soft and comfortable. Just give us a call at the toll-free number listed below to find the store location nearest you. (Lots of parents think of it as the 911 of the fashion world.)

Healthtex
1-800-554-7637

CONSUMER MAGAZINE COLOR 1 PAGE OR SPREAD: SINGLE

244
ART DIRECTOR:
Jamie Mahoney
WRITER:
Raymond McKinney
PHOTOGRAPHER:
Dublin Productions
CLIENT:
Healthtex
AGENCY:
The Martin Agency/ Richmond

245
ART DIRECTOR:
Carolyn McGeorge
WRITER:
Joe Alexander
PHOTOGRAPHER:
Dublin Productions
CLIENT:
Healthtex
AGENCY:
The Martin Agency/ Richmond

246
ART DIRECTOR:
Cliff Sorah
WRITER:
Steve Bassett
PHOTOGRAPHER:
Jim Arndt
CLIENT:
Wrangler Company
AGENCY:
The Martin Agency/ Richmond

247
ART DIRECTOR:
Ashley Jouhar
WRITER:
Dale Haste
ILLUSTRATOR:
Bernard Gudynas
PHOTOGRAPHER:
Sinclair Stammers
CLIENT:
Technics
AGENCY:
McCann-Erickson/ London

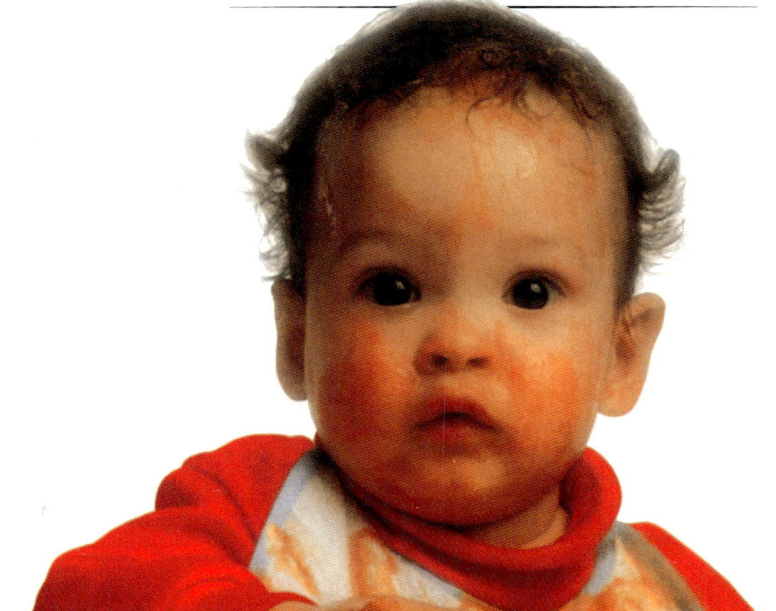

If You Ever See Cowboy Cut Jeans
Ripped At The Knees,
Rest Assured, It Wasn't Done By Some
Fashion Designer Living In Paris.
Double stitching and heavier fabrics make our jeans and shirts almost as tough as Ote Berry, three-time world champ.
If you want real cowboy jeans, make sure you get the only ones designed by real cowboys. Wrangler® 13MWZ® Cowboy Cut® jeans.
Wrangler
The Western Original™

246

A hair on the back of the neck, amplified by Technics.
Technics
For Music Lovers.

247

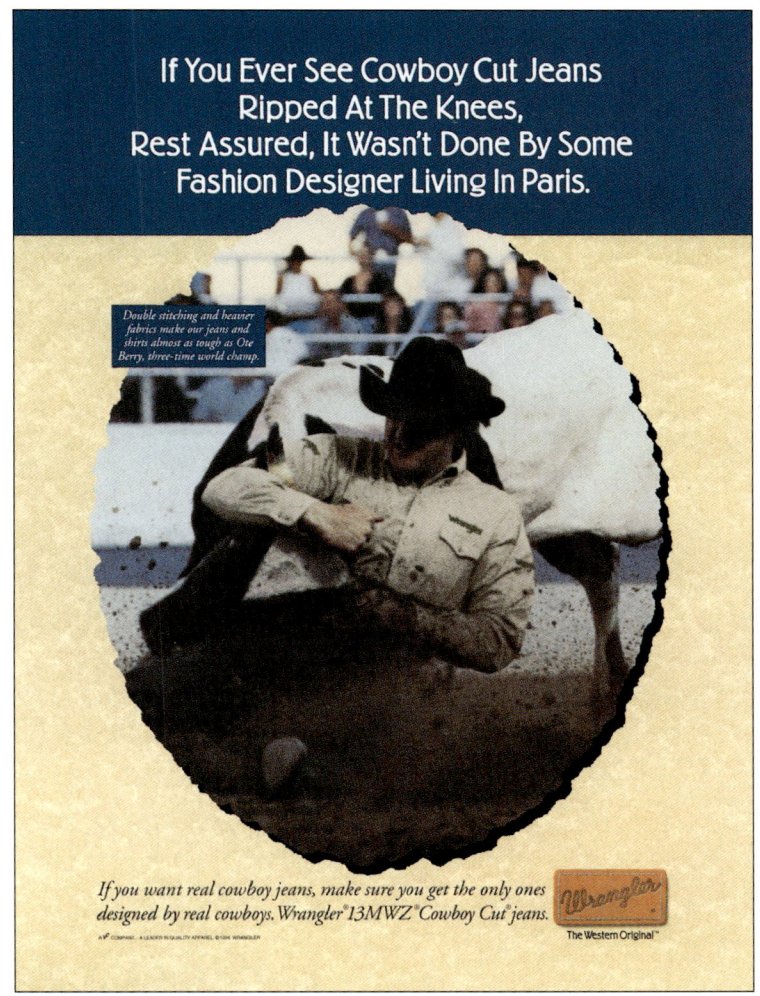

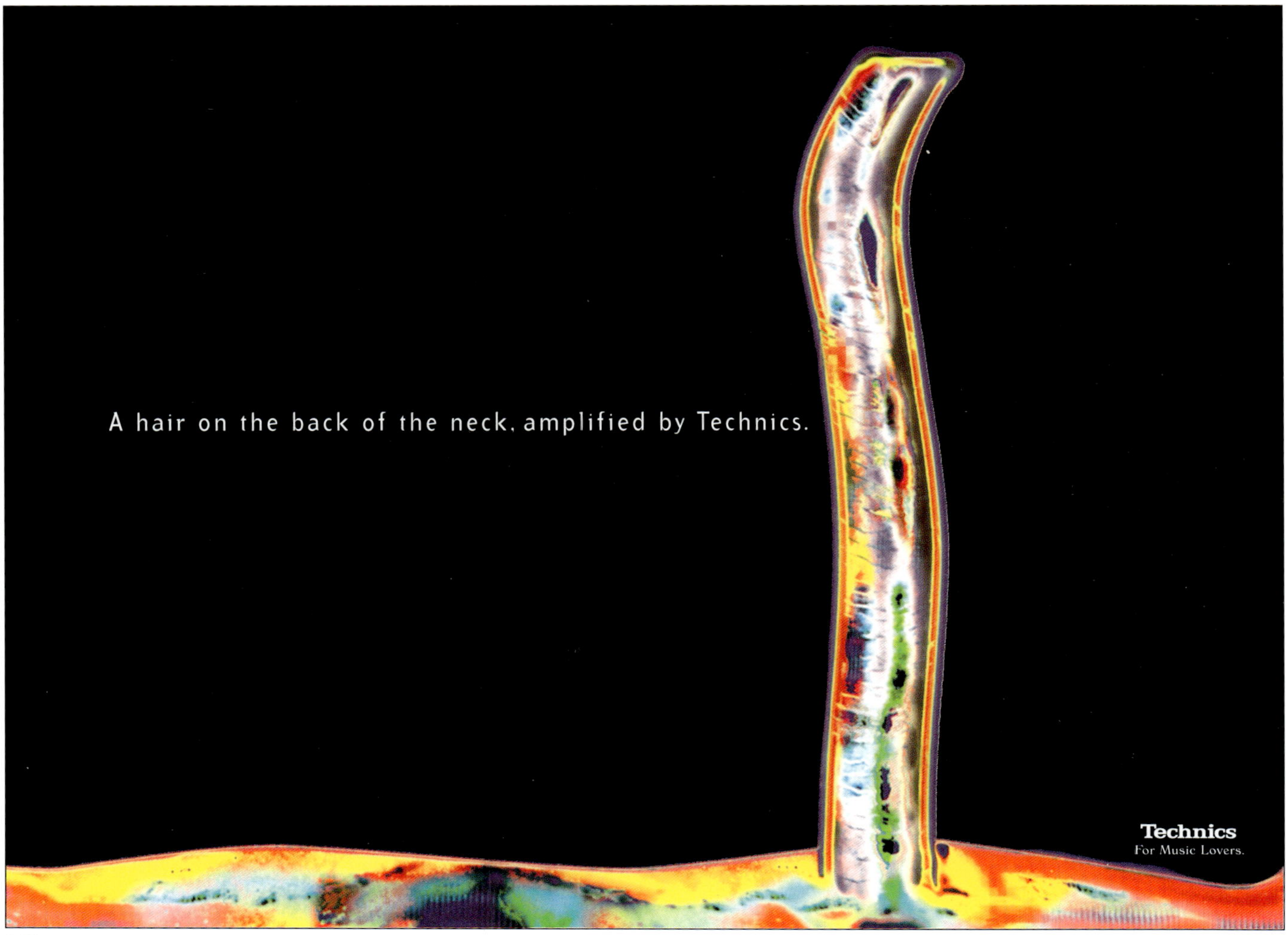

CONSUMER MAGAZINE
COLOR 1 PAGE OR
SPREAD: SINGLE

248
ART DIRECTOR:
Tiger Savage
WRITER:
Paul Silburn
PHOTOGRAPHER:
Nadav Kander
CLIENT:
Nike Sportswear
AGENCY:
Simons Palmer Denton Clemmow & Johnson/ London

249
ART DIRECTOR:
Tiger Savage
WRITER:
Paul Silburn
PHOTOGRAPHER:
Nadav Kander
CLIENT:
Nike Sportswear
AGENCY:
Simons Palmer Denton Clemmow & Johnson/ London

250
ART DIRECTORS:
Maria Kostyk-Petro
Lisa Lipkin
WRITERS:
Lisa Lipkin
Maria Kostyk-Petro
PHOTOGRAPHER:
Ellen Von Unwerth
CLIENT:
Sara Lee Foundations
AGENCY:
TBWA Advertising/ New York

251
ART DIRECTOR:
David Angelo
WRITER:
Glen Wachowiak
PHOTOGRAPHERS:
Shawn Michienzi
Michael Rausch
CLIENT:
Lexus
AGENCY:
Team One Advertising/ El Segundo, CA

248

249

WHO CARES IF IT'S A BAD HAIR DAY?

THE PUSH-UP PLUNGE BRA.

Rejected during inspection No. 1031 at 3:02:56 p.m. on March 17. (.003 oz. too heavy.)

The LS

LEXUS
The Relentless Pursuit Of Perfection.

CONSUMER MAGAZINE
COLOR 1 PAGE OR
SPREAD: SINGLE

252
ART DIRECTOR:
Leeanna Golden
WRITER:
Steve Silver
ILLUSTRATOR:
Antar Dayal
PHOTOGRAPHERS:
Michael Ruppert
Michael Rausch
Vic Huber
CLIENT:
Lexus
AGENCY:
**Team One Advertising/
El Segundo, CA**

253
ART DIRECTOR:
David Angelo
WRITER:
Glen Wachowiak
PHOTOGRAPHERS:
Shawn Michienzi
Michael Rausch
CLIENT:
Lexus
AGENCY:
**Team One Advertising/
El Segundo, CA**

254
ART DIRECTOR:
Leeanna Golden
WRITER:
Glen Wachowiak
PHOTOGRAPHERS:
Holly Stewart
Richard Gillette
CLIENT:
Roederer
AGENCY:
**Team One Advertising/
El Segundo, CA**

255
ART DIRECTOR:
John Vitro
WRITER:
John Robertson
ILLUSTRATOR:
John Craig
PHOTOGRAPHER:
Marshall Harrington
CLIENT:
Odyssey Golf
AGENCY:
VitroRobertson/San Diego

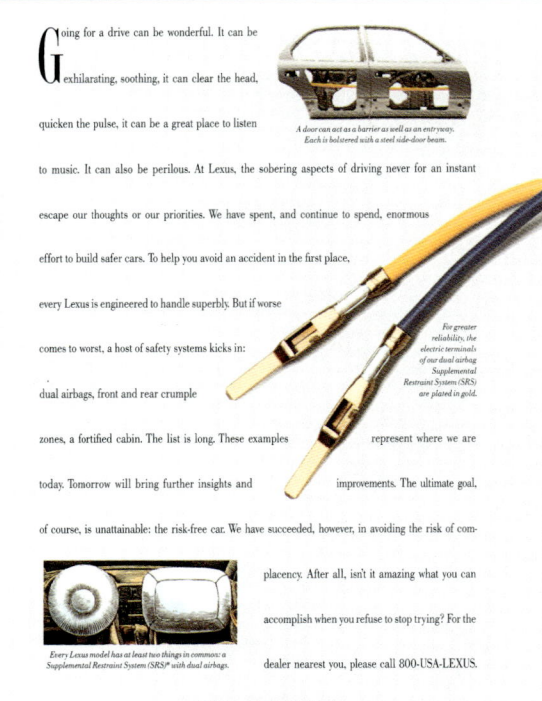

The grapes are vintage 1989.
The roots, however, go all the way back to 1776.

Introducing L'Ermitage from Roederer Estate.

Behind each bottle of our vintage prestige cuvée, you'll find a rather extensive history. That's because L'Ermitage is the result of the House of Louis Roederer's over 200-year commitment to the art of fine wine making in Europe.

For L'Ermitage, we use only the best selection of grapes, which are carefully cultivated at our Anderson Valley Vineyards. A place whose microclimate and long growing season have helped us set a new standard in California sparkling wines.

Naturally, our attention to detail hasn't gone unnoticed by the critics. The *Wine Spectator*, for example, gave L'Ermitage the number-one ranking in their recent poll of California sparklers.

To understand even more about L'Ermitage and Roederer Estate Brut, we invite you to open a bottle. You'll see how 200 years of tradition can make for a memorable evening.

ROEDERER ESTATE

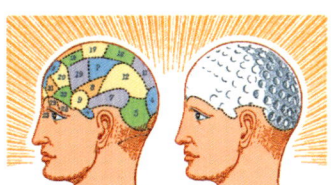

Remember, golf is not brain surgery.

It's harder.

A person can actually learn brain surgery.

A person can never really learn golf.

There are 4,501 brain surgeons in the U.S., with a median income of $500,000.

There are about 50 golfers in the U.S. that make $500,000 or more.

On a brain surgeon, it's the eyes that usually go first.

On a golfer, the brain can pretty much go any day of the week, followed, in quick order, by everything else.

Brain surgeons have, at most, 8 or 10 people watching them.

Golfers have anywhere from 3 to 45 million people watching them.

On bad days, a brain surgeon may sit back and dream about retiring to play golf.

On bad days, which can occur anytime, a golfer may sit back and dream about visiting a brain surgeon. Hey, you've tried everything else. Maybe they've figured out that transplant thing by now.

This'll take a load off your mind.
The Odyssey putter.
In just over two years, it's become the second most popular putter on the PGA Seniors Tour.
And it's moving up on number one.
That mysterious black spot in the face is a big reason why. It's called Stronomic.
It's softer than other materials, for incredible feel and flawless roll.
To feel what we mean, you'll just have to try it.
Call us at 1-800-487-5664.
Then you can put the whole brain surgery thing out of your mind once and for all.

ODYSSEY GOLF

CONSUMER MAGAZINE
COLOR 1 PAGE OR
SPREAD: SINGLE

256
ART DIRECTOR:
Tracy Wong
WRITER:
Craig Hoit
PHOTOGRAPHER:
Larry Prosor
CLIENT:
K2 Skis
AGENCY:
WongDoody/Seattle

CONSUMER MAGAZINE
B/W 1 PAGE OR SPREAD:
CAMPAIGN

257
ART DIRECTORS:
Susan Westre
Maggie Choo
WRITERS:
Chris Wall
John Dullaghan
PHOTOGRAPHER:
Michael O'Brien
CLIENT:
Apple Computer
AGENCY:
BBDO/Los Angeles

CONSUMER MAGAZINE
B/W 1 PAGE OR SPREAD:
CAMPAIGN

258
ART DIRECTOR:
Jon Soto
WRITER:
Tina Hall
PHOTOGRAPHER:
Alexander Ruas
CLIENT:
Shelter
AGENCY:
Mad Dogs & Englishmen/
New York

CONSUMER MAGAZINE
COLOR 1 PAGE OR
SPREAD: CAMPAIGN

259
ART DIRECTOR:
Rob Oliver
WRITER:
Peter Russell
PHOTOGRAPHER:
Nadav Kander
CLIENT:
Cow & Gate
AGENCY:
Abbott Mead Vickers.
BBDO/London

CONSUMER MAGAZINE
COLOR 1 PAGE OR
SPREAD: CAMPAIGN

260
ART DIRECTOR:
Mike Wells
WRITER:
Tim Riley
PHOTOGRAPHER:
Tiff Hunter
CLIENT:
The Whitbread Beer Company
AGENCY:
Bartle Bogle Hegarty/ London

261
ART DIRECTOR:
Graham Watson
WRITER:
Bruce Crouch
PHOTOGRAPHER:
Janet Wooley
CLIENT:
The Whitbread Beer Company
AGENCY:
Bartle Bogle Hegarty/ London

Dehydration was a problem for the boys from Cork, but like the Murphy's they weren't bitter.

The Lotto was split 1,062,437 ways, but like the Murphy's Paddy wasn't bitter.

Eugene kissed goodbye to his bus fare, but like the Murphy's he wasn't bitter.

CONSUMER MAGAZINE
COLOR 1 PAGE OR
SPREAD: CAMPAIGN

262
ART DIRECTOR:
Lye Kok Hong
WRITER:
Jim Aitchison
PHOTOGRAPHER:
Alex Kaikeong
CLIENT:
Mercedes-Benz Asia
AGENCY:
Batey Ads/Singapore

264
ART DIRECTORS:
Andrew Clarke
Grover Tham
WRITER:
Danny Higgins
PHOTOGRAPHER:
Steve Bicknell
CLIENT:
Parker Pen Singapore
AGENCY:
Euro RSCG Ball
Partnership/Singapore

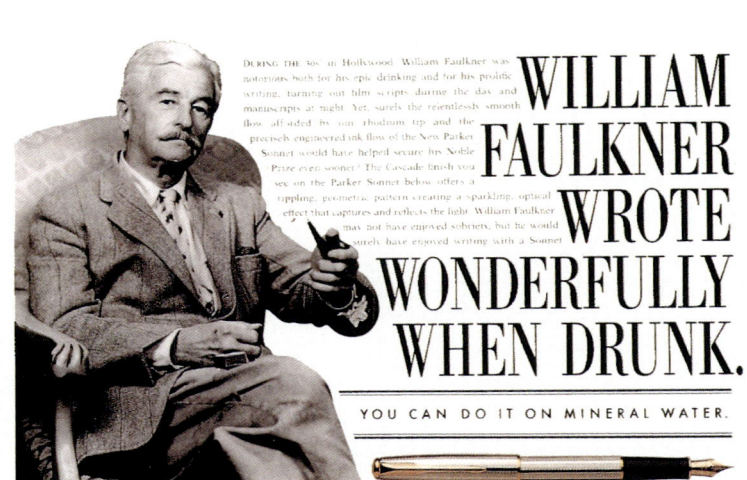

CONSUMER MAGAZINE
COLOR 1 PAGE OR
SPREAD: CAMPAIGN

265
ART DIRECTORS:
J. Liegey
Steve Stone
WRITERS:
Bruce Bildsten
Bill Westbrook
PHOTOGRAPHER:
Shawn Michienzi
CLIENT:
Magnavox
AGENCY:
**Fallon McElligott/
Minneapolis**

266
ART DIRECTOR:
J. Liegey
WRITER:
Mike Gibbs
PHOTOGRAPHER:
Buck Holzemer
CLIENT:
Nikon
AGENCY:
**Fallon McElligott/
Minneapolis**

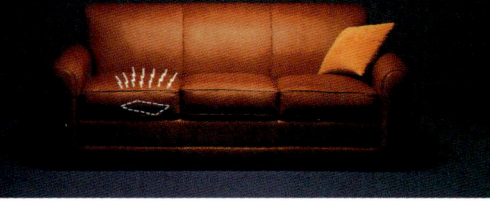

USE YOUR ARMS. USE YOUR LEGS. USE YOUR BODY. FIGHT FOR POSITION. KEEP OPPONENTS BACK. THEN TAKE THE PICTURE.

YOU KNOW THAT FEELING WHEN YOU HEAR THE ROAR OF THE CROWD FROM THE BATHROOM? PHOTOGRAPHERS DON'T.

SWEAT, SPIT, TEARS AND A SPLASH OF CHAMPIONSHIP CHAMPAGNE. ALL WIPED OFF ONE CAMERA.

CONSUMER MAGAZINE
COLOR 1 PAGE OR
SPREAD: CAMPAIGN

267
ART DIRECTOR:
Bob Barrie
WRITER:
Mike Lescarbeau
PHOTOGRAPHER:
Timothy White
CLIENT:
Sunset Marquis Hotel & Villas
AGENCY:
Fallon McElligott/ Minneapolis

268
ART DIRECTOR:
Bob Barrie
WRITER:
Dean Buckhorn
PHOTOGRAPHERS:
Michael Metcalf
Max-Plank Institute for Astronomy
Brian Bohanon
CLIENT:
Time Magazine
AGENCY:
Fallon McElligott/ Minneapolis

When in Hollywood, stay at the original instead of a sequel.

Sunset Marquis Hotel And Villas.
Unique. Even By Hollywood Standards.

1200 North Alta Loma Road, West Hollywood, California 90069-2402 Telephone (310) 657-1333 Fax: (310) 652-5300

If we were any more Hollywood, our pool would be shallow at both ends.

Sunset Marquis Hotel And Villas.
Unique. Even By Hollywood Standards.

1200 North Alta Loma Road, West Hollywood, California 90069-2402 Telephone (310) 657-1333 Fax: (310) 652-5300

Good news for Metallica: Our hotel has a recording studio.

Good news for you: It's soundproof.

Sunset Marquis Hotel And Villas.
Unique. Even By Hollywood Standards.

1200 North Alta Loma Road, West Hollywood, California 90069-2402 Telephone (310) 657-1333 Fax: (310) 652-5300

We covered every moment

of his political career.

Except, of course, for 18 minutes.

Understanding comes with TIME.

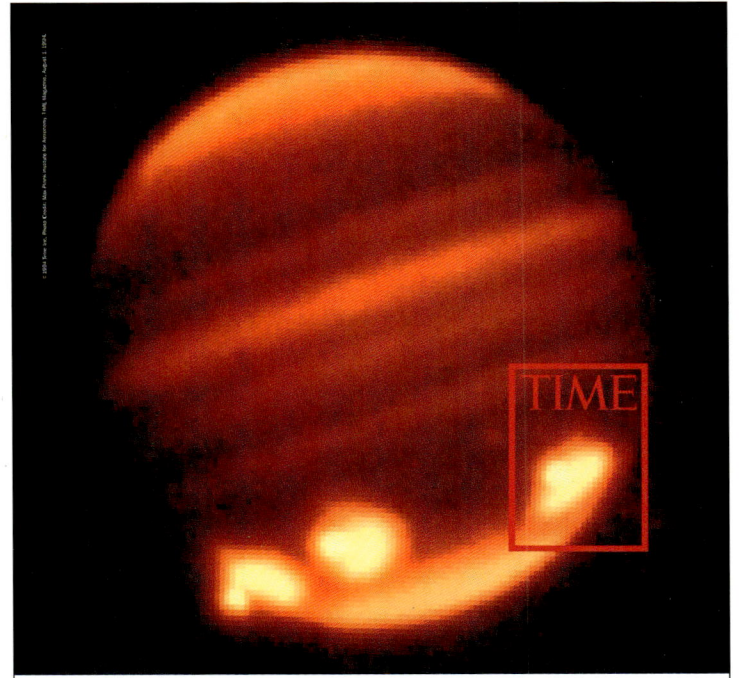

For those without access to

the Hubble telescope, it

was the most detailed view.

Understanding comes with TIME.

Is it legalized murder?

Is it a constitutional right?

Is 30 seconds of TV coverage

enough to decide?

Understanding comes with TIME.

CONSUMER MAGAZINE
COLOR 1 PAGE OR
SPREAD: CAMPAIGN

269
ART DIRECTOR:
Dean Hanson
WRITER:
Bruce Bildsten
PHOTOGRAPHER:
Joe Paczkowski
CLIENT:
Timex Corporation
AGENCY:
**Fallon McElligott/
Minneapolis**

270
ART DIRECTOR:
Gary Goldsmith
WRITER:
Dean Hacohen
ILLUSTRATOR:
Christopher Wormell
CLIENT:
JP Morgan
AGENCY:
**Goldsmith/Jeffrey,
New York**

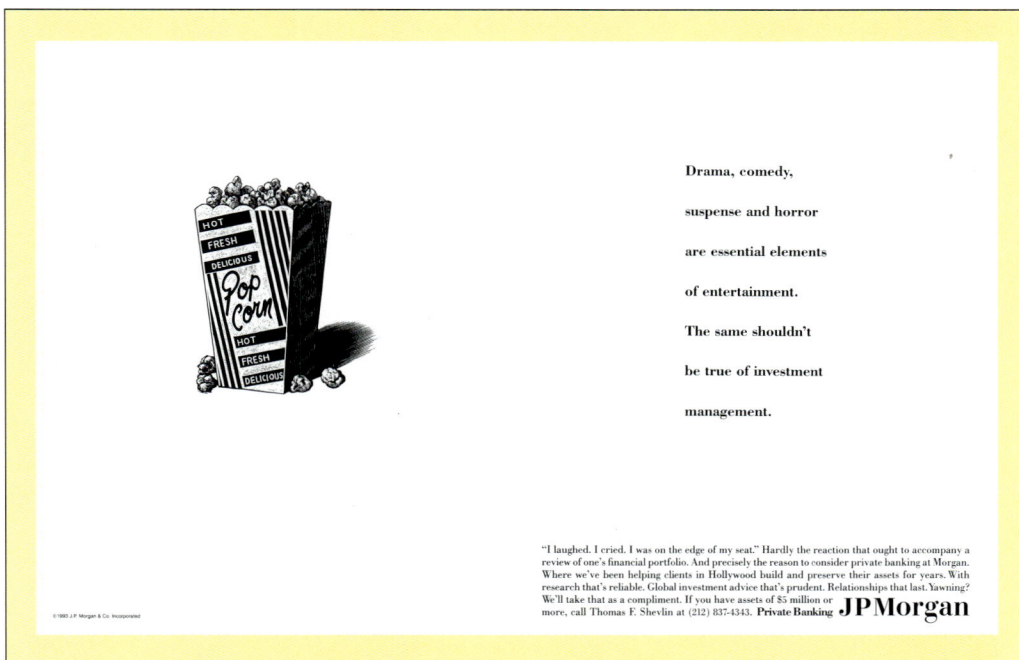

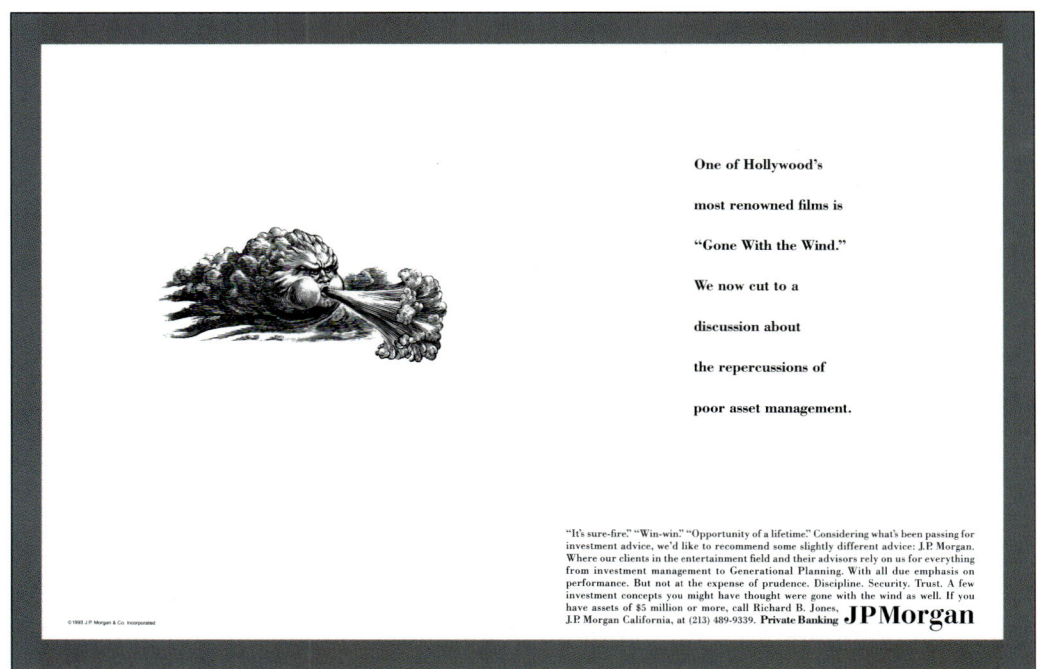

CONSUMER MAGAZINE
COLOR 1 PAGE OR
SPREAD: CAMPAIGN

271
ART DIRECTOR:
Erich Joiner
WRITER:
Bob Kerstetter
PHOTOGRAPHER:
Clint Clemens
CLIENT:
Porsche Cars North America
AGENCY:
Goodby Silverstein & Partners/San Francisco

272
ART DIRECTOR:
Chad Farmer
WRITER:
David Bradley
PHOTOGRAPHER:
Matthew Rolston
CLIENT:
Charles David Footwear
AGENCY:
Lambesis/San Diego

Excuse me sir, do you always talk with your foot in your mouth?

charles david *by Nathalie M*

Dullards and naysayers or anyone who stands in your way, tell them it's not just your feet they can kiss.

charles david *by Nathalie M*

If you really must step on someone to get ahead, use a very sharp heel.

charles david *by Nathalie M*

CONSUMER MAGAZINE
COLOR 1 PAGE OR
SPREAD: CAMPAIGN

273
ART DIRECTOR:
Dave Dye
WRITER:
Tim Delaney
PHOTOGRAPHER:
The Douglas Brothers
CLIENT:
Adidas
AGENCY:
Leagas Delaney/London

274
ART DIRECTOR:
Bob Wyatt
WRITER:
Tom Coleman
PHOTOGRAPHERS:
Robert Whitman
Tony D'Orio
CLIENT:
Schieffelin & Somerset
AGENCY:
Leo Burnett Company/
Chicago

If she asks you what you're drinking, do you really want to say the word "spritzer" to this woman?

Dewar's

A suggestion for those whose perfect evening no longer involves plastic cups, a keg and tipping over a cow.

Dewar's

Gosh, your idea of a big evening sure has changed.

Dewar's

CONSUMER MAGAZINE COLOR 1 PAGE OR SPREAD: CAMPAIGN

275
ART DIRECTOR:
Andy Azula
WRITER:
Ed Jones
PHOTOGRAPHERS:
Harry DeZitter
Steve Murray
CLIENT:
North Carolina Travel & Tourism
AGENCY:
Loeffler Ketchum Mountjoy/Charlotte

276
ART DIRECTOR:
Steve St. Clair
WRITERS:
Andrew Payton
Steve St. Clair
PHOTOGRAPHER:
Chris Kahley
TYPOGRAPHER:
Joseph Pavia
CLIENT:
Pereaux
AGENCY:
Lord Dentsu & Partners/New York

SHOW YOUR CHILDREN THAT NOT ALL ENCHANTED FORESTS EXIST IN FAIRY TALES.

NORTH CAROLINA

IT'S LIKE A LANDSCAPE PAINTING BY MONET OR CÉZANNE. ONLY YOU CAN WALK AROUND IN IT.

NORTH CAROLINA

THINGS MOVE SO SLOWLY OUT HERE, TV DIDN'T ARRIVE UNTIL 1985. CAN HULA HOOPS BE FAR BEHIND?

NORTH CAROLINA

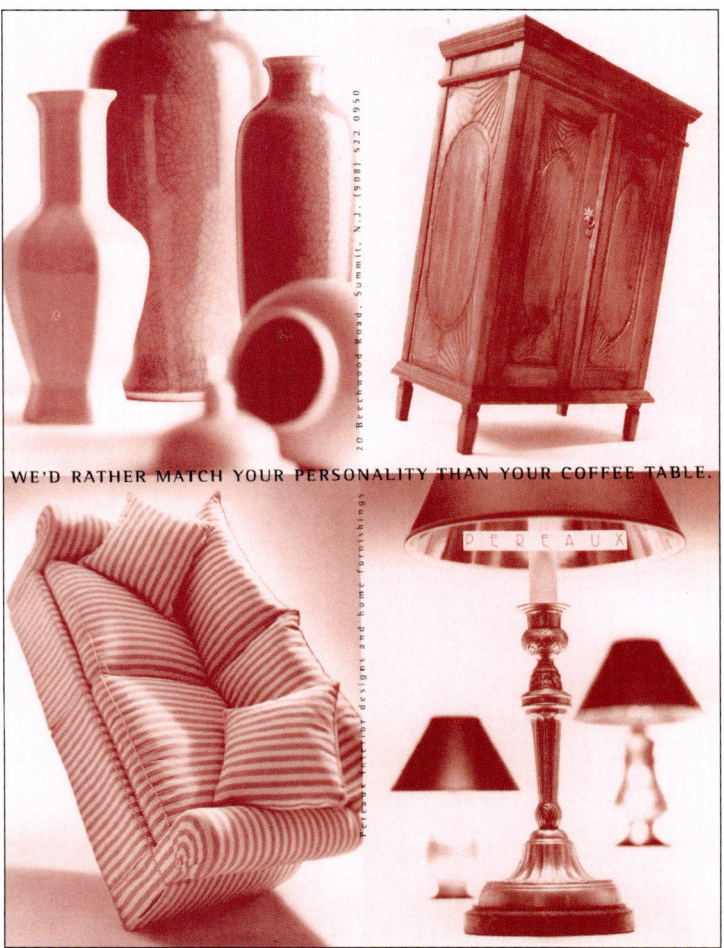

CONSUMER MAGAZINE
COLOR 1 PAGE OR
SPREAD: CAMPAIGN

277
ART DIRECTOR:
Carolyn McGeorge
WRITER:
Joe Alexander
PHOTOGRAPHER:
Dublin Productions
CLIENT:
Healthtex
AGENCY:
The Martin Agency/ Richmond

278
ART DIRECTORS:
Michael Furlong
Gary McKendry
Tom Moore
WRITERS:
Cynthia Gruber
Graham Turner
Michael Ward
ILLUSTRATORS:
Javier Romero Design
Bob Ziering
PHOTOGRAPHER:
Nancy Moran
CLIENT:
American Express
AGENCY:
Ogilvy & Mather/ New York

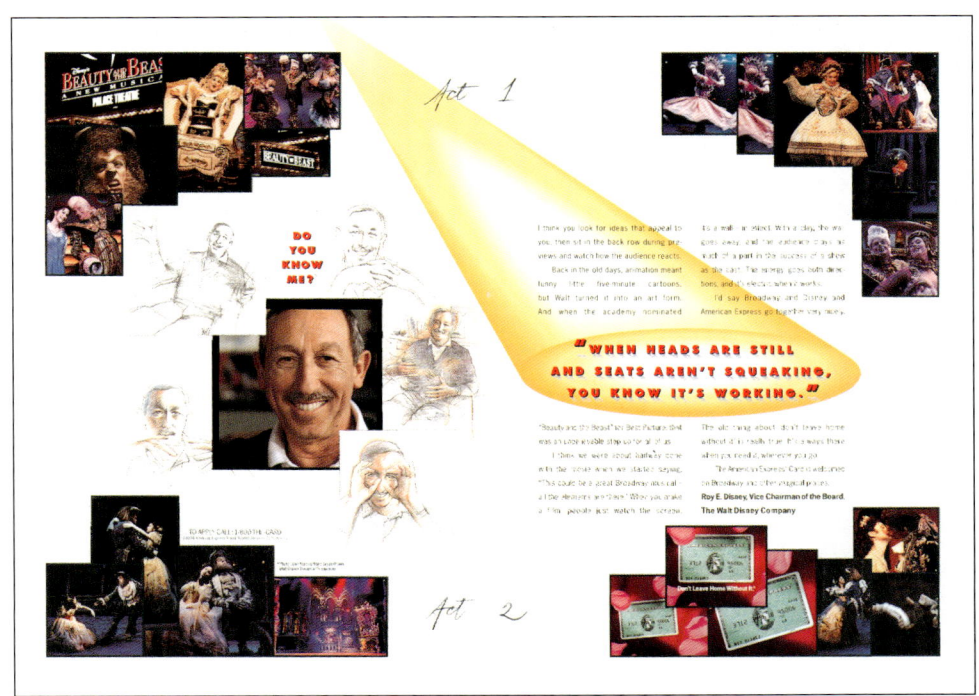

CONSUMER MAGAZINE
COLOR 1 PAGE OR
SPREAD: CAMPAIGN

279
ART DIRECTOR:
Taras Wayner
WRITER:
Kevin Roddy
PHOTOGRAPHER:
Ilan Rubin
CLIENT:
Polygram Video
AGENCY:
Oscar & Cooper/Bethesda

280
ART DIRECTOR:
David Angelo
WRITER:
Glen Wachowiak
PHOTOGRAPHERS:
Shawn Michienzi
Michael Rausch
CLIENT:
Lexus
AGENCY:
Team One Advertising/
El Segundo, CA

Some people say we're too obsessed with a .00039″ tolerance. (Or was it .00038″?)

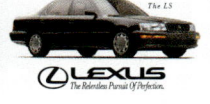

Rejected during inspection No. 1031 at 3:02:56 p.m. on March 17. (.003 oz. too heavy.)

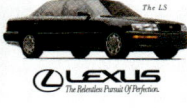

Found on January 17 at 11:34:12 a.m., during inspection No. 756.
We are pleased to note the remaining 1,062 inspections went flawlessly.

CONSUMER MAGAZINE
COLOR 1 PAGE OR
SPREAD: CAMPAIGN

281
ART DIRECTOR:
Darryl McDonald
WRITER:
Jim Riswold
PHOTOGRAPHER:
Eugene Richards
CLIENT:
Nike
AGENCY:
Wieden & Kennedy/
Portland

282
ART DIRECTOR:
Jelly Helm
WRITER:
Jean Rhode
PHOTOGRAPHER:
Michael Jones
CLIENT:
Nike
AGENCY:
Wieden & Kennedy/
Portland

TRUE TENNIS PLAYERS!
Attention!!
ARE WE LETTING DINKERS, MOONBALLERS AND OTHER TENNIS COWARDS POLLUTE OUR SPORT?

Tennis, once a *challenge* for the passionate and athletic has now become a folly for paunch-ridden pushers and white-wearing infidels!

NOT POSSIBLE YOU SAY?? Then consider this:
--WHY DO CERTAIN PEOPLE SULLY THEIR TENNIS SHOES WHILE MOWING THE LAWN OR OTHERWISE INVOLVED IN LEISURE THAT IS NOT RELATED AT ALL TO TENNIS??
--WHY HAS A ONCE VITAL SPORT DEGENERATED TO THE STATUS OF LAWN BOWLING, CROQUET OR BADMINTON? OR PERHAPS A MORE TELLING QUESTION--WHO PROFITS??
--WHY ARE PLAYERS WHO SHOUT "SERVICE" BEFORE THEY SERVE NOT OSTRACIZED AND BANNED FROM PLAY AS THEY SO RICHLY DESERVE?
--WHY HAVE WE HEARD MUCH OF JIM COURIER'S 4 GRAND SLAM WINS YET NOTHING OF THE "VIENNA" INCIDENT?
--WHY ARE IMPERIALIST "SPORT" CORPORATIONS ALLOWED TO PROFITEER FROM THE EVILS OF INFERIOR SHOES...LEADING ULTIMATELY TO THE DEMISE OF OUR SPORT?

Yes, there is NIKE with the AIR ACE LOW shoe that lasts for many playing hours. But answer this: why are not all shoes as honorable? It is time to voice our demands.

TAKE A STAND!
- Commandeer the courts of tennis "players" who are not even keeping score!
- Boycott any partner who has no overhead.
- Confront those who wear TENNIS shoes in tawdry malls and GROCERY stores.
- Do not be intimidated by execrable "shoe" manufacturers that refuse to respect our tennis needs!!

Wake up and smell the freshly opened can of tennis balls!!

Food for thought

TENNIS WOMEN!
Listen To The Truth!!

Are you a woman tennis player?
Or are you an unwitting pawn of the non-tennis playing power-mongers?

It is clear that we, as women tennis players, are not offered suitable respect. An innocent oversight? Or a clear example of the tennis elite trying to monopolize all tennis courts for themselves?

--Why do they pigeonhole us as dainty, non-sweaty beings without muscles in our legs and arms?
--Why do women's matches have only THREE sets?
--Why are women's exciting and vigorous tennis events not given suitable prominence on TV?

You may say this is all much improved since the '70s. But think about this:
Why are not superior Women Tennis Pros featured guests on prominent late night talk shows?
Why is not a Mary Joe Fernandez sponsoring as many products as say a Jim Courier or, say, an Andre Agassi?
Why is Nike's Air La Quinta Mid shoe the only one that stands up to the strong play of women who require footwear that lasts far longer than the other so-called "shoes"?

TAKE A STAND!
- Refuse to surrender the court to the greedy men.
- Protest the conspiracy of talk show hosts and demand the appearance of Mary Joe.
- Ignore "Protocol." Play FIVE sets.

If we do not act, we will not see women's tennis given the air time like that of, say, American baseball or even boxing, which women's tennis so clearly deserves.

TALK IS CHEAP

TENNIS PLAYERS! DO NOT BE SEDUCED BY THE SIREN SONG OF THE SPORTS ESTABLISHMENT!

THEIR TENNIS PROPAGANDA IS LIES! ALL LIES!!

Certain "Sports Imperialists" are openly positioning tennis as a dandy's game for those not strong enough to compete in a real sport.

This could not happen, you say?
- CONSIDER: the Fascistic imposition of white apparel.
- OBSERVE: the Mass-Media's hyped portrayals of athletes such as Andre Agassi or Jim Courier as tame jet-setting "celebrities" instead of the hardened aggressive players that they truly are.
- ASK: Why do shoe interests "engineer" products that are mere foot coverings masquerading as tennis shoes?
- ASK: Why is only Nike bold enough to create a shoe like the Air Ace Low that can stand up to the continual and intense play of the true Player?

CHOOSE WHAT TO BELIEVE:
LIE: Tennis is a social "party game" reserved for white-wearing Victorians.
LIE: Tennis is delicate. It is the place for non-aggressive non-athletes who are weak and complacent.
LIE: Tennis shoes should be dainty white slippers, designed more for prancing and posing than for rabid, aggressive tennis.

As individuals we must refuse to accept any imposition of the will of the Tennis Hegemony! Say NO to puling sports "Commentators" and Shoe Dictators!
Let our present WAR against the Tennis Imperialists end the covert condescension to tennis--FOREVER!!

Think for yourself

CONSUMER MAGAZINE
COLOR 1 PAGE OR
SPREAD: CAMPAIGN

283
ART DIRECTOR:
Tracy Wong
WRITERS:
Craig Hoit
Rene Huey
PHOTOGRAPHERS:
Wade McCoy
Larry Prosor
Chaco Mohler
CLIENT:
K2 Skis
AGENCY:
WongDoody/Seattle

CONSUMER MAGAZINE
LESS THAN A PAGE
B/W OR COLOR: SINGLE

284
ART DIRECTOR:
Frank Guzzone
WRITER:
Paul Hartzell
PHOTOGRAPHER:
Fred Kolhoff
CLIENT:
Austin Nichols & Company/Wild Turkey
AGENCY:
Angotti Thomas Hedge/New York

285
ART DIRECTORS:
Mark Schruntek
Patrick Sutherland
WRITERS:
Patrick Sutherland
Mark Schruntek
CLIENT:
Daffy's
AGENCY:
DeVito/Verdi, New York

Kentucky, home of the nation's most treasured reserves.

(We understand Fort Knox is there, too.)

WILD TURKEY
101 proof, real Kentucky.

WE BELIEVE PEOPLE SHOULD BE PRICE CONSCIOUS.

THEY SHOULD REMAIN CONSCIOUS AFTER THEY SEE THE PRICE.

Don't take the high price of designer clothing lying down. Come into Daffy's, where you'll find men's, women's and children's designer clothes at 40-75% off, every day.

DAFFY'S
CLOTHES THAT WILL MAKE YOU, NOT BREAK YOU.

CONSUMER MAGAZINE
LESS THAN A PAGE
B/W OR COLOR: SINGLE

286
ART DIRECTOR:
Carol Henderson
WRITER:
Dean Buckhorn
CLIENT:
Brit's Pub
AGENCY:
Fallon McElligott/
Minneapolis

287
ART DIRECTORS:
Megan Welsh
Chuck Bennett
WRITERS:
Chuck Guest
Clay Williams
CLIENT:
KCET
AGENCY:
Kresser Stein Robaire/
Santa Monica

CONSUMER MAGAZINE
LESS THAN A PAGE
B/W OR COLOR:
CAMPAIGN

288
ART DIRECTORS:
Rob Carducci
Abi Aron
Patrick Sutherland
Mark Schruntek
Audrey DeVries
WRITERS:
Abi Aron
Rob Carducci
Mark Schruntek
Patrick Sutherland
Audrey DeVries
CLIENT:
Daffy's
AGENCY:
DeVito/Verdi, New York

There's more flavor on the sides of an empty Guinness than in a full Budweiser.

Next time you're in the mood for a true, full-bodied beer, stop by Brit's Pub. After one taste of our Guinness Stout, Fuller's E.S.B, Foster's, Young's Ram Rod or Woodpecker Cider, we think you'll agree. They run rings around most domestics.

Brit's Pub
1110 Nicollet Mall Minneapolis 612-332-3908

FINALLY, YOUR CHANCE TO PLAY MUSIC THAT WILL DRIVE YOUR TEENAGER INSANE.

PERRY COMO'S IRISH CHRISTMAS TONIGHT AT 6:00. JOIN PERRY COMO AND IRELAND'S MOST TALENTED PERFORMERS AS THEY SING THE CHRISTMAS STANDARDS, TO THE DELIGHT OF ALL. OR ALMOST ALL. **KCET/28**

MARRY FOR LOVE AND LOOK LIKE YOU MARRIED FOR MONEY.

At Daffy's, you'll find men's, women's and children's designer clothing at 40-75% off, every day. Good news if the person you married for richer or poorer isn't richer.

DAFFY'S
CLOTHES THAT WILL MAKE YOU, NOT BREAK YOU.

WE BELIEVE PEOPLE SHOULD BE PRICE CONSCIOUS. THEY SHOULD REMAIN CONSCIOUS AFTER THEY SEE THE PRICE.

Don't take the high price of designer clothing lying down. Come into Daffy's, where you'll find men's, women's and children's designer clothes at 40-75% off, every day.

DAFFY'S
CLOTHES THAT WILL MAKE YOU, NOT BREAK YOU.

FRIENDS DON'T LET FRIENDS PAY RETAIL.

If a friend is paying too much for designer clothes, do everything you can to stop them. Tell them about Daffy's where they'll find designer clothing at 40-75% off, every day.

DAFFY'S
CLOTHES THAT WILL MAKE YOU, NOT BREAK YOU.

CONSUMER MAGAZINE
LESS THAN A PAGE
B/W OR COLOR:
CAMPAIGN

289
ART DIRECTOR:
Carol Henderson
WRITER:
Dean Buckhorn
CLIENT:
Brit's Pub
AGENCY:
Fallon McElligott/
Minneapolis

290
ART DIRECTOR:
Andy Azula
WRITER:
Ed Jones
PHOTOGRAPHERS:
Harry DeZitter
Steve Murray
CLIENT:
North Carolina
Travel & Tourism
AGENCY:
Loeffler Ketchum
Mountjoy/Charlotte

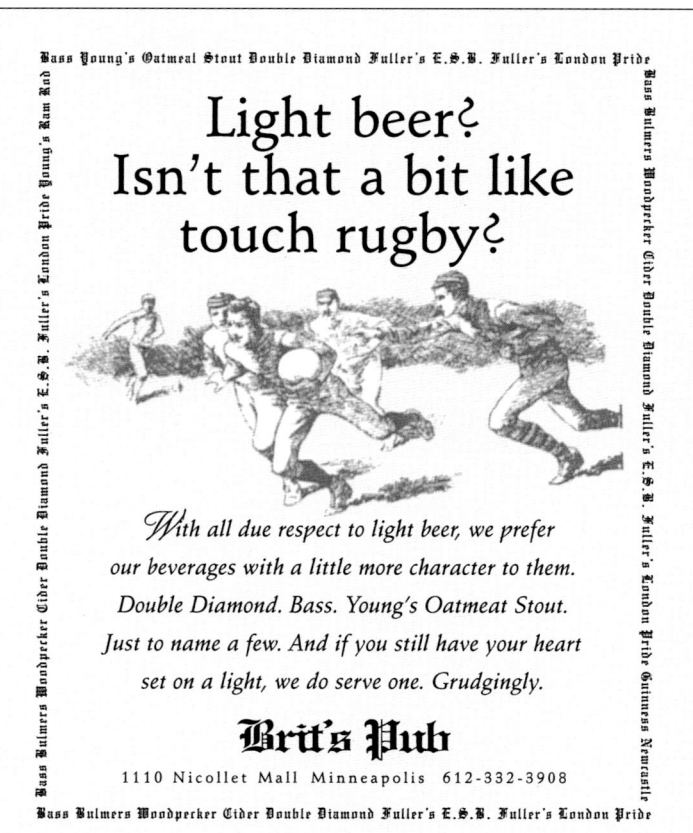

SHOW YOUR CHILDREN THAT
NOT ALL ENCHANTED FORESTS
EXIST IN FAIRY TALES.

NORTH CAROLINA

For a free North Carolina travel guide, call 1-800-VISIT NC.

IT'S LIKE A LANDSCAPE PAINTING
BY MONET OR CÉZANNE. ONLY YOU
CAN WALK AROUND IN IT.

NORTH  AROLINA

For a free North Carolina travel guide, call 1-800-VISIT NC.

THINGS MOVE SO SLOWLY OUT
HERE, TV DIDN'T ARRIVE UNTIL 1985.
CAN HULA HOOPS BE FAR BEHIND?

NORTH CAROLINA

For a free North Carolina travel guide, call 1-800-VISIT NC.

OUTDOOR: SINGLE

291
ART DIRECTOR:
Dan Cohen
WRITER:
Paul Hartzell
PHOTOGRAPHER:
Kevin Logan
CLIENT:
Barron's
AGENCY:
Angotti Thomas Hedge/
New York

292
ART DIRECTOR:
Max Jerome
WRITER:
Steve Biegel
PHOTOGRAPHER:
Jerry Cailor
CLIENT:
Molson Breweries USA/
Foster's
AGENCY:
Angotti Thomas Hedge/
New York

293
ART DIRECTOR:
Tony Angotti
WRITER:
Dion Hughes
PHOTOGRAPHER:
Jerry Cailor
CLIENT:
Molson Breweries USA/
Foster's
AGENCY:
Angotti Thomas Hedge/
New York

294
ART DIRECTOR:
Audrey DeVries
WRITER:
Audrey DeVries
CLIENT:
Daffy's
AGENCY:
DeVito/Verdi, New York

291

292

OUTDOOR: SINGLE

295
ART DIRECTOR:
Dean Hanson
WRITER:
Dean Buckhorn
CLIENT:
Ameritech Corporate
AGENCY:
Fallon McElligott/
Minneapolis

296
ART DIRECTOR:
Henriette Lienke
WRITER:
Tom Miller
CLIENT:
Crain's New York Business
AGENCY:
Goldsmith/Jeffrey,
New York

297
ART DIRECTOR:
Mike Fetrow
WRITER:
Doug Adkins
CLIENT:
Mystic Lake Casino
AGENCY:
Hunt Murray/
Minneapolis

298
ART DIRECTOR:
Dave Dye
WRITER:
Tony Barry
ILLUSTRATOR:
Dave Dye
CLIENT:
GQ
AGENCY:
Leagas Delaney/London

OUTDOOR: SINGLE

299
ART DIRECTOR:
Gina Fortunato
WRITER:
Susan Treacy
CLIENT:
Thom McAn
AGENCY:
Mad Dogs & Englishmen/ New York

300
ART DIRECTOR:
Gina Fortunato
WRITER:
Susan Treacy
CLIENT:
Thom McAn
AGENCY:
Mad Dogs & Englishmen/ New York

301
ART DIRECTOR:
Gerald Schoenhoff
WRITER:
David Rosenberg
CLIENT:
Urban Trans Ad
AGENCY:
Roche Macaulay & Partners/Toronto

302
ART DIRECTOR:
Gerald Schoenhoff
WRITER:
David Rosenberg
CLIENT:
Urban Trans Ad
AGENCY:
Roche Macaulay & Partners/Toronto

You are an individual. Distinct. One of a kind. Just like the thousands of other distinct individuals who, like trained fish, read this subway poster everyday.

Your product *goes* here.

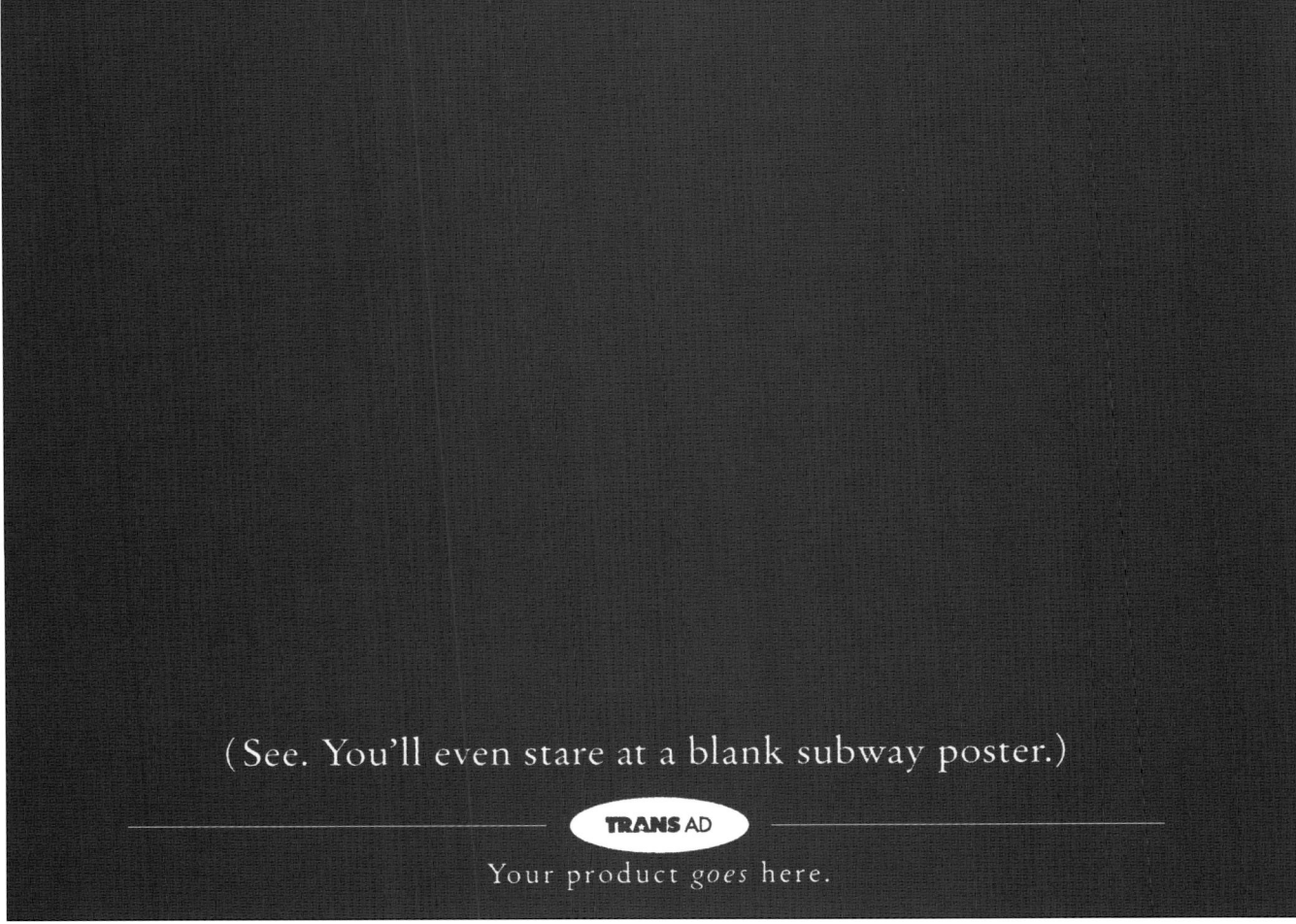

(See. You'll even stare at a blank subway poster.)

Your product *goes* here.

OUTDOOR: SINGLE

303
ART DIRECTORS:
Dan Braun
Bart Slomkowski
WRITERS:
Dan Braun
Bart Slomkowski
PHOTOGRAPHER:
Steve Bronstein
CLIENT:
V&S Vin & Sprit AB
AGENCY:
TBWA Advertising/
New York

304
ART DIRECTORS:
John C. Jay
Imin Pao
WRITER:
Jimmy Smith
PHOTOGRAPHER:
John Huet
CLIENT:
Nike
AGENCY:
Wieden & Kennedy/
Portland

OUTDOOR: CAMPAIGN

305
ART DIRECTORS:
Tony Angotti
Max Jerome
WRITERS:
Dion Hughes
Steve Biegel
PHOTOGRAPHERS:
Jerry Cailor
Jeff Davine
CLIENT:
Molson Breweries USA/
Foster's
AGENCY:
Angotti Thomas Hedge/
New York

303

304

OUTDOOR: CAMPAIGN

306
ART DIRECTOR:
Steve Mitchell
WRITER:
Doug Adkins
CLIENT:
KCBS Television
AGENCY:
Hunt Murray/Minneapolis

307
ART DIRECTOR:
Mike Fetrow
WRITER:
Doug Adkins
PHOTOGRAPHER:
Shawn Michienzi
CLIENT:
Minnesota Brewing
AGENCY:
Hunt Murray/Minneapolis

The cartilage in your nose never stops growing.

A BRUTALLY HONEST BEER.

General Douglas MacArthur's mother dressed him in skirts.

A BRUTALLY HONEST BEER.

At one time there were over 15,000 discos in the U.S.

A BRUTALLY HONEST BEER.

OUTDOOR: CAMPAIGN

308
ART DIRECTORS:
John C. Jay
Imin Pao
WRITER:
Jimmy Smith
PHOTOGRAPHER:
John Huet
CLIENT:
Nike
AGENCY:
Wieden & Kennedy/
Portland

309
ART DIRECTORS:
John C. Jay
Imin Pao
WRITER:
Jimmy Smith
PHOTOGRAPHER:
John Huet
CLIENT:
Nike
AGENCY:
Wieden & Kennedy/
Portland

TRADE
B/W 1 PAGE OR SPREAD:
SINGLE

310
ART DIRECTOR:
Susan Griak
WRITER:
Paul Spencer
CLIENT:
VH-1
AGENCY:
Fallon McElligott Berlin/
New York

311
ART DIRECTOR:
Steve Mitchell
WRITER:
Matt Elhardt
PHOTOGRAPHERS:
Rick Dublin
Joe Lampi
CLIENT:
Dublin Productions
AGENCY:
Hunt Murray/
Minneapolis

312
ART DIRECTOR:
Steve Mitchell
WRITER:
Matt Elhardt
CLIENT:
Dublin Productions
AGENCY:
Hunt Murray/
Minneapolis

313
ART DIRECTORS:
Joe Sciarrotta
Dave Hernandez
WRITER:
Ted Xistris
CLIENT:
The Leap Partnership
AGENCY:
The Leap Partnership/
Chicago

310

311

(Too controversial)

(Too expensive)

(Too dead)

Rick Dublin, Jerry Pope, Jarl Olsen. 414 3rd Ave. N., Minneapolis, MN 55401 (612) 332-8864 **DUBLIN**

Why Sears, Roebuck and Co. stopped making a giant catalogue.

Somewhere up there, Richard Sears and Alvah C. Roebuck are looking down and sharing quite a laugh.

You see, while home shopping networks are being touted as the newest way for the modern consumer to make a purchase decision, these two know they had perfected their own "shop-at-home" service more than a hundred years before anyone ever heard of QVC.

It was called the Sears Catalogue, and on its pages one found anything and everything necessary for a comfortable existence in 20th century America.

You could wake up in the morning to the sound of your Sears alarm clock, throw off your Sears blanket, hop out of your Sears bed and into your Sears suit. Then it was down the stairs and into the kitchen of your Sears-designed home, where you might enjoy a breakfast prepared entirely on Sears electric appliances before going out to the garage to crank up the automobile you recently purchased from Sears (on credit, of course).

In short, you could order your cradle, your coffin, and every conceivable piece of merchandise you might need in between from the Sears Catalogue, and have it shipped directly to your door.

It was a way of doing business that was right for the times.

With much of the country living in rural isolation, Sears and Roebuck figured since the people can't come in to the store, they'd send the store out to the people.

Obviously, this focus on the needs of the consumer worked. The "Big Book" helped make Sears the world's biggest retailer, with the world's biggest selection, in the world's biggest building.

Then times changed.

The population began to grow increasingly mobile, increasingly urban. Competition started to squeeze Sears from both sides, as large "everything-under-one-roof" operations offered lower prices, and smaller, more specialized retailers offered a perception of higher quality.

In an attempt to offset sliding profits, Sears diversified. Soon, they found themselves in the real estate business, the brokerage business, and the credit card business.

Still, the hemorrhaging continued. This "bigger is better" strategy only served to further confuse consumers.

By the 1980s, Sears had lost its identity in the market-place. In trying to mean all things to all people, it ended up not meaning anything to anyone.

Then, with losses at an all-time high, Sears fought back. They sold off those arms not directly related to their core business.

They began to re-focus on the retail customer. And they discontinued the Sears Catalogue.

Why?

It's simple, really. Times had changed. And management knew that Sears must change with them—or face extinction. The catalogue was no longer in step with consumer buying habits. It was big, confusing, and slowly being crushed under the weight of its own bureaucracy.

Today, Sears is well on its way to a healthy recovery. Profits are up, bureaucracy is down, and Wall Street is happy. In fact, Sears is even going back into the catalogue business. Only this time, instead of one giant book for all people, there will be three separate catalogues designed to reach three specific markets.

The Sears Catalogue has been unbundled.

We bring all this up by way of illustration. There are remarkable parallels between the story of Sears and the evolution of the advertising agency business. With one notable exception: While Sears has been able to re-engineer itself to meet the needs of an evolving marketplace, advertising agencies continue to cling stubbornly to the notion that being all things to all clients is the only way to do business.

That's why we started The Leap Partnership.

You see, we realize that the needs of today's sophisticated advertiser are different than they used to be. With the unbundling of media and research functions, clients can get superior service at a reduced cost by working with specialists in those fields.

But for the creative portion of their account, a full-service agency—with all its accompanying inefficiencies— remained the only available option.

Until now.

The Leap Partnership is a creative-only agency. By eliminating the layers of communication and bureaucratic overhead, we can maintain our focus on the one thing that matters most—the development of innovative, brand-building ideas.

Sure, it's a different way of working. But, as Sears discovered, these are different times we're living in.

If you'd like to learn more about the advantages of forming a strategic alliance with The Leap Partnership, give Fred Smith a call at 312-541-7700.

And don't forget to ask for our literature. It's not as big as the Sears Catalogue, but when it comes to creative service you'll find it contains everything you need.

TRADE
B/W 1 PAGE OR SPREAD:
SINGLE

314
ART DIRECTOR:
Bob Meagher
WRITERS:
Mike Hughes
Joe Alexander
CLIENT:
The Martin Agency
AGENCY:
The Martin Agency/
Richmond

TRADE
COLOR 1 PAGE OR
SPREAD: SINGLE

315
ART DIRECTOR:
Darrell Credeur
WRITER:
David Smith
PHOTOGRAPHER:
Craig Cutler
CLIENT:
Thomson Consumer
Electronics/RCA
AGENCY:
Ammirati & Puris/Lintas,
New York

316
ART DIRECTOR:
Bill Schwab
WRITER:
Tony Gomes
PHOTOGRAPHER:
Dennis Blachut
ILLUSTRATORS:
Gerard Huerta
Chris Moore
CLIENT:
Thomson Consumer
Electronics/RCA
AGENCY:
Ammirati & Puris/Lintas,
New York

317
ART DIRECTOR:
John Doyle
WRITER:
Jim Garaventi
PHOTOGRAPHER:
Paul Clancy
CLIENT:
MacTemps
AGENCY:
Berlin Cameron Doyle/
New York

If there's anyone out there who doesn't recognize these two dogs, please write and tell us what it's like living on the Moon.

You'd have to travel pretty far to find someone that hasn't heard of Nipper & Chipper. After all, **99% of all consumers are aware of the RCA brand.** And it doesn't take a degree in calculus to figure out that's powerful brand awareness. Your customers are practically pre-sold on RCA. Which makes your job easier. Not that we don't have confidence in your sales skills.

Here's the RCA 35" Home Theatre. Another in a successful line of RCA televisions. It has one feature your customers will definitely be looking for. The familiar RCA logo.

It's just that **over 50 million people already own an RCA consumer electronics product.** People know us. They like us. At least we assume they like us. We have one of the highest repeat purchase levels in the industry.

So it's not surprising that **RCA is the number one selling color TV brand.** A pretty impressive fact. We're also the number one selling VCR brand. Another impressive fact. But don't worry, we won't rest on our laurels. We'll continue to support the brand with an aggressive national advertising campaign. So people will always see Nipper & Chipper. Unless they live in a cold place often mistaken for green cheese.

The Moon. A cold, dark place some 250,000 miles from Earth. Believe it or not, no one there has ever heard of our popular friend Nipper and his sidekick Chipper. Poor lost souls.

It's quite simple really. Take great products. A strong brand. National advertising support. And a couple of dogs that can be used as merchandising tools. What more do you need? Just think, if you ever start selling products intergalactically, we'll be ready. **Changing Entertainment. Again.** RCA

Any of our temps could talk for hours about Windows **CONFIG.SYS** or **AUTOEXEC.BAT** filing. Just the kind of person you'd love to hire and never ride the elevator with.

Please don't get the wrong idea.

We're not saying our temps favor glasses with tape or shirts with pocket protectors.

It's just that they're quite knowledgeable, even passionate, about working on computers.

Which is only natural, considering they've passed the toughest tests in the business and enjoy the motivation of full-time benefits.

If that sounds like someone you wouldn't mind being stuck with when you need computer help, just call us at 1-800-MACTEMPS.

And if you're ever in the elevator with the person we send over, don't worry. Like everyone else, they can also talk about the weather.

MacTemps

TRADE
COLOR 1 PAGE OR
SPREAD: SINGLE

318
ART DIRECTOR:
Carie Meier
WRITER:
Ryan Ebner
ILLUSTRATOR:
Hanna-Barbara Studios
CLIENT:
The Cartoon Network
AGENCY:
Butler Shine & Stern/
Sausalito

319
ART DIRECTOR:
Christopher Cole
WRITER:
Eric Sorensen
PHOTOGRAPHER:
Joe Lampi
CLIENT:
Great Faces
AGENCY:
Chuck Ruhr Advertising/
Minneapolis

320
ART DIRECTOR:
Bill Karow
WRITER:
Scott Wild
PHOTOGRAPHER:
Gary Hush
CLIENT:
Dr. Martens
AGENCY:
Cole & Weber/Portland

321
ART DIRECTOR:
Tom Lichtenheld
WRITER:
Luke Sullivan
PHOTOGRAPHER:
Mark LaFavor
CLIENT:
Ameritech Enhanced
Business Services
AGENCY:
Fallon McElligott/
Minneapolis

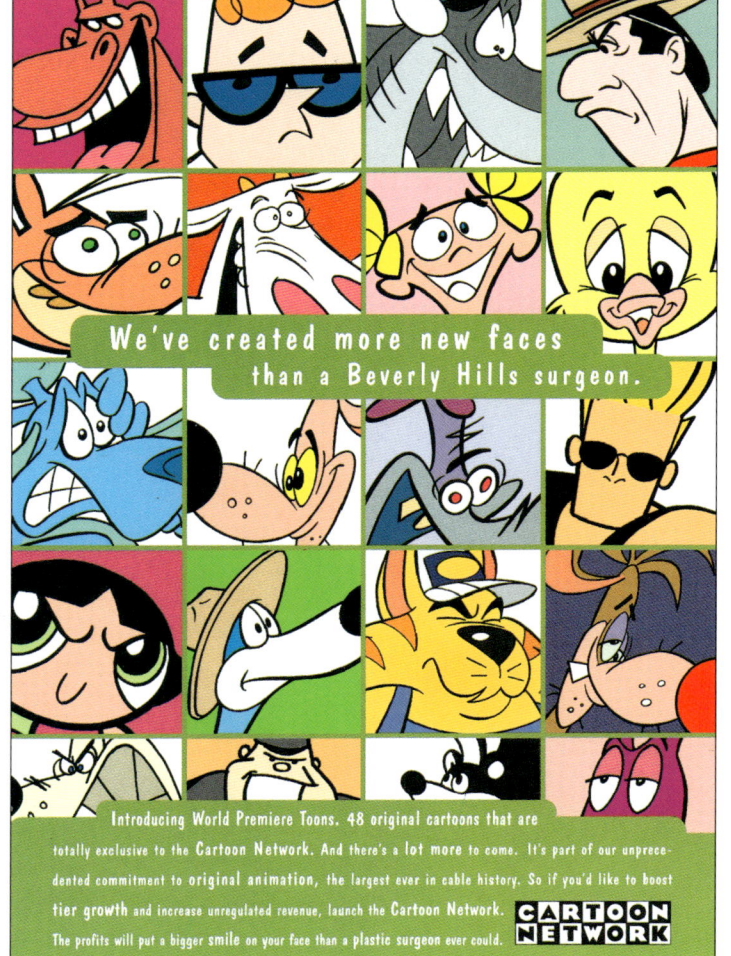

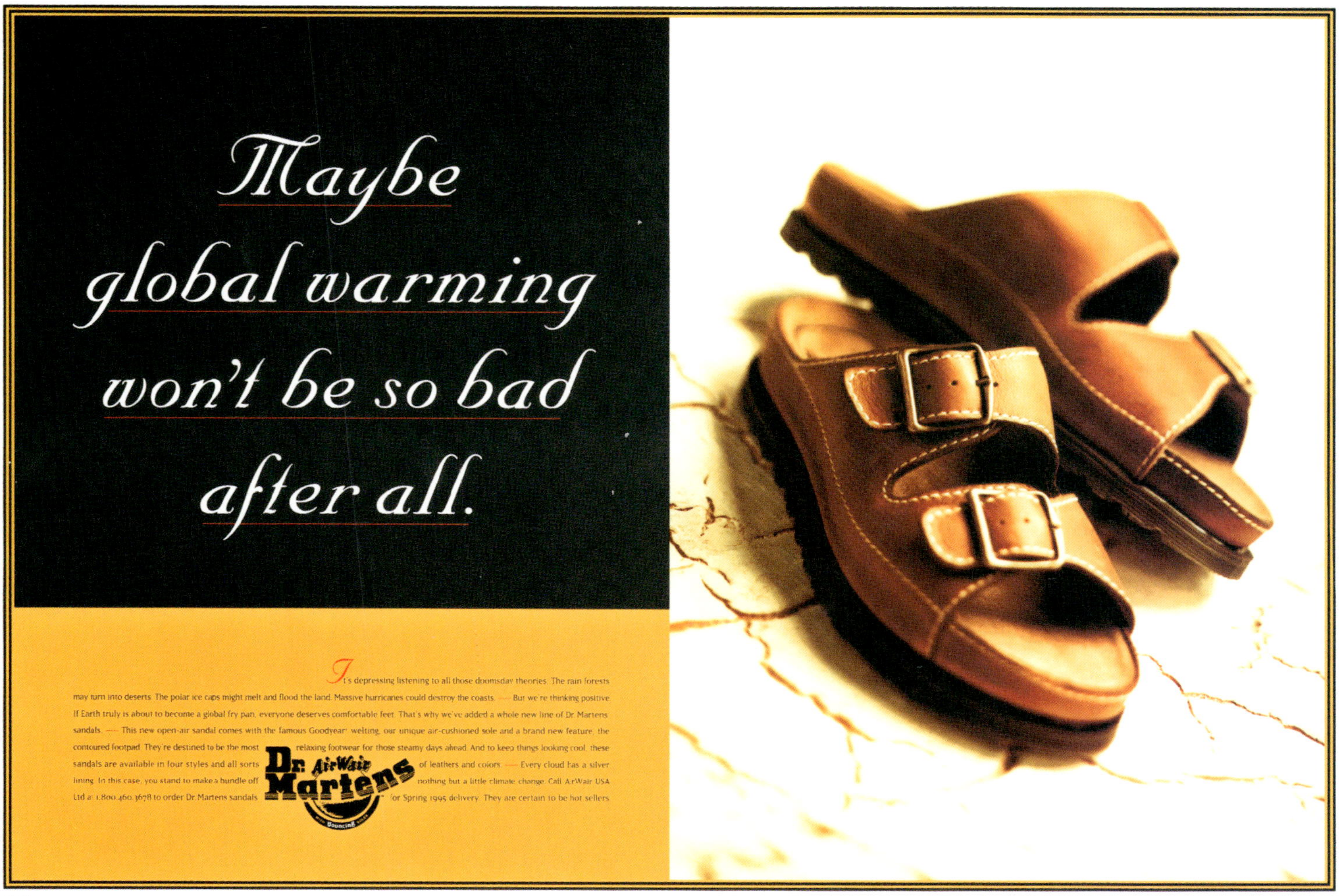
Maybe global warming won't be so bad after all.
It's depressing listening to all those doomsday theories. The rain forests may turn into deserts. The polar ice caps might melt and flood the land. Massive hurricanes could destroy the coasts. — But we're thinking positive. If Earth truly is about to become a global fry pan, everyone deserves comfortable feet. That's why we've added a whole new line of Dr. Martens sandals. — This new open-air sandal comes with the famous Goodyear welting, our unique air-cushioned sole and a brand new feature, the contoured footpad. They're destined to be the most relaxing footwear for those steamy days ahead. And to keep things looking cool, these sandals are available in four styles and all sorts of leathers and colors. — Every cloud has a silver lining. In this case, you stand to make a bundle off nothing but a little climate change. Call AirWair USA Ltd at 1.800.460.3678 to order Dr. Martens sandals for Spring 1995 delivery. They are certain to be hot sellers.
Dr. AirWair Martens

320

Advanced technology isn't much good if you don't know how to use it.
At Ameritech, we do. We also know that in your business, you depend on technology to move information quickly and service your customers.
Every day we partner with banks to provide remote banking using video and screen phone technologies. We help insurance companies process claims faster and more efficiently using our advanced imaging systems. And we help brokerage firms expedite settlements on trades with Confirm and Pay, our innovative new solution based on fax and messaging technologies.
As you can see, we have a lot of ideas in place today. Ideas that can help put you ahead of the competition and in the passing lane of the information highway. To learn more, call 1-800-719-5822, extension 240.
Ameritech
Your Link to Better Communication

321

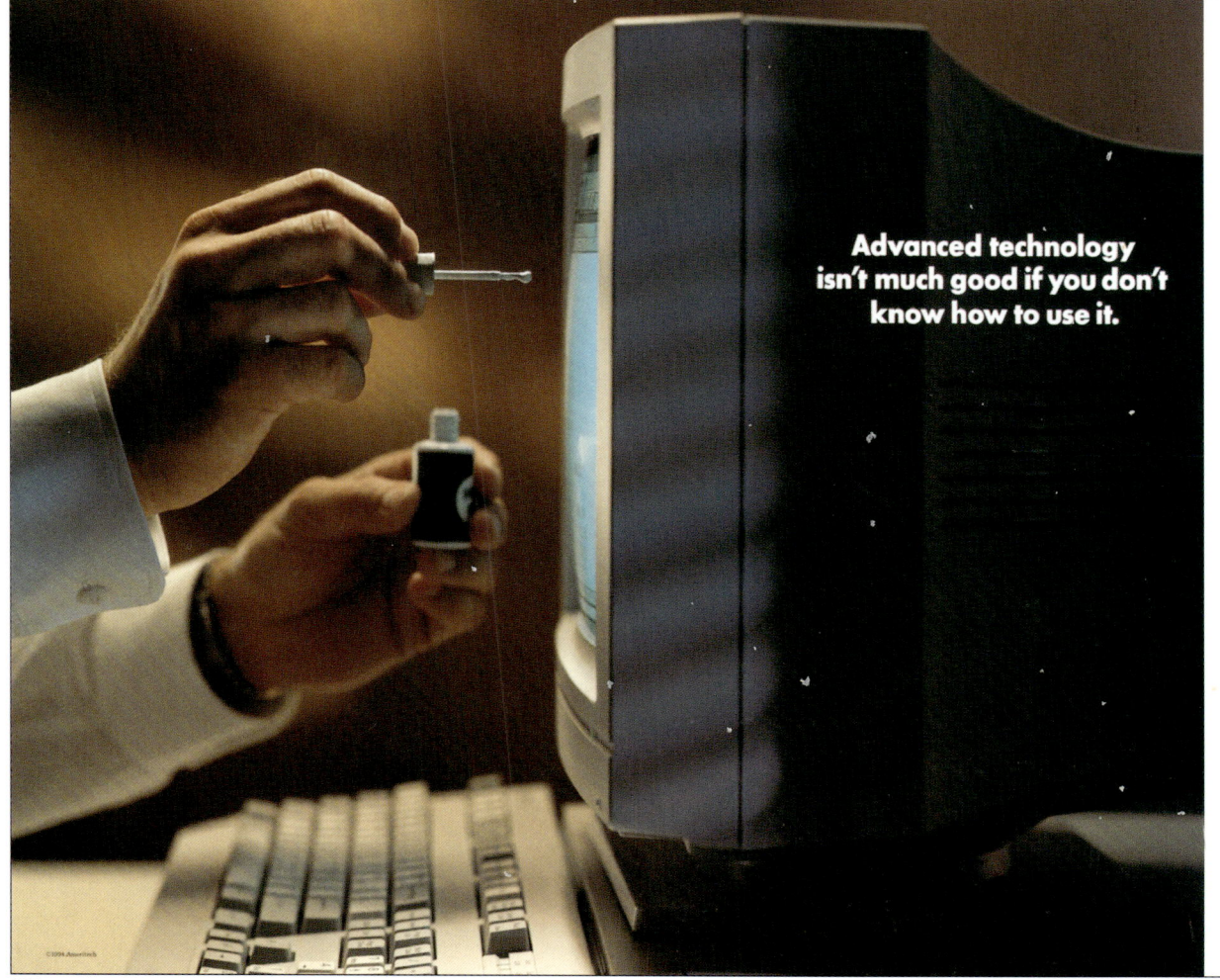

TRADE
COLOR 1 PAGE OR
SPREAD: SINGLE

322
ART DIRECTOR:
Tom Lichtenheld
WRITER:
Luke Sullivan
ILLUSTRATOR:
Tom Lichtenheld
CLIENT:
Ameritech Enhanced Business Services
AGENCY:
Fallon McElligott/ Minneapolis

323
ART DIRECTOR:
Tom Lichtenheld
WRITER:
Luke Sullivan
PHOTOGRAPHER:
Buck Holzemer
CLIENT:
Ameritech Enhanced Business Services
AGENCY:
Fallon McElligott/ Minneapolis

324
ART DIRECTOR:
Tom Lichtenheld
WRITER:
Luke Sullivan
PHOTOGRAPHER:
Buck Holzemer
CLIENT:
Ameritech Enhanced Business Services
AGENCY:
Fallon McElligott/ Minneapolis

325
ART DIRECTOR:
Tom Lichtenheld
WRITER:
Luke Sullivan
PHOTOGRAPHER:
Craig Perman
CLIENT:
Ameritech Enhanced Business Services
AGENCY:
Fallon McElligott/ Minneapolis

Basically, we sell the tape.

Your company has a mainframe at headquarters and computers in the branch offices. Plus a phone system. Your customers have computers. And your key suppliers have computers.

Yet with all that horsepower, how come you still can't get information from one place to another?

Well, you can. Call Ameritech. We have a long history of designing solutions for a variety of business problems. And with our broad range of products and services, we can connect all the systems you need access to; making the information your people need available anywhere and anytime.

Welcome to the passing lane on the information highway. Just call 1-800-719-5822, extension 17.

Ameritech
Your Best Link To Better Communication

By June of '95, the SEC will require that you settle all security transaction requests in three days. You can add personnel to handle increased paperwork and hope that you'll conform to the regulation. Or you can call Ameritech and ask about Confirm and Pay,™ a service that can confirm and settle all your trades, often within 24 hours. Probably for less than what you're paying now. With Confirm and Pay, confirmations are automatically sent out on your own company forms by fax, e-mail, telex, or mail. You can also, if you choose, debit your customer's bank account via electronic funds transfer. Less printing. Less handling. In less time. And all with less hassle. For details, call Ameritech today at the number below.

Ameritech
Your Link to Better Communication

Two things you can tear out to deal with the latest SEC regulation.

TRADE
COLOR 1 PAGE OR
SPREAD: SINGLE

326
ART DIRECTOR:
Bob Brihn
WRITER:
Dean Buckhorn
PHOTOGRAPHER:
Joe Lampi
CLIENT:
AudioMaster
AGENCY:
Fallon McElligott/
Minneapolis

327
ART DIRECTOR:
Joe Paprocki
WRITER:
Luke Sullivan
PHOTOGRAPHER:
Joe Lampi
CLIENT:
Family Life
AGENCY:
Fallon McElligott/
Minneapolis

328
ART DIRECTOR:
Joe Paprocki
WRITER:
Luke Sullivan
PHOTOGRAPHER:
Craig Perman
CLIENT:
Family Life
AGENCY:
Fallon McElligott/
Minneapolis

329
ART DIRECTOR:
Mark Johnson
WRITER:
Mike Gibbs
PHOTOGRAPHER:
Shawn Michienzi
CLIENT:
Lee Printwear
AGENCY:
Fallon McElligott/
Minneapolis

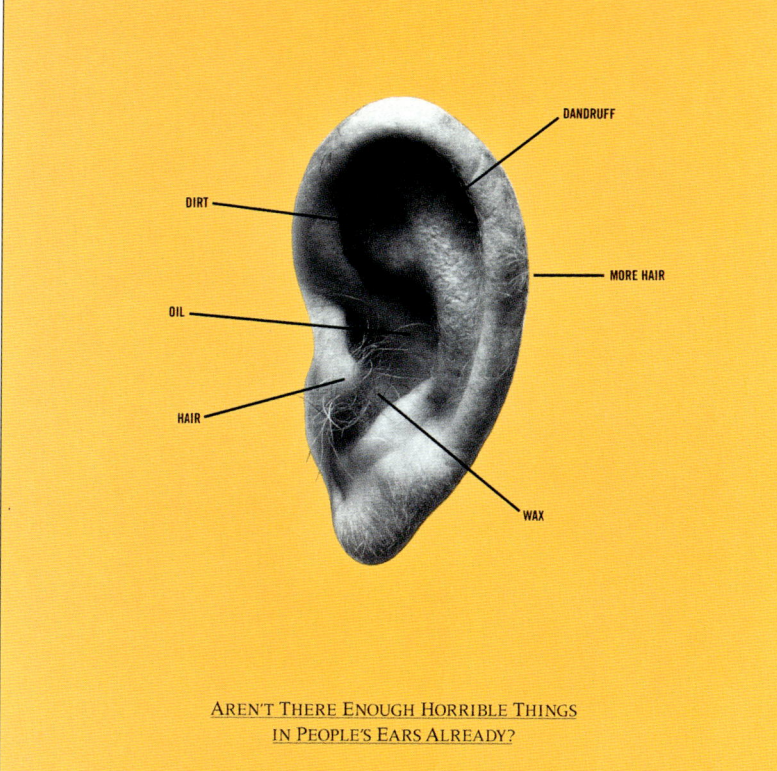

On your deathbed, will you wish you spent more time with the company controller?

The Baby Boomers finally have families of their own. They want to do it right this time around. Only one magazine is written just for them.

MACHINE WASH WARM

ONLY NON-CHLORINE BLEACH

TUMBLE DRY LOW

GENEROUS CUT

The grade-A fit and choice cut customers hunger for. We've added 2" in circumference to our Lee Total Cotton tees and 9 oz. 50/50 Heavyweight sweatshirts. Now you get more prime printing area. And a brand name consumers can sink their teeth into.

Lee
The brand that fits.

**TRADE
COLOR 1 PAGE OR
SPREAD: SINGLE**

330
ART DIRECTOR:
Ellen Steinberg
WRITER:
Mike Lescarbeau
CLIENT:
Nikon
AGENCY:
Fallon McElligott/
Minneapolis

331
ART DIRECTOR:
Ellen Steinberg
WRITER:
Mike Lescarbeau
CLIENT:
Nikon
AGENCY:
Fallon McElligott/
Minneapolis

332
ART DIRECTOR:
Bob Barrie
WRITER:
Dean Buckhorn
PHOTOGRAPHER:
David Burnett
CLIENT:
Time Magazine
AGENCY:
Fallon McElligott/
Minneapolis

333
ART DIRECTOR:
Dean Hanson
WRITER:
Tina Hall
PHOTOGRAPHER:
Buck Holzemer
CLIENT:
Weyerhaeuser Paper
Company
AGENCY:
Fallon McElligott/
Minneapolis

330

331

It was centuries of hatred.

It was years of bloodshed.

It was less than a minute on the evening news.

Understanding comes with TIME.

332

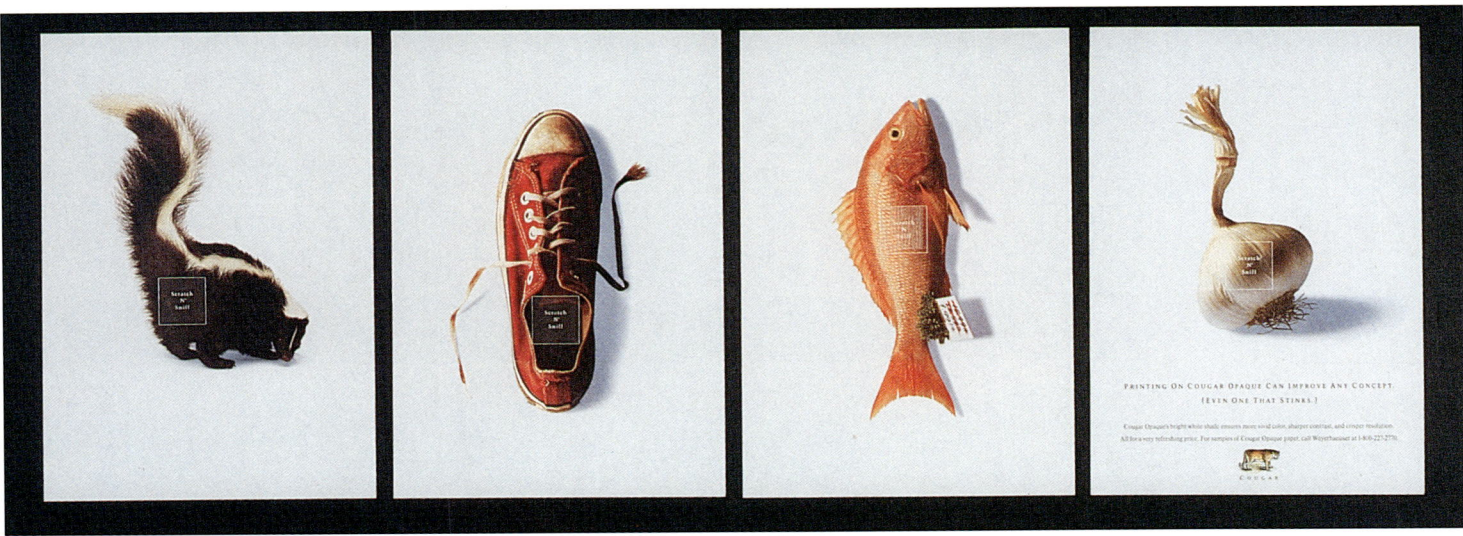

333

TRADE
COLOR 1 PAGE OR
SPREAD: SINGLE

334
ART DIRECTOR:
Rachel Gorenstein
WRITER:
Blake Daley
PHOTOGRAPHERS:
Tom Tracy
RJ Muna
CLIENT:
Norwegian Cruise Line
AGENCY:
Goodby Silverstein & Partners/San Francisco

335
ART DIRECTOR:
Steve Mitchell
WRITER:
Doug Adkins
PHOTOGRAPHER:
Mark LaFavor
CLIENT:
Parallel Productions
AGENCY:
Hunt Murray/
Minneapolis

336
ART DIRECTOR:
Mark Cohen
WRITER:
David Locascio
PHOTOGRAPHER:
Richard Dailey
CLIENT:
Warner Bros. Records
AGENCY:
Kresser Stein Robaire/
Santa Monica

337
ART DIRECTOR:
Greg Bokor
WRITER:
Kara Goodrich
PHOTOGRAPHER:
Nora Scarlett
CLIENT:
Polaroid
AGENCY:
Leonard/Monahan,
Providence

334

335

TRADE
COLOR 1 PAGE OR
SPREAD: SINGLE

338
ART DIRECTOR:
Bob Meagher
WRITER:
Joe Alexander
PHOTOGRAPHERS:
Mark Scott
Dean Hawthorne
CLIENT:
Wrangler Company
AGENCY:
The Martin Agency/
Richmond

339
ART DIRECTOR:
Rick Rabe
WRITER:
David Leite
PHOTOGRAPHER:
Brigette Lancombe
CLIENT:
The Wool Bureau
AGENCY:
Merkley Newman Harty/
New York

340
ART DIRECTOR:
Larry Frey
WRITER:
Glenn Cole
PHOTOGRAPHER:
Peggy Sirota
CLIENT:
ESPN
AGENCY:
Wieden & Kennedy/
Portland

TRADE
LESS THAN A PAGE
B/W OR COLOR: SINGLE

341
ART DIRECTOR:
Chuck Finkle
WRITER:
Dean Hacohen
PHOTOGRAPHER:
Ilan Rubin
CLIENT:
NYNEX Business to
Business Directory
AGENCY:
Goldsmith/Jeffrey,
New York

338

339

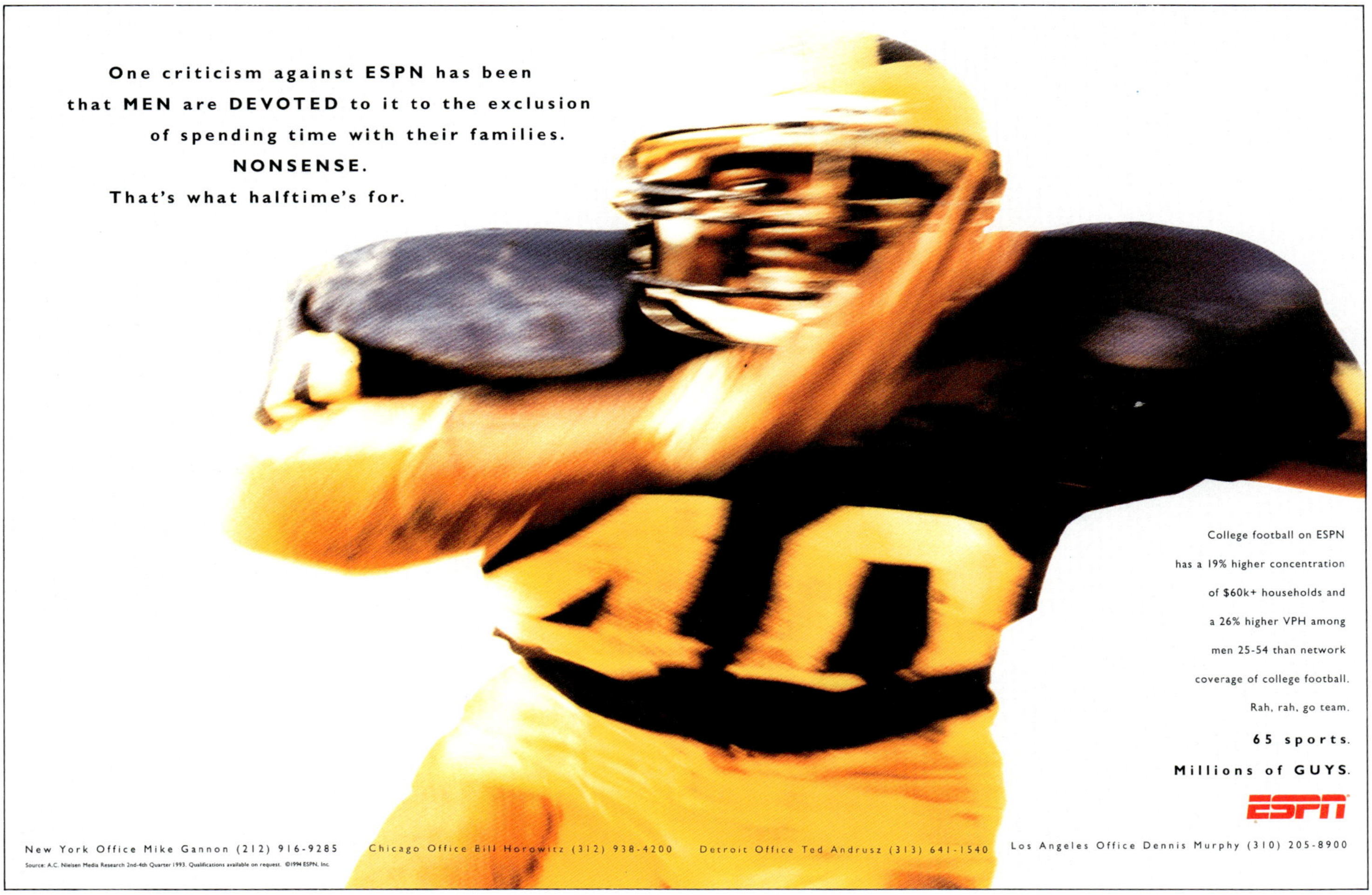
One criticism against ESPN has been
that MEN are DEVOTED to it to the exclusion
of spending time with their families.
NONSENSE.
That's what halftime's for.
College football on ESPN
has a 19% higher concentration
of $60k+ households and
a 26% higher VPH among
men 25-54 than network
coverage of college football.
Rah, rah, go team.
65 sports.
Millions of GUYS.
ESPN
New York Office Mike Gannon (212) 916-9285
Chicago Office Bill Horowitz (312) 938-4200
Detroit Office Ted Andrusz (313) 641-1540
Los Angeles Office Dennis Murphy (310) 205-8900
Source: A.C. Nielsen Media Research 2nd-4th Quarter 1993. Qualifications available on request. ©1994 ESPN, Inc.

340

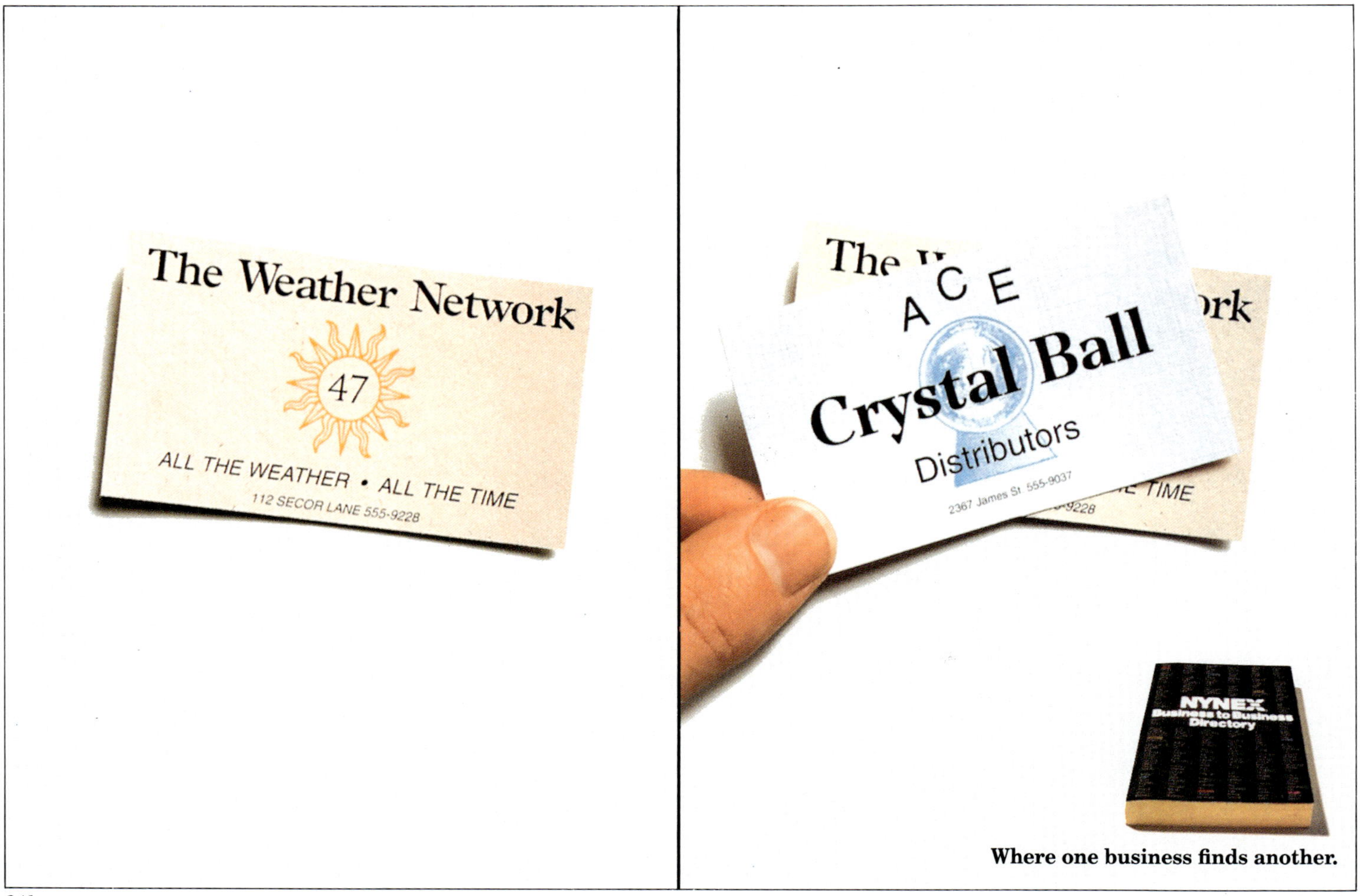
The Weather Network
47
ALL THE WEATHER • ALL THE TIME
112 SECOR LANE 555-9228
ACE
Crystal Ball
Distributors
2367 James St. 555-9037
NYNEX
Business to Business
Directory
Where one business finds another.

TRADE
LESS THAN A PAGE
B/W OR COLOR: SINGLE

342
ART DIRECTOR:
Mark Wenneker
WRITER:
Derrick Ogilvie
PHOTOGRAPHER:
Jamie Biondo
CLIENT:
Clark Candy Company
AGENCY:
McCann-Erickson/
San Francisco

343
ART DIRECTOR:
Brian Burke
WRITER:
Chris Wigert
PHOTOGRAPHER:
Steve Umland
CLIENT:
Fred Arbogast
AGENCY:
TBWA Wolfe Freeman/
St. Louis

TRADE
ANY SIZE
B/W OR COLOR:
CAMPAIGN

344
ART DIRECTOR:
Tom Lichtenheld
WRITER:
Luke Sullivan
PHOTOGRAPHERS:
Buck Holzemer
Mark LaFavor
CLIENT:
Ameritech Enhanced
Business Services
AGENCY:
Fallon McElligott/
Minneapolis

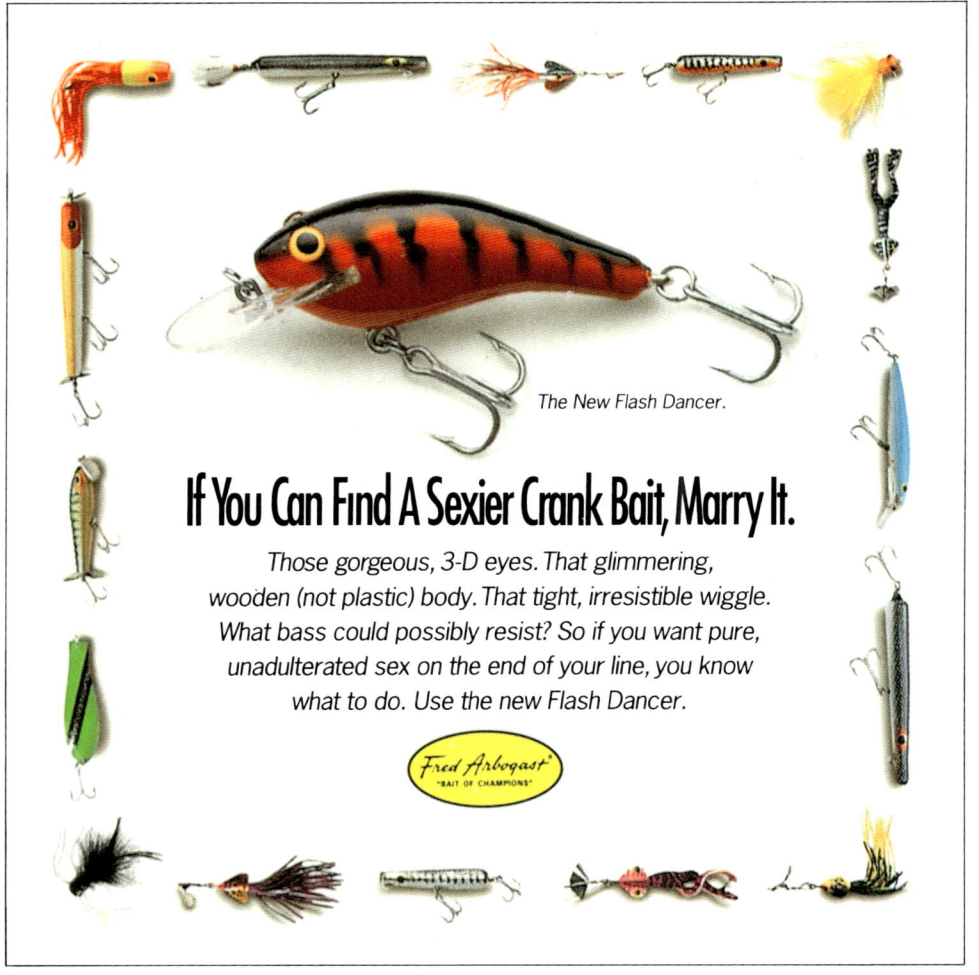

TRADE
ANY SIZE
B/W OR COLOR:
CAMPAIGN

345
ART DIRECTOR:
Ellen Steinberg
WRITER:
Mike Lescarbeau
CLIENT:
Nikon
AGENCY:
Fallon McElligott/
Minneapolis

346
ART DIRECTOR:
Henriette Lienke
WRITER:
Tom Miller
CLIENT:
Crain's New York Business
AGENCY:
Goldsmith/Jeffrey, New York

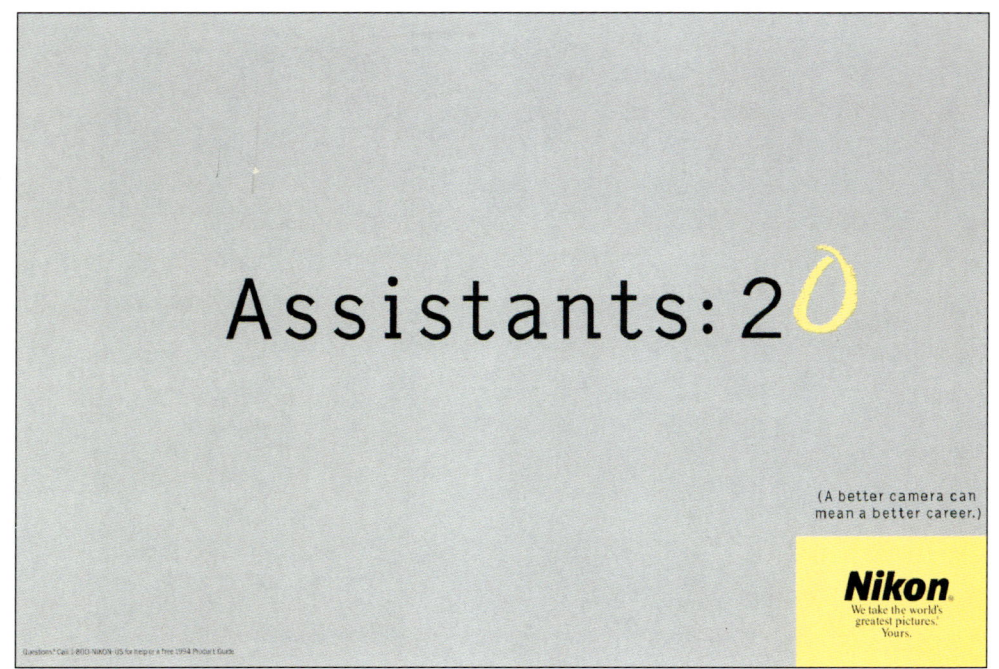

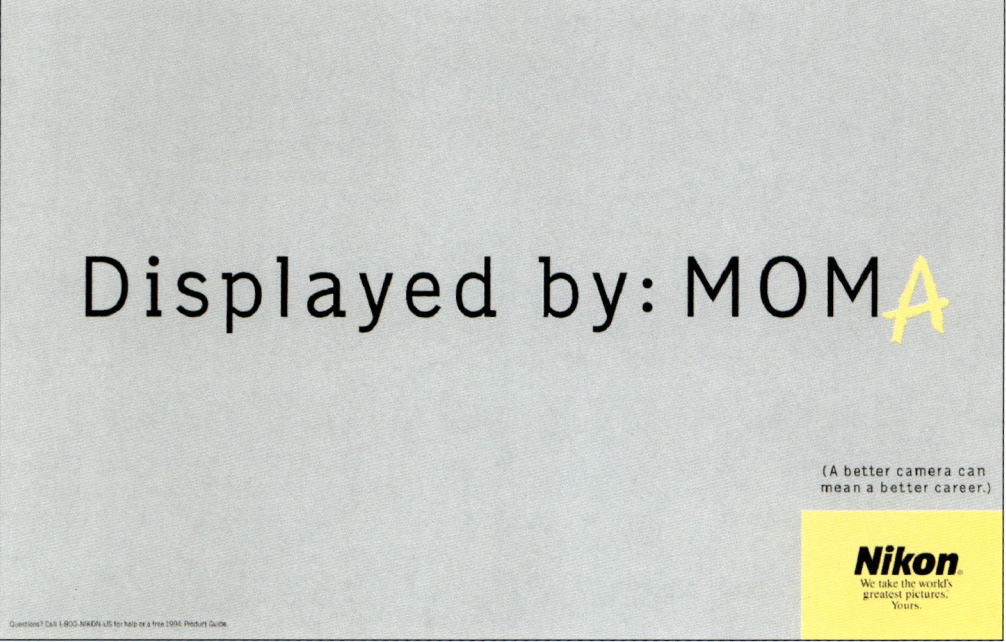

TRADE
ANY SIZE
B/W OR COLOR:
CAMPAIGN

347
ART DIRECTOR:
Chuck Finkle
WRITER:
Dean Hacohen
PHOTOGRAPHER:
Ilan Rubin
CLIENT:
NYNEX Business to Business Directory
AGENCY:
Goldsmith/Jeffrey, New York

COLLATERAL
BROCHURES OTHER
THAN BY MAIL

348
ART DIRECTOR:
Vinny Matassa
WRITERS:
Sheldon Clay
Jim Nelson
PHOTOGRAPHER:
Clint Clemens
CLIENT:
Harley-Davidson
AGENCY:
Carmichael Lynch/ Minneapolis

349
ART DIRECTOR:
Sally Morrow
WRITER:
David Baldwin
PHOTOGRAPHERS:
Lars Topelmann
Gary Hush
CLIENT:
Dr. Martens
AGENCY:
Cole & Weber/Portland

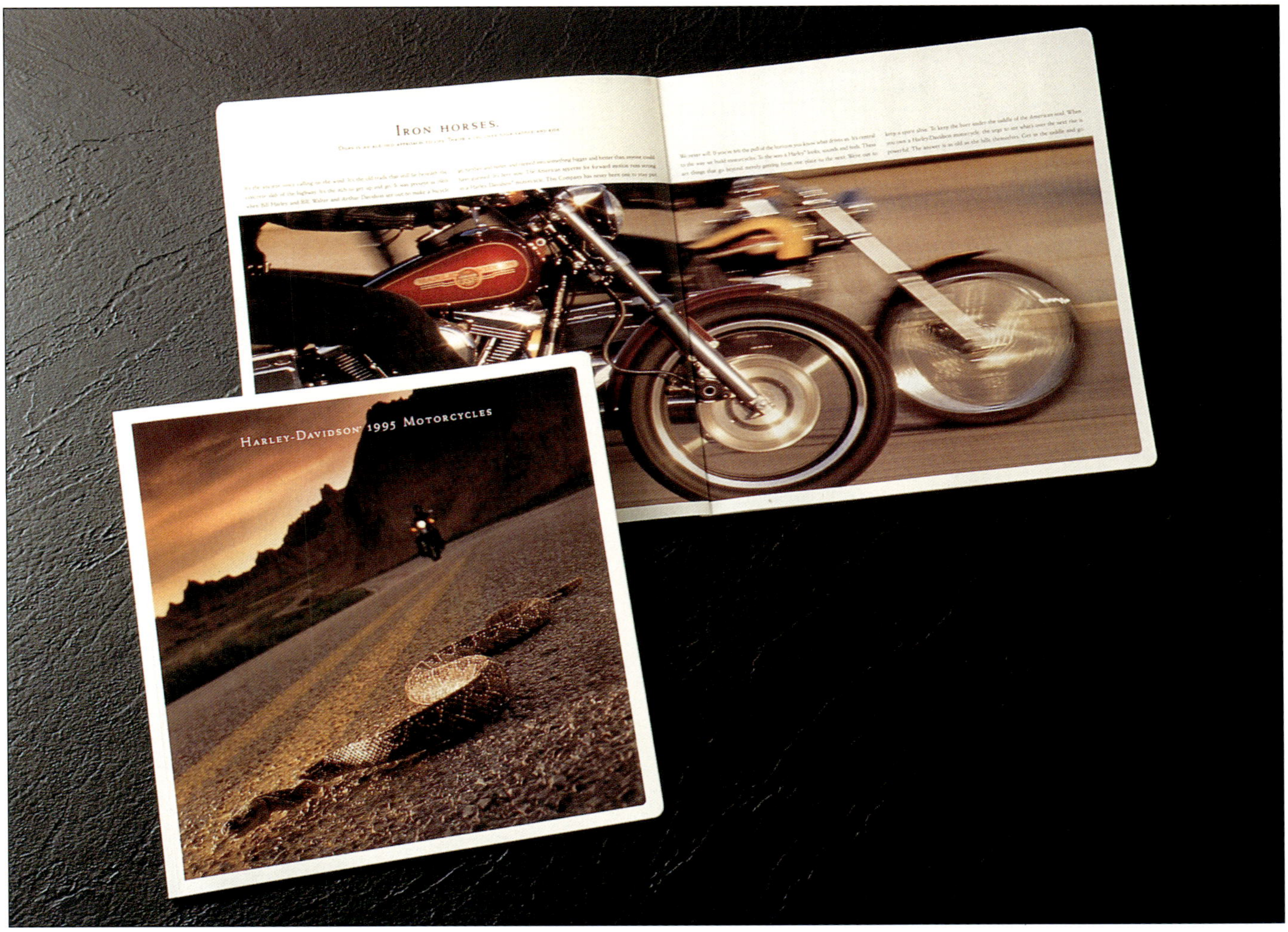
Iron horses.
Harley-Davidson 1995 Motorcycles

348

Walk
a mile
in somebody else's
shoes--
and
you'll
understand
their problems--
Walk
a mile in
somebody else's
Dr. Martens--
and
you probably
won't
give them back.

349

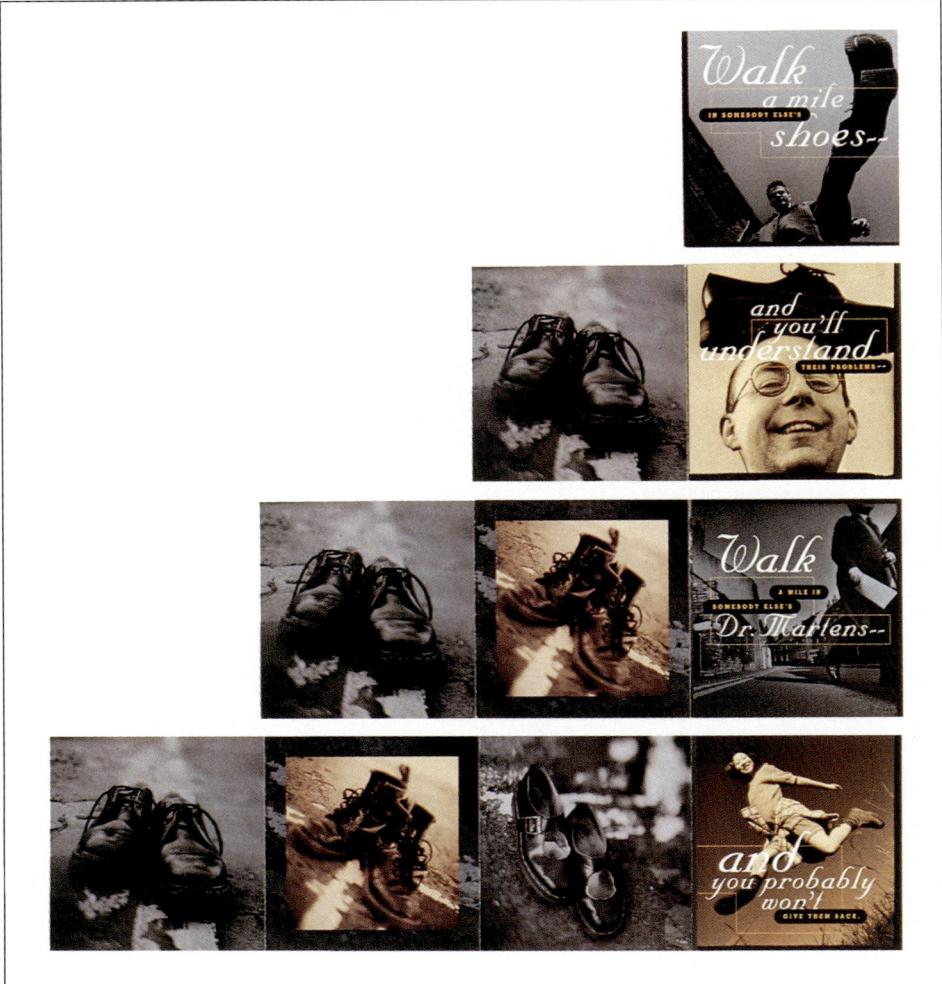

COLLATERAL
BROCHURES OTHER
THAN BY MAIL

350
ART DIRECTORS:
Peter Rae
Paul Holden
ILLUSTRATORS:
Mike Chan
Dennis Ou
PHOTOGRAPHER:
Arthur Schulten
CLIENT:
Reebok International
AGENCY:
Leo Burnett/Hong Kong

351
ART DIRECTOR:
Julie Markle
WRITER:
Barnaby Southgate
PHOTOGRAPHER:
Rick Rusing
ILLUSTRATORS:
Paul Cox
Jerzy Kolacz
James Marsh
CLIENT:
General Motors
of Canada/
Oldsmobile Aurora
AGENCY:
MacLaren Lintas/Toronto

352
ART DIRECTOR:
John Swisher
WRITERS:
Laurie Habeeb
John Swisher
PHOTOGRAPHER:
Tom Cwenar
CLIENT:
Family Health Council
AGENCY:
Marc Advertising/
Pittsburgh

350

351

Jessica Rose Tate
Born October 15
10:43 a.m.
Weighed 7 lbs. 3 ozs.
She Had All Ten Fingers
And All Ten Toes.

There's Only One Complication.

This Is Her Mom.

COLLATERAL
BROCHURES OTHER
THAN BY MAIL

353
ART DIRECTORS:
Steve Sandstrom
Charlotte Moore
WRITERS:
Jean Rhode, Peter Wegner
ILLUSTRATORS:
Daniel Clowes
Charles Burns
PHOTOGRAPHER:
Doug Petty
CLIENT:
The Coca-Cola Company
AGENCY:
Sandstrom Design/
Portland

354
ART DIRECTORS:
Scott Bremner
Gabrielle Mayeur
WRITERS:
Rebecca Rivera
Neil Szigethy
ILLUSTRATOR:
Joe Dominic
PHOTOGRAPHERS:
Craig Cutler, RJ Muna
Vic Huber, Rick Rusing
Holly Stewart, Bret Lopez
Michael Ruppert
CLIENT:
Lexus
AGENCY:
Team One Advertising/
El Segundo, CA

COLLATERAL
SALES KITS

355
ART DIRECTORS:
Paul Curtin
Keith Anderson
WRITER:
Rob Price
PHOTOGRAPHERS:
Jim Erickson
James Wojack
Bruce Deboar
CLIENT:
Haggar Apparel Company
AGENCY:
Goodby Silverstein &
Partners/San Francisco

356
ART DIRECTORS:
Freeman Lau Siu Hong
Eddy Yu Chi Kong
DESIGNERS:
Freeman Lau Siu Hong
Eddy Yu Chi Kong
Janny Lee Yin Wa
PHOTOGRAPHERS:
CK Wong, Idea Vision
CLIENT:
Membership Etc.
AGENCY:
Kan Tai-Keung Design/
Hong Kong

353

354

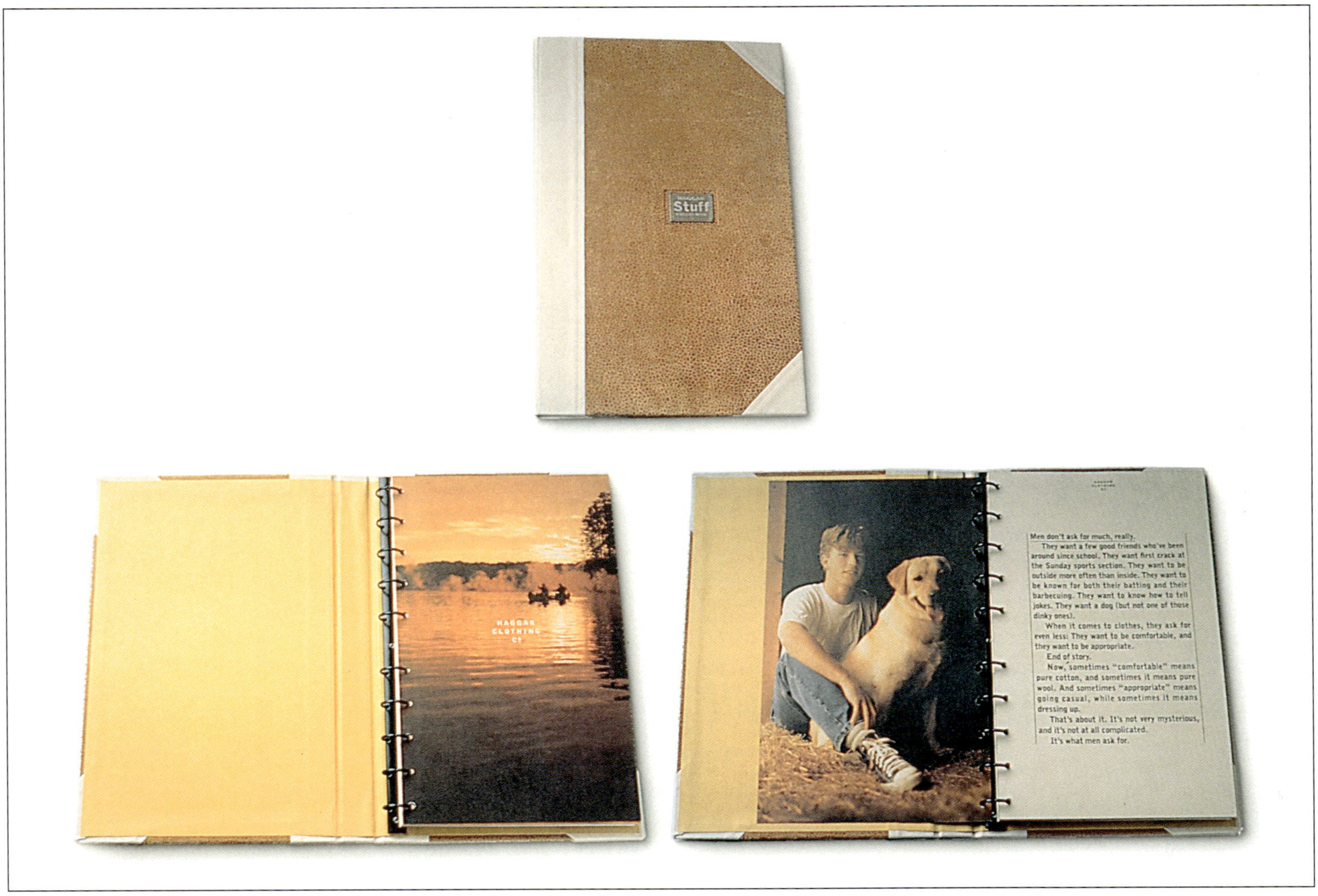
Stuff
HAGGAR CLOTHING CO
Men don't ask for much, really.
They want a few good friends who've been around since school. They want first crack at the Sunday sports section. They want to be outside more often than inside. They want to be known for both their batting and their barbecuing. They want to know how to tell jokes. They want a dog (but not one of those dinky ones).
When it comes to clothes, they ask for even less: They want to be comfortable, and they want to be appropriate.
End of story.
Now, sometimes "comfortable" means pure cotton, and sometimes it means pure wool. And sometimes "appropriate" means going casual, while sometimes it means dressing up.
That's about it. It's not very mysterious, and it's not at all complicated.
It's what men ask for.

355

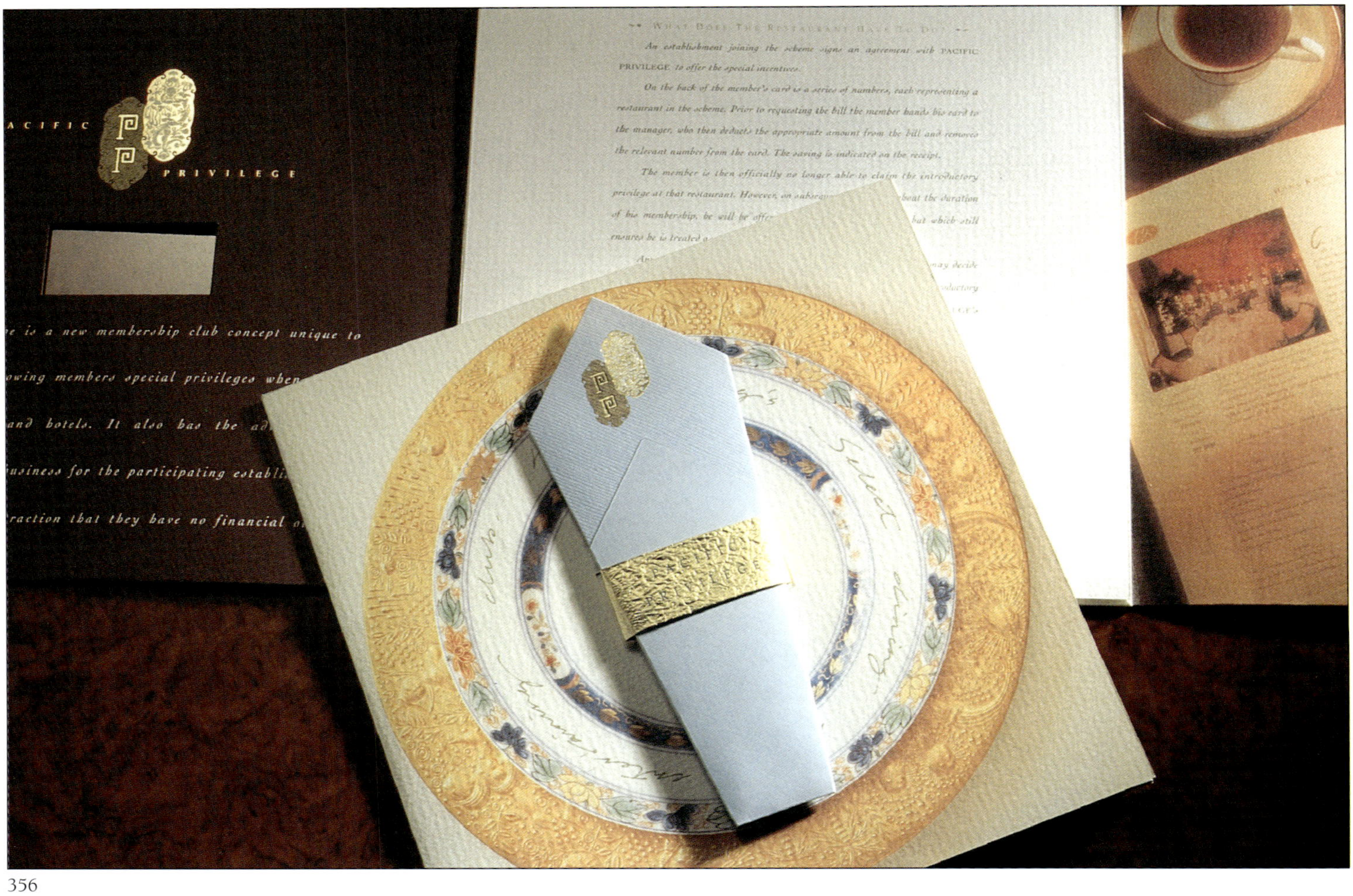
PACIFIC
PRIVILEGE
What Does The Restaurant Have To Do?
An establishment joining the scheme signs an agreement with PACIFIC PRIVILEGE to offer the special incentives.
On the back of the member's card is a series of numbers, each representing a restaurant in the scheme. Prior to requesting the bill the member hands his card to the manager, who then deducts the appropriate amount from the bill and removes the relevant number from the card. The saving is indicated on the receipt.
The member is then officially no longer able to claim the introductory privilege at that restaurant.
is a new membership club concept unique to
owing members special privileges when
and hotels. It also has the
business for the participating
traction that they have no financial

356

COLLATERAL
DIRECT MAIL: SINGLE

357
ART DIRECTOR:
Ronnie Cooke
WRITER:
Glenn O'Brien
ILLUSTRATOR:
Jean-Philippe Delhomme
CLIENT:
Barneys New York
AGENCY:
Barneys New York Advertising/New York

358
ART DIRECTOR:
Terry Schneider
WRITER:
Greg Eiden
PHOTOGRAPHER:
Pete Stone
CLIENT:
Columbia Sportswear
AGENCY:
Borders Perrin & Norrander/Portland

359
WRITERS:
Rob Schapiro
Ty Harper
CLIENT:
Richmond Ad Club
AGENCY:
Earle Palmer Brown/Richmond

360
ART DIRECTOR:
Joe Paprocki
WRITER:
Doug de Grood
CLIENT:
The Lee Company
AGENCY:
Fallon McElligott/Minneapolis

357

358

359

(MUSIC: MOTEL 6 THEME)

TOM: Hi, Tom Bodett here for the Richmond Ad Club. You know, I've made a good living as the spokesman in all those Motel 6 radio commercials. But, the truth is somebody else wrote most of 'em. Hard to believe, I know. Well his name's David Fowler and he's comin' to Richmond to talk to you about advertising. He's won a whole bunch of national awards for his work. A lot more in some years, a little less in others, but always one heck of a showing. Now, I know what you're saying: "Tom, just how much is this gonna cost me?" Well, that's the beauty of this whole thing. It's free for members and just forty bucks for non-members. For that you get to rub elbows with a big time advertising guy and eat your fill of pate de foie gras, whatever that is. So come on down to the Commonwealth Club, Tuesday, March 22nd. The small talk starts at 5:30 and Dave'll start a little bit later. For reservations call 747-7855 by Friday, March 18th. I'm Tom Bodett for the Richmond Ad Club, and we'll keep a seat saved for you.

360

COLLATERAL
DIRECT MAIL: SINGLE

361
ART DIRECTOR:
Todd Grant
WRITER:
Bo Coyner
PHOTOGRAPHER:
Clint Clemens
CLIENT:
Porsche
AGENCY:
Goodby Silverstein & Partners/San Francisco

362
ART DIRECTOR:
Anthony Katalinic
WRITER:
Michael Hush
CLIENT:
Hannah Dee
AGENCY:
Hush-a-linic Advertising/Chicago

363
ART DIRECTOR:
Megan Wisheart
WRITER:
Andrew Cox
CLIENT:
United Distillers Australia
AGENCY:
Leo Burnett Connaghan & May/North Sydney

364
ART DIRECTOR:
John Scavnicky
WRITER:
Craig Astler
CLIENT:
Willen Dental Associates
AGENCY:
Meldrum & Fewsmith Advertising/Cleveland

361

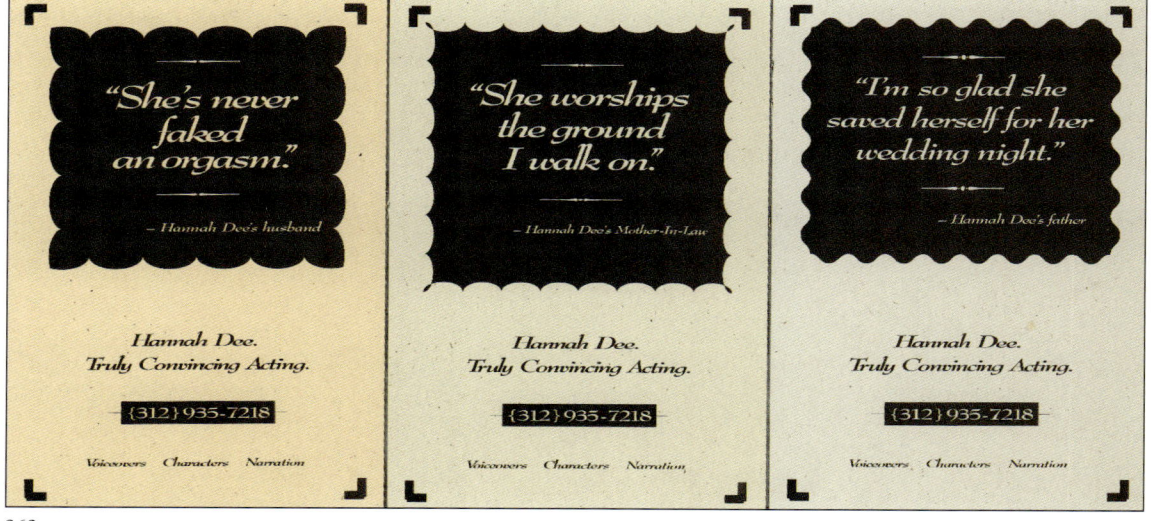
362

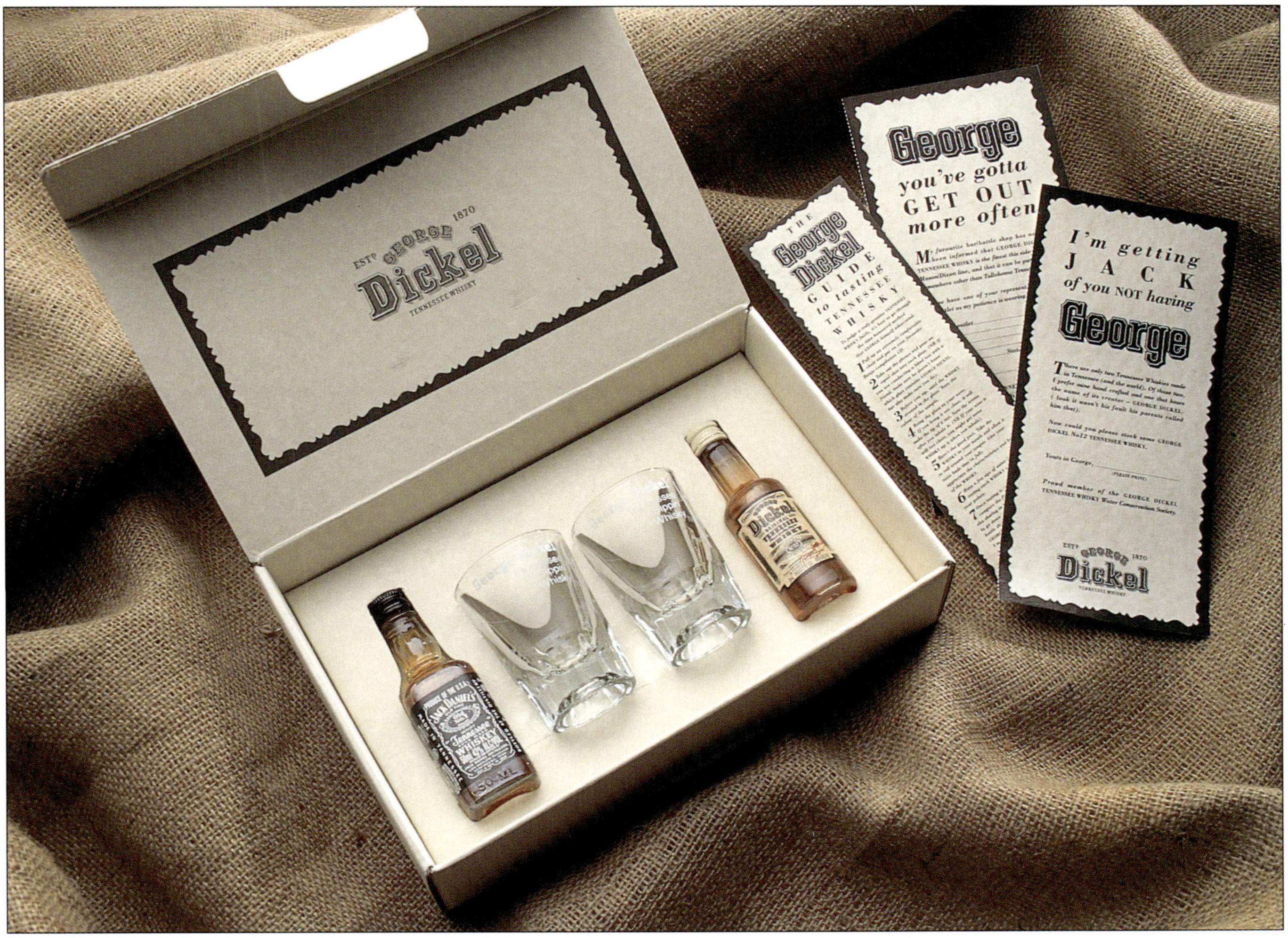
ESTD GEORGE 1870
Dickel
TENNESSEE WHISKY
THE George Dickel GUIDE to tasting TENNESSEE WHISKY
George
you've gotta
GET OUT
more often
I'm getting
J A C K
of you NOT having
George
There are only two Tennessee Whiskies made in Tennessee (and the world). Of those two, I prefer mine hand crafted and one that bears the name of its creator – GEORGE DICKEL. (look it wasn't his fault his parents called him that).
Now could you please stock some GEORGE DICKEL No.12 TENNESSEE WHISKY.
Yours in George,
(PLEASE PRINT)
Proud member of the GEORGE DICKEL TENNESSEE WHISKY Water Conservation Society.
ESTD GEORGE 1870
Dickel
TENNESSEE WHISKY

363

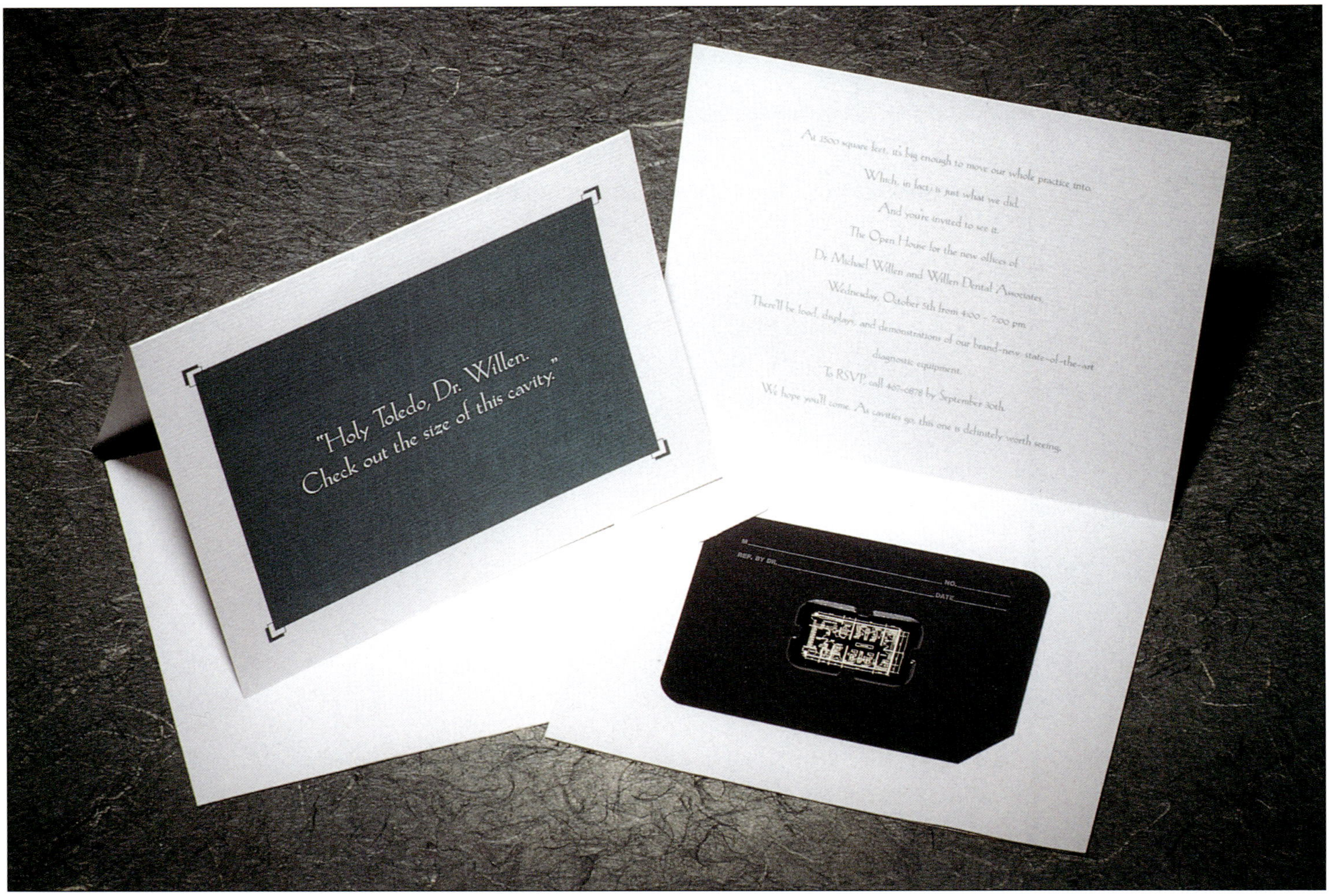
"Holy Toledo, Dr. Willen.
Check out the size of this cavity."
At 1500 square feet, it's big enough to move our whole practice into.
Which, in fact, is just what we did.
And you're invited to see it.
The Open House for the new offices of
Dr. Michael Willen and Willen Dental Associates,
Wednesday, October 5th from 4:00 - 7:00 pm.
There'll be food, displays, and demonstrations of our brand-new state-of-the-art
diagnostic equipment.
To RSVP, call 467-6878 by September 30th.
We hope you'll come. As cavities go, this one is definitely worth seeing.
REF. BY DR.
NO.
DATE

364

COLLATERAL
DIRECT MAIL: SINGLE

365
ART DIRECTOR:
Robert Hamilton
WRITER:
Tim Cawley
CLIENT:
Zarod Paving
AGENCY:
Pagano Schenck & Kay/Boston

366
ART DIRECTORS:
Eric C. King
Andrew Christou
WRITER:
Stephen P. Gill
CLIENT:
Dennis Laminating
AGENCY:
The Trauma Unit/Boston

367
ART DIRECTORS:
Eric C. King
Andrew Christou
WRITER:
Stephen P. Gill
CLIENT:
Dennis Laminating
AGENCY:
The Trauma Unit/Boston

368
ART DIRECTOR:
Brad Ramsey
WRITER:
Jeff Cole
CLIENT:
Atlanta Print Production Association
AGENCY:
Tucker Wayne/Luckie & Company, Atlanta

369
ART DIRECTOR:
Heward Jue
WRITER:
Troy Torrison
CLIENT:
The Nation
AGENCY:
Weiss Whitten Stagliano/New York

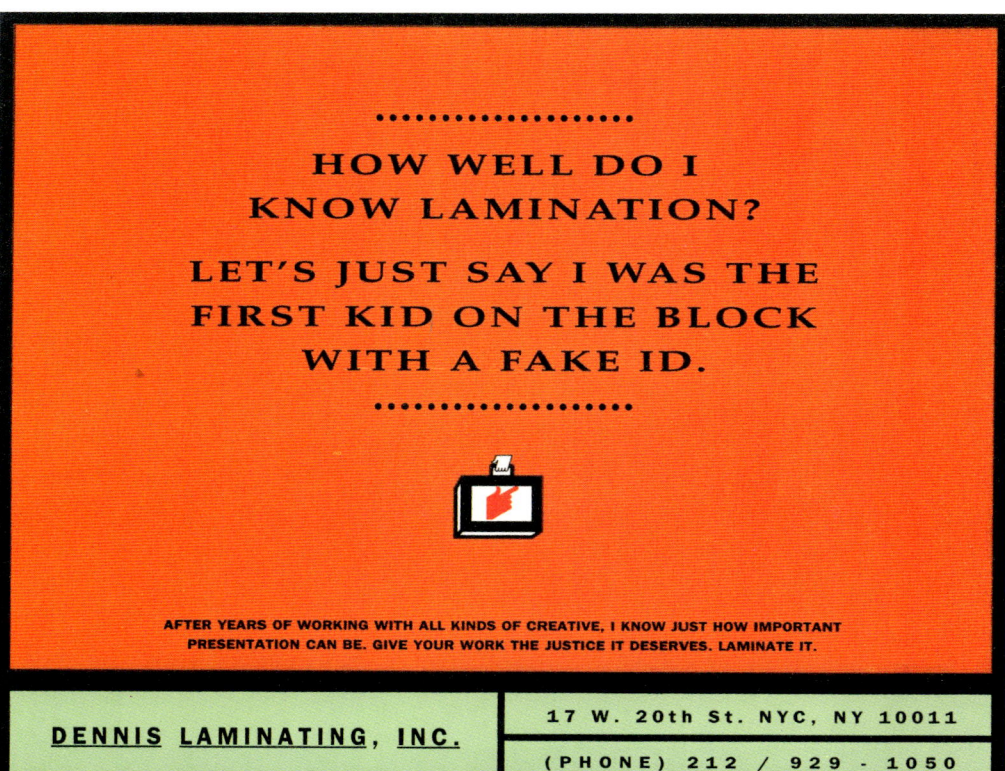

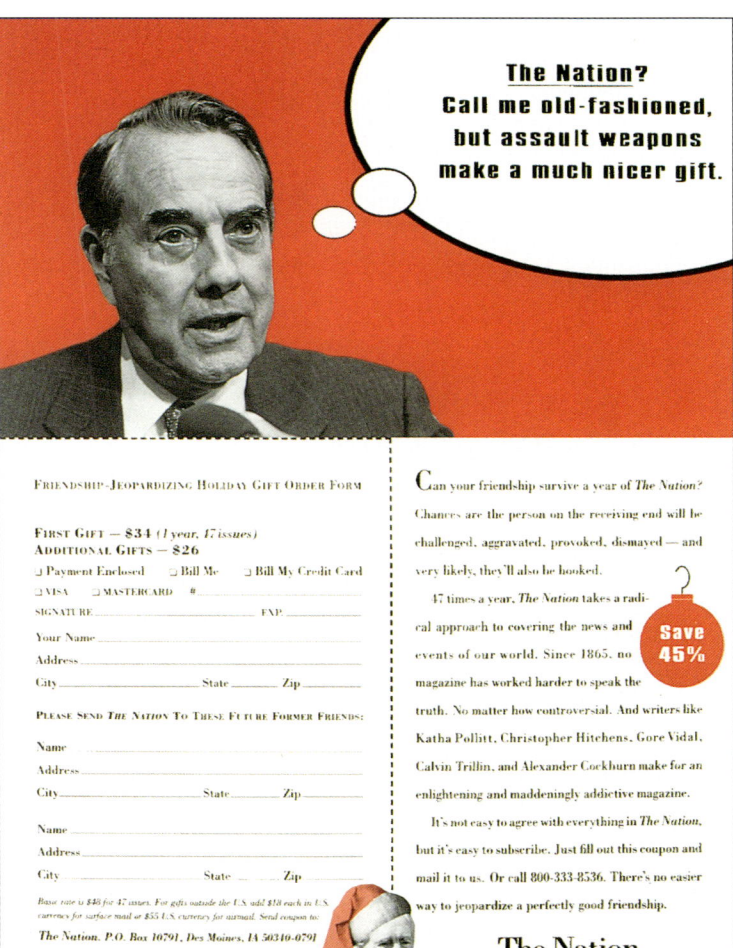

COLLATERAL
DIRECT MAIL: SINGLE

370
ART DIRECTOR:
Danielle Flagg
WRITER:
Marty Weiss
CLIENT:
Weiss Whitten Stagliano
AGENCY:
Weiss Whitten Stagliano/ New York

371
ART DIRECTOR:
Charlotte Moore
WRITER:
Peter Wegner
CLIENT:
The Coca-Cola Company
AGENCY:
Wieden & Kennedy/ Portland

COLLATERAL
DIRECT MAIL: CAMPAIGN

372
ART DIRECTORS:
Eric C. King
Andrew Christou
WRITER:
Stephen P. Gill
CLIENT:
Dennis Laminating
AGENCY:
The Trauma Unit/Boston

....
OK, FINE. LAMINATING RELEASES
HARMFUL CHLOROFLUOROCARBONS
INTO THE ATMOSPHERE
WHICH DEPLETES THE OZONE LAYER
AND DIRECTLY CONTRIBUTES TO
THE GREENHOUSE EFFECT.

BUT BOY DOES IT MAKE YOUR BOOK
LOOK REALLY, REALLY COOL.
....

OF COURSE THE ENVIRONMENT IS IMPORTANT. BUT SO IS YOUR BOOK.
GIVE YOUR WORK THE JUSTICE IT DESERVES. LAMINATE IT.

DENNIS LAMINATING, INC. — 17 W. 20th St. NYC, NY 10011 — (PHONE) 212 / 929 - 1050

....
HOW WELL DO I
KNOW LAMINATION?

LET'S JUST SAY I WAS THE
FIRST KID ON THE BLOCK
WITH A FAKE ID.
....

AFTER YEARS OF WORKING WITH ALL KINDS OF CREATIVE, I KNOW JUST HOW IMPORTANT
PRESENTATION CAN BE. GIVE YOUR WORK THE JUSTICE IT DESERVES. LAMINATE IT.

DENNIS LAMINATING, INC. — 17 W. 20th St. NYC, NY 10011 — (PHONE) 212 / 929 - 1050

....
FOR AWARD-WINNING ADS,
WE HAVE 10 MIL LAMINATION.

FOR ALL OTHERS,
WE RECOMMEND OUR
HIGH GLOSS, RIGID VINYL
30 MIL LAMINATION
WITH A SOFT, LUXURIOUS
VELVET BACKING.
....

YOU'VE GOT ONE SHOT AT MAKING A FIRST IMPRESSION IN THE WORLD OF ADVERTISING.
SO DON'T BLOW IT. GIVE YOUR WORK THE JUSTICE IT DESERVES. LAMINATE IT.

DENNIS LAMINATING, INC. — 17 W. 20th St. NYC, NY 10011 — (PHONE) 212 / 929 - 1050

COLLATERAL
POINT OF PURCHASE
AND IN-STORE

373
ART DIRECTOR:
Kent Suter
WRITER:
Derek Barnes
PHOTOGRAPHER:
Doug Petty, in memoriam
CLIENT:
All That Glitters
AGENCY:
Borders Perrin & Norrander/Portland

374
ART DIRECTOR:
Simon McQuoid
WRITER:
Steve Callen
PHOTOGRAPHER:
Studio 9D
CLIENT:
Lotteries Commission of South Australia
AGENCY:
Clemenger Adelaide/ Eastwood, Australia

375
ART DIRECTOR:
Jeff Nixon
WRITER:
Larry Lipson
PHOTOGRAPHER:
Beth Canzano
CLIENT:
Daisy
AGENCY:
Cramer-Krasselt/Chicago

376
ART DIRECTOR:
Kris Jenson
WRITER:
Tom Rosen
PHOTOGRAPHER:
Scott Lanza
CLIENT:
Museum of Questionable Medical Devices
AGENCY:
Cramer-Krasselt/ Milwaukee

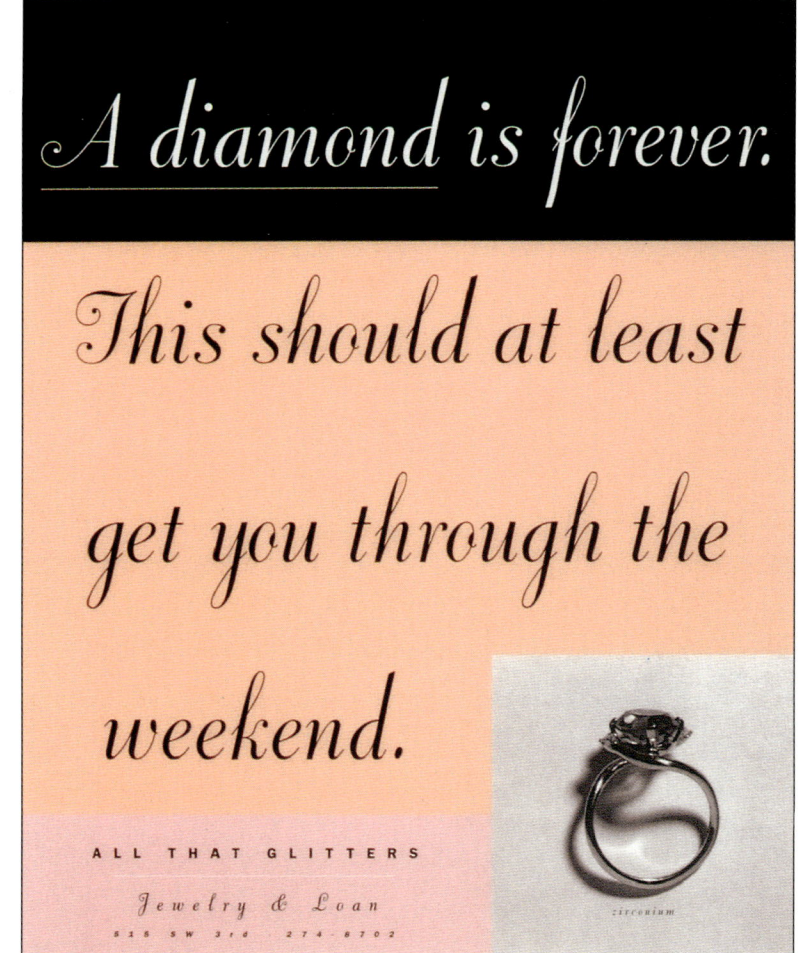
373

374

375

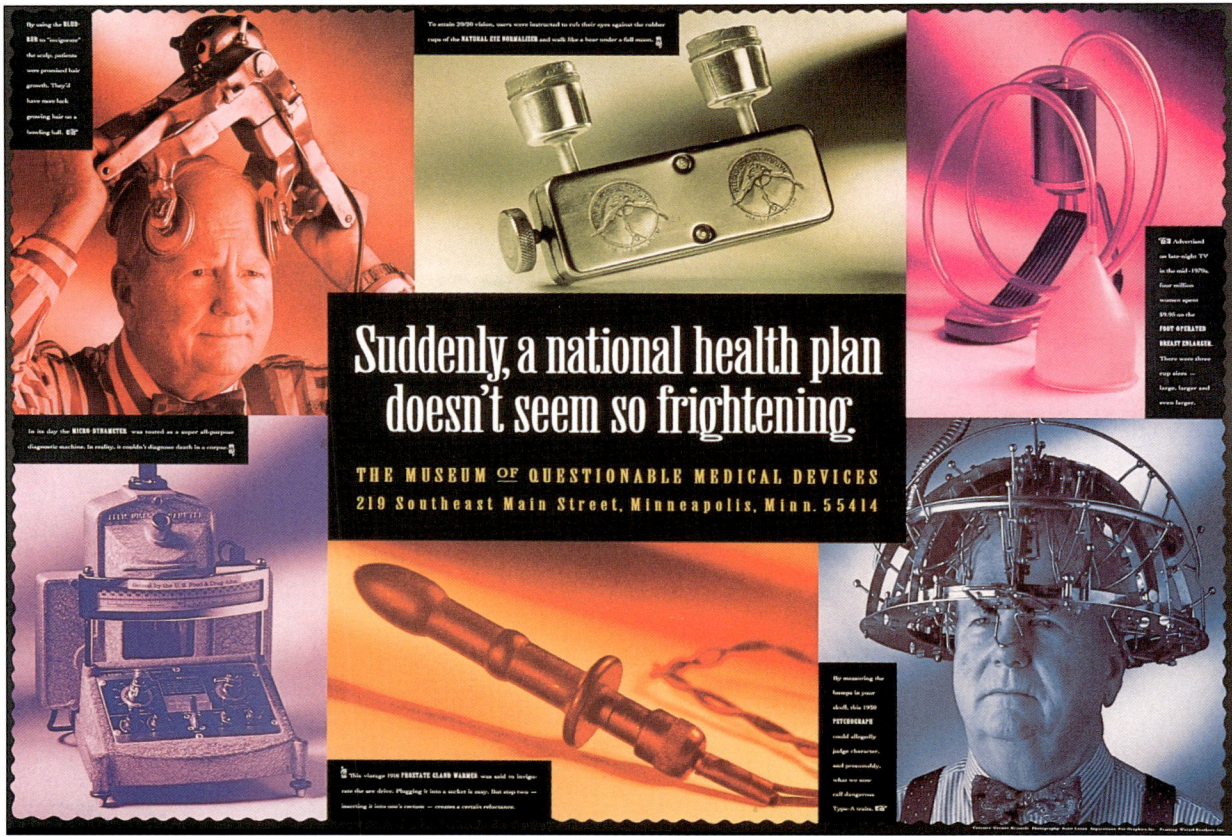

376

COLLATERAL
POINT OF PURCHASE
AND IN-STORE

377
ART DIRECTOR:
J. Kent Pepper
WRITER:
Daniel Swanson
PHOTOGRAPHER:
Henderson/Cartledge
CLIENT:
The Zoo Doo Compost Company
AGENCY:
DRK/Boston

378
ART DIRECTOR:
J. Kent Pepper
WRITER:
Daniel Swanson
PHOTOGRAPHER:
Henderson/Cartledge
CLIENT:
The Zoo Doo Compost Company
AGENCY:
DRK/Boston

379
ART DIRECTOR:
Robert Shaw West
WRITER:
Kelly Simmons
ILLUSTRATOR:
Square One Studio
PHOTOGRAPHER:
Steve Belkowitz
CLIENT:
Style of Man
AGENCY:
Earle Palmer Brown/ Philadelphia

380
ART DIRECTOR:
Nic York
WRITER:
Sally Hogshead
CLIENT:
Leapin' Lizards
AGENCY:
Fallon McElligott/ Minneapolis

377

378

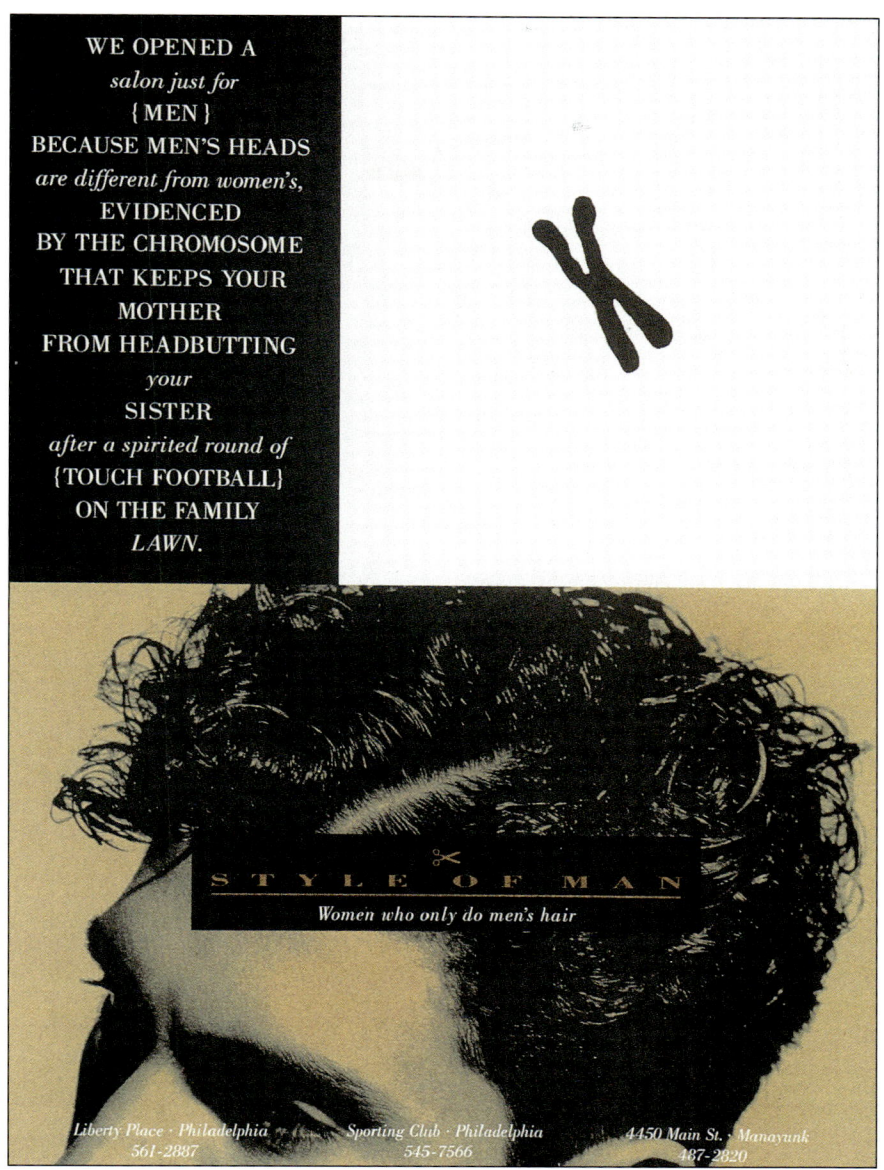

COLLATERAL
POINT OF PURCHASE
AND IN-STORE

381
ART DIRECTOR:
Joe Paprocki
WRITER:
Doug de Grood
CLIENT:
The Lee Company
AGENCY:
Fallon McElligott/
Minneapolis

382
ART DIRECTOR:
J. Liegey
WRITER:
J. Liegey
CLIENT:
Sir Freddie's Pale Ale
AGENCY:
Fallon McElligott/
Minneapolis

383
ART DIRECTOR:
J. Liegey
WRITER:
J. Liegey
CLIENT:
Sir Freddie's Pale Ale
AGENCY:
Fallon McElligott/
Minneapolis

384
ART DIRECTOR:
J. Liegey
WRITER:
J. Liegey
CLIENT:
Sir Freddie's Pale Ale
AGENCY:
Fallon McElligott/
Minneapolis

381

382

383

384

COLLATERAL
POINT OF PURCHASE
AND IN-STORE

385
ART DIRECTOR:
Brent Ladd
WRITER:
Brian Brooker
PHOTOGRAPHER:
Dennis Fagan
CLIENT:
Rootin' Ridge
AGENCY:
GSD&M Advertising/
Austin

386
ART DIRECTOR:
Brent Ladd
WRITER:
Brian Brooker
PHOTOGRAPHER:
Dennis Fagan
CLIENT:
Rootin' Ridge
AGENCY:
GSD&M Advertising/
Austin

387
ART DIRECTOR:
Brent Ladd
WRITER:
Brian Brooker
PHOTOGRAPHER:
Dennis Fagan
CLIENT:
Rootin' Ridge
AGENCY:
GSD&M Advertising/
Austin

388
ART DIRECTOR:
Brent Ladd
WRITER:
Brian Brooker
PHOTOGRAPHER:
Dennis Fagan
CLIENT:
Rootin' Ridge
AGENCY:
GSD&M Advertising/
Austin

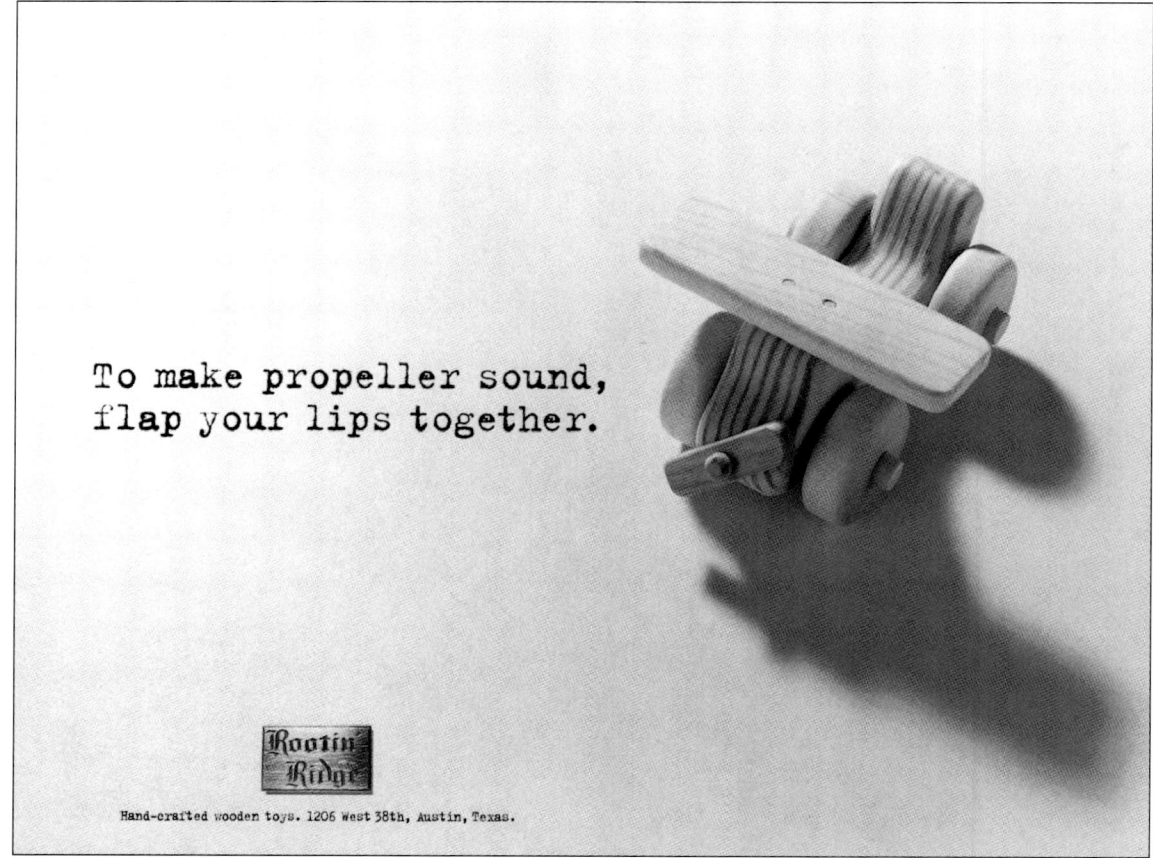
385

386

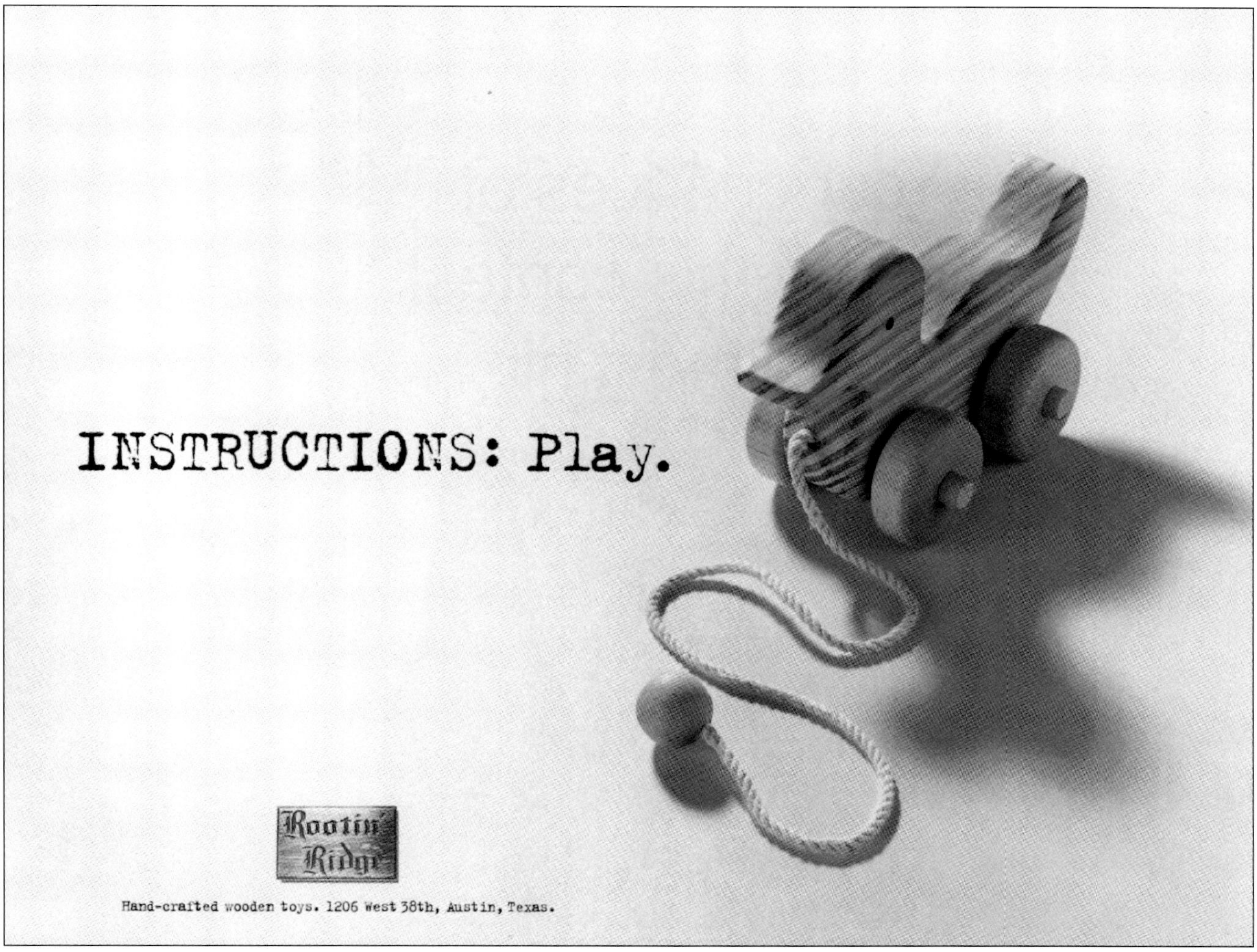
INSTRUCTIONS: Play.
Rootin' Ridge
Hand-crafted wooden toys. 1206 West 38th, Austin, Texas.

387

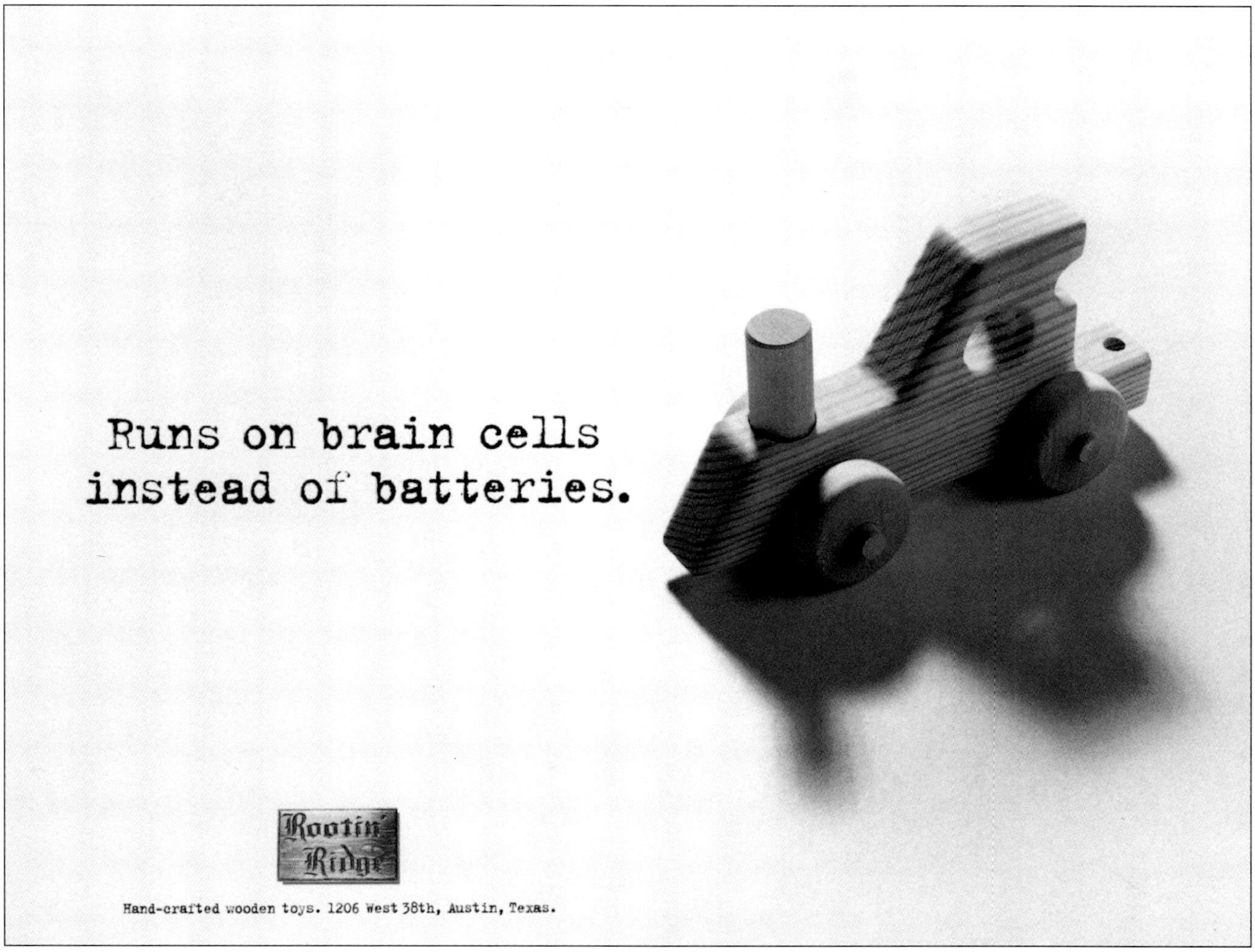
Runs on brain cells
instead of batteries.
Rootin' Ridge
Hand-crafted wooden toys. 1206 West 38th, Austin, Texas.

388

COLLATERAL
POINT OF PURCHASE
AND IN-STORE

389
ART DIRECTOR:
Mike Fetrow
WRITER:
Doug Adkins
PHOTOGRAPHER:
Shawn Michienzi
CLIENT:
Minnesota Brewing
AGENCY:
Hunt Murray/
Minneapolis

390
ART DIRECTORS:
Tan Shen Guan
Kelvin Hung
Paul Regan
WRITERS:
Paul Regan
Iris Lo
PHOTOGRAPHER:
Raymond Ng
CLIENT:
Kraft General Foods
AGENCY:
J. Walter Thompson/
Hong Kong

391
ART DIRECTOR:
Rob Rich
WRITER:
Kara Goodrich
CLIENT:
Stork's Landing
AGENCY:
Leonard/Monahan,
Providence

392
ART DIRECTOR:
Jon Soto
WRITER:
Tina Hall
PHOTOGRAPHER:
Alexander Ruas
CLIENT:
Shelter
AGENCY:
Mad Dogs & Englishmen/
New York

389

390

No food or drink allowed in store.

Unless it has a nipple attached.

Stork's Landing

COLLATERAL
POINT OF PURCHASE
AND IN-STORE

393
ART DIRECTOR:
Gina Fortunato
WRITER:
Susan Treacy
CLIENT:
Thom McAn
AGENCY:
Mad Dogs & Englishmen/
New York

394
ART DIRECTOR:
Tom Kim
WRITER:
Scott Eirinberg
TYPOGRAPHER:
Tom Kim
CLIENT:
K. James Kim, M.D.
AGENCY:
McConnaughy Stein
Schmidt Brown/Chicago

395
ART DIRECTOR:
Michael Kadin
WRITER:
Rick Rosenberg
PHOTOGRAPHER:
Craig Saruwatari
CLIENT:
Attila Photography
School
AGENCY:
Not a Division of
Omnicom Advertising/
Los Angeles

396
ART DIRECTOR:
Tom Sullivan
WRITER:
Jeff Bitsack
PHOTOGRAPHER:
Lars Topelmann
CLIENT:
Andromeda Body
Piercing
AGENCY:
Verge/New York

393

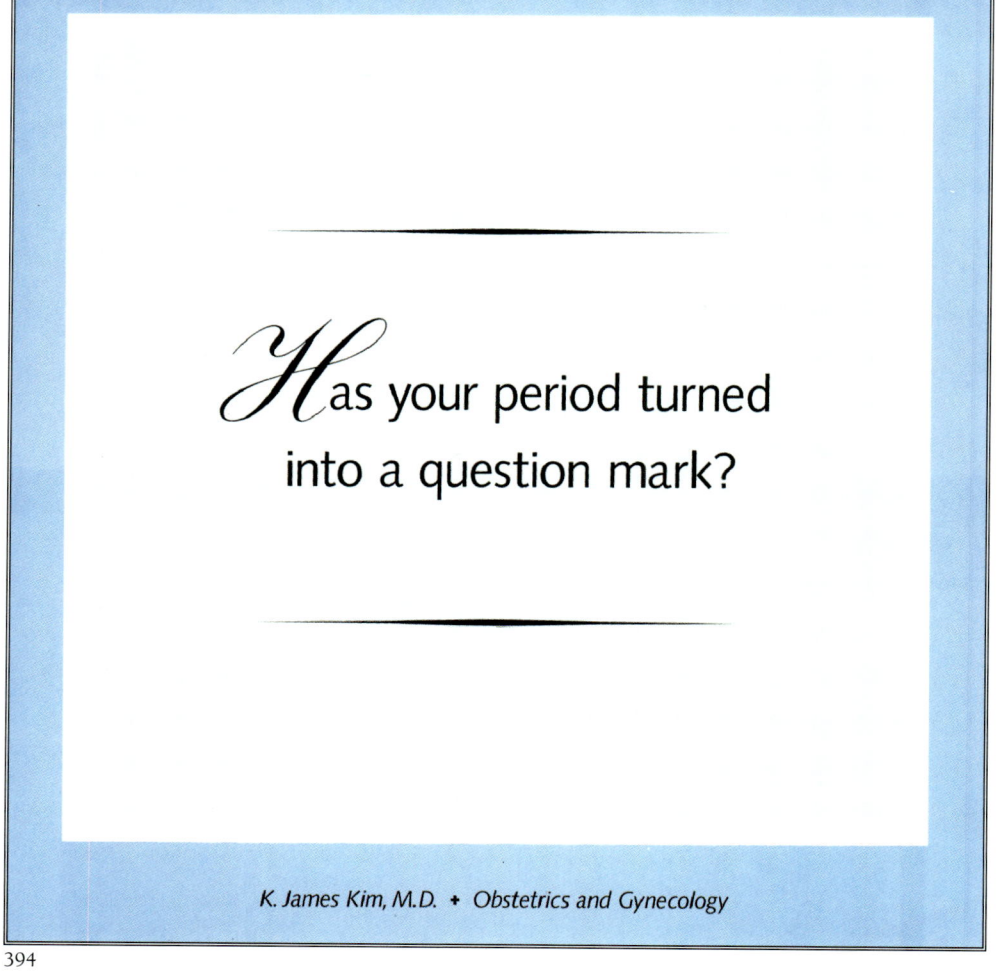
394

395

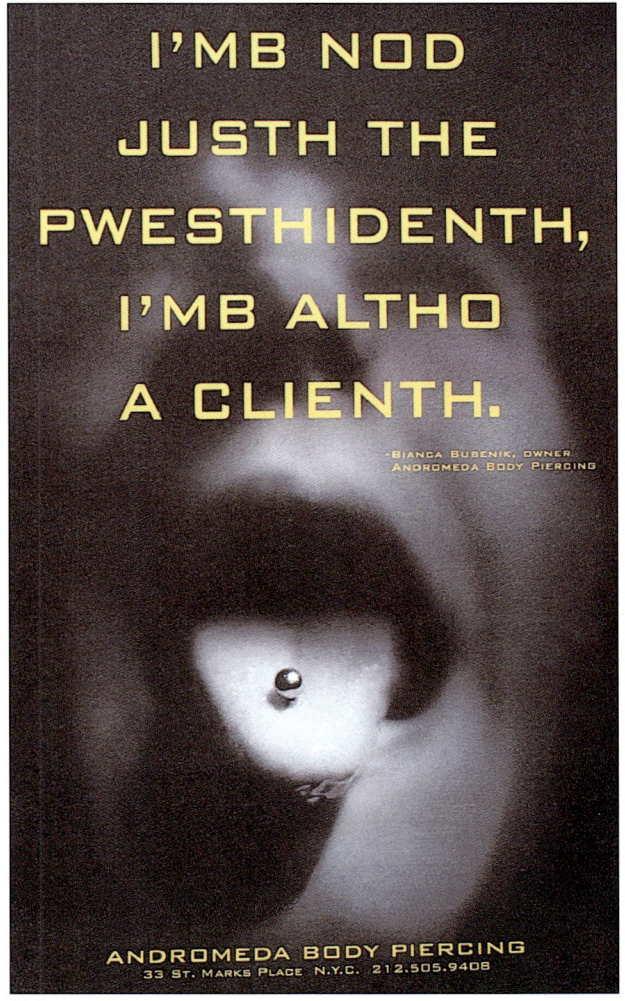

396

COLLATERAL
SELF-PROMOTION

397
ART DIRECTOR:
John Gellos
WRITER:
Kevin Mooney
PHOTOGRAPHER:
Peter Reitzfeld
CLIENT:
Altschiller & Company
AGENCY:
Altschiller & Company/
New York

398
ART DIRECTOR:
Steve Kimura
WRITER:
Steve Skibba
PHOTOGRAPHER:
Gary McGuire
CLIENT:
BBDO
AGENCY:
BBDO/Los Angeles

399
ART DIRECTOR:
Jeff Kling
WRITER:
Jeff Kling
ILLUSTRATOR:
Jeff Kling
CLIENT:
Jeff Kling

COLLATERAL
POSTERS

400
ART DIRECTOR:
Marc Klein
WRITER:
Ray Johnson
PHOTOGRAPHER:
Mark Weiss
CLIENT:
Billy's Topless
AGENCY:
Big Bear/New York

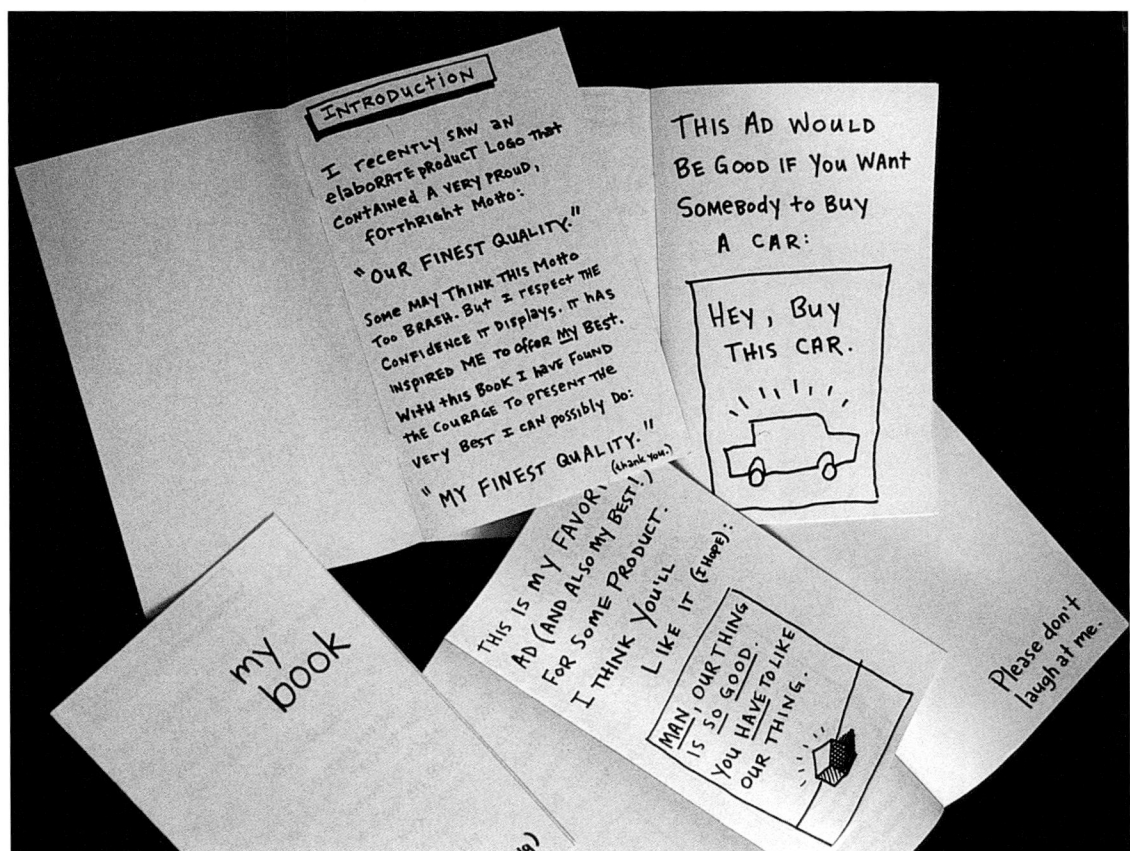

COLLATERAL
POSTERS

401
ART DIRECTOR:
Dave Dickey
WRITER:
Scott Jorgensen
PHOTOGRAPHER:
Steve Umland
CLIENT:
Bozell Worldwide/
Minneapolis
AGENCY:
Bozell Worldwide/
Minneapolis

402
ART DIRECTOR:
Heidi Flora
WRITER:
Kevin Jones
ILLUSTRATOR:
Heidi Flora
CLIENT:
Winterbrook/Africola
AGENCY:
Cole & Weber/Seattle

403
ART DIRECTOR:
Roger Bentley
WRITER:
Scott Wild
ILLUSTRATOR:
Ken Anderson
CLIENT:
The Big House
AGENCY:
Dalbey & Denight
Advertising/Portland

404
ART DIRECTOR:
Roger Bentley
WRITER:
Scott Wild
PHOTOGRAPHER:
Ken Anderson
CLIENT:
The Big House
AGENCY:
Dalbey & Denight
Advertising/Portland

401

402

WE DIDN'T STEAL OUR DESIGNS FROM LEVI'S®.

BUT EVEN IF WE DID, WHAT ARE YOU GOING TO DO, THROW US IN JAIL?

SOMETIMES OUR JEANS LAST LONGER THAN THE GUYS WHO MAKE THEM.

COLLATERAL POSTERS

405
ART DIRECTOR:
Nic York
WRITER:
Sally Hogshead
PHOTOGRAPHER:
Liz Banfield
CLIENT:
Leapin' Lizards
AGENCY:
Fallon McElligott/
Minneapolis

406
ART DIRECTOR:
Nic York
WRITER:
Nic York
PHOTOGRAPHER:
Chris Sheehan
CLIENT:
PMS Clinic
AGENCY:
Fallon McElligott/
Minneapolis

407
ART DIRECTOR:
Henriette Lienke
WRITER:
Tom Miller
CLIENT:
Crain's New York Business
AGENCY:
Goldsmith/Jeffrey,
New York

408
ART DIRECTOR:
Damon Williams
WRITER:
Chris Jacobs
DESIGNER:
Troy King
PHOTOGRAPHER:
Chris Davis
CLIENT:
The Skydiving Center
AGENCY:
Hughes Advertising/
Atlanta

407

408

COLLATERAL
POSTERS

409
ART DIRECTORS:
Mike Fetrow
Mike Murray
WRITER:
Doug Adkins
PHOTOGRAPHER:
Richard Hamilton Smith
CLIENT:
Advanced Aerobatic Flight Training
AGENCY:
Hunt Murray/
Minneapolis

410
ART DIRECTOR:
Steve Mitchell
WRITER:
Kristine Larsen
ILLUSTRATOR:
Tom Larson
CLIENT:
Minnesota Brewing
AGENCY:
Hunt Murray/
Minneapolis

411
ART DIRECTOR:
Joe Hemp
WRITER:
Bryan Behar
CLIENT:
91.5 KUSC Radio
AGENCY:
Ketchum Advertising/
Los Angeles

412
ART DIRECTOR:
Rob Rich
WRITER:
Kara Goodrich
CLIENT:
Stork's Landing
AGENCY:
Leonard/Monahan,
Providence

409

410

COLLATERAL
POSTERS

413
ART DIRECTOR:
Wayne Thompson
WRITER:
Christopher Wilson
ILLUSTRATOR:
Brad Palm
PHOTOGRAPHER:
Joe Lampi
CLIENT:
Grand Groomers
AGENCY:
Martin/Williams,
Minneapolis

414
ART DIRECTOR:
Jeff Jahn
WRITER:
Pete Smith
ILLUSTRATOR:
Scott McCulley
PHOTOGRAPHER:
Scott McCulley
CLIENT:
Graphic Technologies
AGENCIES:
Martin/Williams,
Minneapolis and
Pete Smith Advertising/
Minneapolis

416
ART DIRECTOR:
Marta Ibarrondo
WRITER:
Tom Givone
CLIENT:
Printbox
AGENCY:
Mezzina/Brown,
New York

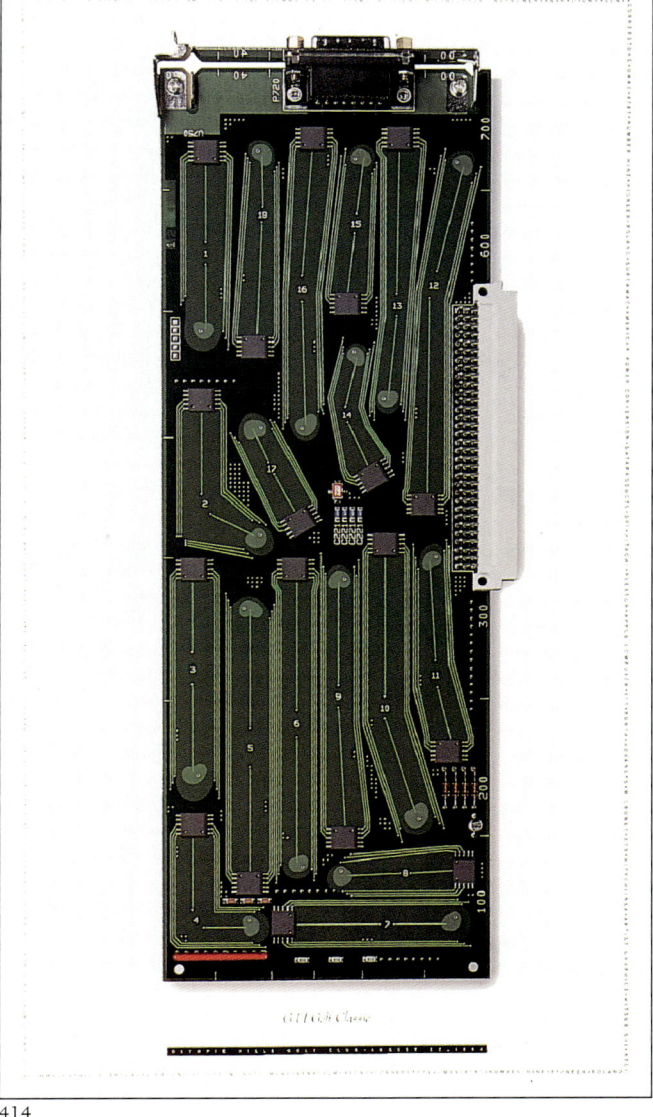

COLLATERAL POSTERS

417
ART DIRECTOR:
Keith Weinman
WRITERS:
Stephen P. Gill
Ben Resnikoff
PHOTOGRAPHER:
Michael Furman
CLIENT:
BMW of North America
AGENCY:
Mullen Advertising/
Wenham, MA

418
ART DIRECTOR:
Mark Bell
WRITERS:
Doug James
Ernest Lupinacci
PHOTOGRAPHER:
Tom Seawell
CLIENT:
Golden Gate Rugby Club
AGENCY:
Odiorne Wilde Narraway
Groome/San Francisco

419
ART DIRECTOR:
Mark Bell
WRITERS:
Doug James
Ernest Lupinacci
PHOTOGRAPHER:
Tom Seawell
CLIENT:
Golden Gate Rugby Club
AGENCY:
Odiorne Wilde Narraway
Groome/San Francisco

420
ART DIRECTORS:
Michael Wilde
Brad Webb
WRITERS:
Eric Weltner
Jeff Odiorne
PHOTOGRAPHER:
Terry Husebye
CLIENT:
Medicine Bow Guest Ranch
AGENCY:
Odiorne Wilde Narraway
Groome/San Francisco

417

418

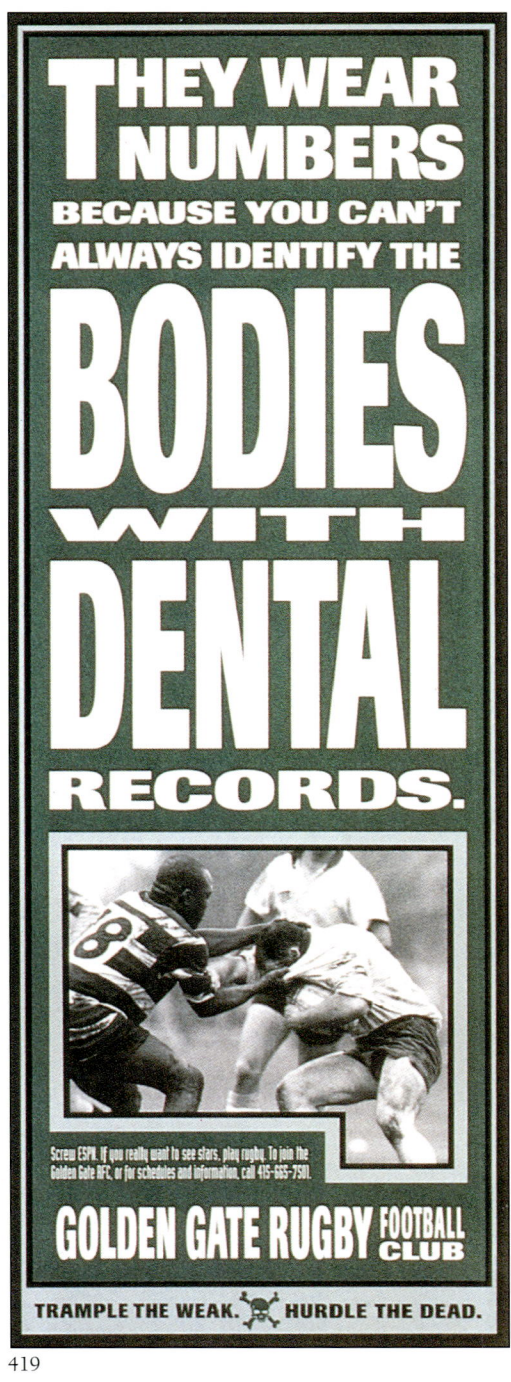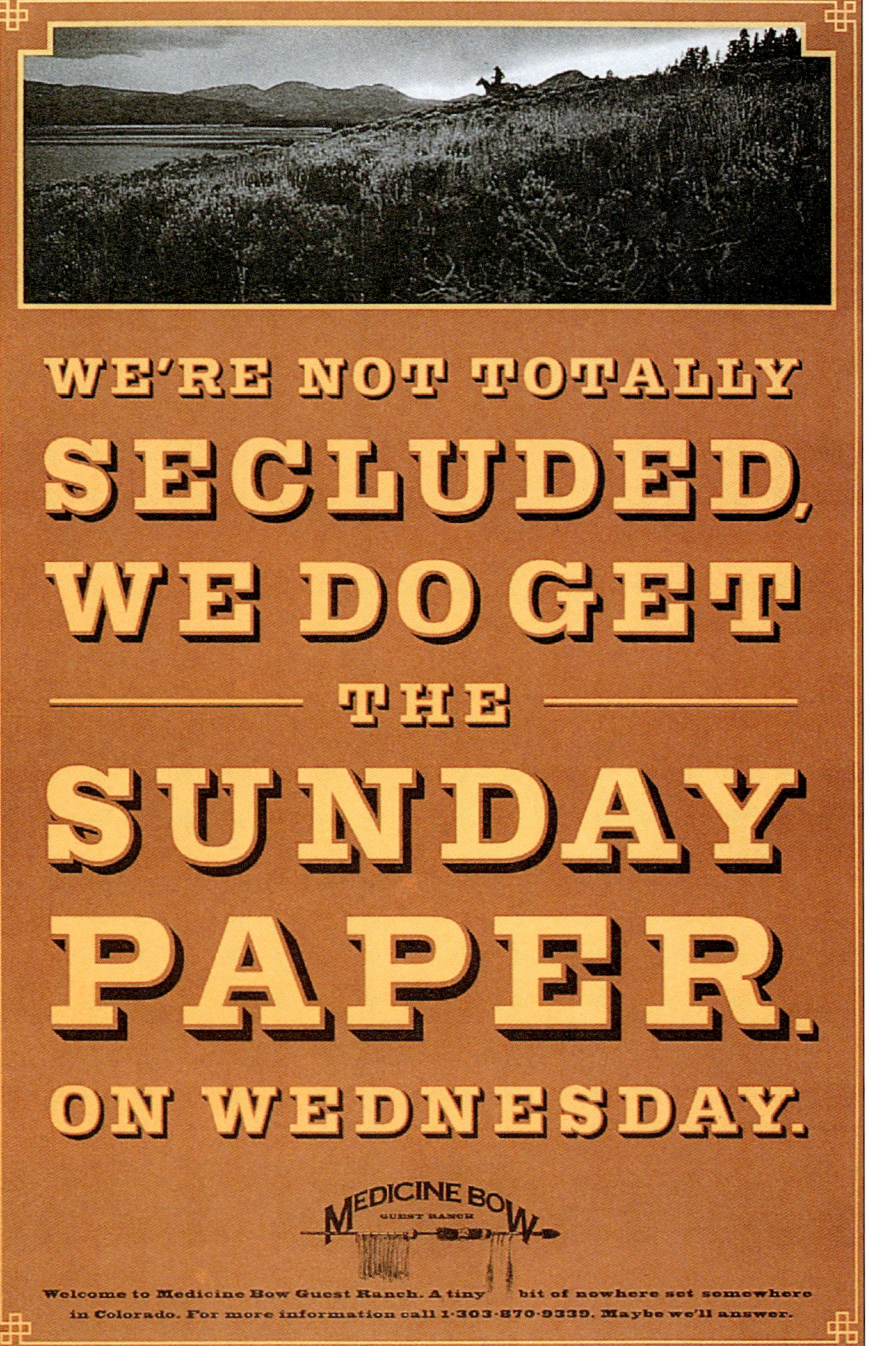

COLLATERAL POSTERS

421
ART DIRECTORS:
Michael Wilde
Brad Webb
WRITERS:
Jeff Odiorne
Eric Weltner
PHOTOGRAPHER:
Terry Husebye
CLIENT:
Medicine Bow Guest Ranch
AGENCY:
Odiorne Wilde Narraway Groome/San Francisco

422
ART DIRECTORS:
Maria Kostyk-Petro
Lisa Lipkin
WRITERS:
Lisa Lipkin
Maria Kostyk-Petro
CLIENT:
Sara Lee Foundations
AGENCY:
TBWA Advertising/New York

423
ART DIRECTOR:
Tracy Wong
WRITER:
Craig Hoit
PHOTOGRAPHER:
Larry Prosor
CLIENT:
K2 Skis
AGENCY:
WongDoody/Seattle

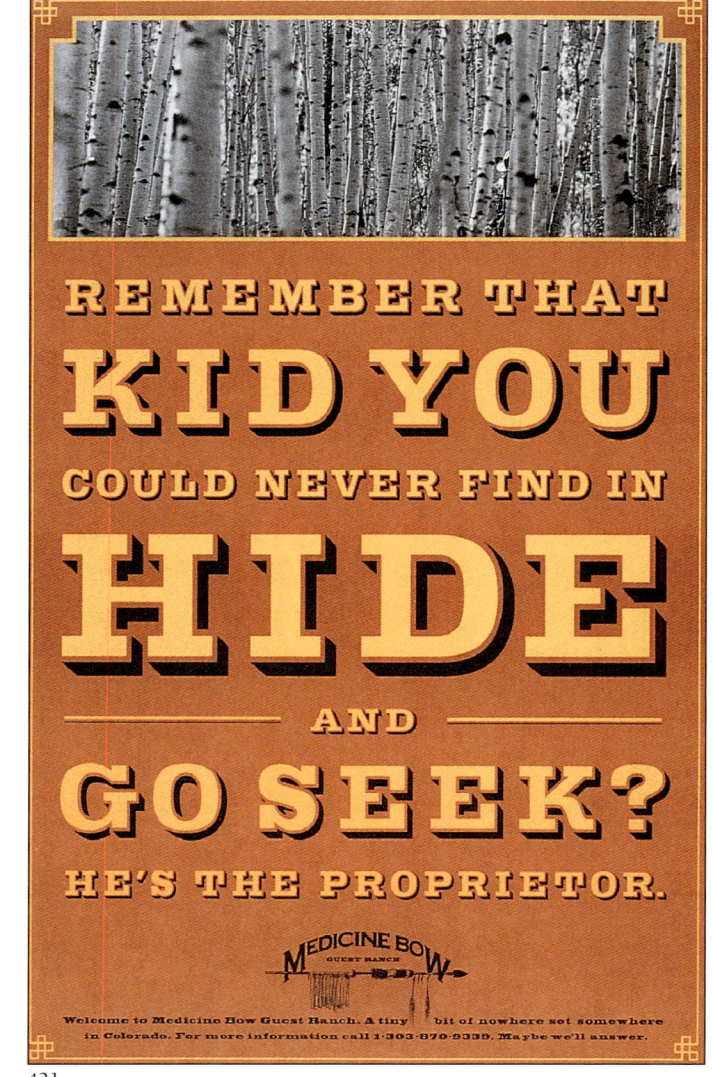
421

422

Public Service
&
Political Finalists

PUBLIC SERVICE/
POLITICAL NEWSPAPER
OR MAGAZINE: SINGLE

424
ART DIRECTOR:
Greg Martin
WRITER:
Nick Bell
CLIENT:
RSPCA
AGENCY:
Abbott Mead Vickers.
BBDO/London

425
ART DIRECTOR:
Robert Richter
WRITER:
Michael Dean
PHOTOGRAPHER:
Bill Tucker
CLIENT:
Off The Street Club
AGENCY:
Bayer Bess Vanderwarker/
Chicago

426
ART DIRECTORS:
Roger Bentley
Jerry Ketel
WRITER:
Scott Wild
ILLUSTRATOR:
John Bileski
PHOTOGRAPH:
Family Archives
CLIENT:
Hanford Health
Information Network
AGENCY:
Big Ads/Portland

427
ART DIRECTOR:
Ian Morton
WRITER:
Mick Hunter
TYPOGRAPHER:
Kristian Molloy
PHOTOGRAPHER:
Simon Harsent
CLIENT:
NSW Police Service
AGENCY:
The Campaign Palace/
New South Wales,
Australia

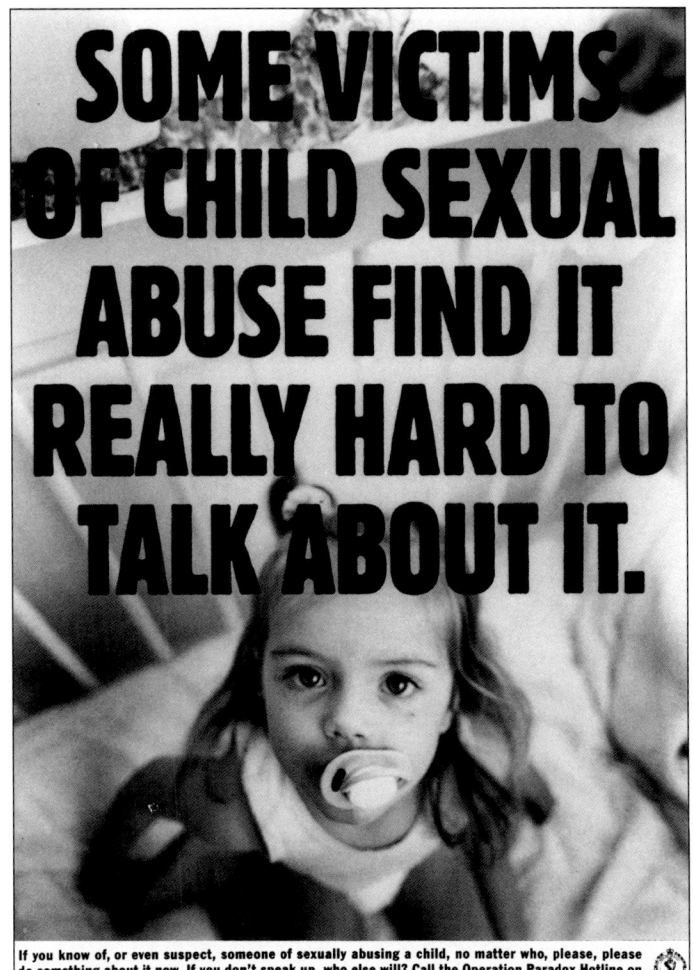

PUBLIC SERVICE/ POLITICAL NEWSPAPER OR MAGAZINE: SINGLE

428
ART DIRECTOR:
Cliff Sorah
WRITER:
Joe Alexander
PHOTOGRAPHER:
Martin Adler
CLIENT:
American Red Cross
AGENCY:
The Martin Agency/ Richmond

429
ART DIRECTORS:
Chris Bleackley
Len Cheeseman
WRITERS:
Maggie Mouat
Kim Thorp
CLIENT:
New Zealand AIDS Foundation
AGENCY:
Saatchi & Saatchi/ Wellington, New Zealand

PUBLIC SERVICE/ POLITICAL NEWSPAPER OR MAGAZINE: CAMPAIGN

430
ART DIRECTOR:
Greg Martin
WRITER:
Nick Bell
CLIENT:
RSPCA
AGENCY:
Abbott Mead Vickers. BBDO/London

428

Dear Eric,

There is a virus spreading through our community which is claiming a life every week. It is spread through contaminated blood or sexual contact. I'm sure you know what I'm talking about. HIV and ultimately AIDS.

The only way we can stop it spreading is to spread the word faster than the virus.

And the word is condoms. Practise safe sex and use them. It's that simple.

Now take this letter and copy it 6 times. Send them to people who you consider make the world a better place. Don't be embarrased, we could all do with a reminder.

If you send the letter on to six people this week, and each of these people do the same, by the end of the month 7,776 people will be better informed. If you choose to do nothing, by the end of the year several million people will have missed our message.

We owe it to everyone to spread the word and beat the virus.

SIGNED: Someone who cares

PS. If you could afford to send a donation to the Aids Foundation they would very much appreciate it. Their address is:

NZ AIDS Foundation.
PO Box 7287,
Wellington,
New Zealand.

429

Sorry if this is hard hitting but so was the man who did it.

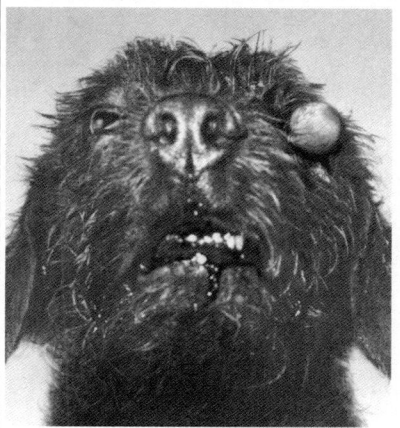

Max was beaten over the head with a garden spade.

According to witnesses, he was beaten repeatedly and viciously.

His teeth were shattered, his jaw was broken, his left eye was knocked out of its socket.

Our Inspector said they were the most horrific injuries he'd encountered in ten years with the RSPCA.

All year round, we're called to the aid of suffering animals like Max.

Last year, our Inspectors responded to nearly 100,000 reports of animal cruelty.

Reports of horses that had been starved, dogs that had been beaten, kittens that had been kicked and maimed.

Our policy is never to refuse a call for help. But, of course, it's an expensive one.

The current cost of training, equipping and putting just one new Inspector on the road for a year is £32,407.

Which is why we need your help so desperately.

The RSPCA receives no funding from the Government.

We rely entirely on the generosity of the public.

Indeed, it's thanks to people like you that we were able to save Max.

So please send as much money as you can.

Because it's cruelty like this that needs beating.

Investigating this wasn't difficult. We had a lead.

We found Trudy tethered round the neck by a piece of rusting curtain wire.

Her three small puppies were just a few feet away.

Where Trudy had struggled to get to them, the sharp, rusty coil of the wire had cut deep into her throat.

From the depth of the wound and the amount of scar tissue formed, our vet estimated she had been tethered in this way for at least five weeks.

In his opinion, she would have suffered considerably.

All year round, our Inspectors are called to the aid of suffering animals like Trudy.

Last year alone, we responded to nearly 100,000 reports of animal cruelty. Reports of horses that had been starved, dogs that had been beaten, kittens that had been kicked and maimed.

Our policy is never to refuse a call for help. But, of course, it's an expensive one.

The current cost of training, equipping and putting just one new Inspector on the road for a

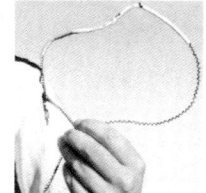

year is £32,407. Which is why we so desperately need your help.

The RSPCA doesn't receive any funding from the Government.

We rely entirely on the public's generosity.

Thanks to people like you, we were able to find a loving new home for Trudy and her puppies.

So please send as much money as you can. And help us save a few more necks.

"How I put on 35lbs in just 8 weeks."
Spot of Ipswich.

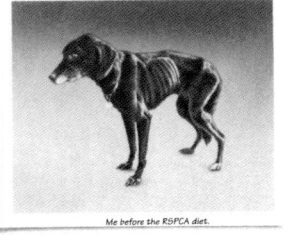
Me before the RSPCA diet.

Me after.

"Eighteen months ago, I had a weight problem.

My eyes were sunken, my ribs were showing; I looked awful.

Then I discovered the RSPCA. Or rather, they discovered me.

In no time, they had me eating sensibly again.

Plenty of the right things every day - even the occasional treat.

After just eight weeks, I'd reached my target weight."

When we discovered Spot, she was terribly underweight.

She had severe muscle wastage, she was weak with hunger and hadn't been fed properly for weeks.

But Spot is one of our many success stories. Because our Inspector reached her in time, we were able to save her and find her a loving new home.

Many animals aren't as fortunate.

All year round, our Inspectors are called to the aid of suffering animals like Spot.

Last year alone, we responded to nearly 100,000 reports of animal cruelty.

Reports of horses that had been starved, dogs that had been beaten, kittens that had been kicked and maimed.

Our policy is never to refuse a call for help. But, of course, it's an expensive one.

The current cost of training, equipping and putting just one new Inspector on the road for a year is £32,407.

Which is why we desperately need your help.

The RSPCA receives no funding from the Government.

We rely entirely on the generosity of people like you.

Please send as much money as you can.

We know plenty more animals that could do with a few pounds.

PUBLIC SERVICE/
POLITICAL NEWSPAPER
OR MAGAZINE:
CAMPAIGN

431
ART DIRECTOR:
Tom Lichtenheld
WRITER:
Sally Hogshead
PHOTOGRAPHER:
Buck Holzemer
CLIENT:
Children's Defense Fund
AGENCY:
Fallon McElligott/
Minneapolis

432
ART DIRECTOR:
Denise Crandall
WRITER:
Court Crandall
CLIENT:
St. Joseph's
AGENCY:
Ground Zero/Venice

NORTH HOLLYWOOD 1 bd, $550, 1bd + loft $650. Central air/heat, pool, spa. Near studios. (818)985-1592.

PARK BENCH If you wouldn't want to live here, you're not alone. Please help the homeless, call The St. Joseph Center at (310) 396-6468.

PRIME MELROSE AREA Spanish-style, lg. 1bd, Hardwood floors throughout, new paint, new blinds, spacious kitchen w/ Stove/refridge, lots of closets space, laundry, parking. 832-840 1/2 Atla Vist $675/mo. 310-659-5944.

BRIGHT, AIRY, LARGE 1 bd Hollywood. $510 Hardwood floors, french windows, stove, cabinets, tile bath, cable, garage available. 1173 N. Ardmore (213) 666-7523.

CARDBOARD BOX If you have the luxury of considering another home on this page, please help the people who don't. Support the homeless, call the St. Joseph Center at (310)396-6468.

CHARMING HISTORICAL 7-STORY BLDG Wilshire & Normandie. All utilities paid by landlord. 1 Bedroom. 1/2 blk from transportation and shopping. No security deposit, subject to approval. (213)388-2101

HANCOCK PARK ADJ 3bd/2ba 2000 S.F. Bay windows, hardwood floors, garage parking. 1 Month Free! $500 deposit OAC $1150/mo. 213-381-5443.

HEATING GRATE With all the homes in this section, it's a shame so many people have to settle for this one. Help the homeless, call the St. Joseph Center at (310)396-6468.

HOLLYWOOD CLASSIC Courtyard bungalow. Hardwood floors, lots of light, built-in bookcases, dining table, benches. Singles $420/mo. 10-unit building w/ laundry. 1135 N. Lodi Place. (213) 931-8715

PUBLIC SERVICE/
POLITICAL OUTDOOR
AND POSTERS

433
ART DIRECTORS:
Roger Bentley
Jerry Ketel
WRITER:
Scott Wild
ILLUSTRATOR:
John Bileski
PHOTOGRAPH:
Family Archives
CLIENT:
Hanford Health
Information Network
AGENCY:
Big Ads/Portland

434
ART DIRECTOR:
Tom Lichtenheld
WRITER:
Sally Hogshead
PHOTOGRAPHER:
Buck Holzemer
CLIENT:
Children's Defense Fund
AGENCY:
Fallon McElligott/
Minneapolis

435
ART DIRECTOR:
Tom Lichtenheld
WRITER:
Sally Hogshead
PHOTOGRAPHER:
Buck Holzemer
CLIENT:
Children's Defense Fund
AGENCY:
Fallon McElligott/
Minneapolis

436
ART DIRECTORS:
Dave Hernandez
John Fuller
WRITER:
Dean Wei
PHOTOGRAPHER:
Chris Feinstein
CLIENT:
National Head Injury
Foundation
AGENCY:
The Leap Partnership/
Chicago

433

434

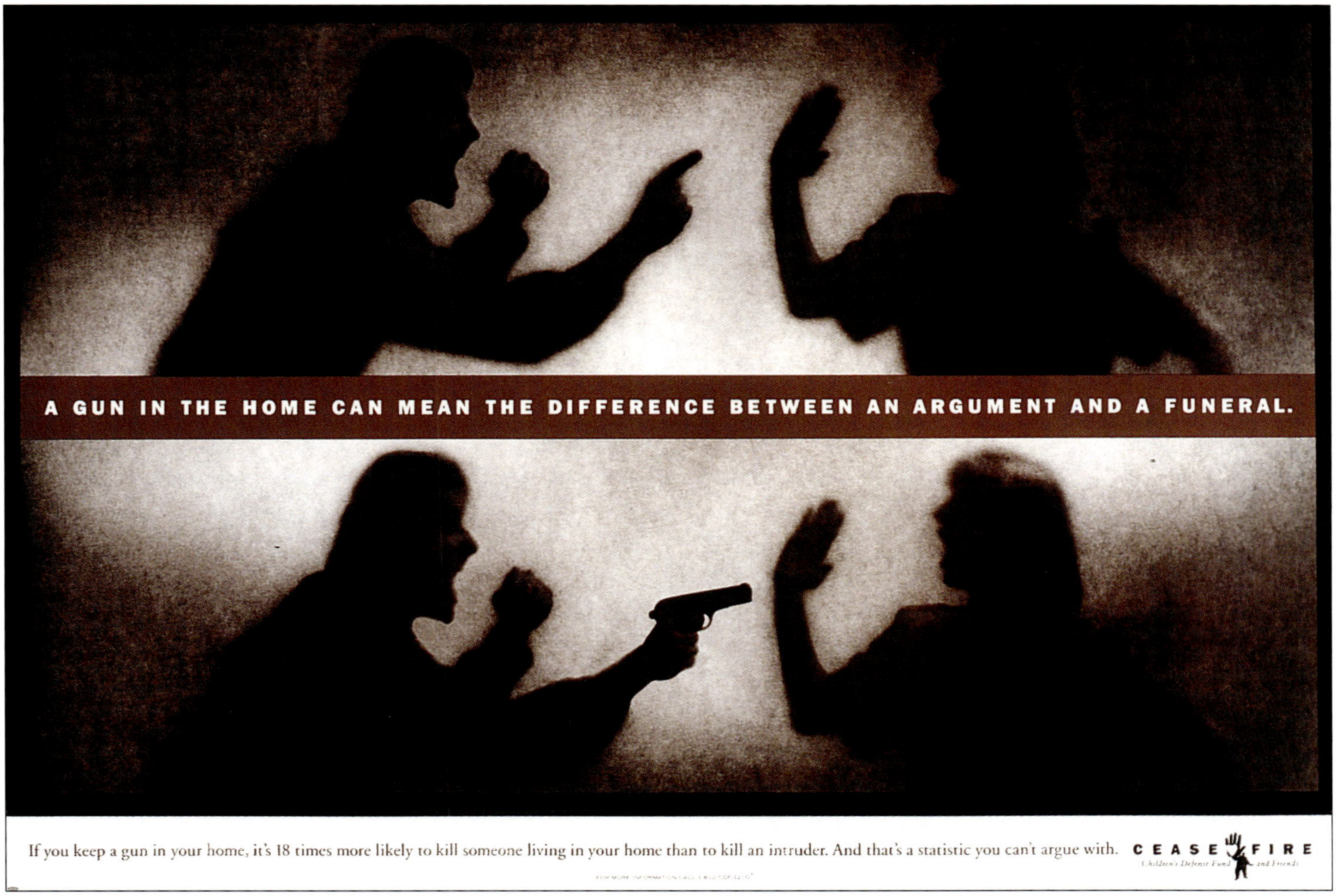
A GUN IN THE HOME CAN MEAN THE DIFFERENCE BETWEEN AN ARGUMENT AND A FUNERAL.
If you keep a gun in your home, it's 18 times more likely to kill someone living in your home than to kill an intruder. And that's a statistic you can't argue with.
CEASE FIRE
Children's Defense Fund and Friends

435

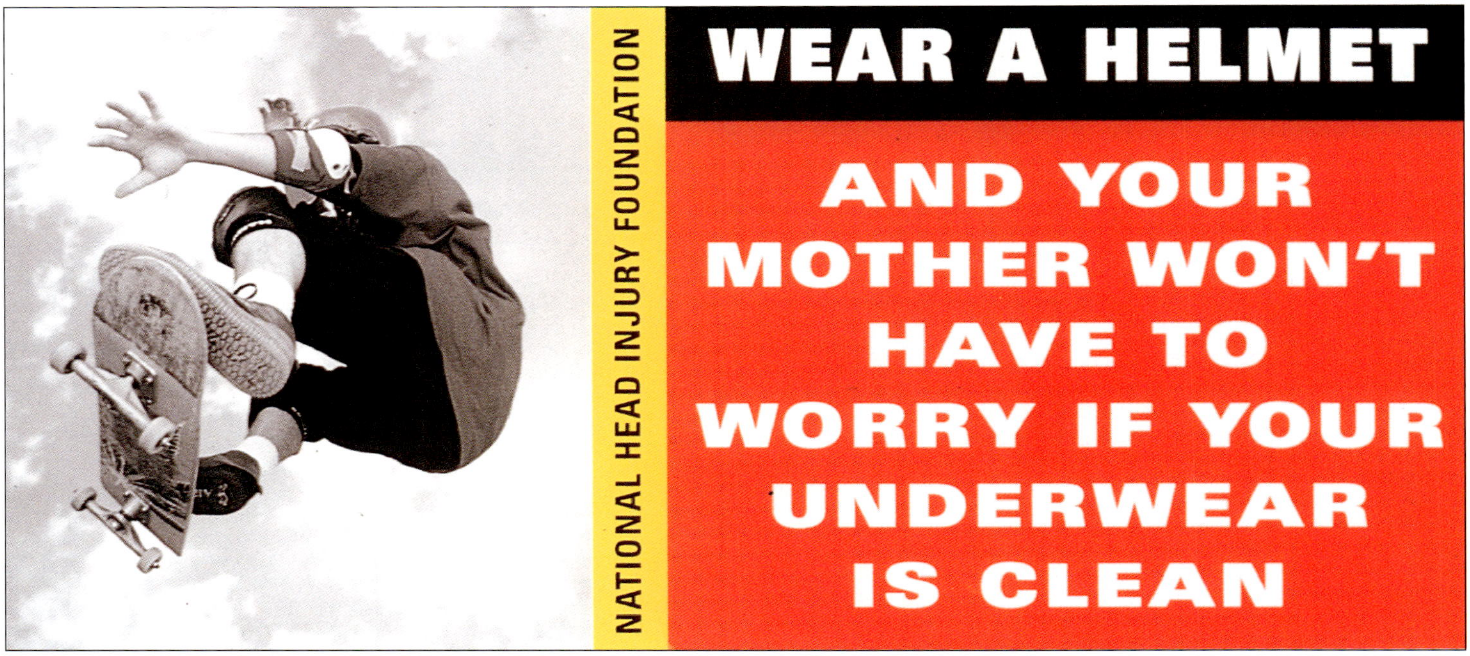
NATIONAL HEAD INJURY FOUNDATION
WEAR A HELMET
AND YOUR MOTHER WON'T HAVE TO WORRY IF YOUR UNDERWEAR IS CLEAN

436

PUBLIC SERVICE/
POLITICAL OUTDOOR
AND POSTERS

437
ART DIRECTOR:
Pat Tom
WRITER:
Steve Skibba
CLIENT:
California Department of Health Services
AGENCY:
Livingston & Company/ Los Angeles

438
ART DIRECTOR:
Cliff Sorah
WRITER:
Joe Alexander
PHOTOGRAPHER:
Martin Adler
CLIENT:
American Red Cross
AGENCY:
The Martin Agency/ Richmond

439
ART DIRECTOR:
Alan Schutte
WRITER:
Alan Schutte
PHOTOGRAPHER:
Craig Brewer
CLIENT:
City of Hampton/Pentran
AGENCY:
Raoust & Gearhart/ Hampton, VA

PUBLIC SERVICE/ POLITICAL RADIO: SINGLE

440
WRITERS:
Steve Dunkley
Kevin Gammon
AGENCY PRODUCER:
James Mahoney
PRODUCTION COMPANY:
Chicago Recording Company
CLIENT:
Earth Share
AGENCY:
Foote Cone & Belding/ Chicago

441
WRITER:
Suzy Davidson
AGENCY PRODUCER:
Noeleen Burley
PRODUCTION COMPANY:
Sonovision
CLIENT:
The Salvation Army
AGENCY:
Sonnenberg Murphy Leo Burnett/Johannesburg

PUBLIC SERVICE/ POLITICAL TELEVISION: SINGLE

442
ART DIRECTOR:
Benjamin Vendramin
WRITER:
Robert McDougall
AGENCY PRODUCER:
Audrey Telfer
PRODUCTION COMPANY:
Stripes
DIRECTOR:
Drew Jarvis
CLIENT:
The Urban Alliance on Race Relations
AGENCY:
Bozell Palmer Bonner/ Toronto

443
ART DIRECTOR:
Ty Harper
WRITER:
Rob Schapiro
AGENCY PRODUCER:
Frank Soukup
PRODUCTION COMPANY:
Johns + Gorman Films
DIRECTOR:
Gary Johns
CLIENT:
Eastern Veterinary Blood Bank
AGENCY:
Earle Palmer Brown/ Richmond

440
(SFX: SHOWER RUNNING)

GUY (SINGING VEGAS STYLE): *You are my baby. You're the kind of lady that deserves fine things. The kind of lady who wears pearls like you were born in them. Yeah. You know that a limousine is made for driving. Yeah. And she's got hair that flows in the breeze like a salmon swimming upstream against the current.*
(MAKES GUITAR NOISES, KEEPS SINGING)

ANNCR: If you think this is going on too long, you're right. Remember, shorter showers save water. This message sponsored by the Ad Council and Earth Share.

441
WOMAN: My name ith Theila. I am not taalking thith thway becauthe I am drunk. I am not deaf or mentally dithabled. I am a dormal woman, mother (SOBS) . . . and wife. I am talking thth thway, becauthe thth ith the thway my huthband wanth me to talk. I know thth, becauthe he bwrock my dose, an' knocked out my teeth lath night when I tried to taalk to him like a dormal human being.

ANNCR: Every year the Salvation Army provides shelter for thousands of women, who can't take a little discipline.

WOMAN: I'm juth glad that taalking to you like thith . . . you can't thee me, becauthe I know I thound (CRYING) muth better than I look.

ANNCR: Help us to help them.

442

(MUSIC: THROUGHOUT)

SUPER: MICHAEL CONRAD. MALE. AGE 28. ARMED ROBBERY. ASSAULT AND BATTERY. RAPE. MURDER. APPREHENDED AUGUST 1994 BY POLICE LIEUTENANT JOSEPH CRUTHERS, SHOWN HERE.

SUPER: URBAN ALLIANCE ON RACE RELATIONS.

443

ANNCR: Not long ago, the big dog on the left donated blood to help save the cute little guy on the right. Pepe, is there anything you'd like to say to Max?

PEPE (BARKING LIKE A GERMAN SHEPARD): Thank you.

ANNCR: Ask your dog to give blood. What's he gonna say, no?

SUPER: EASTERN VETERINARY BLOOD BANK. (410) 224-BANK.

PUBLIC SERVICE/ POLITICAL TELEVISION: SINGLE

444
ART DIRECTOR:
Dave Gardiner
WRITERS:
Ken Lewis
Stu Cooperrider
AGENCY PRODUCER:
Harry McCoy
PRODUCTION COMPANIES:
Palomar, Picture Park
DIRECTOR:
Neil Abramson
CLIENT:
Massachusetts Department of Public Health
AGENCY:
Houston Effler Herstek Favat/Boston

445
ART DIRECTOR:
Dave Gardiner
WRITERS:
Ken Lewis
Stu Cooperrider
AGENCY PRODUCER:
Harry McCoy
PRODUCTION COMPANIES:
Palomar, Picture Park
DIRECTOR:
Neil Abramson
CLIENT:
Massachusetts Department of Public Health
AGENCY:
Houston Effler Herstek Favat/Boston

446
ART DIRECTOR:
Sean Riley
WRITERS:
Joe Alexander
Raymond McKinney
AGENCY PRODUCER:
Randy Shreve
CLIENT:
Stay In School
AGENCY:
The Martin Agency/ Richmond

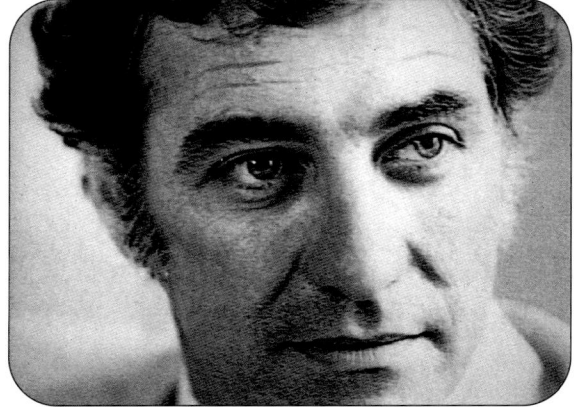

444
VICTOR CRAWFORD: Maybe they'll get your little brother or sister. Or maybe the kid down the block. But one thing is perfectly clear to me, tobacco companies are after children. Why? Because tobacco companies know that 90 percent of smokers start as children before they know any better. Of course, marketing to kids is unethical, so they just deny it. I'm Victor Crawford. I was a tobacco lobbyist for five years so I know how tobacco companies work. I lied. And I'm sorry.

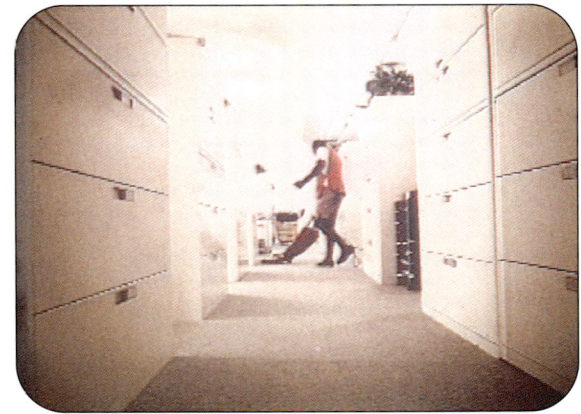
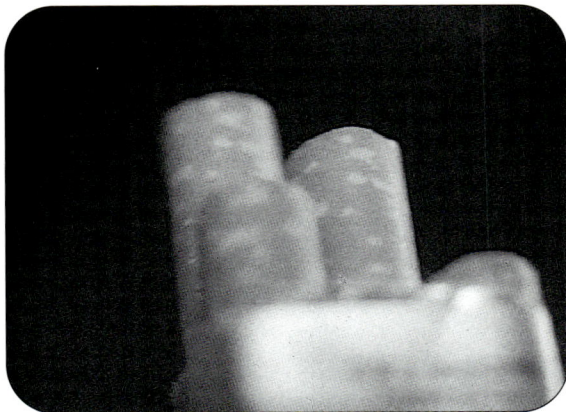

445

PATRICK REYNOLDS: Do you know what's in cigarettes? No. Because the last thing tobacco companies want is for you to know how many poisonous chemicals there are in cigarettes. So they just don't tell you. Not on the pack, not in their ads. I'm Patrick Reynolds, the grandson of RJ Reynolds. My family's name is printed on the side of seven billion packs a year. Why am I telling you this? I want my family to be on the right side for a change.

446

(SFX: SOUND OF A VACUUM)
SUPER: STAY IN SCHOOL.

PUBLIC SERVICE/ POLITICAL TELEVISION: SINGLE

447
ART DIRECTOR:
Jim Henderson
WRITER:
Alan Marcus
AGENCY PRODUCER:
Rebecca Keller
PRODUCTION COMPANY:
Matre Rajtar
DIRECTOR:
Tom Matre
CLIENT:
Minnesota Department of Natural Resources
AGENCY:
Martin/Williams, Minneapolis

448
ART DIRECTOR:
Matthew Schwartz
WRITER:
David George
AGENCY PRODUCER:
Jerry Boyle
CLIENT:
Partnership for a Drug-Free America
AGENCY:
Saatchi & Saatchi/ New York

449
ART DIRECTOR:
Peter Cohen
WRITER:
Jay Taub
AGENCY PRODUCERS:
Peter Cohen
Jay Taub
PRODUCTION COMPANIES:
NYU Films
Pittman Hensley
DIRECTOR:
Daniel Fisher
CLIENT:
Coalition for the Homeless
AGENCY:
StreetSmart Advertising/ New York

447
ANNCR: What happens when you combine the world's finest German hops with rare Canadian malted barley and add the ice cold, clear waters of a spring fed Minnesota lake? How about big trouble?

SUPER: DON'T DRINK AND BOAT.

SUPER: MINNESOTA DEPARTMENT OF NATURAL RESOURCES.

448

(SFX: SOUND OF PROJECTOR, CLICK OF EACH SLIDE THROUGHOUT)

ANNCR: In advertising, they say one of the surest ways to get your message across is to put celebrities in your commercial. We hope they're right.

SUPER: PARTNERSHIP FOR A DRUG-FREE AMERICA.

449

(SFX: CITY STREET SOUNDS THROUGHOUT)

SUPER: PLEASE DON'T LITTER.

SUPER: PEOPLE HAVE TO SLEEP HERE.

SUPER: COALITION FOR THE HOMELESS. 212-964-5900.

Radio Finalists

CONSUMER RADIO: SINGLE

450
WRITER:
Gary Mueller
AGENCY PRODUCER:
Gary Mueller
PRODUCTION COMPANY:
Independent Sound
CLIENT:
Schaeffer's Foods
AGENCY:
Birdsall-Voss & Kloppenburg/Milwaukee

451
WRITER:
Mike Shine
AGENCY PRODUCER:
Adrienne Cummins
CLIENT:
Millers Outpost
AGENCY:
Butler Shine & Stern/Sausalito

452
WRITERS:
David Corr
Eric Silver
David Shane
AGENCY PRODUCER:
Roxanne Karsch
PRODUCTION COMPANY:
Are These My Shoes? Productions
CLIENT:
NYNEX Yellow Pages
AGENCY:
Chiat/Day, New York

453
WRITERS:
Arthur Bijur
Jeff Watzman
Harold Einstein
AGENCY PRODUCER:
Anne Kurtzman
PRODUCTION COMPANIES:
Clack Sound Studio
Radio Ranch
CLIENT:
Staples
AGENCY:
Cliff Freeman & Partners/New York

450
(SFX: DUCK MOANING)
ANNCR: Donald Duck Orange Juice. It's that good. Donald Duck Orange Juice is now available at Schaefer's Food Mart. Schaefer's. Over 1,000 brands under one nicely re-shingled roof.
(SFX: DUCK MOANS)

452
MIKE: Life is full of questions. Fortunately, the NYNEX Yellow Pages is full of answers. Just ask the Human Balloon, Zoltan Krasznai.
ZOLTAN: Like it says in my ad, Mike, I'm the answer to your entertainment needs.
MIKE: Right. So Zoltan, what, exactly, makes you the human balloon?
ZOLTAN: Well, lemme show you Mike.
(SFX: BALLOON INFLATING)
MIKE: Now, is that, uh, helium?
ZOLTAN (WITH VOICE A LITTLE HIGHER): Yes it is, Mike.
MIKE: Not too much, wouldn't want you to explode.
ZOLTAN: Mike, I'm a pro.
MIKE: Zoltan . . . you're uh . . . beginning to float.
ZOLTAN: Just hold on to my string, Mike, and I'll be fine. Don't let go.
MIKE: Isn't this kind of dangerous?
ZOLTAN: Not if you steer me clear of those electrical wires, Mike.
MIKE: I'm trying. Now, if you go left do I pull right or left?
ZOLTAN: Mike, I'm not a physicist, I'm a balloon man.
MIKE: Well, if you're looking for answers to your entertainment needs . . .
ZOLTAN: Left, Mike, left!!
MIKE: I'm trying, geez . . . look no further than the NYNEX Yellow Pages.
ZOLTAN: Oh boy, that's it, Mike, now I'm stuck! Real good, Mike, real good.
MIKE: Sorry, sorry. NYNEX. More information. More solutions. More stuff.
ZOLTAN: Now I'm going to be late for little Bobby Hershfield's birthday party.
MIKE: I'm sure he'll be devastated.
ZOLTAN: You bet he will, pal, you bet he will.

451
(SFX: TWO MALE VOICES ON LANGUAGE TAPE)
"Welcome to Let's Speak French. Please listen and repeat."
"Hello." "Allo."
"How nice to see you." "C'est bien a te voir."
"Please come in." "Entre, s'il vous plait."
"May I take your coat?" "Puis-je prendre taveste?"
"It makes you look like a cheeseball." "Quelle taveste comme le balle de fromage."
"But I see that your shirt is even cheesier." "Mais je vois que ta chemise comme la frommage-ier."
"Have you shopped at all since the Reagan era?" "Es tu n' alle pas faire des courses depuis lepoque de Reagan?"
"I have not seen so much cheese since my last trip to Switzerland." "Je nai pas vu autant fromage que ma voyage au Switzerland."
ANNCR: Hey, maybe it's time for you to take a study break and head over to Millers Outpost. They've got tons of non-cheesy clothes, and right now you can get 40 percent off all men's flannel shirts, denim shirts, and outerwear. Millers Outpost. Why pay the price of shopping someplace else?
(SFX: LANGUAGE TAPE)
"If your clothes were any more cheesy . . ." "Si tes vetements a comme le fromage . . ."
". . . I could spread you on a cracker." ". . . Je te mett rai sur une biscotte."

453
MAN: I know, I'll start my own business. I'll start . . . an advertising agency!
ANNCR: Staples has everything you need to start a business.
MAN: I'll name it after . . . me.
ANNCR: Nameplates.
MAN: I'll look out on Madison Avenue.
ANNCR: Desk sets.
MAN: No, no I'll be on Park Avenue.
ANNCR: Oak desk sets.
MAN: And I'll hire artists.
ANNCR: Markers.
MAN: Copywriters.
ANNCR: Typewriters.
MAN: Account Executives.
ANNCR: Attaché cases.
MAN: And hundreds of other people who will call me sir.
ANNCR: Employment application forms.
MAN: I'll just sit around all day dreaming up clever slogans.
ANNCR: Dictation machines.
MAN: And I'll schmooze clients to get their business.
ANNCR: Pen and pencil gift sets.
MAN: And they'll beg to see my brilliant ideas.
ANNCR: Overhead projectors.
MAN: 'Course they'll be nervous.
ANNCR: Restroom signs.
MAN: But in the end we'll shake on it.
ANNCR: Hand soap.
ANNCR: At Staples you'll find over 5000 office products at the guaranteed low price. Everything you need to start and grow a business. Staples, yeah we've got that.
MAN: And then some big company will try and take me over and that's when things will get rough.
ANNCR: First aid kits.
MAN: (LAUGHS)

454

ANNCR: On the bank of the East River at 88th Street sits a two-story private residence known as Gracie Mansion. It is within these walls that the mayor, his family, and frequent guests have been known to openly discuss radical new plans for the city. If you are a New York executive looking to benefit from advance notice of the sweeping changes that could very well affect your business, we regret to inform you that the positions of chef, butler and housekeeper have been filled. *Crain's New York Business,* however, is at newsstands everywhere.

456

MAN 1: Hey, little bunny. Want to come to my birthday bash?
MAN 2 (OVER SPEAKER): Again. Take 52.
MAN 1: Hey, little bunny. Want to come to my birthday bash?
MAN 2: Lighter.
MAN 1: Hey, little bunny. Want to come to my birthday bash?
MAN 2: No, it's a cartoon. Goofy.
MAN 1: Hey, little bunny. Want to come to my birthday bash?
MAN 2: Let's take five.
(SFX: DIALING)
MAN 3: Ace Helium Suppliers.
MAN 1 (IN HELIUM VOICE): Hey, little bunny. Want to come to my birthday bash?
ANNCR: The NYNEX Business to Business Directory. Where one business finds another.

458

(MUSIC: '50S STYLE COMMERCIAL JINGLE)
SINGERS: *All the gals come runnin when it's . . .*
ANNCR (OVER SINGERS): Chevys.
SINGERS: *. . . that you wear. Can't keep their hands off ya when you have that . . .*
ANNCR (OVER SINGERS): Fresh Mex.
SINGERS: *. . . scent in your hair.*
ANNCR: Boy, oh boy did we get a great deal on these old canned commercials. And you know us. At Chevys, we never miss a chance to pass the savings on to you, the customer.
SINGERS: *When you use . . .*
ANNCR (OVER SINGERS): Chevys.
SINGERS: *. . . the gals think you're a dream . . .*
ANNCR (OVER SINGERS): Fresh Mex.
SINGERS: *. . . formula really makes 'em scream.*
ANNCR: Yes, at Chevys our commercials may be canned, but that's the only thing that is. We're the home of the Fresh Mex pledge. That means we promise to deliver our fresh tortillas to your table piping hot. And those babies roll off our specially designed El Machino every 63 seconds or so. We'd never serve you something that's been sitting around for awhile. Present commercial excepted.
SINGERS: *No gal can resist from Poughkeepsie to Pomona 'cuz when you have . .*
ANNCR (OVER SINGERS): Chevys.
SINGERS: *. . . in your hair you get that . . .*
ANNCR (OVER SINGERS): Fresh Mex.
SINGERS: *. . . aroma . . .*
ANNCR (OVER SINGERS): Chevys. Chevys. Fresh Mex.

455

ANNCR: Up on the West Side, across from Central Park, stands New York's most famous planetarium. Inside, under a large dome, the heavens light up and rotate, revealing the precise points in the year when the moon passes Venus, Jupiter aligns with Mars, and Mercury is retrograde. If you are a New York executive attempting to pinpoint the correct moment in time to execute your next business deal, feel free to bring a notepad to the planetarium. We strongly recommend, however, you also consult the weekly information in *Crain's New York Business.*

457

(MUSIC: STRING QUARTET)
ATTORNEY: And now we'll commence with the reading of the will.
WIFE: He was a good husband (SOB). God knows he may have strayed a time or two but (SOB) there was a special bond between us.
DAUGHTER: Yeah, it's called thirty million bucks mother, let's get on with this.
WIFE (WAILING): I loved that man so!
SON: Yeah mom, so what if he missed all my little league games, my wedding, my bone marrow transplant.
ATTORNEY: I, Colin Champion Probert, being of sound mind and body, do hereby bequeath all my earthly possessions . . .
WIFE: (LOUD SOB)
ATTORNEY: My stocks, bonds and considerable cash holdings . . .
DAUGHTER: Yes!
ATTORNEY: To my faithful dog, Mr. Stinky.
FAMILY: What?
ATTORNEY: Yes, it says right here; nothing for my wife and children because they always forgot the milk for my cookies.
WIFE: There must be a mistake!
ATTORNEY: Nope. It says you forgot his milk and you're all a bunch of big losers and he wants you to die alone, miserable and penniless. Well, have a nice day.
(MUSIC: DRIVING)
ANNCR: Ah, wholesome goodness the entire family can enjoy. Got milk?

CONSUMER RADIO: SINGLE

454
WRITER:
Dean Hacohen
PRODUCTION COMPANY:
Soundtrack Studios
CLIENT:
Crain's New York Business
AGENCY:
Goldsmith/Jeffrey, New York

455
WRITER:
Dean Hacohen
PRODUCTION COMPANY:
Soundtrack Studios
CLIENT:
Crain's New York Business
AGENCY:
Goldsmith/Jeffrey, New York

456
WRITER:
Dean Hacohen
CLIENT:
NYNEX Business to Business Directory
PRODUCTION COMPANY:
Are These My Shoes? Productions
AGENCY:
Goldsmith/Jeffrey, New York

457
WRITER:
Ron Saltmarsh
AGENCY PRODUCER:
Taryn Holland
CLIENT:
California Fluid Milk Processor Advisory Board
AGENCY:
Goodby Silverstein & Partners/San Francisco

458
WRITER:
Erik Moe
AGENCY PRODUCER:
Betsy Flynn
CLIENT:
Chevys Mexican Restaurants
AGENCY:
Goodby Silverstein & Partners/San Francisco

CONSUMER RADIO: SINGLE

459
WRITER:
Erik Moe
AGENCY PRODUCER:
Betsy Flynn
CLIENT:
Chevys Mexican Restaurants
AGENCY:
Goodby Silverstein & Partners/San Francisco

460
WRITER:
Sam Pond
AGENCY PRODUCER:
Greg Martinez
CLIENT:
Prego
AGENCY:
Goodby Silverstein & Partners/San Francisco

461
WRITER:
Jack Low
AGENCY PRODUCER:
Jack Low
CLIENT:
Genesee Brewing Company
AGENCY:
Pedone & Partners/New York

462
WRITER:
Jack Low
AGENCY PRODUCER:
Steffi Binder
PRODUCTION COMPANY:
Pomann Music
CLIENT:
Genesee Brewing Company
AGENCY:
Pedone & Partners/New York

463
WRITERS:
Terry O'Reilly
Rick Shurman
PRODUCTION COMPANY:
Pirate Radio/Toronto
CLIENT:
Interactive Media Corporation/Telepersonals

459
(MUSIC: '50S STYLE COMMERCIAL JINGLE)
SINGERS: *Brush, brush, brush with . . .*
ANNCR (OVER SINGERS): Chevys.
SINGERS: *. . . Every single day. Tasty . . .*
ANNCR (OVER SINGERS): Fresh Mex..
SINGERS: *. . . flavor cavities will stay away!*
ANNCR: A while back this guy came into Chevys and gave us a great deal on these old commercials. And you know us. We never miss a chance to pass the savings on to you, the customer.
SINGERS: *Brush, brush, brush with . . .*
ANNCR (OVER SINGERS): Chevys.
SINGERS: *. . . white teeth, delicious taste your family and your dentist love that . . .*
ANNCR (OVER SINGERS): Fresh Mex.
SINGERS: *. . . paste.*
ANNCR: At Chevys, the commercials may be canned but that's the only thing that is. We're the home of Fresh Mex. That means everything in the place is fresh. For instance all our delicious tamales are handmade every morning. And that's just part of our pledge to make everything from only the freshest ingredients. That is, everything but our commercials.
SINGERS: *Brush, brush, brush with . . .*
ANNCR (OVER SINGERS): Chevys.
SINGERS: *. . . every single day. Tasty . . .*
ANNCR (OVER SINGERS): Fresh Mex.
SINGERS: *. . . flavor cavities will stay away.*
ANNCR: Chevys. Fresh Mex.

461
ANNCR: The celebrated and world renowned mime Marcel Marceau once said . . . He was also quoted more than once as saying . . . And on the subject of mandatory street permits for mimes, the seldom outspoken Marceau was overheard to say . . . Ooh, harsh words for a man of such a quiet disposition. Now if Marceau was still around today, what would he have said about new Genny Ice beer?
(SFX: BEER POURING)
ANNCR: Would he have burst forth proclaiming . . . ? Seems we can only wonder what the great mime would have said about new Genny Ice. But with a beer this good, it's fair to say that even the great Marceau would not have been at a loss for words. New Genny Ice . . .
(SFX: CAN OPENING)
ANNCR: The perfect ice.

460
PAULO: It is I, Paulo. At the fabulous Prego resaurant, I am Italian once again. I say "grazie" to the hostess. I say "per favore." I say "ciao." I say it again. I say "ciao" so many times the manager asks me to stop. It is annoying the other customers. But I am home again with the smell of Italian herbs and the heat of the brick ovens and the women. A brunette looks at her watch. She is wondering what is keeping me from her perhaps? I am patient. I let her simmer, like my parmigiana di melanzane. Warm and wholesome inside, certain to bubble over if forgotten. I wink at her. Ah, no response. I wink again. She does not notice. I wink with my left eye and then my right eye. Then I double wink with both eyes and then alternate left to right . . . it is a wild Morse code of love! The manager approaches, he asks me if I require an ambulance. His concern is touching. Oh, Paulo! Prego, Union Street. See. Be seen. Be seen eating.

462
ANNCR: Recently, we received a lot of mail from folks all over the country who have tried our new Genny Ice Beer. So we thought we'd invite them to our studio here in New York to share their letters with us on the air. Our first letter is from Paul Lippinachi from Exit 8 in New Jersey who writes . . .
(SFX: WRITING SOUNDS)
ANNCR: Allan Pafenbach of Breakneck Ski Area in Vermont sends us this kind note . . .
(SFX: WRITING SOUNDS)
ANNCR: And finally, Betty Keepin from Godblessyou Falls, Illinois writes . . .
(SFX: ERASING SOUNDS)
ANNCR: Well actually, she erases first . . .
(SFX: BLOWING SOUNDS)
ANNCR: . . . then writes . . .
(SFX: WRITING SOUNDS)
ANNCR: . . . and writes . . .
(SFX: WRITING SOUNDS)
ANNCR: . . . and hey Betty, what is this, *War and Peace*? . . . Let's get to the point.
(SFX: MORE WRITING, FINAL PERIOD)
ANNCR: Thanks. Well now, there you have it. Written proof that Genny Ice Beer is the one ice beer folks love most. New Genny Ice, the perfect ice.

463
ANNCR: You can spend your life looking for the perfect woman.
(SFX: COCKTAIL PIANO BAR)
ANNCR: Hi, can I buy you a drink?
GAL: No.
ANNCR: How about lunch?
GAL: No.
ANNCR: A car perhaps?
GAL: No.
ANNCR: Fortunately, I called Telepersonals, with over 3,000 personal ads from people looking for long term or casual relationships. It's free to listen to ads 24 hours a day and leaving a message costs less than a beer.
(SFX: BEEP)
ANNCR: Hi, this is Norm, I'm looking for a woman. Well, that about sums it up. Call me.

464

TOM: Hi, Tom Bodett for Motel 6 with some thoughts about the big baseball strike. You know a lot of the players are probably using this time off to take a rare summer get-away. And with those million dollar salaries on hold, it only makes sense that they stay at Motel 6. Of course they wouldn't get the pamperin' they're used to at those big fancy hotels, but they would get a clean, comfortable room for the lowest prices of any national chain. And since the owners aren't exactly makin' money hand-over-fist right now, they could stay at Motel 6 on their vacations, too. Well, just picture it. They run into the players down at the ice machine and hang out together watchin' free in-room movies—like that heart-warming one where the guy builds a ballpark in his cornfield. Everybody gets all misty-eyed and they sit down and settle their differences right then and there. Could happen. Well, I'm Tom Bodett, part-time mediator, for Motel 6 and we'll leave the light on for you.

466

(SFX: TYPEWRITER)

COW: Dear Greenpeace, I've got a little problem here. It's called Bum Steer. A great steak house. There lies the problem. I'm a cow. Anyway, heard you saved a few whales. Well how 'bout us cows? Don't we count? It's not like you need to charter a boat. Just get on some bikes and start swervin' like maniacs in front of people headed for the Bum Steer. Anyway, the more I worry, the more I eat, which means time's running out. Signed, Cow.

ANNCR: The Bum Steer. Great Steaks at Sixty-fourth and O.

COW: Bummer.

465

ANNCR: In polite society, yelling at the top of one's lungs is considered completely unacceptable and most uncouth. For example, witness such behavior at a symphony . . .

(MUSIC: MOZART SYMPHONY)

MAN: You stupid cellist! Mozart must be spinning in his grave!

ANNCR: What about laying Uncle Hubert to rest .

(MUSIC: FUNERAL ORGAN)

(SFX: CRYING)

MAN: Hubie you're goin' down! Take it to the hole baby!! Six feet under baby!!!

ANNCR: And your cousin's wedding . . .

(MUSIC: WEDDING MARCH)

WOMAN: You call this a wedding? Where'd you get the cake? Prison? And that dress! Why it could fit an elephant!

ANNCR: While polite society provides no place for such behavior, there is the Tacoma Dome, this year's home to the SuperSonics.

(SFX: BASKETBALL GAME)

MAN: Uncle Hubie could take you . . .

ANNCR: For the socially unacceptable, we recommend Sonics seven-game plans. With these mini-season tickets, you are assured seats when the NBA's stars come to town. Call 283-DUNK while packages still remain.

WOMAN: "Thunder Dan?" Make that "Blunder Dan?" Woo!! Woo!! Woo!! Woo!!

467

DOG: Hey, Red Dog here.

I got a bone to pick. Not with you in particular. Unless your one of them dogs I see barking up the wrong tree. Never mind for a moment whether you got the wrong tree or the right tree—why are you barking up a freakin' tree in the first place?

See, makes no sense. If there's somethin' up there, it sure as hell ain't gonna come down with you barkin' your fool head off. Quit your yelping. Walk away. Sooner or later whatever's up there's gonna come down.

Now I don't care if you spend all night howlin' up a tree but you're keeping me up at night. And believe me when I don't get my beauty sleep, I am not a pretty sight.

ANNCR: Red Dog Beer. You are your own dog.

CONSUMER RADIO: SINGLE

464
WRITERS:
Mike Bales
Tim Wood
AGENCY PRODUCERS:
Thomas Hripko
Harvey Lewis
PRODUCTION COMPANIES:
Clear Shot
Real to Reel
CLIENT:
Motel 6
AGENCY:
The Richards Group/Dallas

465
WRITER:
Craig Hoit
AGENCY PRODUCER:
Joyce Schmidtbauer
PRODUCTION COMPANY:
Clatter & Din
CLIENT:
Seattle SuperSonics
AGENCY:
WongDoody/Seattle

CONSUMER RADIO: CAMPAIGN

466
WRITERS:
Laura Crawford
Carter Weitz
AGENCY PRODUCERS:
Laura Crawford
Carter Weitz
PRODUCTION COMPANY:
Soundscapes
CLIENT:
Bum Steer Steakhouse
AGENCY:
Bailey Lauerman & Associates/Lincoln, NE

467
WRITER:
Stephen Creet
AGENCY PRODUCER:
Marie Robertson
PRODUCTION COMPANY:
Harris Cole Wilde
CLIENT:
Molson Breweries
AGENCY:
BBDO/Toronto

CONSUMER RADIO: CAMPAIGN

468
WRITERS:
David Corr
David Shane
AGENCY PRODUCER:
Roxanne Karsch
PRODUCTION COMPANY:
Are These My Shoes? Productions
CLIENT:
Nick at Nite
AGENCY:
Chiat/Day, New York

469
WRITER:
Michelle Roufa
AGENCY PRODUCERS:
Mary Ellen O'Brien
Maresa Wickham
PRODUCTION COMPANIES:
Kamen Audio
Clack Sound Studio
CLIENT:
Little Caesars
AGENCY:
Cliff Freeman & Partners/New York

470
WRITER:
Randy Hibbitts
AGENCY PRODUCER:
George Young
CLIENT:
Kia Motors America
AGENCY:
Goldberg Moser O'Neill/San Francisco

471
WRITERS:
Trevor Robinson
Alan Young
AGENCY PRODUCER:
Emma Palfrey-Rogers
CLIENT:
Mercury Communications
AGENCY:
Howell Henry Chaldecott Lury & Partners/London

468
(SFX: TELEPHONE RINGING)

NICK AT NITE MAN: Hello, Nick at Nite Hotline. May I help you?

CALLER: Yeah. I'm having trouble with my shoe phone.

NICK A NITE MAN: You have a shoe phone?

CALLER: Yeah, I mean my shoe phone is the same model Maxwell Smart wears, so I figured you guys at Nick at Nite would be able to help.

NICK AT NITE MAN: I don't know, actually.

CALLER: Well, put Max on. He'll no how to fix it.

NICK AT NITE MAN: Well . . . ah, he's not here.

CALLER: Okay, let me speak to 99.

NICK AT NITE MAN: She's not here either.

CALLER: How about Hymie? I bet Hymie will know what to do.

NICK AT NITE MAN: You know, Hymie actually just stepped out.

CALLER: I don't believe it. Hymie wouldn't just go steppin' out, he's a robot.

NICK AT NITE MAN: Robots step out . . . they do . .

CALLER: Well, he's got no free will of his own.

NICK AT NITE MAN: M-M-Maybe you should, you know, round out your viewing habits a little.

CALLER: What?

NICK AT NITE MAN: You know kind of count on us for all your classic TV; a Mary Tyler Moore, a little Dragnet, a Bob Newhart for example.

CALLER: Bob Newhart? As in Dr. Bob Hartley?

NICK AT NITE MAN: Yeah . . . Uh-huh.

CALLER: I . . . I . . . don't need a shrink, I need a new rotary for my wing tip.

NICK AT NITE MAN: Up . . . look who . . . just . . . walked in but . . . Hymie . . . Hang on one second, I'll . . . a . . . (CLEARS THROAT) Hello I am Hymie . . .

CALLER: Hymie.

NICK AT NITE MAN (IN CHANGED VOICE): How may I help you?

CALLER: The man was trying to tell me you weren't there.

NICK AT NITE MAN: I am here now.

CALLER: Can you fix my shoe?

NICK AT NITE MAN: No problem.

ANNCR: Watch Nick at Nite, every night, all night. It's classic TV. To get cable call 1-800-OK-CABLE.

470
(MUSIC: FAST, DRIVING MUSIC)

ANNCR: Hi, I'm here for Kia Motors America with a hypothetical situation for you. Imagine there's a big old pothole on the road ahead of you. What do you do? Well, if you're driving your own car, you swerve. But how about if you're in a rent-a-car? You step on the gas and see how hard you can nail the sucker. So what does this have to do with the new Sephia sedan we've just introduced to America? Well, we tested them by sticking about two thousand Kias in rental fleets where people were confronted with hard choices like this every day. And we heard some suggestions on how to improve our car. And now, our cars are ready for sale, starting at under 8,900 dollars. Check 'em out. They're tested not just by robots and engineers, but by wild, reckless yahoos. Like you and me. Introducing Kia. Because it's about time everyone had a well-made car.

469
ANNCR: Not long ago, Little Caesars asked America to speak out for what they really want . . .

MAN 1 IN CROWD: I want a new car!

WOMAN IN CROWD: Money!

MAN 2 IN CROWD: A tub full of pudding and a supermodel!

ANNCR: Unable to meet their initial requests, we asked how many would like more cheese and toppings on their pizzas . . .

CROWD: Yeah!

(MUSIC: TRIUMPHANT, PATRIOTIC)

ANNCR: Introducing the new Little Caesars Pleasers Menu. Pizzas with more meat. More cheese. More toppings. Get any two for $9.98, or one for $5.99!

LITTLE CAESAR: Pizza! Pizza!

471
(SFX: STATIC)

GRAYSON: Attention. This is London. Introducing Mercury MiniCall. Once purchased you never pay another bean, because you give the number to friends and they pay to contact you using secret numerical codes. There now follows some vital coded messages for Mercury MiniCall users.

One-seven-seven. A famous comedian has just caught fire.

Six-nine-one. Henry the Eighth enjoys corgis.

Two-four-one. The beast has ironed your socks.

Eight-five-five. Uncle Albert's new frock is full of mirth.

Zero-zero-one. I'll biff you in the perishin' conk.

Heed these warnings! Mercury MiniCall is free to use but walls have ears.

ANNCR: FreeCall 0500-505-505 for the splendid details. Mercury MiniCall's ripping gizmo is brought to you courtesy of Motorola.

472

SINGERS: *Back Hoe . . . Back Hoe . . . Back Hoe . . . Back Hoe Bob.*

BOB: Quiet. Today I got one of my heavy duty Battaluco Scrap Iron sweatshirts, cost 45 dollars and one of those official NFL Chicago Bears sweatshirts, cost 60 dollars. We're gonna see which one's tougher. I've strung the sweatshirts up between two I-beams. Now while Tony is walking from one beam to the other acrosss his Battaluco sweatshirt, it's a good time for me to tell you that Back Hoe Bob clothing is all tough-as-steak fat, honest-to-goodness work wear. And I only made a few so you won't see 'em on every corncob on the street. All right, Tony. Now the Bears sweatshirt.

(SFX: CLOTH RIPPING, MAN YELLING, CRASH)

BOB: Oh geez. Look, if you want a tough, comfortable sweatshirt, you gotta buy one of mine. Or, get hurt with some other piece of crap.

SINGERS: *Sturdy clothes worn by everyday joes.*

BOB: Shut up.

ANNCR: Back Hoe Bob apparel available exclusively at Pride of Milwaukee in the Grand Avenue.

474

ANNCR: Samuel F. B. Morse, creator of the Morse code, once said:

(SFX: SERIES OF BEEPS AND DASHES)

ANNCR: He uttered these famous words at the unveiling of his transmitting system in 1837:

(SFX: SERIES OF LONG BEEPS AND DASHES)

ANNCR: And shouted:

(SFX: ONE LONG BEEP)

ANNCR: Whoa, you don't have to know code to figure that one out. Now if Morse were still around today, what would he have said about new Genny Ice Beer?

(SFX: VERY LONG SERIES OF BEEPS AND DASHES, FOLLOWED BY BEER OPENING, POURING)

ANNCR: Would he have prattled on and on about it's exceptional drinkability and smooth taste?

(SFX: MORE BEEPS AND DASHES UNDER UNTIL END)

ANNCR: He did have a tendency to prattle. While no one can know for sure what the great inventor would have said about new Genny Ice Beer, this we do know, Samuel Morse had his finger on the pulse of the information superhighway and yet tragically, never had the chance to lay that same finger on the pull tab of a Genny Ice Beer.

(SFX: BEER OPENING, POURING)

ANNCR: New Genny Ice. The Perfect Ice.

473

GUY: So like my girlfriend—she's always talking about our relationship—and she's like, "You like Devil Dogs more than you like me." And I'm like, "That's crazy." And she goes, "Then why did you leave my party so early?" And I'm like, "Cause you didn't have any Yodels or Funny Bones or Ring Dings or nothin'." And she's like, "I had chips." And I go, "I need more than that." And she's like, "You're so stupid." And I'm like, "Heah"—like I'm the one who forgot to buy the Devil Dogs. And she's like crying and I'm really bumming out cause she got my Yodel all soggy.

ANNCR: Drakes cookies, pies and cakes. They're all consuming.

475

ANNCR: When goldfish die, do they go to the same heaven people do, or is there a separate goldfish heaven? You there, Yonni Ouray, Marine Biologist, what say you?

YONNI: Well, a popular notion is that heaven is the place that exists up above the world we live in. If a goldfish is pulled up through the surface of the water, which ironically would look to him very bright and hazy . . . much like our own mental image of heaven . . .

ANNCR: Wrap it up, man.

YONNI: Yes, um, well, a fish out of water could be in so to speak . . . fish heaven, although not a very pleasant one.

(SFX: BONGOS)

ANNCR: Oh man, that's deep. Deep like Mamma Ilardo's pizza. Thick, deep crust, deep cheese, deep toppings. It's deep, man.

CONSUMER RADIO: CAMPAIGN

472
WRITER:
Steve Koeneke
AGENCY PRODUCER:
Darlene Stimac
CLIENT:
Back Hoe Bob
AGENCY:
Kohnke Koeneke/ Milwaukee

473
WRITER:
Kathy Kiely
AGENCY PRODUCER:
Matt Pedone
PRODUCTION COMPANY:
Jay West Productions
CLIENT:
Drakes Bakeries
AGENCY:
Pedone & Partners/ New York

474
WRITER:
Jack Low
AGENCY PRODUCER:
Steffi Binder
PRODUCTION COMPANIES:
Pomann Music
Mixed Nuts
CLIENT:
Genesee Brewing Company
AGENCY:
Pedone & Partners/ New York

475
WRITERS:
Jane King
Jeff Alphin
David McMillan
Marc Lichtenstein
AGENCY PRODUCER:
Rick Hemmert
PRODUCTION COMPANY:
Flite Three Recordings
CLIENT:
Mamma Ilardo's
AGENCY:
TBC Advertising/ Baltimore

Television Finalists

CONSUMER TELEVISION OVER :30 SINGLE

476
ART DIRECTOR:
John Horton
WRITER:
Richard Foster
AGENCY PRODUCER:
Lindsay Hughes
PRODUCTION COMPANY:
Smith Hadfield
DIRECTOR:
David Smith
CLIENT:
The Economist
AGENCY:
Abbott Mead Vickers.
BBDO/London

477
ART DIRECTOR:
Walter Campbell
WRITER:
Tom Carty
AGENCY PRODUCER:
Lindsay Hughes
PRODUCTION COMPANY:
Tony Kaye Films
DIRECTOR:
Tony Kaye
CLIENT:
Volvo Cars UK
AGENCY:
Abbott Mead Vickers.
BBDO/London

478
ART DIRECTOR:
Don Schneider
WRITER:
Michael Patti
AGENCY PRODUCER:
Regina Ebel
PRODUCTION COMPANY:
Pytka
DIRECTOR:
Joe Pytka
CLIENT:
Pepsi Cola International
AGENCY:
BBDO/New York

479
ART DIRECTOR:
Don Schneider
WRITERS:
Ted Sann
Michael Patti
AGENCY PRODUCER:
Regina Ebel
PRODUCTION COMPANY:
Pytka
DIRECTOR:
Joe Pytka
CLIENT:
Pepsi Cola
AGENCY:
BBDO/New York

476
GEORGE: So, have we found the man for the job?
HAMISH: Two excellent candidates. I liked the second chap.
GEORGE: Really?
HAMISH: What's this?
GEORGE: A little candid camera I arranged with the security people.
HAMISH: Despicable!
GEORGE: Observation, Hamish, observation. Now, observe candidate one. There . . . see? He reads *The Economist*. Good sign. Now here's your man.
HAMISH: So, he picks up the car magazine.
GEORGE: Precisely. Bit of a giveaway don't you think?
HAMISH: Oh absolutely, an interest in cars, thoroughly reprehensible. How's the Aston by the way?
GEORGE: I'm just saying, given the choice, I'd choose *The Economist* reader.
HAMISH: Rewind the tape a bit. There. Freeze it.
GEORGE: What?
HAMISH: In the briefcase, George. Now that's an *Economist* reader.
GEORGE: Well I'll be . . . well spotted, Hamish.
HAMISH: Observation, George, observation.
SUPER: THE ECONOMIST.

477
STUNTMAN: I used to be a stunt kid before I was a stuntman. I learnt one thing early on—belief is everything. My interest in cars started on my fourth birthday, I've loved driving cars ever since. This car is great to drive. I do stunts people think can't be done. They think my stunts are crazy. I've never been afraid of heights, never. I guess I have a pretty healthy fear of death. You can conquer fear through knowledge. One centimeter this way or that and its four hundred miles down. When I ask it to do something it responds. Control. I'm a control freak. You know some people say I'll believe it when I see it, I prefer to say you'll see it when you believe it. They think my stunts are crazy.

SUPER: VOLVO. A CAR YOU CAN BELIEVE IN.

478

ANNCR: To see if there is any difference between Pepsi and Coke, we are delving into their sub-molecular structures to discover the very essence of what they are made of. First the Coke . . .

(SFX: GUY MOWING LAWN)

ANNCR: And now the Pepsi. Just as we expected, there is no difference.

(SFX: CINDY CRAWFORD MOWING LAWN)

(MUSIC: *Could this be magic my dear, my heart's all aglow . . .*)

SUPER: PEPSI. THE CHOICE OF A NEW GENERATION.

479

GUY 1: Here come those darn hippies again.

GUY ON LOUDSPEAKER: Testing . . . 1, 2 . . . 1 . . . check, check, okay. Stay away from the green pesto sauce, it is a real bummer.

MAN: Is that you Sunflower?

WOMAN: Pigpen!

GUY 2: Place hasn't changed in twenty-five years.

GUY 3: Yeah, it's a shame, you know they should have put in some condos by now.

GUY 4: I'm on a low-sodium, low-fat diet.

GUY 5: Well, how do you feel?

GUY 4: Terrible.

GUY 6: Green marble goes in the upstairs bathroom!

KID 1: This is the anniversary of a historic event.

KID 2: Which one?

KID 1: Watergate.

GUY ON LOUDSPEAKER: Let's have a warm welcome for Country Joe MacDonald.

JOHN SEBASTIAN: Joe, remember when we did this twenty-five years ago?

COUNTRY JOE: No.

ANNCR: Wouldn't it be nice if your youth was as easy to hold on to as an ice cold Pepsi?

KID 1: Do you think they'll go skinny dippin' again?

KID 2: I hope not.

SUPER: BE YOUNG, HAVE FUN, DRINK PEPSI.

CONSUMER TELEVISION OVER :30 SINGLE

480
ART DIRECTORS:
Steve Hudson
Victoria Fallon
WRITERS:
Victoria Fallon
Steve Hudson
AGENCY PRODUCER:
Sarah Pollitt
PRODUCTION COMPANY:
Paul Weiland Film Company
DIRECTOR:
Frank Budgen
CLIENT:
Powerbreaker
AGENCY:
BMP DDB Needham/London

481
ART DIRECTOR:
Malcolm Poynton
WRITER:
Simon Collins
AGENCY PRODUCER:
Bea Bisits
PRODUCTION COMPANY:
Bunton Films
DIRECTOR:
Tony Sherwood
CLIENT:
Holeproof
AGENCY:
The Campaign Palace/Melbourne

480
ANNCR: Tonight Mr. and Mrs. Hudson have decided to stay in. At the moment they are enjoying Chicken Kiev in the dining room. Now they're having coffee and after dinner mints in the comfort of the lounge. Ah, Mrs. Hudson has gone upstairs to unwind in a nice hot bath. Finally they both retire for the evening to snuggle up in bed. Mr. and Mrs. Hudson are staying at the Grand Hotel, Brighton. And what you've been watching are their Kingshield Security Time Switches in action. If they fooled you, they could fool a burglar.
(SFX: SECURITY TIME SWITCH TICKING, THEN CLICKS OFF)
SUPER: KINGSHIELD. WE DO EVERYTHING TO MAKE YOU FEEL SECURE.

481
(SFX: BEEP)
SECURITY GUARD 1: Shirt. Shirt.
(SFX: BEEP)
SECURITY GUARD 1: Pants please.
(MUSIC: *One day . . .*)
(SFX: BEEP)
SECURITY GUARD 2: One day, you're going to get caught.
SECURITY GUARD 1: He's probably gay.
SUPER: HOLEPROOF UNDERDAKS.

CONSUMER TELEVISION OVER :30 SINGLE

482
ART DIRECTOR:
Dean Hanson
WRITER:
Dean Buckhorn
AGENCY PRODUCER:
Wil McDonald
PRODUCTION COMPANY:
Spots Films
DIRECTOR:
Tarsem
CLIENT:
The Coca-Cola Company
AGENCY:
Fallon McElligott/Minneapolis

483
ART DIRECTOR:
Stephanie Halverson
WRITER:
Annie Kinscherff
AGENCY PRODUCERS:
Ann J. Storm
Allison Gerrish
PRODUCTION COMPANY:
Propaganda Films
DIRECTOR:
Dominic Sena
CLIENT:
Saturn Corporation
AGENCY:
Hal Riney & Partners/San Francisco

482
(MUSIC: '30S ROMANTIC)
SUPER: ALWAYS FEELS RIGHT.

483
ERIN WALLING (ANNCR): I thought the days of women being treated differently than men were long gone.
SALESMAN 1: Hey, how ya doin'? What's your name again? Karen, right?
ERIN: Erin.
SALESMAN 2: Ariel, let me show you . . . Erin, I'm sorry.
ERIN (ANNCR): Then I tried to buy a car. Something reliable.
CAR SALESMAN 3: You, uh, want to buy a car, huh?
ERIN (ANNCR): Sporty.
SALESMAN 2: What a great day to buy a car.
ERIN (ANNCR): With lots of standard features.
SALESMAN 4: This is the vanity mirror so you can check your make-up.
SALESMAN 5: You're gonna love it.
ERIN (OFF CAMERA): Tell me about the mileage.
SALESMAN 3: It has no miles on it yet.
ERIN: Okay, what about safety features?
SALESMAN 4: You feel safe. It's safe.
SALESMAN 1: How much you lookin' to spend?
ERIN (OFF CAMERA): I want to spend about twelve thousand dollars.
SALESMAN 1: Rich! Rich can help you out. I'll be back to you.
ERIN (ANNCR): When I got to Saturn, I didn't know what to expect. But Dave Pierce actually took the time to answer all my questions. Not only did I buy a Saturn, I thought it might be fun to sell them. You know what I like best about working here? Showing guys the vanity mirror.
SUPER: A DIFFERENT KIND OF COMPANY. A DIFFERENT KIND OF CAR. SATURN.

CONSUMER TELEVISION
OVER :30 SINGLE

484
ART DIRECTOR:
Jane Evans
WRITER:
Jane Caro
AGENCY PRODUCER:
Brad Steinwede
PRODUCTION COMPANY:
Cranbrook Films
DIRECTOR:
Roger Tompkins
CLIENT:
Lever Rexona
AGENCY:
J. Walter Thompson/ Sydney

485
ART DIRECTOR:
Joe Sciarrotta
WRITER:
Terry Cosgrove
AGENCY PRODUCER:
Mike Diedrich
PRODUCTION COMPANY:
HSI Productions
DIRECTOR:
Tom DeCerchio
CLIENT:
Miller Lite
AGENCY:
The Leap Partnership/ Chicago

486
ART DIRECTOR:
Lloyd Stein
WRITER:
Geoff Whalen
PHOTOGRAPHER:
Tom Richmond
AGENCY PRODUCER:
Abby Terkuhle
PRODUCTION COMPANY:
In-House
DIRECTOR:
Lloyd Stein
CLIENT:
MTV
AGENCY:
MTV/New York

487
ART DIRECTOR:
Steve Thomas
WRITER:
Mark Davis
AGENCY PRODUCER:
Barney Miller
DIRECTOR:
Barney Miller
CLIENT:
Nickelodeon
AGENCY:
Nickelodeon/New York

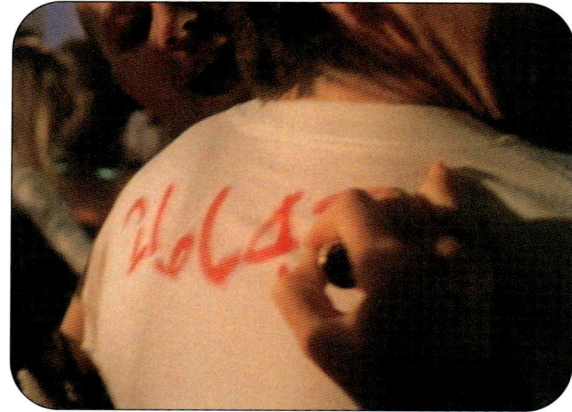
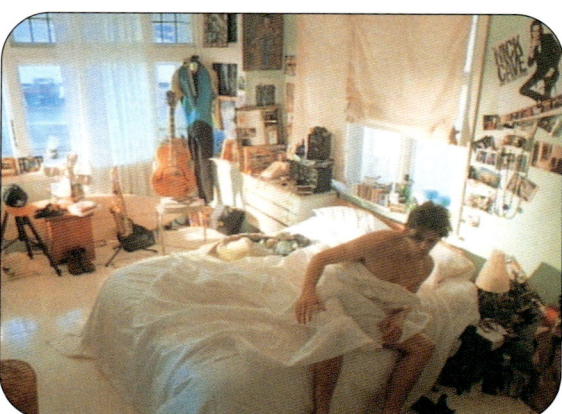

484
WOMAN: You got a pen? Paper?
MAN: John!!
MAN: John, the washing machine . . . the stuff in my room?
ROOMMATE: Yeah, it's my turn.
ANNCR: As you can see, with double action Drive, the toughest stains will come out in the wash.
SUPER: DOUBLE ACTION.

485
ANNCR: At Super Bowl I, a little known quarterback named Elmer Bruker was on the sidelines for the Green Bay Packers. He did not play. Nine years later with the Steelers, he was slated to start but was injured during the coin toss. And where was he when they wanted to send him in Super Bowl XXI? Searching for his lost contact lens. Although he's never played, Elmer Bruker was a member of every winning Super Bowl team until he retired last year from the world champion Cowboys.

ELMER: I look at it this way. I had a great seat for every game.

ANNCR: To Elmer and armchair quarterbacks everywhere, Miller Lite says thanks for letting us play a part in the Super Bowl.

ELMER: It feels weird not being there.
JIMMY JOHNSON: Tell me about it.
SUPER: A PROUD SPONSOR OF SUPER BOWL XXIX.

486

SIXTIES STYLE SINGING GROUP:
From when you wake up, 'til you go to bed at night
television that makes you feel all right.
We care about you, we're on your side
spend time with us, we'll show our pride.

We're music, we're MTV
we care about you and your family
puppies and laughter, bright sunny skies
where everyone's happy and nobody cries.

We're music, we're MTV
just turn us on, check out the quality.
Everyone, every color, across the land
plug in, everybody, lend a hand.

487

WOMAN (SINGING):
Da da da da da da da da
da da da da da da da da
I am sitting on the sofa
There's a TV in the corner
I am watching Major Nelson
He is played by Larry Hagman.

LARRY HAGMAN: Jeannie!

WOMAN: *And he found a little bottle*
And out popped Barbara Eden
But she couldn't show her belly button
All she did was blink

(SFX: JEANNIE BLINK)

WOMAN: *Tony Nelson works at NASA*
With suspicious Doctor Bellows
And there's also Roger Healy
Who would become Howard Borden

LARRY HAGMAN: Jeannie!

WOMAN: *And Jeannie always means well*
But they get in wacky trouble
She folds her arms and blinks her eyes
It's kind of like Bewitched.

Da da da da . . .

Oh the reruns will continue
On the TV as I'm watching
The pink smoke of her bottle
I am dreaming of Jeannie

Da da da da . . .

CONSUMER TELEVISION
OVER :30 SINGLE

488
ART DIRECTORS:
Bruce Bousman
Leslie Dektor
Bill Hamilton
Bruce Davidson
WRITERS:
Charlie Tercek
Bill Hamilton
AGENCY PRODUCERS:
Bruce Davidson
Lee Weiss
PRODUCTION COMPANY:
Dektor Higgins & Associates
DIRECTOR:
Leslie Dektor
CLIENT:
IBM
AGENCY:
Ogilvy & Mather/ New York

489
ART DIRECTOR:
Jim Baldwin
WRITER:
Mike Renfro
AGENCY PRODUCER:
Jessica Coats
PRODUCTION COMPANY:
Smilie Films
CLIENT:
G. Heileman Brewing Company/Henry Weinhard's Beer
AGENCY:
The Richards Group/ Dallas

488
(IN FRENCH WITH ENGLISH SUBTITLES)

MAN 1: My hard drive's maxed out. I've got to back up 500 megabytes or else.
MAN 2: Bummer. You know, I heard they're working on a new way of using lasers to store information.
MAN 1: Lasers? Who?
MAN 2: IBM. Yes, IBM. They say it'll hold ten times the data.
MAN 1: Cool.
SUPER: SOLUTIONS FOR A SMALL PLANET.

489
ANNCR: In the old West new ideas were sometimes slow to catch on.
RANCH OWNER: You a good horseman?
COWGIRL: Horse-person.
RANCH OWNER: How about ropin' and brandin'?
COWGIRL: Well, I ain't here to clean.
ANNCR: Some change was downright unwelcome.
RANCH OWNER: I'm sorry, but we just can't use anybody like you, Miss . . .
COWGIRL: Ms. Weinhard.
ANNCR: With one notable exception.
RANCH OWNER: Weinhard, huh? Like Henry Weinhard?
COWGIRL: Yessir, he's my uncle.
COWBOY: I haven't had a Henry's in a long time.
RANCH OWNER: Weinhard, huh?
ANNCR: And who knows, maybe Henry's helped some things change just a little faster.
RANCH OWNER: That Weinhard lady — she'd make a pretty good foreman.
COWBOY: Fore-person.

CONSUMER TELEVISION
OVER :30 SINGLE

490
ART DIRECTOR:
Carlos
WRITER:
Keith Bickel
AGENCY PRODUCER:
Tim Berriman
PRODUCTION COMPANY:
Spots Films
DIRECTOR:
Paul Meijer
CLIENT:
British Airways
AGENCY:
Saatchi & Saatchi/London

491
ART DIRECTORS:
Alexandra Taylor
Nik Studzinski
WRITERS:
Adam Kean
Jason Fretwell
AGENCY PRODUCER:
Jim Baker
PRODUCTION COMPANY:
Paul Weiland Film Company
DIRECTOR:
Mike Stephenson
CLIENT:
Schweppes GB
AGENCY:
Saatchi & Saatchi/London

490

(SFX: ALARM)
MAN: Carol? Carol?
(SFX: FOOTSTEPS ON STAIRS)
MAN (SHOUTING): Where is everybody?
SUPER: RIO £299. LA £199. ROME £99. PARIS £59. NEW YORK £168. BRITISH AIRWAYS WORLD OFFER.

491

ORANGEE TANG: I know what you're thinking . . . why? Why does an orangee tang like me come to a lunatic asylum like California? For the women? I don't think so. Bodies too long, arms too short—get me out of here. Why? To get a facelift? Five thousand miles for a tummy tuck, buttock suck, all over pluck? Not me pal. Collagen injections? With my lips? Hey what's the matter lady, someone stolen your wheels? A word of advice Mr. LA — never eat a chili before you take a bath. Why California? Sunkist is why. You want real taste, you gotta have real oranges. Okay so this place got one thing right. Hey you guys got something against long hair or what?

SUPER: FOR A REAL ORANGEE TANG.

CONSUMER TELEVISION OVER :30 SINGLE

492
ART DIRECTOR:
Jelly Helm
WRITER:
Stacy Wall
AGENCY PRODUCER:
Bill Davenport
PRODUCTION COMPANY:
Pytka
DIRECTOR:
Joe Pytka
CLIENT:
Nike
AGENCY:
Wieden & Kennedy/ Portland

493
ART DIRECTOR:
Jelly Helm
WRITER:
Stacy Wall
AGENCY PRODUCER:
Bill Davenport
PRODUCTION COMPANY:
Pytka
DIRECTOR:
Joe Pytka
CLIENT:
Nike
AGENCY:
Wieden & Kennedy/ Portland

494
ART DIRECTOR:
Rick McQuiston
WRITER:
Jamie Barrett
AGENCY PRODUCER:
Donna Portaro
PRODUCTION COMPANY:
Palomar
DIRECTOR:
Melodie McDaniel
CLIENT:
Nike
AGENCY:
Wieden & Kennedy/ Portland

CONSUMER TELEVISION :30/:25 SINGLE

495
ART DIRECTOR:
Dan Cohen
WRITER:
Paul Hartzell
AGENCY PRODUCER:
Fran Cosentino
PRODUCTION COMPANY:
Pomann Sound
CLIENT:
Saab Cars USA
AGENCY:
Angotti Thomas Hedge/ New York

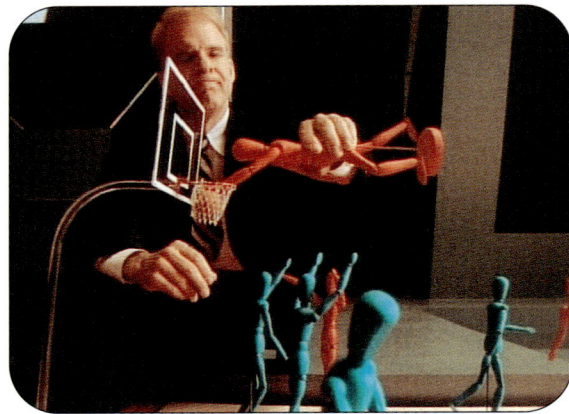

492
STEVE MARTIN: Good evening America. I'm Steve Martin. A few months ago the world was shocked by Michael Jordan's retirement.
SUPER: OCTOBER 6, 1993.
MICHAEL JORDAN: It's time for me to move away from the game of basketball.
STEVE: Three weeks later I received a mysterious package from a fan of the Billings Bandits: "Dear Steve, this guy Motorboat Jones looks a lot like Michael Jordan."
SUPER: DRAMATIZATION.
STEVE: When I spoke of this on a national talk show . . .
SUPER: REGIS & KATHY LEE, NOVEMBER 1993.
STEVE: At first I think it's just another kook. But then, then I realize this actually could be Michael Jordan.
. . . The flood gates opened. Incredible stories of exceptional basketball players — players who all uncannily resembled Michael Jordan. Then this audio tape turned up.
MYSTERIOUS VOICE: Yeah, I faked my retirement. So what?
CHRIS MULLIN: I don't think that was him. He didn't come back yet, but he's thinking about it.
DAVID ROBINSON: I don't think he faked his retirement.
HAROLD MINER: You know, with that guy you never know what he's gonna do next.
MICHAEL IRVIN: You can't blame him, man. The man just wants to play the game.
STEVE: Did Michael Jordan fake his retirement? In the second half I will show you the Popcorn Tape — the tape someone doesn't want you to see.
SUPER: TO BE CONTINUED.
SUPER: NIKE.

493
STEVE MARTIN: Is Kilroy Jordan?
SUPER: DECEMBER 20, 1993.
PHIL JACKSON: Uh, I don't want to answer any questions about Kilroy.
STEVE: What are you afraid of Coach Jackson? This? December 20th. A routine game. Bulls vs. Hornets. The only recorded evidence of this game is a fan's home video, the Popcorn tape.
SUPER: COURTESY MANNY COURTELIS.
STEVE: On this night an unknown player, Johnny Kilroy, scores 79 points in only one quarter of play. Johnny Kilroy or a cleverly disguised Michael Jordan? Alonzo take us back to that night.
ALONZO MOURNING: Well Steve, I was standing right about here . . .
SUPER: CHARLOTTE, NC.
ALONZO: . . . then Kilroy cuts through the lane and dunks right over me.
MARV ALBERT: The only person who could have made that move is Michael Jordan.
ALONZO: That was Jordan all right. Kilroy is Jordan.
STEVE: Conclusion: Michael Jordan, the greatest basketball player of all time, is letting nothing stand in the way of what he loves to do. And that's just play basketball.
SUPER: NIKE.

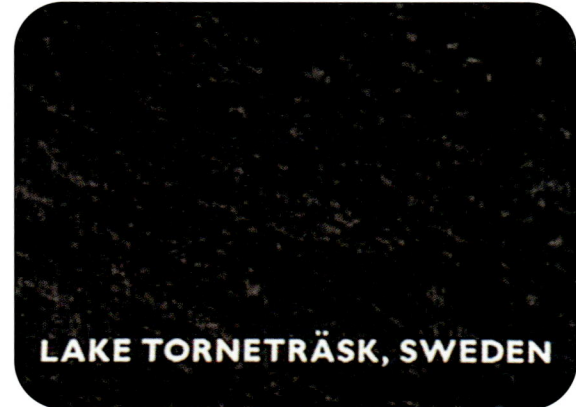

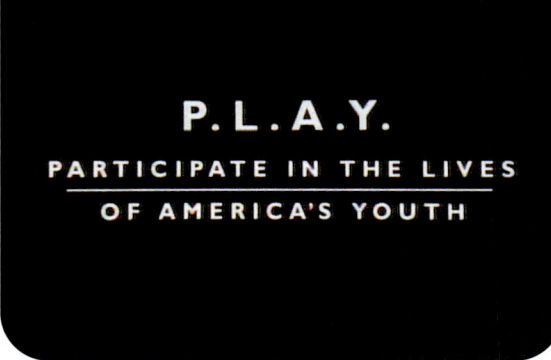

494

MICHAEL JORDAN: What if there were no sports? What if there were no last second shots? Would there be such a thing as adrenaline? Would old men still exchange high fives? And when would 90,000 people get together and sing? What if there were no sports?

If you couldn't join a team what would you join? If you couldn't shoot hoops, what would you shoot? If you couldn't dream of touchdowns, what would you dream? What if you did something? What if you cleaned up an old ballfield? Or put up a new rim? What if you coached a team? What if? What if there were no sports? Where would I be? Where would you be? Would I still be your hero?

SUPER: P.L.A.Y. PARTICIPATE IN THE LIVES OF AMERICA'S YOUTH.

SUPER: CALL 1-800-929-PLAY.

SUPER: NIKE

495

(SFX: HOWLING WIND)

SUPER: KALKUTJAKKAK, SWEDEN.

ANNCR: Saabs are designed to endure winters in the north of Sweden.

(SFX: GALE)

SUPER: KIRUNA, SWEDEN.

ANNCR: Winters so severe that for a whole month . . .

(SFX: BLIZZARD)

SUPER: LAKE TORNETRÄSK, SWEDEN.

ANNCR: . . . the sun never rises.

(SFX: BIRDS CHIRPING)

ANNCR: But let's not forget there's a whole month of summer . . .

(SFX: CAR ROOF GOING DOWN)

ANNCR: . . . when the sun never sets.

(MUSIC: CALYPSO)

ANNCR: The Saab Convertible.

SUPER: SAAB.

CONSUMER TELEVISION
:30/:25 SINGLE

496
ART DIRECTOR:
Ian Barry
WRITER:
Steve Dolbinksi
AGENCY PRODUCER:
Sylvia Kahn
PRODUCTION COMPANY:
Johns + Gorman Films
DIRECTOR:
Jeff Gorman
CLIENT:
The Los Angeles County Coroner's Office Gift Shop
AGENCY:
Arnold Finnegan Martin/ Richmond

497
ART DIRECTORS:
Tom Mackechney
Scott Carrelli
WRITERS:
Tom Mackechney
Joshua Koppel
AGENCY PRODUCER:
Dennis Bannon
PRODUCTION COMPANY:
Backyard Productions
DIRECTOR:
Rob Pritts
CLIENT:
Illinois Lottery
AGENCY:
Bayer Bess Vanderwarker/ Chicago

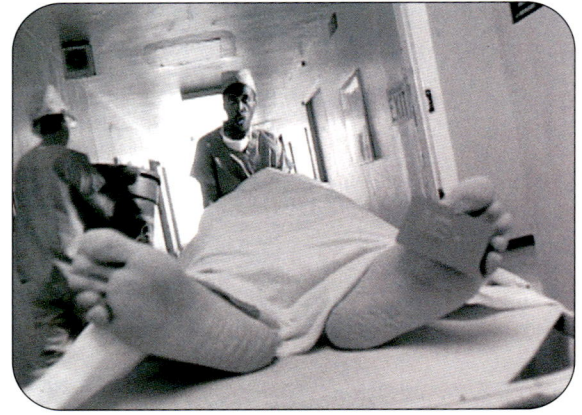

496
(SFX: DOORS OPENING, GURNEY WHEELING DOWN CORRIDOR)
SUPER: THE LOS ANGELES COUNTY CORONER'S OFFICE GIFT SHOP.

497
(MUSIC: '60S MUZAK)

CLERK: So you're looking for a birthday gift? We have some very sporty sport shirts. This is ambrosia. Maybe something practical? Cool, comfortable.

ANNCR: For the Lottery's 20th birthday, we got you something special.

CLERK: Oh, this is nice. How about a million dollars?

ANNCR: So what'd you expect? A tie? . . . New Birthday Millions from the Illinois Lottery. You can win eight times on a single ticket. And a million dollars instantly.

CLERK: Now, if they don't like this, they can always return it.

ANNCR: New Birthday Millions. Got a second? Play this instant.
SUPER: PLAY THIS INSTANT.

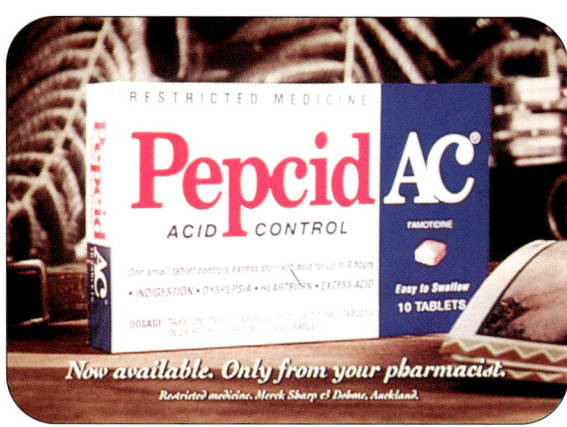

502
(SFX: WIND)
(MUSIC: THROUGHOUT)
SUPER: THERE'S ONLY ONE JEEP.

503
ANNCR: If you suffer from the effects of excess stomach acid try Pepcid AC. Pepcid AC can give you relief for up to nine hours.
SUPER: SEE YOUR CHEMIST.

CONSUMER TELEVISION
:30/:25 SINGLE

504
ART DIRECTOR:
Ron Mather
WRITER:
Lionel Hunt
AGENCY PRODUCER:
Ivan Robinson
PRODUCTION COMPANY:
Thirty-Second Street
DIRECTOR:
Mary Cooke
CLIENT:
Hanimex
AGENCY:
The Campaign Palace/
Woolloomooloo, Australia

505
ART DIRECTORS:
Mike Rosen
Duncan Milner
WRITER:
Marty Cooke
AGENCY PRODUCERS:
Peter Cline
Andrew Chinich
PRODUCTION COMPANIES:
Click 3X
Farenheit Films
DIRECTOR:
Greg Ramsey
CLIENT:
Fruitopia
AGENCY:
Chiat/Day, New York

504
ANNCR: Fuji Color film. As recommended by the world's top photographers.

505
SUPER: THE APPLES DON'T FIGHT THE PINEAPPLES IN FRUIT INTEGRATION. PEOPLE COULD LEARN A LOT FROM FRUIT. FRUITOPIA FROM MINUTE MADE. FOR THE *MIND, BODY, PLANET.*

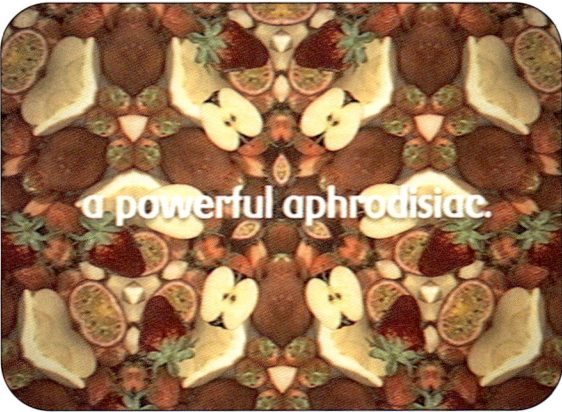

CONSUMER TELEVISION :30/:25 SINGLE

506
ART DIRECTORS:
Mike Rosen
Duncan Milner
WRITER:
Marty Cooke
AGENCY PRODUCERS:
Peter Cline
Andrew Chinich
PRODUCTION COMPANIES:
Click 3X
Farenheit Films
DIRECTOR:
Greg Ramsey
CLIENT:
Fruitopia
AGENCY:
Chiat/Day, New York

507
ART DIRECTOR:
Steve Sweitzer
WRITER:
Bob Rice
AGENCY PRODUCER:
Andrew Chinich
PRODUCTION COMPANIES:
Media Lab
Chelsea Pictures
DIRECTOR:
Kevin Godley
CLIENT:
NYNEX Yellow Pages
AGENCY:
Chiat/Day, New York

506
SUPER: THE ANCIENT MAORI BELIEVED PASSION FRUIT WAS A POWERFUL APHRODISIAC. HEY, IT COULDN'T HURT. TRY STRAWBERRY PASSION AWARENESS. FRUITOPIA. FROM MINUTE MADE. FOR THE *MIND, BODY, PLANET.*

507
SAXON: Excuse me, is it too much to ask to put up a wet paint sign? I'm supposed to be storming a village in Gaul tommorow and I've got absolutely nothing to wear. No, it's no good. I'm too upset. I'm going home.

SENTRY: Sorry.

SAXON: You're sorry.

ANNCR: NYNEX. More information. More Solutions. More stuff.

CONSUMER TELEVISION
:30/:25 SINGLE

508
ART DIRECTOR:
Jerry Gentile
WRITER:
Scott Vincent
AGENCY PRODUCER:
Michelle Burke
PRODUCTION COMPANY:
Johns + Gorman Films
DIRECTOR:
Jeff Gorman
CLIENT:
California Sunkist Pistachios
AGENCY:
Chiat/Day, Venice

509
ART DIRECTOR:
Donna Weinheim
WRITER:
Arthur Bijur
AGENCY PRODUCER:
Anne Kurtzman
PRODUCTION COMPANY:
Harmony Pictures
DIRECTOR:
Charles Wittenmaier
CLIENT:
Little Caesars
AGENCY:
Cliff Freeman & Partners/ New York

510
ART DIRECTOR:
Greg Bell
WRITER:
Michelle Roufa
AGENCY PRODUCER:
Anne Kurtzman
PRODUCTION COMPANY:
Crossroads Films
DIRECTOR:
Mark Story
CLIENT:
Little Caesars
AGENCY:
Cliff Freeman & Partners/ New York

511
ART DIRECTOR:
Bruce Hurwit
WRITER:
Arthur Bijur
AGENCY PRODUCER:
MaryEllen Duggan
PRODUCTION COMPANY:
Crossroads Films
DIRECTOR:
Bruce Hurwit
CLIENT:
Little Caesars
AGENCY:
Cliff Freeman & Partners/ New York

508

BUDDY: My angel name is Sanfernandinaki. People call me Buddy.
(SFX: BUDDY CHANTING, CHIME)
(SFX: HEAVY BREATHING SOUNDS FROM BUDDY, MORE CHANTING)
BUDDY: We have spiritual parties at our house about once every other month. If you're at all interested, we'll invite you.
SUPER: EVERYBODY KNOWS THE BEST NUTS COME FROM CALIFORNIA.
ANNCR: Sunkist California Pistachios. Now that's a nut.
SUPER: CALIFORNIA PISTACHIOS.

509

GRANNY: Have you ever seen anything more amazing than Little Caesars Italian Sausage Pizza?
BABY (SINGING): *Give my regards to Broadway . . .*
FATHER: No.
ANNCR: Italian Sausage Pizza! Loaded with sausage, peppers and onions. The newest from a whole menu of Little Caesars Pleasers. Any two for $9.98.
LITTLE CAESAR: Pizza! Pizza!
ANNCR: Or get one for $5.99!
LITTLE CAESAR: Pizza!

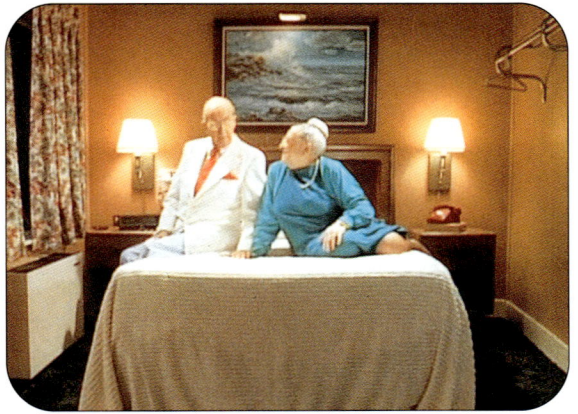

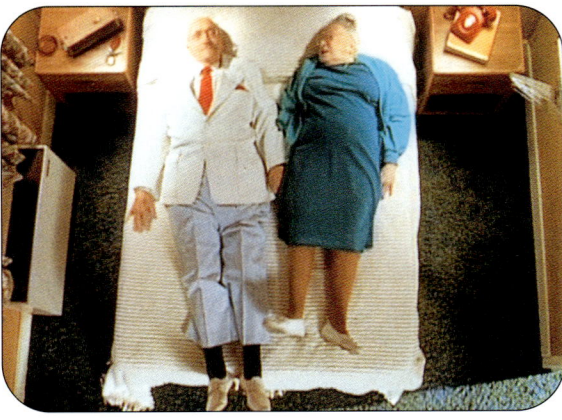

510
(MUSIC: ROMANTIC, ON RADIO)
(SFX: DOLLAR INSERTED INTO MACHINE, BED VIBRATING)
WOMAN: We should've gotten the pizza.
SUPER: $1.
ANNCR: Pizza for a buck! Now when you buy two pizzas with two toppings for $8.98, you get a third pizza for a buck!
SUPER: LITTLE CAESARS.
LITTLE CAESAR: Pizza! Pizza!

511
ANNCR (THROUGH SPEAKER): One banana? Or two bananas?
(SFX: BUZZ)
ANNCR: One female orangutan? Or two female orangutans?
(SFX: BUZZ)
ANNCR: One pizza for $9.98? Or two for $9.98?
ANNCR: He seems to prefer two.
ANNCR: Two is better than one, so why settle for one supreme pizza when you can get two at Little Caesars for just $9.98!
LITTLE CAESAR: Pizza! Pizza!

CONSUMER TELEVISION
:30/:25 SINGLE

512
ART DIRECTORS:
Matt Vescovo
Greg Bell
WRITER:
Steve Dildarian
AGENCY PRODUCERS:
Anne Kurtzman
MaryEllen Duggan
PRODUCTION COMPANY:
Industrial Artists
DIRECTOR:
Henry Holtzman
CLIENT:
Staples
AGENCY:
Cliff Freeman & Partners/
New York

513
ART DIRECTOR:
Heidi Flora
WRITER:
Kevin Jones
AGENCY PRODUCER:
Sam Walsh
PRODUCTION COMPANY:
Straight Cut
EDITOR:
Johnna Turiano
CLIENT:
Seattle International
Film Festival
AGENCY:
Cole & Weber/Seattle

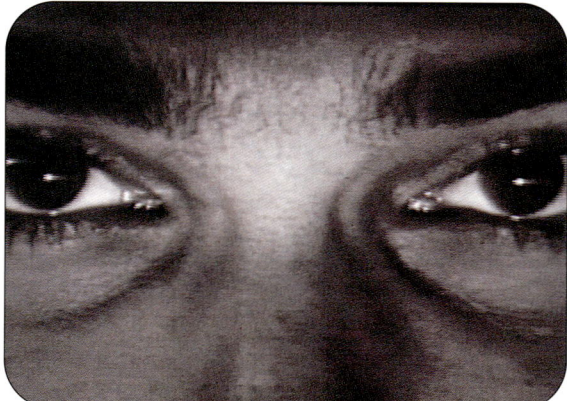

512
(MUSIC: "THE MOST WONDERFUL TIME OF THE YEAR")
ANNCR: It's that time of year again. They're going back! It's back to school time at Staples! Over 5,000 school supplies at the guaranteed low price.
SUPER: STAPLES.
ANNCR: Staples. Yeah, we've got that.

513
SUPER: ALL PARTICLES OF LIGHT TRAVEL AT EXACTLY THE SAME SPEED. 186,282 MILES PER SECOND.
SUPER: SOME JUST HIT YOU HARDER THAN OTHERS.
SUPER: CINEMA SEATTLE PRESENTS THE SEATTLE INTERNATIONAL FILM FESTIVAL XX.
SUPER: SEE WHAT THE WORLD IS COMING TO MAY 20 – JUNE 12.

**CONSUMER TELEVISION
:30/:25 SINGLE**

514
ART DIRECTORS:
Ken Ferris
David Angelo
WRITERS:
Ken Shuldman
Rob Slosberg
AGENCY PRODUCER:
Steve Amato
PRODUCTION COMPANY:
Paul Weiland Film Company
DIRECTOR:
Paul Weiland
CLIENT:
Seiko
AGENCY:
DDB Needham Worldwide/New York

515
ART DIRECTOR:
Pat Epstein
WRITER:
Rob Jamieson
DIRECTOR:
Brian Belefant
CLIENT:
WQHS
AGENCY:
Dog Eat Dog/New York

514
ANNCR: One day, Dan Brooks was walking down the street minding his own business. What he didn't realize is that he was about to bump into a beautiful woman. The woman who would have his three children The woman who would graduate from law school and go on to become a successful politician. The woman who would change his life forever. But rather than insisting on a Seiko, Dan settled for an ordinary watch. And unfortunately, Dan was running one second late.

ANNCR: Seiko. Built for life.

515
(MUSIC: COUNTRY)
ANNCR: The average Texas radio station plays the same song 23 times every day.
DJ (ON RADIO): Y'all liked that one so much, I'm going to play it one more time.
ANNCR: Texas is the mass murder capital of the country.
(SFX: SHOTGUN BLAST)
ANNCR: You do the math.
SUPER: WQHS.

CONSUMER TELEVISION
:30/:25 SINGLE

516
ART DIRECTOR:
Pat Epstein
WRITER:
Rob Jamieson
DIRECTOR:
Brian Belefant
CLIENT:
WQHS
AGENCY:
Dog Eat Dog/New York

517
ART DIRECTOR:
Robert Shaw West
WRITER:
Ken Cills
AGENCY PRODUCER:
Joe Mosca
PRODUCTION COMPANY:
In-House
CLIENT:
WMMR 93.3 FM
AGENCY:
Earle Palmer Brown/ Philadelphia

518
ART DIRECTOR:
Rohitash Rao
WRITER:
Eric Silver
AGENCY PRODUCER:
Nancy Hacohen
PRODUCTION COMPANY:
HKM Productions
DIRECTOR:
Jesse Dylan
CLIENT:
Good Guys Auto
AGENCY:
Earle Palmer Brown/ Richmond

519
ART DIRECTOR:
Rohitash Rao
WRITER:
Eric Silver
AGENCY PRODUCER:
Nancy Hacohen
PRODUCTION COMPANY:
HKM Productions
DIRECTOR:
Jesse Dylan
CLIENT:
Good Guys Auto
AGENCY:
Earle Palmer Brown/ Richmond

516
(MUSIC: COUNTRY)
ANNCR: A recent study of 49 metropolitan areas has found that the more people listen to country music, the higher the suicide rate.
SUPER: WQHS.

517
SUPER: DOCTORS HAVE THIS THEORY THAT IF YOU PLAY CLASSICAL MUSIC TO INFANTS THEY'LL GROW UP WITH A BETTER UNDERSTANDING OF COMPLEX RELATIONSHIPS, LIKE MATH. THEY DON'T KNOW WHAT EFFECT ROCK AND ROLL WILL HAVE BUT I PLAY THIS STUFF FOR HIM ANYWAY. I FIGURE THE WORLD CAN LIVE WITH ONE LESS ACCOUNTANT.

518

MECHANIC: It's an American car . . . Cadillac. . . . Power windows . . . power steering. . . . And the air conditioning is on the fritz.

SUPER: GOOD GUYS AUTO. WE KNOW CARS SO WELL, IT'S KINDA CREEPY.

519

MECHANIC: That's gonna be a Buick . . . Skylark . . . Convertible. Could you shut the right door for me? The car has 126,000 miles on it. . . . And it was in an accident in 1978.

SUPER: GOOD GUYS AUTO. WE KNOW CARS SO WELL, IT'S KINDA CREEPY.

MECHANIC: May third I believe.

CONSUMER TELEVISION
:30/:25 SINGLE

520
ART DIRECTORS:
Jason Peterson
Paul Hirsch
Izzy DeBellis
WRITERS:
Izzy DeBellis
Paul Hirsch
Jason Peterson
AGENCY PRODUCER:
Deborah Sullivan
PRODUCTION COMPANY:
Epoch Films
DIRECTOR:
Jeff Priess
CLIENT:
NBA
AGENCY:
Fallon McElligott Berlin/ New York

521
ART DIRECTORS:
Jason Peterson
Paul Hirsch
Izzy DeBellis
WRITERS:
Izzy DeBellis
Paul Hirsch
Jason Peterson
AGENCY PRODUCER:
Deborah Sullivan
PRODUCTION COMPANY:
Epoch Films
DIRECTOR:
Jeff Priess
CLIENT:
NBA
AGENCY:
Fallon McElligott Berlin/ New York

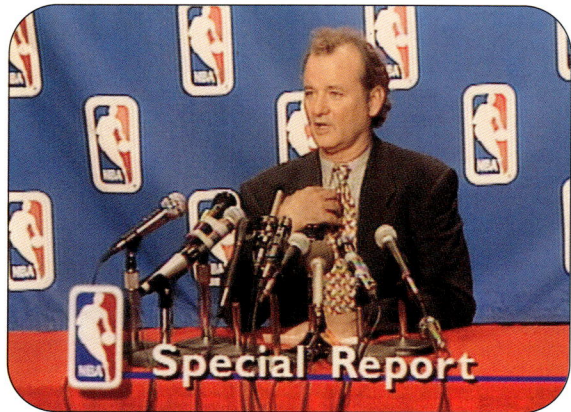
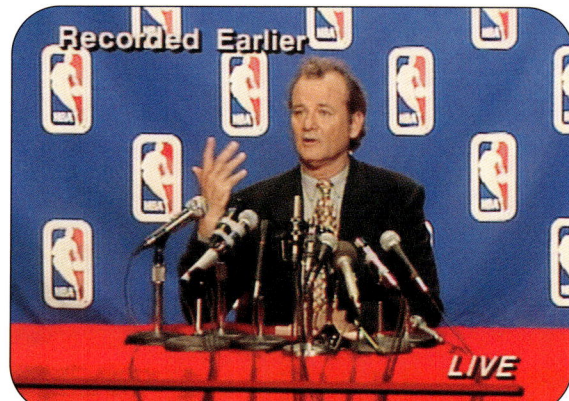
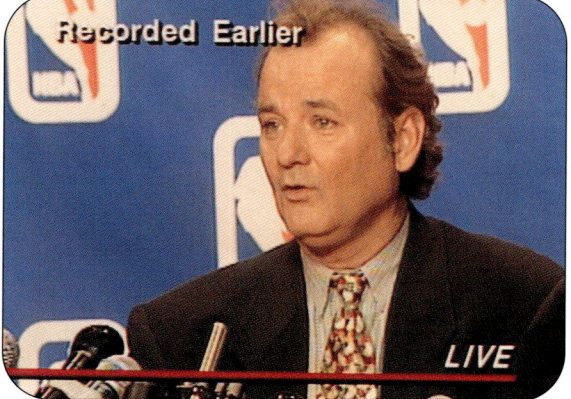

520
BILL MURRAY: What I got to worry about is the road, man. Hotel rooms, you know, room service food. I'm gonna bring a vegetable juicer with me, you know just travel with it. When I get to a town I'm just going to find a farmer's market, go get fresh vegetables and juice. I got a really powerful will, but I just don't know where to direct it sometimes, you know. Like, I knew I was hungry and I knew I had to get food and I did. You know, that's an example of my will power. You know, I just didn't have time to get the vegetables this morning.

521
BILL MURRAY: You know, I don't understand why you're being so tough on me, Mr. Rashad. You weren't this tough on Michael Jordan or Scottie Pippen. I mean, just because I want to play? Maybe you and I should play sometime, you know?

AHMAD RASHAD: Mr. Murray, I'm not trying to play in the National Basketball Association.

BILL: You can call me Bill, I mean, not "Mr. Murray," you know, I know it's . . . think of this as the locker room.

AHMAD: You were calling a press conference saying that you were going to play basketball and we found out here today you never played in college—you never played in high school.

BILL: S-So.

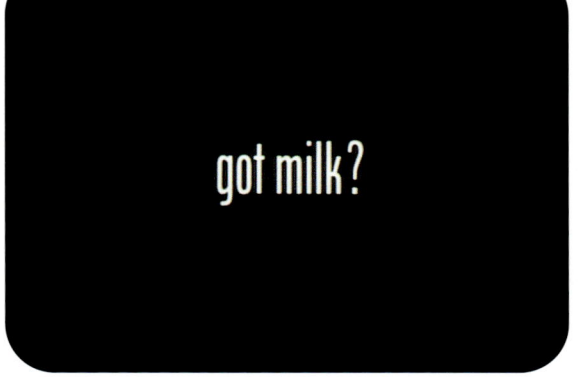

**CONSUMER TELEVISION
:30/:25 SINGLE**

522
ART DIRECTOR:
Joe Shands
WRITER:
Chuck McBride
AGENCY PRODUCER:
Cindy Epps
PRODUCTION COMPANY:
Propaganda Films
DIRECTOR:
Michael Bay
CLIENT:
California Fluid Milk
Processor Advisory Board
AGENCY:
Goodby Silverstein &
Partners/San Francisco

523
ART DIRECTOR:
Steve Luker
WRITER:
Steve Simpson
AGENCY PRODUCER:
Elizabeth O'Toole
PRODUCTION COMPANY:
Ritts/Hayden
DIRECTOR:
Carlton Chase
CLIENT:
Norwegian Cruise Line
AGENCY:
Goodby Silverstein &
Partners/San Francisco

522

(MUSIC: CHANTING)

PRIEST: Mmmmm. Hmmm! Hmmm! Mmmmm. Hmmm! Hmmm! Mmm . . . Milllkkk!

(SFX: STRAINED SOUNDING VENDING MACHINE)

(SFX: SLAM, THEN ECHO)

(SFX: REPEATED SLAMS, THEN ECHOES)

ANNCR: Got Milk?

523

(MUSIC: "BLUE MOON" BY THE COWBOY JUNKIES)

SUPER: OUT HERE THE MEMORY FACTORY WORKS OVERTIME. WORRY DISSOLVES IN SALTWATER. FANTASY AND REALITY TRADE PLACES. THE MUSCLES IN YOUR NECK RELAX. IT'S DIFFERENT OUT HERE.

SUPER: NORWEGIAN CRUISE LINE.

CONSUMER TELEVISION
:30/:25 SINGLE

524
ART DIRECTOR:
Tom Routson
WRITER:
Bob Kerstetter
AGENCY PRODUCER:
Kim Noble
PRODUCTION COMPANY:
Red Dog Films
DIRECTOR:
Marc Chiat
CLIENT:
Sega of America
AGENCY:
Goodby Silverstein & Partners/San Francisco

525
ART DIRECTOR:
Philip Andrew
WRITERS:
Peter Robertson
Philip Andrew
AGENCY PRODUCER:
Lisa Faircloth
PRODUCTION COMPANY:
Motion Pictures Auckland
DIRECTOR:
Dennis Hitchcock
CLIENT:
Scandinavian Vehicle Distributors
AGENCY:
HKM Advertising/Wellington, New Zealand

526
ART DIRECTORS:
Steve Mitchell
Mike Murray
WRITER:
Kristine Larsen
PRODUCTION COMPANY:
Reelworks
DIRECTOR:
Tom Larson
CLIENT:
Minnesota Brewing
AGENCY:
Hunt Murray/Minneapolis

527
ART DIRECTOR:
Dante Lombardi
WRITERS:
Paul Venables
Neil Leinwohl
AGENCY PRODUCER:
Linda Tesa Olken
PRODUCTION COMPANY:
Barking Weasel
DIRECTOR:
Tenney Fairchild
CLIENT:
Comedy Central
AGENCY:
Korey Kay & Partners/New York

524
(SFX: SQUEAKY BABY CARRIAGE, GAMEBOY SOUNDS)
BOY: (SIGHS)
(SFX: WHAM!)
(SFX: PSYCHEDELIC SITAR-LIKE SOUNDS)
BOY: Woah . . . Color.
(MUSIC: HARD ROCK)
ANNCR: Hey. There's an easier way to get color. Get a Game Gear. The full-color portable with over 150 games, like the new Echo, Mortal 2, and Sonic Triple Trouble.
SQUIRREL: Sega!

525
(SFX: HAMMER AND CHISEL)
SUPER: THE NEW STREAMLINED VOLVO. A CAR YOU CAN BELIEVE IN.

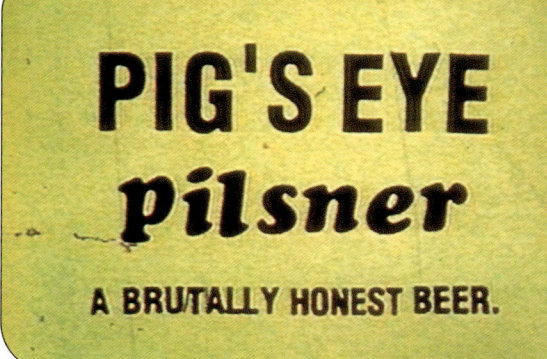

526

(MUSIC: '40S CRIME STORY TUNE)

PIG'S EYE: Are you staring at me? What are you looking at? My patch? Underneath that patch is something so gnarled, so grizzly, so ugly, they named me after it. You still wanna see it? Are you happy now? Quit starin' at it. Go get a Pig's Eye and stare at that instead.

SUPER: PIG'S EYE PILSNER. A BRUTALLY HONEST BEER.

527

(SFX: CHANNELS CHANGING AS MAN TRIES TO PUT OUT FLAMES)

ANNCR: Maybe you could use a little Comedy Central too. Call your cable company. Comedy Central. What the hell's going on here?

CONSUMER TELEVISION
:30/:25 SINGLE

528
ART DIRECTOR:
Mark Oosthuizen
WRITER:
John Condon
AGENCY PRODUCER:
David Moore
PRODUCTION COMPANY:
HKM Productions
DIRECTOR:
Graham Henman
CLIENT:
Miller Brewing Company
AGENCY:
Leo Burnett Company/ Chicago

529
ART DIRECTOR:
Andy Hirsch
WRITERS:
Lee Garfinkel
Barbara Siegel
AGENCY PRODUCER:
Rachel Novak
PRODUCTION COMPANY:
Harmony Pictures
DIRECTOR:
Charles Wittenmaier
CLIENT:
Diet Coke/ The Coca-Cola Company
AGENCY:
Lowe & Partners/SMS, New York

530
ART DIRECTOR:
Bob Meagher
WRITER:
John Mahoney
AGENCY PRODUCER:
Pam Campagnoli
PRODUCTION COMPANY:
Crossroads Films
DIRECTOR:
Mark Story
CLIENT:
Residence Inn
AGENCY:
The Martin Agency/ Richmond

531
ART DIRECTOR:
Kristy Willson
WRITER:
John Schofield
AGENCY PRODUCER:
Michelle Woodruff
PRODUCTION COMPANY:
Blue Goose
DIRECTOR:
Ron Gross
CLIENT:
Seattle Mariners Baseball Club
AGENCY:
McCann-Erickson/Seattle

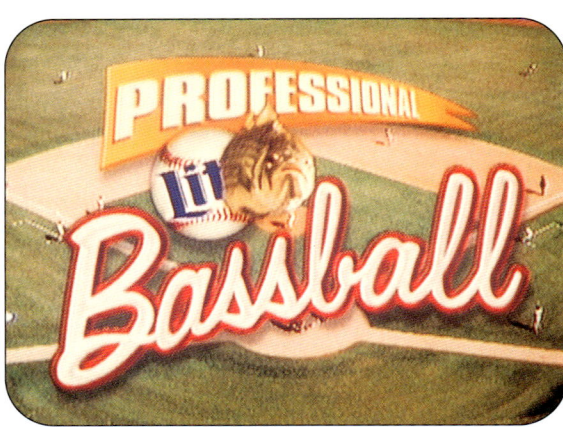

528
BARTENDER: Okay guys, baseball or bass fishing.
GUY 1: Baseball.
GUY 2: Baseball.
GUY 3: Bass fishing.
BARTENDER: Hey guys, watch this.
(SFX: BOTTLE HITS TV)
(MUSIC: THROUGHOUT)
ANNCR: Miller Lite presents professional bassball!
GUYS: Oh!
ANNCR: Roger calls for a fresh bass. There's the wind-up, and the fish!
(SFX: BALL BEING HIT)
CROWD: Whoaa!
ANNCR: It's a high fly bass! Brought to you by Miller Lite. If you can combine great taste and less filling, you can combine anything. Here comes the play at the plate . . .
UMP: You're out!
ANNCR: Great taste, less filling. Can your beer do this?
GUY: Whoa!

529
(MUSIC: "SABRE DANCE")
SUPER: SLO-MO. INSTANT REPLAY.
SUPER: THIS IS REFRESHMENT.

530

ANNCR: Can you tell which man is at home? And which man is at the Residence Inn hotel room?

WIFE: Honey, can you take out the garbage?

ANNCR: That was a hint. Residence Inn by Marriot. The next best thing to home.

531

ANNCR: Please welcome, from Seattle, a very funny man. Jay Buhner.

BUHNER: Here's one for you. A horse walks into a bar. Bartender says, "Hey, why the long face?" Here's one for you . . .

ANNCR: Aren't you glad he decided to play for the Mariners instead?

CONSUMER TELEVISION
:30/:25 SINGLE

532
ART DIRECTOR:
Jim Walker
WRITER:
Jim Copacino
AGENCY PRODUCER:
Branson Veal
PRODUCTION COMPANY:
Blue Goose
DIRECTOR:
Ron Gross
CLIENT:
Washington State Lottery
AGENCY:
McCann-Erickson/Seattle

533
ART DIRECTORS:
Bruce Bousman
Leslie Dektor
Bill Hamilton
Bruce Davidson
WRITERS:
Charlie Tercek
Bill Hamilton
AGENCY PRODUCERS:
Bruce Davidson
Lee Weiss
PRODUCTION COMPANY:
Dektor Higgins & Associates
DIRECTOR:
Leslie Dektor
CLIENT:
IBM
AGENCY:
Ogilvy & Mather/ New York

532

BOSS (ON PHONE): Schofield, you were told to be in front of my apartment at 8:05 sharp. I don't like to be kept waiting. You're incompetence is unacceptable. Time is money, Schofield. My money! Keep this up and you'll never drive for me again.

RADIO VOICE: Here's something to brighten up someone's rainy morning. There was one winner in last night's Washington State Lotto drawing. The winning numbers: 7, 15, 26, 37, 40 and 44.

(SFX: WATER SPLASHES)

BOSS: Schofield?

ANNCR: Lotto. Do you feel lucky?

533

(IN FRENCH WITH ENGLISH SUBTITLES)

NUN 1: I'm trying to get that new operating system, Chicago, but they keep pushing back the release date.

NUN 2: That new OS/2 Warp from IBM looks pretty hot.

NUN 1: OS/2 Warp?

NUN 2: I just read about it in *Wired*. You get true multitasking, easy access to the internet.

NUN 1: I'm dying to surf the 'net.

(SFX: PAGER BEEPING)

NUN 1: Whoops. My beeper.

SUPER: SOLUTIONS FOR A SMALL PLANET.

CONSUMER TELEVISION
:30/:25 SINGLE

534
ART DIRECTOR:
Susan Hoffmann
WRITER:
Evelyn Monroe
AGENCY PRODUCER:
Jane Brimblecombe
PRODUCTION COMPANY:
Propaganda Films
DIRECTOR:
David Fincher
CLIENT:
Nike International
AGENCY:
Wieden & Kennedy/ Amsterdam

535
ART DIRECTOR:
Warren Eakins
WRITER:
Bob Moore
AGENCY PRODUCER:
Jane Brimblecombe
PRODUCTION COMPANY:
Pytka
DIRECTOR:
Joe Pytka
CLIENT:
Nike International
AGENCY:
Wieden & Kennedy/ Amsterdam

534
(SFX: PAGES RUSTLING, RACQUET HITTING BALL)
JOHN McENROE: What the . . .
(SFX: GRUNT, RACQUET HITTING BALL)
(SFX: GLASS BREAKING)
(SFX: BALL BEING CAUGHT, AUDIENCE APPLAUDING)
(SFX: NEWSPAPER RUSTLING)
LINEMAN: Fault!
(SFX: DOOR OPENING, RUNNING FOOTSTEPS)
(SFX: GRUNTING, BALL BEING HIT, PAGES FLICKING OVER)
(SFX: LOUD GRUNT, BALL FLYING, GLASS SMASHING)
COURIER AND KRAJICEK: Shhhh.
(SFX: GLASS BEING SWEPT)

535
CANTONA: I've been punished for striking a goalkeeper, for spitting at a supporter, for throwing my shirt at a referee, and for calling my manager a bag of shit. Then I called the jury who punished me a bunch of idiots. I thought I might have trouble finding a sponsor.
SUPER: NIKE.

CONSUMER TELEVISION
:30/:25 SINGLE

536
ART DIRECTOR:
Tim Hanrahan
WRITER:
Glenn Cole
AGENCY PRODUCER:
Jennifer Smieja
PRODUCTION COMPANY:
Tiny Films
DIRECTOR:
Robin Willis
CLIENT:
ESPN
AGENCY:
Wieden & Kennedy/ Portland

537
ART DIRECTOR:
Tim Hanrahan
WRITER:
Hank Perlman
AGENCY PRODUCER:
Jennifer Smieja
PRODUCTION COMPANY:
Backyard Productions
DIRECTOR:
Rob Pritts
CLIENT:
ESPN
AGENCY:
Wieden & Kennedy/ Portland

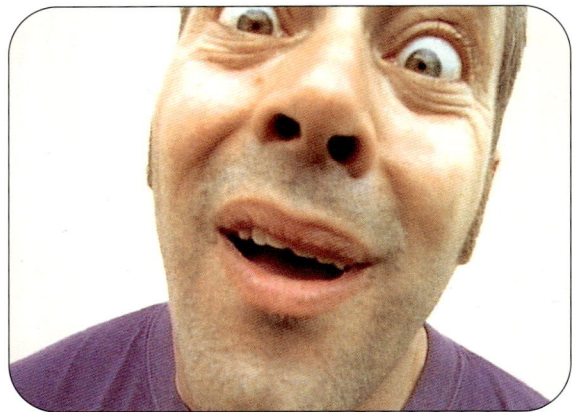

536

(MUSIC: THROUGHOUT)

ANNCR: Howdy partners. Now you people think guys like Bo and Shaq are special. I mean when was the last time "Mr. Shaq" faced a 70 mph leather ball with only gloves to protect him? Hey, you try stopping a shot in a space this big.

537

DENNIS LEARY: You know what I like about hockey? I like that everybody gets to carry a stick. I like the skating, the scoring, the passing. I like that you don't shake hands with your opponent until the very end of the play-off series. I like the Zamboni. I like the hitting. I love the Bruins. I like how they throw a dead octopus on the ice in Detroit during the play-offs.

I like that when somebody does something bad they go to the box. I like the fact that right now I'm on a break-away with the greatest player of all time. I don't like the fact that he's not passing to me. Come on, hog.

SUPER: HOCKEY. A LOT LIKE LIFE. ONLY MORE TO LIKE.
SUPER: THE STANLEY CUP PLAY-OFFS ON ESPN.

CONSUMER TELEVISION
:30/:25 SINGLE

538
ART DIRECTOR:
John Boiler
WRITER:
Stacy Wall
AGENCY PRODUCERS:
Jeff Selis
Bill Davenport
PRODUCTION COMPANY:
Pytka
DIRECTOR:
Joe Pytka
CLIENT:
Nike
AGENCY:
Wieden & Kennedy/ Portland

539
ART DIRECTORS:
Andrew Christou
Eric C. King
WRITERS:
Derek Barnes
James LeMaitre
AGENCY PRODUCER:
Donna Portaro
PRODUCTION COMPANY:
Pytka
DIRECTOR:
Joe Pytka
CLIENT:
Nike
AGENCY:
Wieden & Kennedy/ Portland

538
(MUSIC: THROUGHOUT)
DENNIS HOPPER: Troy Aikman. Michael Irvin. They have ESP, man. I've seen them on the field like cosmic twins . . . ESP. This is a special message for Michael and Troy.
SUPER: NIKE.

539
SUPER: DAY 15.
(SFX: PITCHING MACHINE)
SUPER: PLAY BALL.
SUPER: PLEASE.
SUPER: NIKE.

CONSUMER TELEVISION
:30/:25 SINGLE

540
ART DIRECTORS:
Andrew Christou
Eric C. King
WRITERS:
Derek Barnes
James LeMaitre
AGENCY PRODUCER:
Donna Portaro
PRODUCTION COMPANY:
Pytka
DIRECTOR:
Joe Pytka
CLIENT:
Nike
AGENCY:
Wieden & Kennedy/
Portland

541
ART DIRECTOR:
Darryl McDonald
WRITER:
Jamie Barrett
AGENCY PRODUCER:
Ben Grylewicz
PRODUCTION COMPANY:
Palomar
DIRECTOR:
Melodie McDaniel
CLIENT:
Nike
AGENCY:
Wieden & Kennedy/
Portland

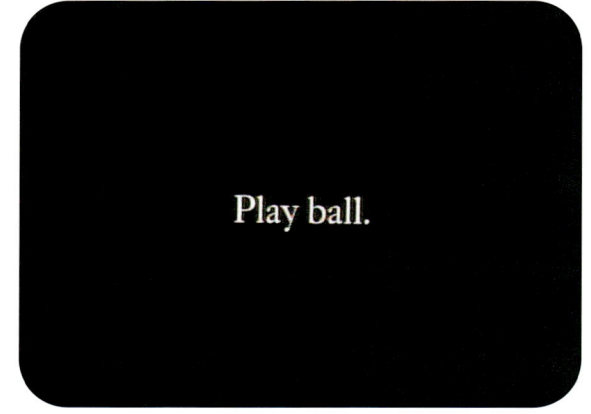

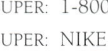

540
SUPER: DAY 10.
(MUSIC: ORGAN PLAYING BASEBALL WARM-UP)
(MUSIC: CHOPSTICKS)
SUPER: PLAY BALL.
SUPER: PLEASE.
SUPER: NIKE.

541
(MUSIC: THROUGHOUT)

CHARLES BARKLEY: Every 24 hours, somewhere in this country a kid takes a gun and shoots another kid. Sometimes it's over a girl. Sometimes it's over pride. Sometimes it's because they have nothing better to do. Can you think of something better to do? I can.

SUPER: P.L.A.Y. PARTICIPATE IN THE LIVES OF AMERICA'S YOUTH.
SUPER: 1-800-929-PLAY.
SUPER: NIKE.

**CONSUMER TELEVISION
:30/:25 SINGLE**

542
ART DIRECTORS:
Andrew Christou
Eric C. King
WRITERS:
Derek Barnes
James LeMaitre
AGENCY PRODUCER:
Donna Portaro
PRODUCTION COMPANY:
Pytka
DIRECTOR:
Joe Pytka
CLIENT:
Nike
AGENCY:
**Wieden & Kennedy/
Portland**

543
ART DIRECTOR:
John C. Jay
WRITER:
Jimmy Smith
AGENCY PRODUCER:
Renee Raab
PRODUCTION COMPANY:
Radical Media
DIRECTOR:
Robert Leacock
CLIENT:
Nike
AGENCY:
**Wieden & Kennedy/
Portland**

542
SUPER: DAY 24
SUPER: PLAY BALL.
SUPER: PLEASE.
SUPER: NIKE.

543
EARL MONROE: One of the things I've tried to squash is that I was a hot dog. Of course having names like "Black Jesus," "Magic" and "Pearl" y'know hasn't really helped. All that Hurky-Jerky, Jack-knifing and spinning was necessary for me to get my shot off. So if he moves that way and you go that way, then you movin' and you movin' and doin' it, your little dips and dos and what not. Sometimes I suprise myself. Sometimes when I spin, I do somethin' in the midst of doin' it, I say, "Damn Earl, that was beautiful."

CONSUMER TELEVISION :30/:25 SINGLE

544
ART DIRECTOR:
John Boiler
WRITER:
Glenn Cole
AGENCY PRODUCERS:
Peter Wiedensmith
Jeff Selis
PRODUCTION COMPANY:
Wiedensmith Productions
CLIENT:
Oregon Tourism
AGENCY:
Wieden & Kennedy/ Portland

CONSUMER TELEVISION :30/:25 CAMPAIGN

545
ART DIRECTORS:
Mike Rosen
Duncan Milner
WRITER:
Marty Cooke
AGENCY PRODUCERS:
Peter Cline
Andrew Chinich
PRODUCTION COMPANIES:
Click 3X
Farenheit Films
DIRECTOR:
Greg Ramsey
CLIENT:
Fruitopia
AGENCY:
Chiat/Day, New York

544
(SFX: WATERFALLS)
FISH 1: Oh, this is nice. Oregon rivers are so clean.
FISH 2: You know, my uncle in the Rogue says the whole state's like this.
FISH 1: No kidding.
FISH 2: Yeah.
FISH 1: Well, I'm going to give this another shot. Uungh!
FISH 2: Ooo. Almost. Hey, let's let these guys go ahead.
FISH 1: Oh, give it up.
FISH 2: Yeah, nice try guys. Oh, and here goes, here goes Alan.
SUPER: OREGON. THINGS LOOK DIFFERENT HERE.
FISH 2: Hah. Coordination.
FISH 1: Let's just spawn here.

545
SUPER: THE FOLLOWING 30 SECONDS WILL NOT INSPIRE: VIOLENT CRIME. A RELIGIOUS EXPERIENCE. CONSPICUOUS CONSUMPTION. IT MAY, HOWEVER, MAKE YOU THIRSTY. FRUITOPIA FROM MINUTE MADE. FOR THE *MIND, BODY, PLANET.*

CONSUMER TELEVISION :30/:25 CAMPAIGN

546
ART DIRECTOR:
Bill Karow
WRITER:
David Baldwin
AGENCY PRODUCER:
Olivia Sitea
CLIENT:
The Oregonian
AGENCY:
Cole & Weber/Portland

547
ART DIRECTORS:
Jason Peterson
Paul Hirsch
Izzy DeBellis
WRITERS:
Izzy DeBellis
Paul Hirsch
Jason Peterson
AGENCY PRODUCER:
Deborah Sullivan
PRODUCTION COMPANY:
Epoch Films
DIRECTOR:
Jeff Priess
CLIENT:
NBA
AGENCY:
Fallon McElligott Berlin/New York

546

DAD: Nature's most perfect paper is the new *Oregonian*. Perfect for nourishment, perfect for health. And a mighty informative newspaper. Here's to the new *Oregonian*.

MOM: Three sections every day.

GIRL: Four for me. I'm still growing.

DAD: Well now that we have the house all decorated for your party, I'm gonna relax and enjoy this paper.

MOM: It's the perfect paper for when you're tired, it's refreshing and satisfying.

DAD: Make every day an *Oregonian* day. And remember you never outgrow your need for the new *Oregonian*.

547

BILL MURRAY: Check it. I got a foul.

KID: Foul.

BILL: Right here.

KID: It wouldn't have been a foul if you made the shot.

BILL: It's the first one I've called, man, come on. Still game point. Okay, you ready? What is this, your mother coming to get you here?

KID: Where?

BILL: See that, in the NBA, when some guy starts talking about your momma you don't listen up. You stay right here. My mother, my father, my dog, my brothers and sisters, I'm all about the game. Baby . . .

KID: I got it.

BILL: . . . you better get hungry or you're not going to be there with me.

CONSUMER TELEVISION
:30/:25 CAMPAIGN

548
ART DIRECTOR:
Leslie Caldwell
WRITER:
Mike Koelker
AGENCY PRODUCER:
Anna Frost
PRODUCTION COMPANY:
Pytka
DIRECTOR:
Joe Pytka
CLIENT:
Levi Strauss & Company
AGENCY:
Foote Cone & Belding/ San Francisco

549
ART DIRECTORS:
Steve Mitchell
Mike Murray
WRITER:
Kristine Larsen
PRODUCTION COMPANY:
Reelworks
DIRECTOR:
Tom Larson
CLIENT:
Minnesota Brewing
AGENCY:
Hunt Murray/Minneapolis

550
ART DIRECTORS:
Jeff Martin
Katherine Petillo
WRITERS:
Jack Becker
Kevin Sutton
AGENCY PRODUCERS:
Keith Brown
Jim Frame
PRODUCTION COMPANY:
Truth
DIRECTOR:
Eric McClellan
CLIENT:
First Commerce Corporation
AGENCY:
Lawler Ballard Van Durand/Birmingham

551
ART DIRECTOR:
Glenn Ribble
WRITER:
Glenn Ribble
AGENCY PRODUCER:
Abby Terkuhle
PRODUCTION COMPANY:
In-House
DIRECTOR:
Glenn Ribble
CLIENT:
MTV
AGENCY:
MTV/New York

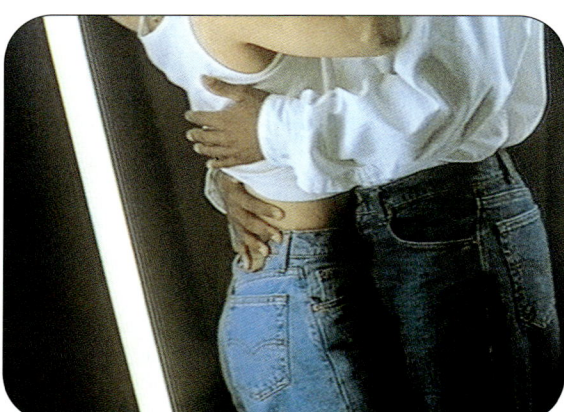

548

(MUSIC: THROUGHOUT)

ANNCR: This time around we'll dance. We'll dance down the rooftops. Dance up the thunder. And we will ride the rhythm, because everything's possible this time around.

SUPER: LEVI'S. LOOSE FITTING JEANS.

549

(MUSIC: SITAR)

PIG'S EYE (WITH FAKE INDIAN ACCENT): To live in the past is to ignore the future. To ignore the future is to ignore the progress of humankind. Ha ha . . . Had you goin' for a sec' didn't I?

(MUSIC: '50S MUZAK)

PIG'S EYE: Don't worry, I haven't become an existential transcendentalist or a follower of Zen. It's just the sam ol' me, Pig's Eye. So keep believin' what you've always believed.

(MUSIC: SITAR MUSIC)

PIG'S EYE (WITH INDIAN ACCENT): And keep Pig's Eye on your mind.

SUPER: PIG'S EYE PILSNER. A BRUTALLY HONEST BEER.

550

SUPER: YOU'VE JUST WITNESSED A BANK FAILURE.

SUPER: WITNESS BANKING FROM A DIFFERENT POINT OF VIEW.

SUPER: PERSONAL BANKING FROM FIRST NBC. PART OF THE STRONGEST FAMILY OF BANKS IN LOUISIANA. MEMBER FDIC.

551

ANNCR: Make your own MTV logo with materials found around the house. Cut open some old tin cans and flatten them with a hammer. Stich them together with twine. Affix cloth with household glue. Using tin snips, cut an MTV logo out of sheet metal. If you don't have sheet metal, tinfoil will do. Add details with hobby paint. Don't forget to circle the "R". Nail your logo to the background and frame it. Old iron nails add even more character. Your MTV logo is ready to use.

CONSUMER TELEVISION
:30/:25 CAMPAIGN

552
ART DIRECTORS:
Bruce Bousman
Leslie Dektor
Bill Hamilton
Bruce Davidson
WRITERS:
Charlie Tercek
Bill Hamilton
AGENCY PRODUCERS:
Bruce Davidson
Lee Weiss
PRODUCTION COMPANY:
Dektor Higgins & Associates
DIRECTOR:
Leslie Dektor
CLIENT:
IBM
AGENCY:
Ogilvy & Mather/ New York

553
ART DIRECTOR:
Jim Baldwin
WRITER:
Mike Renfro
AGENCY PRODUCER:
Jessica Coats
PRODUCTION COMPANY:
In-House
DIRECTOR:
Jim Baldwin
CLIENT:
American Spirit
AGENCY:
The Richards Group/ Dallas

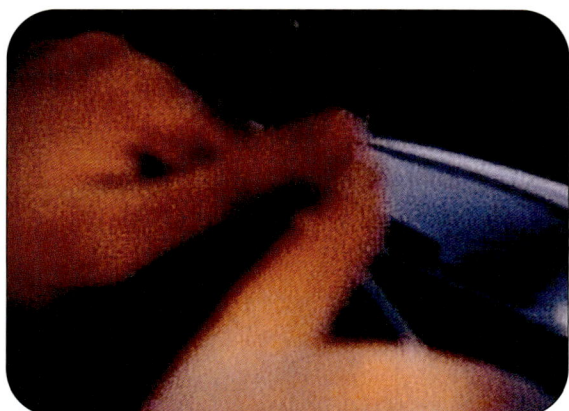

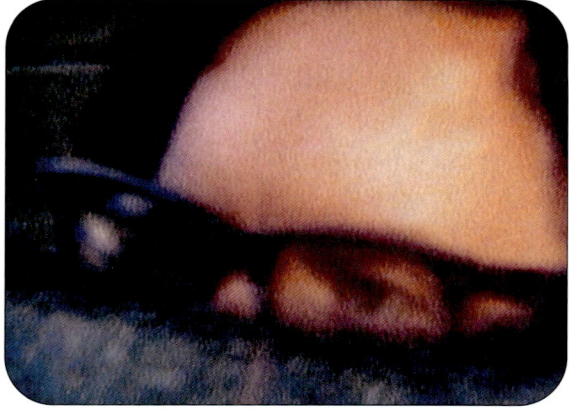

552
(IN ARABIC WITH ENGLISH SUBTITLES)

MAN 1: Man, I'm so stressed. Corporate wants our systems talking to each other. Hey, I'm no wirehead.
MAN 2: You check out IBM?
MAN 1: No.
MAN 2: Look. IBM can make your stuff work with their stuff . . . anybody's stuff.
MAN 1: Got there number?
MAN 2: Sure. I'll e-mail it to you.
SUPER: SOLUTIONS FOR A SMALL PLANET.

553
(SFX: OLD CAR RATTLING DOWN THE ROAD)

MAN (ANNCR): Recently, the Association of Scrap Metal Dealers and Auto Salvage Professionals named me their man of the year for the third consecutive time. I've been involved in so many accidents, that until recently, I thought dashboards were one of the four major food groups. What's even scarier, I'm about to get on the freeway with you.
SUPER: SOME PEOPLE DESERVE HIGH INSURANCE PREMIUMS. WE SPECIALIZE IN THOSE WHO DON'T.
SUPER: AMERICAN SPIRIT.

 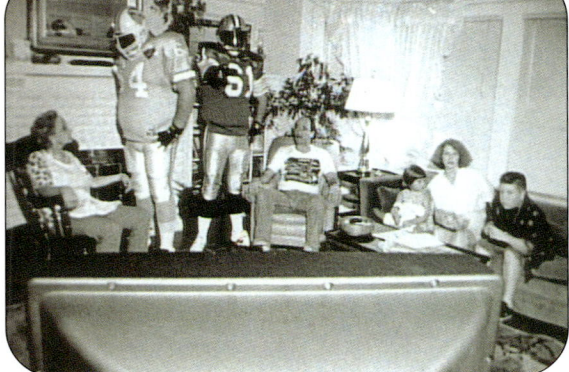

CONSUMER TELEVISION
:30/:25 CAMPAIGN

554
ART DIRECTOR:
Larry Frey
WRITER:
Scott Wild
AGENCY PRODUCER:
Jill Andresevic
PRODUCTION COMPANY:
Tony Kaye Films
DIRECTORS:
Tony Kaye
Larry Frey
CLIENT:
ESPN
AGENCY:
Wieden & Kennedy/ Portland

555
ART DIRECTOR:
Larry Frey
WRITER:
Hank Perlman
AGENCY PRODUCER:
Beth Harding
PRODUCTION COMPANY:
Sandbank Kamen & Partners
DIRECTORS:
Frank Todaro
Bryan Buckley
CLIENT:
ESPN
AGENCY:
Wieden & Kennedy/ Portland

554

PREACHER: To understand the loyalty, you must understand the hostility. These pockets of ill-will are the only places where animosity remains politically correct. It may even be unclear what matters more, your team's victory, or the other team's defeat. These rivalries, they may be nasty. These rivalries, they may be wrathful. These rivalries, they are not pretty. But my, oh my, they are fun.

555

BOOMER: Hi, I'm Boomer Esiason and I'm here to tell you about some very special work being done on behalf of the NFL and ESPN. It's a program in which players are reaching into communities to help people see the value of setting aside Sunday nights for football on ESPN. It's called the W.A.T.C.H. program. Players from around the league are getting the word out to people just like you, and you know what — the program is working! We kindly ask everyone to W.A.T.C.H. this Sunday Night Football.

CONSUMER TELEVISION
:30/:25 CAMPAIGN

556
ART DIRECTOR:
Tim Hanrahan
WRITER:
Glenn Cole
AGENCY PRODUCER:
Jennifer Smieja
PRODUCTION COMPANY:
Tiny Films
DIRECTOR:
Robin Willis
CLIENT:
ESPN
AGENCY:
Wieden & Kennedy/ Portland

557
ART DIRECTORS:
Andrew Christou
Eric C. King
WRITERS:
Derek Barnes
James LeMaitre
AGENCY PRODUCER:
Donna Portaro
PRODUCTION COMPANY:
Pytka
DIRECTOR:
Joe Pytka
CLIENT:
Nike
AGENCY:
Wieden & Kennedy/ Portland

556

FAN: So novice soccer fans. Ever see the mayhem after a world cup goal?

ANNCRS: Goooaaaaallllll! Alberto Beneeeeee! Aahh Ahhh Ahhh! . . . and the substitute has scored! . . . Dramatic finale!

SUPER: ESPN WORLD CUP SOCCER '94.

SUPER: ESPN. STARTS JUNE 17.

FAN: Whoa! Who do you love, who do you love? I'm not done yet.

557

SUPER: DAY 12.
SUPER: PLAY BALL.
SUPER: PLEASE.
SUPER: NIKE.

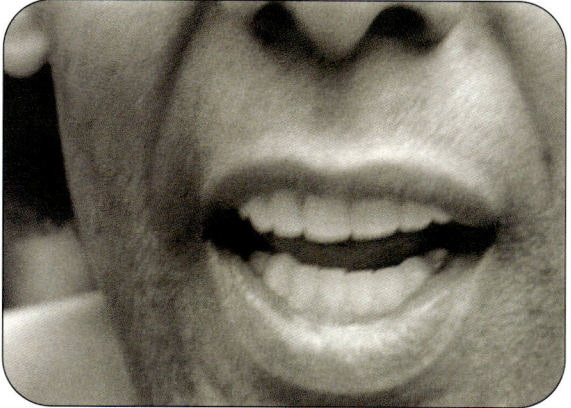

CONSUMER TELEVISION :30/:25 CAMPAIGN

558
ART DIRECTOR:
John C. Jay
WRITER:
Jimmy Smith
AGENCY PRODUCER:
Renee Raab
PRODUCTION COMPANY:
Radical Media
DIRECTOR:
Robert Fernandez
CLIENT:
Nike
AGENCY:
Wieden & Kennedy/ Portland

559
ART DIRECTOR:
John C. Jay
WRITER:
Ken Wieden
AGENCY PRODUCER:
Ben Grylewicz
PRODUCTION COMPANY:
Radical Media
DIRECTORS:
Robert Leacock
Joe DeSalvo
CLIENT:
Nike
AGENCY:
Wieden & Kennedy/ Portland

558

PLAYER: Then I bring him back out 'cause I wanna embarrass him. I wanna shake him and fake him, and I'm lookin' at his face sayin', whatcha want me to do make a layup, make a jumpshot? Make up your mind watcha want me to do. Bam bam bam, I'm goin' through my legs twice, then I'm gonna reverse, hesitate, stop. I freeze then I pull up on him, then I back up on him. "Yeah c'mon nah nah uh oh you ain't guardin' me, oh here I'm back again, oh I thought you was guardin' me." An' I'm sayin', "Now let's go, push up, push up, push up now." Up, he's in the air I done faked him but I goin' back and fake him again and I goin' to the basket, layin' it up, behind my back double reverse fake head fake, and I'm lookin' at him sayin', "Hey you can't guard me man. I got so many moves last game I shook myself."

559

DWAYNE McGEE: You know and stuff like basketball man, basketball is the game of the city, not football, not baseball, not soccer, not hockey. You don't see them playing. There's a blizzard out there, and you don't see nobody in the city playing football. But you say come on let's go play some ball, let's clear the court of ice and they'll ball. And they'll sweat and they'll take their shirts off and it will be zero degrees and people be going, these boys is crazy, but they ballin'.

CONSUMER TELEVISION :20 AND UNDER: SINGLE

560
ART DIRECTOR:
Tony Angotti
WRITER:
Dion Hughes
AGENCY PRODUCER:
Jill Meschino
PRODUCTION COMPANY:
Independent Films
DIRECTOR:
John Marles
CLIENT:
Molson Breweries USA/ Foster's
AGENCY:
Angotti Thomas Hedge/ New York

561
ART DIRECTOR:
Warren Brown
WRITER:
Paul Fishlock
AGENCY PRODUCER:
Alison Chambers
PRODUCTION COMPANY:
Ibbetson Cherry & Dean
DIRECTOR:
Peter McIntosh
CLIENT:
Australian Meat & Live-Stock Corporation
AGENCY:
The Campaign Palace/ Woolloomooloo, Australia

562
ART DIRECTOR:
Jarl Olsen
WRITER:
Jarl Olsen
PRODUCTION COMPANY:
Dublin Productions
DIRECTOR:
Jarl Olsen
CLIENT:
MTV

563
ART DIRECTOR:
Houman Pirdavari
WRITERS:
Scott Burns
Jarl Olsen
AGENCY PRODUCERS:
Shelly Predovich-Eisner
Deborah Sullivan
PRODUCTION COMPANY:
Coppos Films
DIRECTOR:
Buddy Cone
CLIENT:
Volkswagen
AGENCY:
Fallon McElligott Berlin/ New York

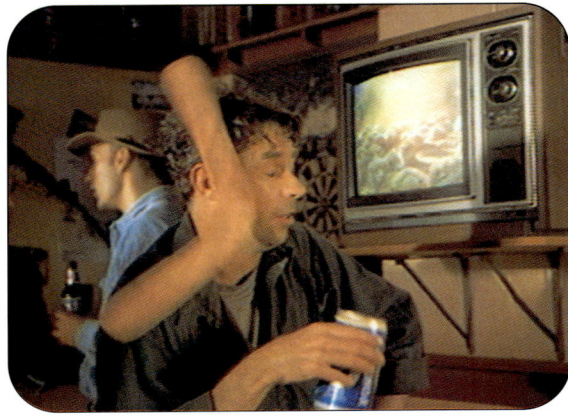 

560
ANNCR: How to speak Australian. Remote Control. Beer. Foster's. Australian for beer.

561
ANNCR: This steamed snapper, or this grilled lean rump steak will give you half your daily iron needs. So let's see them side by side.
SUPER: LEAN BEAF: YOUR BEST SOURCE OF ESSENTIAL DAILY IRON.

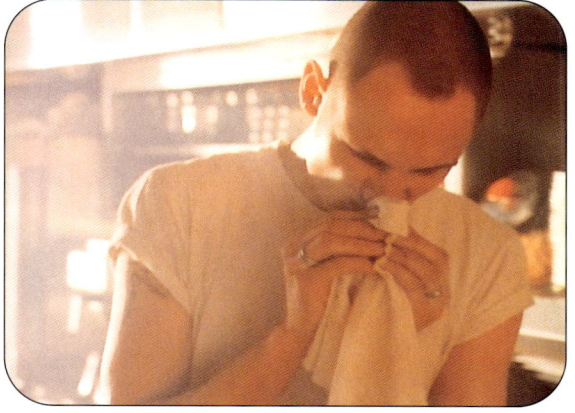

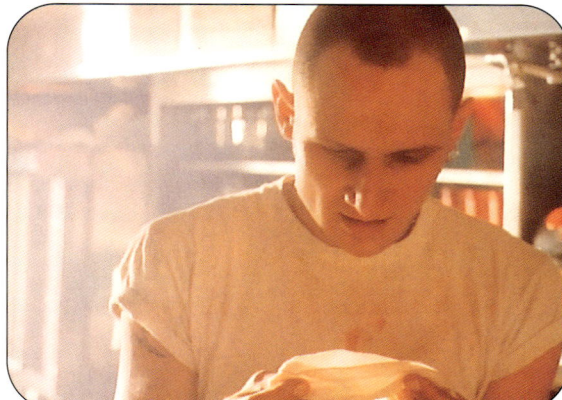

562

(SFX: MAN BLOWING NOSE)

MAN: Oh look, I made an MTV logo. Wanna see? (SHOUTING) Well, I didn't wanna show it to you anyway.

563

ANNCR: The new Volkswagon Golf features a track correcting rear axel and an improved turning radius of just $32^{1}/2$ feet. All of which makes the tight-handling Golf the perfect car for the city.

SUPER: THE NEW GOLF.

CONSUMER TELEVISION :20 AND UNDER: SINGLE

564
ART DIRECTOR:
Tom Routson
WRITER:
Bob Kerstetter
AGENCY PRODUCER:
Mark Tripp
PRODUCTION COMPANY:
Propaganda Films
DIRECTOR:
David Kellogg
CLIENT:
Sega of America
AGENCY:
Goodby Silverstein & Partners/San Francisco

565
ART DIRECTOR:
Hal Tench
WRITER:
Ron Huey
AGENCY PRODUCER:
Morty Baran
PRODUCTION COMPANY:
Dektor Higgins & Associates
DIRECTOR:
Thom Higgins
CLIENT:
Wrangler Company
AGENCY:
The Martin Agency/Richmond

566
ART DIRECTOR:
Tom McConnaughy
WRITER:
Jim Schmidt
AGENCY PRODUCER:
Jon Wyville
CLIENT:
Walgreen Company
AGENCY:
McConnaughy Stein Schmidt Brown/Chicago

567
ART DIRECTOR:
Kent Johnson
WRITERS:
David Coats
Kevin Sutton
AGENCY PRODUCER:
Carol Leftwich
PRODUCTION COMPANY:
Crossroads Films
DIRECTOR:
Robert Hannant
CLIENT:
EyeMasters
AGENCY:
The Richards Group/Dallas

564
(MUSIC: THROUGHOUT)
ANNCR: Sega's new NFL '95 has a brand new feature . . .
(SFX: GRUNTS OF PLAYERS)
ANNCR: . . . that let's you see 65 yards down field. Just like in real life.
FAT GUY: Go deeeeeeeep Joe!
JOE: Oh my Go—!
(SFX: CRUNCHING, TACKLING)
(SFX: CROWD GASP)
(SFX: MORE TACKLING)
(SFX: WHISTLE)
HOT DOG: Sega!

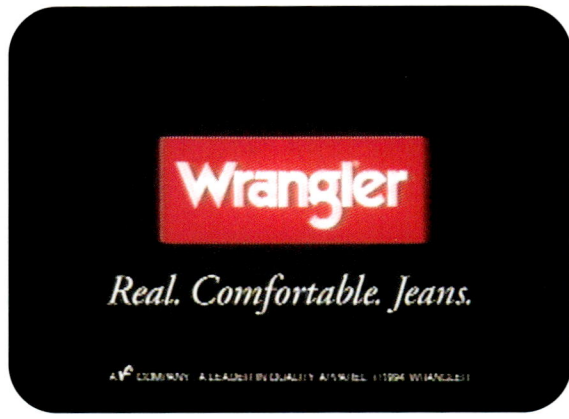

565
(MUSIC: GUITAR)
ANNCR: Wrangler jeans have always been worn by cowboys. But nowadays, even horses wear them.
SUPER: WRANGLER. REAL. COMFORTABLE. JEANS.

566

ANNCR: For some, it's a reminder of their honeymoon. For others, of their nose during cold season.

SUPER: WALGREENS. THE PHARMACY AMERICA TRUSTS.

567

(SFX: PHONE RINGING)

GUY: Hello.

ANNCR: Time to have your eyes checked?

(SFX: DOG YELPS)

ANNCR: We'll pay for your eye exam, up to fifty dollars. Right now at EyeMasters.

SUPER: EYEMASTERS. YOUR EYES. OUR FOCUS.

CONSUMER TELEVISION
:20 AND UNDER: SINGLE

568
ART DIRECTOR:
Tim Hanrahan
WRITER:
Hank Perlman
AGENCY PRODUCER:
Ben Grylewicz
PRODUCTION COMPANY:
Radical Media
DIRECTORS:
Bryan Buckley
Frank Todaro
CLIENT:
ESPN
AGENCY:
Wieden & Kennedy/ Portland

569
ART DIRECTORS:
Andrew Christou
Eric C. King
WRITERS:
Derek Barnes
James LeMaitre
AGENCY PRODUCER:
Donna Portaro
PRODUCTION COMPANY:
Pytka
DIRECTOR:
Joe Pytka
CLIENT:
Nike
AGENCY:
Wieden & Kennedy/ Portland

568
SUPER: MIKE RICHTER. NEW YORK RANGERS.
(SFX: SLAP SHOTS)
(SFX: SQUEAKING AS PLEXIGLASS IS WIPED CLEAN)
SUPER: NEW YORK ISLANDERS VS. NEW YORK RANGERS.
SUPER: THE STANLEY CUP PLAYOFFS. ESPN.

569
SUPER: DAY 27.
FAN: Hey, atta boy buddy, huh!!?? Good job!! Way ta go, huh!!?? Atta boy!!
SUPER: PLAY BALL.
SUPER: PLEASE.
SUPER: NIKE.

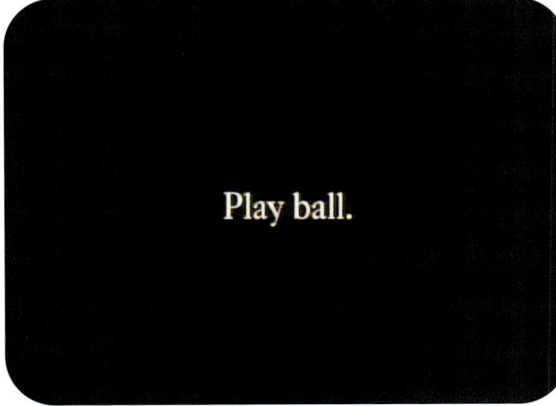

CONSUMER TELEVISION :20 AND UNDER: CAMPAIGN

570
ART DIRECTOR:
Andrew Christou
Eric C. King
WRITERS:
Derek Barnes
James LeMaitre
AGENCY PRODUCER:
Donna Portaro
PRODUCTION COMPANY:
Pytka
DIRECTOR:
Joe Pytka
CLIENT:
Nike
AGENCY:
Wieden & Kennedy/ Portland

CONSUMER TELEVISION VARYING LENGTHS CAMPAIGN

571
ART DIRECTORS:
Jason Peterson
Paul Hirsch
Izzy DeBellis
WRITERS:
Izzy DeBellis
Paul Hirsch
Jason Peterson
AGENCY PRODUCER:
Deborah Sullivan
PRODUCTION COMPANY:
Epoch Films
DIRECTOR:
Jeff Priess
CLIENT:
NBA
AGENCY:
Fallon McElligott Berlin/ New York

570
SUPER: DAY 8.
FAN: Get off the field! You're a bum! You don't deserve to be on a baseball field! You! Yeah, you! I'm talking to you! Don't make me come out there!
SUPER: PLAY BALL.
SUPER: PLEASE.
FAN: You know I'm talking to ya!
SUPER: NIKE.

571
BILL MURRAY (ANNCR): It's like a religion with me. I believe in myself. I'm there for me. I believe in the ball and the ball is there for me. I believe in the court. But I just can't find the court. I know it's out there somewhere.

CONSUMER TELEVISION
VARYING LENGTHS
CAMPAIGN

572
ART DIRECTORS:
Sean Ehringer
Joe Shands
WRITERS:
Harry Cocciolo
Chuck McBride
AGENCY PRODUCER:
Cindy Epps
PRODUCTION COMPANY:
Propaganda Films
DIRECTORS:
Jeffrey Goodby
Michael Bay
CLIENT:
California Fluid Milk Processor Advisory Board
AGENCY:
Goodby Silverstein & Partners/San Francisco

573
ART DIRECTOR:
Amy Nicholson
WRITER:
Risa Mickenberg
AGENCY PRODUCER:
Bruce Wellington
PRODUCTION COMPANY:
HSI Productions
DIRECTOR:
Stephen Kessler
CLIENT:
Snapple Beverage Corporation
AGENCY:
Kirshenbaum & Bond/New York

572
MAN: Tom, can I make a suggestion? You're fired!!!
(SFX: TRUCK HORN WAILING)
MAN: Aaaaaaaaaaah!!!!!
(SFX: CHIMES, FLAPPING BIRD WINGS)
WOMAN: Welcome to eternity.
(MUSIC: PIANO INTRO, SLOW JAZZ)
(SFX: DOOR SHUTTING, TICKING, CAT PURRING)
MAN: Heaven! . . . Yes! . . . Hmmm . . . milk! . . . Wait a minute. Where am I ?
ANNCR: Got Milk?

573
WENDY: Hi from Snapple. An iced tea drinker from Atlanta writes: "Are your commercials for real, or are the people just actors?" Ask them yourself.

DETENTION GUY: Luther!

LUTHER: The detention guy. Yeah. Come in . . . come in . . . come in, Shane. . . . Oh I can't believe it.

COLONEL: The only good thing that ever came out of New York, and I've been in New York and had an unusual experience there, and uhh.

NANCY: Come on. Can you say Snapple? Shaney.

DETENTION GUY: I held the record last year for having the most detentions. I had 75.

GLASS MAKER: So, you don't think the people are real. Well, we're real, Luther.

LUTHER: I believe you now. I believe you now.

WENDY: Snapple. Made from the best stuff on earth.

LUTHER: I'm a real person.

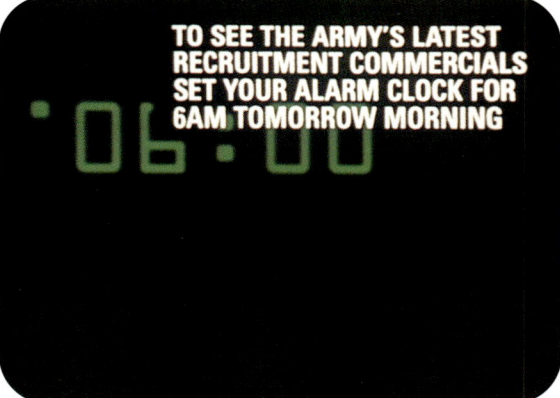

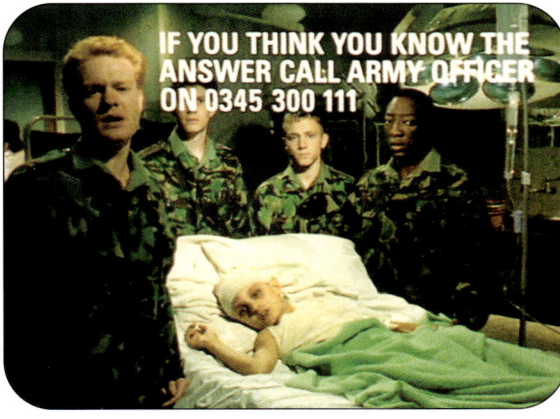

CONSUMER TELEVISION
VARYING LENGTHS
CAMPAIGN

574
ART DIRECTOR:
Alexandra Taylor
WRITER:
Adam Kean
AGENCY PRODUCER:
David Eddon
PRODUCTION COMPANY:
Arden Sutherland-Dodd
DIRECTOR:
Thomas Krygier
CLIENT:
COI/Army
AGENCY:
Saatchi & Saatchi/London

575
ART DIRECTOR:
John Boiler
WRITER:
Stacy Wall
AGENCY PRODUCERS:
Bill Davenport
Jeff Selis
PRODUCTION COMPANY:
Pytka
DIRECTOR:
Joe Pytka
CLIENT:
Nike
AGENCY:
Wieden & Kennedy/Portland

574
ANNCR: To see the Army's latest recruitment commercials, set your alarm clock for 6AM tommorow morning.
SUPER: THE ARMY. BE THE BEST.

575
(MUSIC: THROUGHOUT)
SUPER: NIKE.

CONSUMER TELEVISION
UNDER $50,000 BUDGET

576
ART DIRECTOR:
Robert Shaw West
WRITER:
Ken Cills
AGENCY PRODUCER:
Joe Mosca
PRODUCTION COMPANY:
In-House
CLIENT:
WMMR 93.3 FM
AGENCY:
Earle Palmer Brown/Philadelphia

577
ART DIRECTOR:
Lindsey Redding
WRITER:
Adrian Jeffery
AGENCY PRODUCER:
Tim Maguire
PRODUCTION COMPANY:
Tony Kaye Films
DIRECTOR:
Jonathan Barnbrook
CLIENT:
BBC Radio Scotland
AGENCY:
Faulds Advertising/Edinburgh

578
ART DIRECTOR:
Kirk Souder
WRITER:
Court Crandall
AGENCY PRODUCER:
Claudia Plasencia
PRODUCTION COMPANY:
Windmill Lane
DIRECTOR:
Meiert Avis
CLIENT:
The Daily Grill
AGENCY:
Ground Zero/Venice

576
SUPER: DOCTORS HAVE THIS THEORY THAT IF YOU PLAY CLASSICAL MUSIC TO INFANTS THEY'LL GROW UP WITH A BETTER UNDERSTANDING OF COMPLEX RELATIONSHIPS, LIKE MATH. THEY DON'T KNOW WHAT EFFECT ROCK AND ROLL WILL HAVE BUT I PLAY THIS STUFF FOR HIM ANYWAY. I FIGURE THE WORLD CAN LIVE WITH ONE LESS ACCOUNTANT.

577

ANNCR 1: An excercise I often do is write words like "bombaize" and "forfoughen" and words like that up on the board you see. And they think things like, a foggie bummer, what's a foggie bummer? Then we'll ask one another, you see, and . . .

ANNCR 2: What is a foggy bummer?

ANNCR 1: A bumble bee! (LAUGHS)

ANNCR 2: I was away to say you could have got us struck off the air then!

ANNCR 1: Oh no, no, no, no! It's not that bad!

SUPER: REDISCOVER THE POWER OF THE SPOKEN WORD.

SUPER: BBC RADIO SCOTLAND.

SUPER: UK NATIONAL STATION OF THE YEAR.

578

(MUSIC: SITAR)

POTATO (THINKING): Is the universe finite? Is there a divine being? Is there a cosmic plan? Where do I fit in?

SUPER: DAILY GRILL.

SUPER: LA'S ONLY GREAT AMERICAN MEAL.

CONSUMER TELEVISION UNDER $50,000 BUDGET

579
ART DIRECTOR:
Terence Reynolds
WRITER:
Todd Tilford
AGENCY PRODUCER:
Diana Lawless
PRODUCTION COMPANY:
Bednarz Films
DIRECTOR:
Robb Debenport
CLIENT:
94.5 FM/The Edge
AGENCY:
The Richards Group/
Dallas

NON-BROADCAST: CINEMA

580
ART DIRECTORS:
Mike Rosen
Duncan Milner
WRITER:
Marty Cooke
AGENCY PRODUCERS:
Peter Cline
Andrew Chinich
PRODUCTION COMPANIES:
Click 3X
Farenheit Films
DIRECTOR:
Greg Ramsey
CLIENT:
Fruitopia
AGENCY:
Chiat/Day, New York

581
ART DIRECTOR:
Lyn Smith
WRITER:
Larry Kopald
AGENCY PRODUCER:
Jacqueline Lebovitz
CLIENT:
Earth Communications Office
AGENCY:
The Kopald Group/
Los Angeles

579

(MUSIC: "VASELINE" BY THE STONE TEMPLE PILOTS)

SUPER: GUARANTEED TO KEEP YOUR PARENTS OUT OF YOUR BEDROOM.

SUPER: 94.5 FM. THE EDGE.

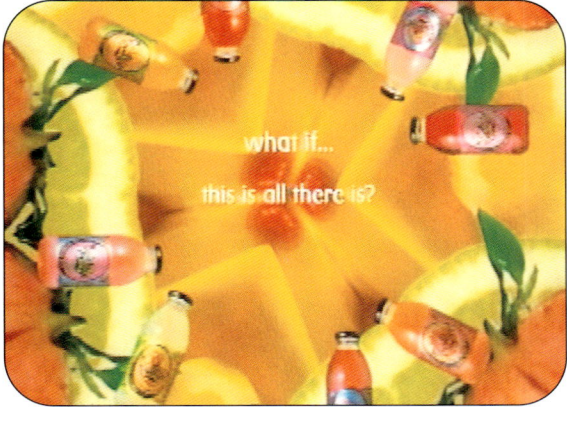

580

SUPER: WHAT IF . . . NOBODY VOTED? THERE REALLY IS SOMEONE OUT THERE? EVERYBODY WAS THE SAME COLOR? EXTRATERRESTRIALS ARE US, NOT THEM? YOU DIE NOT KNOWING? YOU NEVER FALL IN LOVE? THE EXPERTS ARE WRONG? FASHION DOESN'T MATTER? VIRTUAL REALITY IS REALITY? CHILDREN RAN THE WORLD? ROCK AND ROLL IS DEAD? PEOPLE STOP READING? NOBODY LAUGHED? THERE WERE NO LAST NAMES? YOU ARE ALONE? YOU NEVER READ MADAME BOVARY? THE CYNICS ARE RIGHT? THE BOMB DIDN'T EXIST? HISTORY COULD BE REWRITTEN? YOU SPILL YOUR POPCORN? GEORGE WASHINGTON HAD BEEN AN AFRICAN AMERICAN? EVERYBODY COULD DRAW? EVERYBODY COULD SING? POLITICAL CORRECTNESS HAD A SENSE OF HUMOR? YOU NEVER NEEDED A PASSPORT? THEY NEVER INVENTED ARTIFICIAL TURF? NOBODY WAS HUNGRY? TRIBES DIDN'T EXIST? YOU WERE INVISIBLE? YOU'RE THIRSTY? BLACK IS WHITE? AND VICE VERSA? THE END IS NEAR? THIS MOVIE CHANGES YOUR LIFE? NOBODY HAD TO SLEEP ALONE? BIG BROTHER HAD A SENSE OF HUMOR? COMPUTERS TAKE OVER THE WORLD? NOBODY CRIED? YOUR PET IS YOUR BEST FRIEND? YOU DIDN'T ATTEND WOODSTOCK? YOU HUGGED THE PERSON NEXT TO YOU? THIS IS ALL THERE IS? FRUITOPIAN QUERIES HAVE NO ANSWERS? FRUTOPIA FOR THE *MIND, BODY, PLANET*.

581

SUPER: IT'S NOT A THING. IT'S ALIVE.

ANNCR: Long ago, before the first human was born, before the first tree began reaching for the sun, her life began. She breathes. And grows. Her blood rushes through her veins. She can speak her mind. And, she can feel pain. She can feed us when we're hungry. She can heal us when we're sick. She has the power to give us energy. And the power to make us smile. She is not a thing. She's the Earth. And there is a reason we call her Mother.

Every day nineteen more of earth's species disappear. Forever. But thanks to your efforts, whales are beginning to return, the bald eagle is off the endangered list, and one million acres of rainforest were protected. Forever.

We only have one planet. We only get one chance. Our mother needs our help. Do something. Anything.

SUPER: YOU HAVE THE POWER.

SUPER: 1-800-ONE POWER.

SUPER: EARTH COMMUNICATIONS OFFICE.

SUPER: MADE POSSIBLE BY THE GENEROSITY OF THE TERESA & H. JOHN HEINZ III FOUNDATION, THE EASTMAN KODAK COMPANY AND THE NATIONAL ASSOCIATION OF THEATRE OWNERS.

NON-BROADCAST:
OUT-OF-HOME

582
ART DIRECTOR:
James Dalthorp
WRITER:
Joe O'Neill
AGENCY PRODUCER:
Victoria Waldock
PRODUCTION COMPANY:
Dektor Higgins & Associates
DIRECTOR:
Leslie Dektor
CLIENT:
Buena Vista Home Video
AGENCY:
Hal Riney & Partners/ San Francisco

583
ART DIRECTOR:
Steve Mitchell
WRITER:
Doug Adkins
PRODUCTION COMPANY:
Dublin Productions
DIRECTOR:
Rick Dublin
CLIENT:
Dublin Productions
AGENCY:
Hunt Murray/Minneapolis

INTERNATIONAL FOREIGN LANGUAGE COMMERCIAL: TELEVISION

584
ART DIRECTOR:
David Caballero
WRITER:
Pablo Monzon
AGENCY PRODUCER:
Toni Segarra
PRODUCTION COMPANY:
Jodaf and Joao Daniel Films
DIRECTOR:
Joao Tikhomiroff
CLIENT:
Spanish Cancer Association
AGENCY:
Delvico Bates/Barcelona

582

CLARENCE: The overall memory of it. I . . . I can close my eyes and I can see them walking along.

(MUSIC: *Heigh ho, heigh ho*)

AGNES: Doc was the leader, and Dopey, of course, was the one at the end that was always trying to catch up.

GINA: Tripping and falling on everything.

MICK (SINGING): *Heigh ho, heigh ho.*

REBECCA: All with such different personalities.

AGNES: Doc, Dopey . . .

CLARENCE: Grumpy. How many is that?

SARAH: Sleepy.

MICK: Happy.

SANDRA: Bashful.

CLARENCE: Two guys . . . we got two missing dwarfs.

ANNCR: Snow White and the Seven Dwarfs. On video for the first time.

CLARENCE: Was there one that was forgetful? I don't remember.

583

(ALL VOICES OFF CAMERA)

(MUSIC: THROUGHOUT)

WOMAN 1: For shame, Mr. Dublin. Is it the dog's fault that it has big ears? Don't you think it has suffered enough embarrassment and ridicule from small-eared dogs without you drawing further attention to its affliction? Bad director! Bad, bad director . . .

MAN 1: I am tormented by terrifying visions of your evil froggy character. To the world it is but a frog—but I know better! I know that it is actually Satan's valet, conceived in the deepest depths of hell . . .

MAN 2: Do you enjoy making fun of a poor sports car's anatomy? For this transgression you shall be kicked. Your uncles, kicked. Pets, kicked. I shall dig your ancestors out of the grave and kick them. None shall escape the kicking. The kicking shall be indiscriminate and eternal. Kick, kick, kick, kick . . .

MAN 3: Before you attempt another golf commercial, ask yourself Mr. Dublin, why the blood of the grass stains permanent. May the anguish of the grass come back upon you a thousand-fold, staining your very soul with . . .

WOMAN 2: Dear Mr. Dublin: I like your ads. Nay, I love them. And—dare I say it—I love you, Rick. I love you, and I must have you. Oh, you will be mine, all mine. I've been watching you, Rick. And recording your telephone conversations. At night while you sleep, I sneak into your room and gaze at your naked body, twisted in the sheets . . .

SUPER: RICK DUBLIN. ADS PEOPLE NOTICE.

584

ANNCR: If you feel ashamed about showing your two breasts, imagine showing just one. Visit your gynecologist once a year.

SUPER: SPANISH CANCER ASSOCIATION.

College Finalists

COLLEGE COMPETITION
ASSIGNMENT: BRAND
NAME BAR SOAP

585
ART DIRECTOR:
Chris Fullwood
WRITER:
Chris Fullwood
COLLEGE:
East Texas State
University/Commerce, TX

586
ART DIRECTOR:
Mike Calienes
WRITER:
Mike Calienes
COLLEGE:
Miami Ad School/Miami

587
ART DIRECTOR:
Bobby Appleby
WRITER:
Kimberly Anne Mattig
COLLEGE:
Miami Ad School/Miami

588
ART DIRECTORS:
Dee Reed
Lynn Sarnow
WRITER:
Dee Reed
COLLEGE:
Miami Ad School/Miami

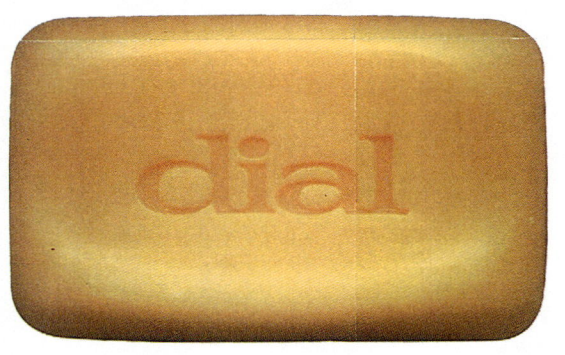

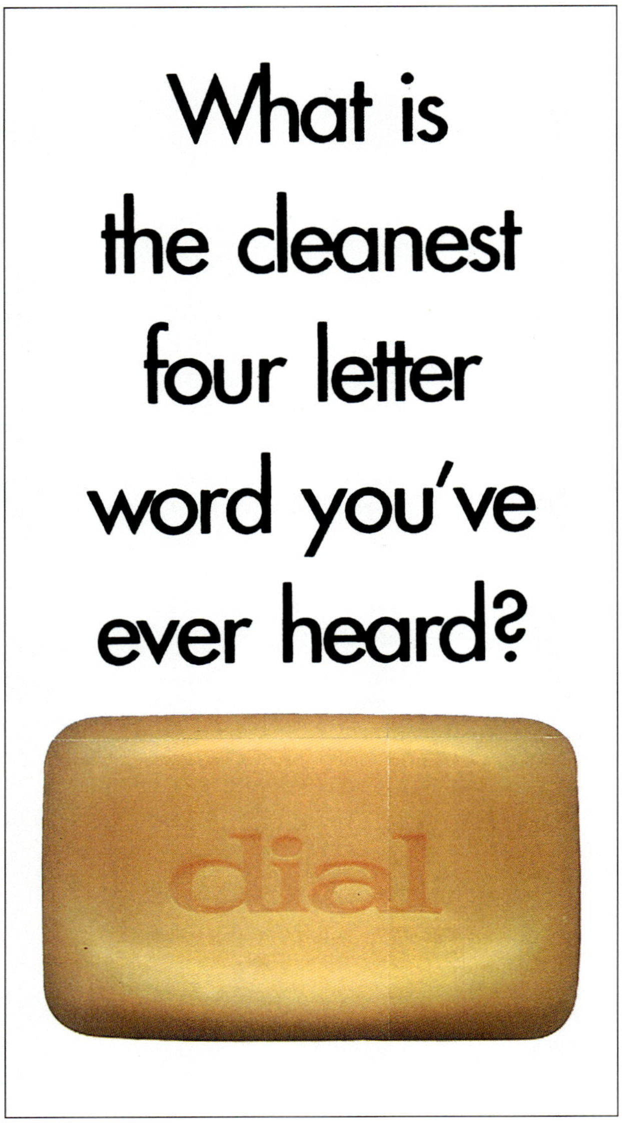
What is
the cleanest
four letter
word you've
ever heard?
dial
585

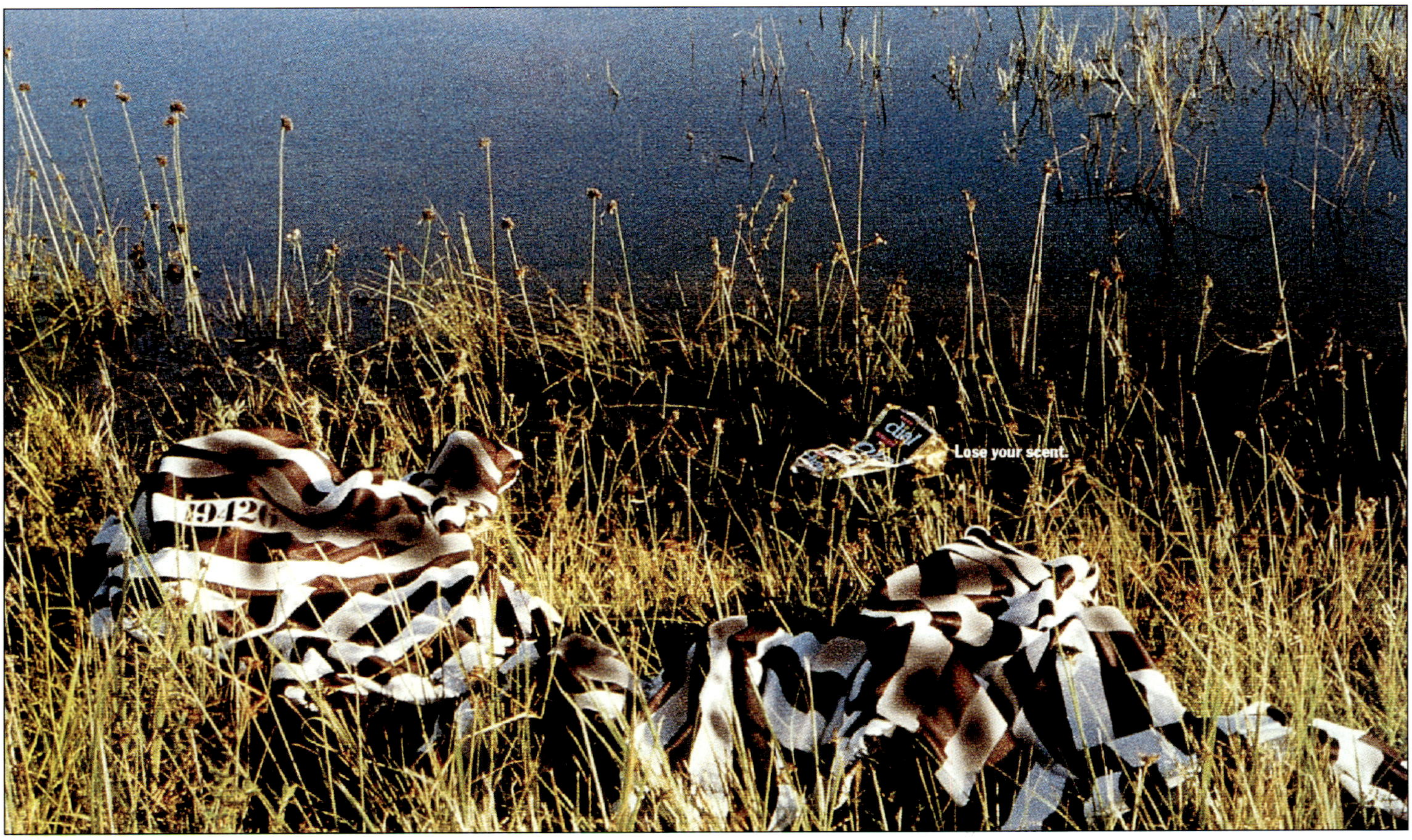
dial
Lose your scent.
586

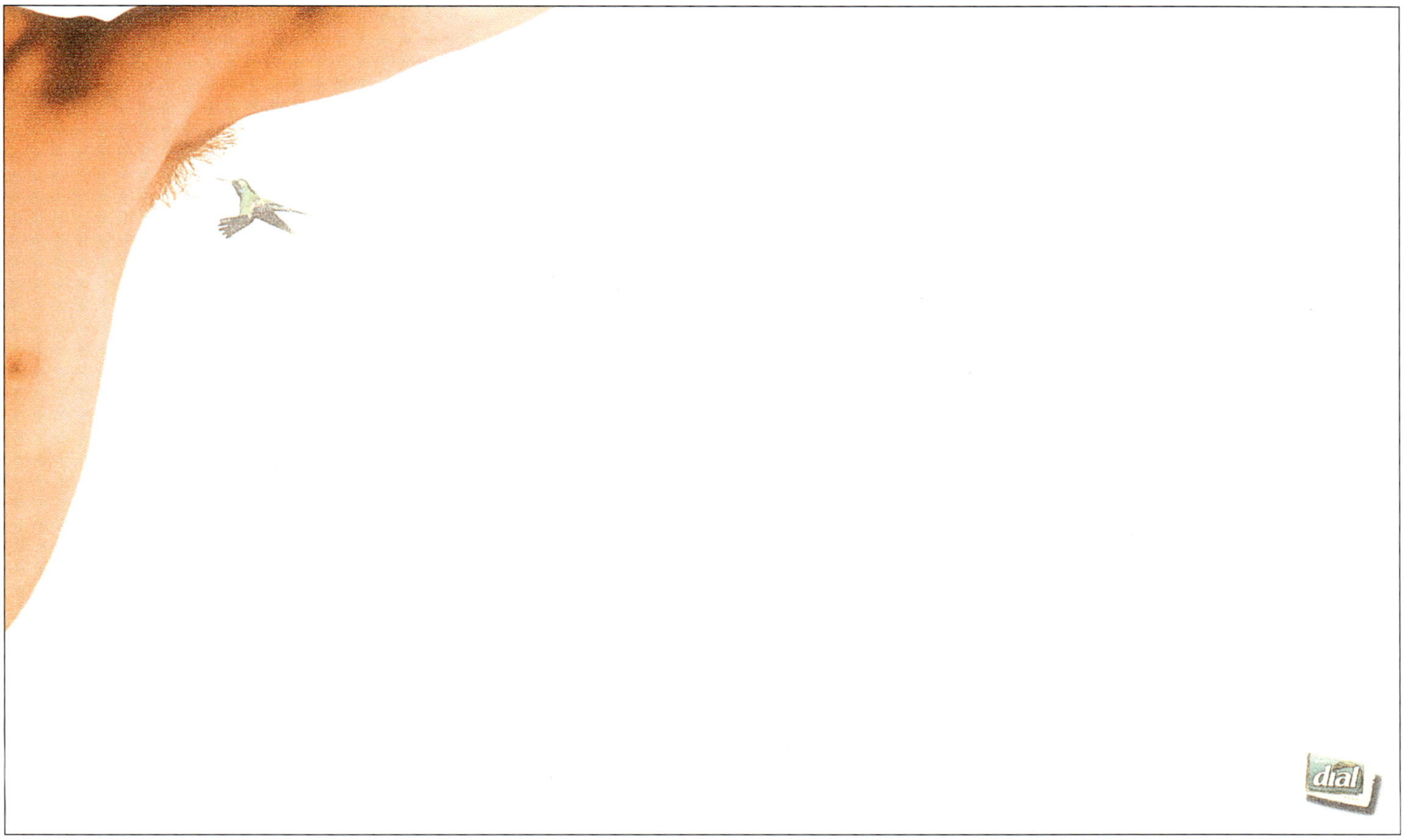
dial

587

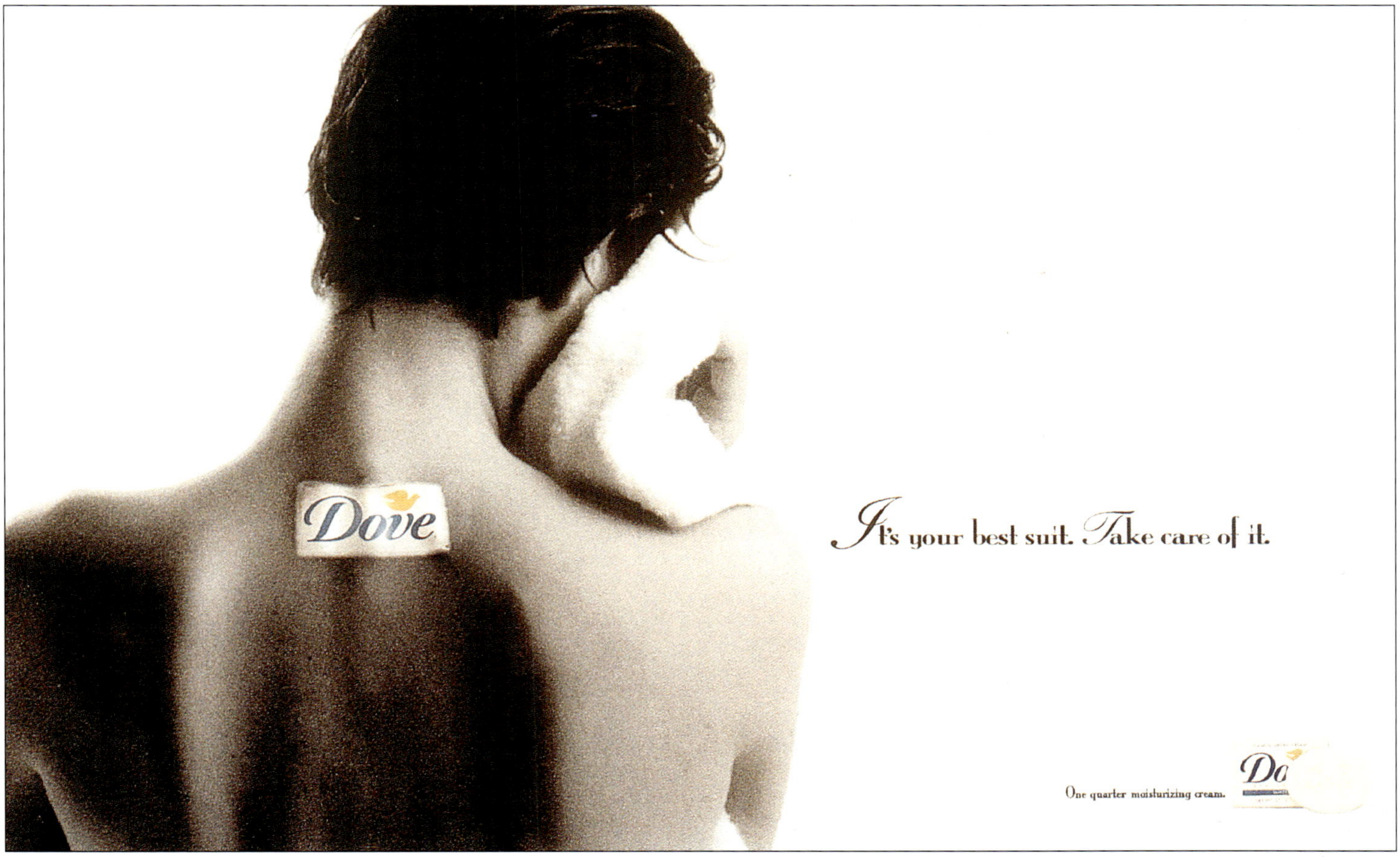
Dove
It's your best suit. Take care of it.
One quarter moisturizing cream.

588

COLLEGE COMPETITION
ASSIGNMENT: BRAND
NAME BAR SOAP

589
ART DIRECTOR:
Jim Genell
WRITER:
Steve Murray
PHOTOGRAPHER:
David Emmite
COLLEGE:
Portfolio Center/Atlanta

590
ART DIRECTORS:
Ahmer Kalam
Rich DeSimone
WRITER:
Ken Herbst
COLLEGE:
Portfolio Center/Atlanta

591
ART DIRECTOR:
Judy Engelman
WRITER:
Robert Havlena
COLLEGE:
Portfolio Center/Atlanta

592
ART DIRECTOR:
Chris Parks
WRITER:
Dave Loew
COLLEGE:
Portfolio Center/Atlanta

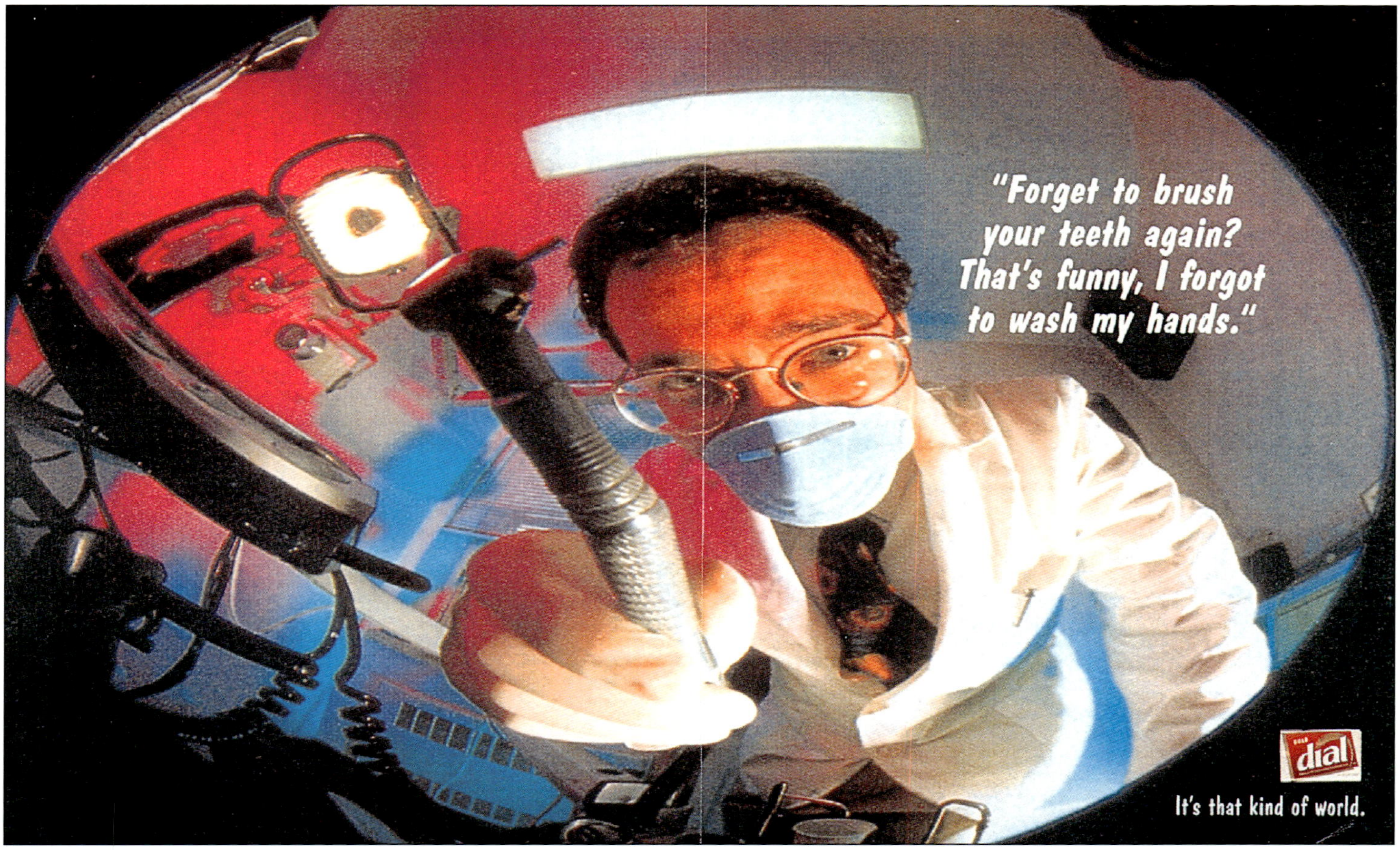

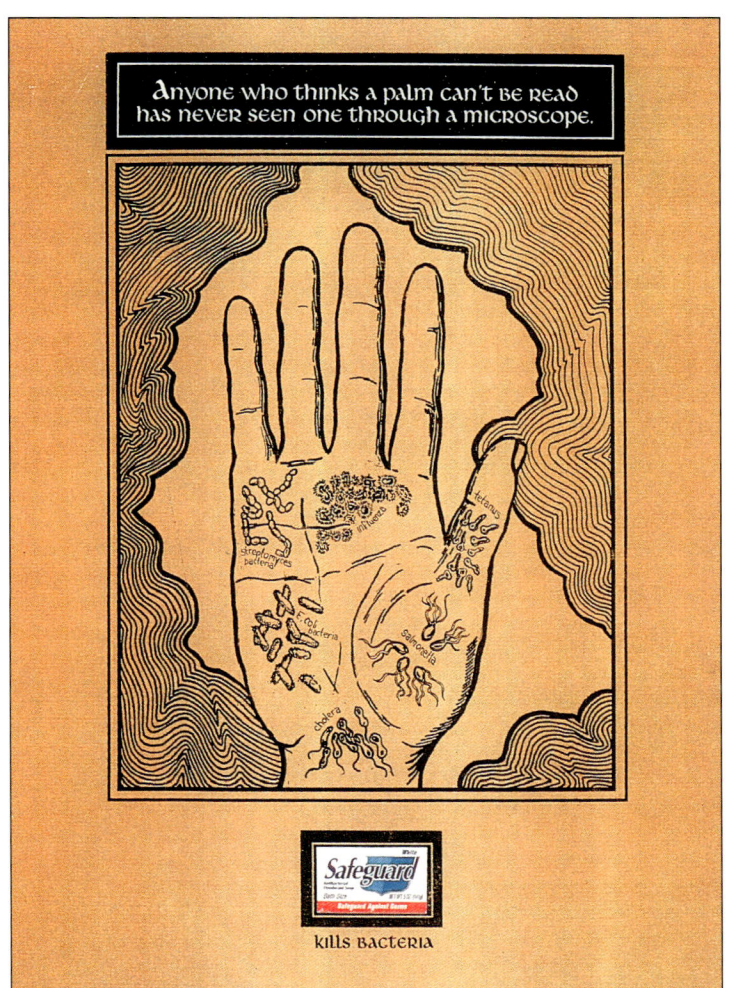

591

592

COLLEGE COMPETITION ASSIGNMENT: BRAND NAME BAR SOAP

593
ART DIRECTOR:
Jennifer Van Blarcom
WRITER:
Jennifer Van Blarcom
COLLEGE:
School of Visual Arts/New York

594
ART DIRECTOR:
Christopher Turner
WRITER:
Christopher Turner
COLLEGE:
School of Visual Arts/New York

595
ART DIRECTOR:
Ted Guidotti
WRITER:
Ted Guidotti
PHOTOGRAPHER:
Ryan Eastwood
COLLEGE:
Syracuse University/Syracuse

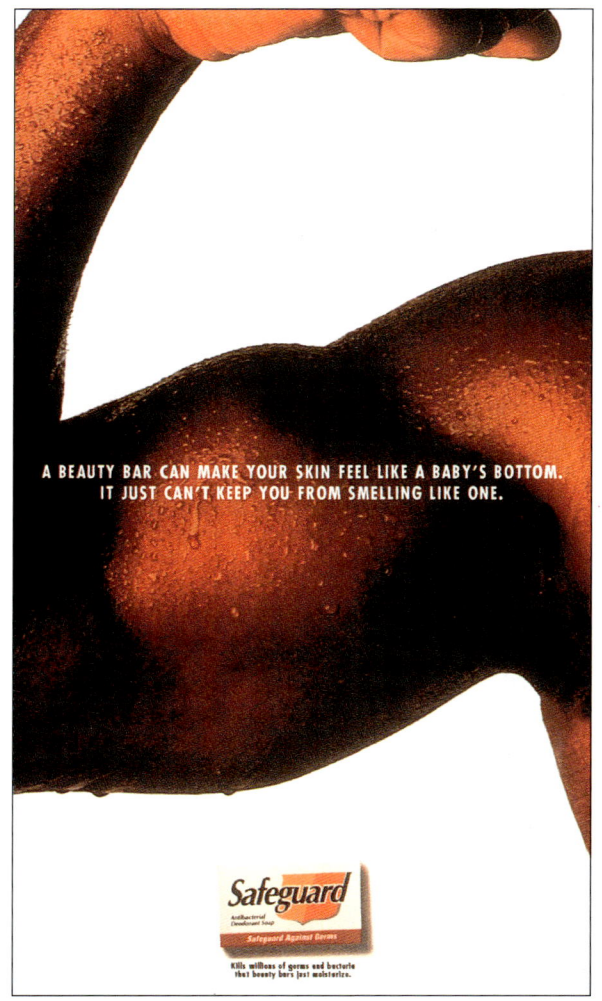

Index

AGENCIES

Abbott Mead Vickers. BBDO/ London 4, 26, 51, 82, 83, 84, 123, 124, 125, 186, 259, 424, 430, 476, 477

Altschiller & Company/ New York 397

Ammirati & Puris/Toronto 85, 86, 87, 88, 126, 127

Ammirati & Puris/Lintas, New York 315, 316

Angotti Thomas Hedge/ New York 89, 187, 188, 189, 284, 291, 292, 293, 305, 495, 560

Arnold Finnegan Martin/ Richmond 39, 496

Bailey Lauerman & Associates/Lincoln, NE 466

Barneys New York Advertising/New York 357

Bartle Bogle Hegarty/London 190, 191, 260, 261

Bates/Hong Kong 7

Batey Ads/Singapore 90, 192, 262

Bayer Bess Vanderwarker/ Chicago 425, 497

BBDO/Los Angeles 193, 194, 195, 257, 398, 498

BBDO/New York 478, 479, 499, 500, 501

BBDO/Toronto 467

Berlin Cameron Doyle/ New York 20, 91, 128, 145, 146, 196, 197, 198, 199, 317

Berry Bush De Villiers Di Bella Bellamy/Cape Town 92

Big Ads/Portland 426, 433

Big Bear/New York 400

Birdsall-Voss & Kloppenburg/ Milwaukee 450

BMP DDB Needham/London 480

Borders Perrin & Norrander/ Portland 358, 373

Bozell Palmer Bonner/Toronto 442

Bozell Worldwide/ Minneapolis 401

Bozell Worldwide/Southfield, MI 502

Butler Shine & Stern/Sausalito 56, 59, 93, 129, 200, 318, 451

Campaign Palace, The/ Auckland 503

Campaign Palace, The/ Melbourne 481

Campaign Palace, The/ New South Wales, Australia 427

Campaign Palace, The/ Woolloomooloo, Australia 504, 561

Carmichael Lynch/ Minneapolis 176, 201, 202, 348

CF2GS/Seattle 23

Chiat/Day, New York 452, 468, 505, 506, 507, 545, 580

Chiat/Day, Venice 18, 65, 67, 70, 177, 203, 204, 205, 206, 207, 508

Chuck Ruhr Advertising/ Minneapolis 319

Clarity Coverdale Fury/ Minneapolis 46

Clarke Goward/Boston 94, 95

Clemenger Adelaide/ Eastwood, Australia 147, 178, 374

Cliff Freeman & Partners/ New York 63, 75, 453, 469, 509, 510, 511, 512

Cole & Weber/Portland 2, 10, 11, 12, 13, 96, 97, 98, 130, 148, 149, 150, 151, 152, 179, 208, 209, 320, 349, 546

Cole & Weber/Seattle 77, 402, 513

Cramer-Krasselt/Chicago 375

Cramer-Krasselt/Milwaukee 376

Crispin & Porter/Miami 210, 211

Dalbey & Denight Advertising/Portland 40, 99, 100, 131, 403, 404

DDB Needham Worldwide/ New York 24, 38, 514

DDB Needham Worldwide/ North Sydney 153

Delvico Bates/Barcelona 45, 584

Dentsu Young & Rubicam/ Singapore 101

DeVito/Verdi, New York 212, 213, 285, 288, 294

dGWB/Irvine 35

Dog Eat Dog/New York 515, 516

DRK/Boston 377, 378

Earle Palmer Brown/Bethesda 48

Earle Palmer Brown/ Philadelphia 379, 517, 576

Earle Palmer Brown/ Richmond 72, 76, 102, 359, 443, 518, 519

Elgin Syferd/DDB Needham, Seattle 9

Euro RSCG Ball Partnership/ Singapore 264

Fallon McElligott Berlin/ New York 61, 68, 71, 310, 520, 521, 547, 563, 571

Fallon McElligott/Minneapolis 8, 29, 32, 37, 44, 47, 103, 104, 105, 132, 133, 154, 155, 156, 157, 180, 181, 214, 215, 216, 217, 218, 219, 220, 221, 222, 223, 265, 266, 267, 268, 269, 286, 289, 295, 321, 322, 323, 324, 325, 326, 327, 328, 329, 330, 331, 332, 333, 344, 345, 360, 380, 381, 382, 383, 384, 405, 406, 431, 434, 435, 482

Faulds Advertising/Edinburgh 577

Foote Cone & Belding/ Chicago 440

Foote Cone & Belding/ San Francisco 548

Goldberg Moser O'Neill/ San Francisco 470

Goldsmith/Jeffrey, New York 28, 31, 57, 184, 270, 296, 341, 346, 347, 407, 454, 455, 456

Goodby Silverstein & Partners/San Francisco 14, 15, 16, 17, 19, 25, 62, 64, 134, 224, 225, 226, 227, 228, 271, 334, 355, 361, 457, 458, 459, 460, 522, 523, 524, 564, 572

Grace & Rothschild/New York 5, 159, 229

Griffith/Lovering, New York 160, 161, 182

Griswold-Eshleman/Cleveland 158

Ground Zero/Venice 43, 432, 578

GSD&M Advertising/Austin 385, 386, 387, 388

Hal Riney & Partners/Chicago 162

Hal Riney & Partners/ San Francisco 230, 483, 582

HKM Advertising/Wellington, New Zealand 525

Houston Effler Herstek Favat/ Boston 49, 50, 54, 231, 232, 444, 445

Howell Henry Chaldecott Lury & Partners/London 58, 471

Hughes Advertising/Atlanta 41, 408

Hunt Murray/Minneapolis 33, 106, 297, 306, 307, 311, 312, 335, 389, 409, 410, 526, 549, 583

Hush-a-linic Advertising/ Chicago 362

Ingalls Quinn & Johnson/ Boston 107

J. Walter Thompson/ Hong Kong 135, 390

J. Walter Thompson/London 233, 234

J. Walter Thompson/Sydney 484

Kan Tai-Keung Design/ Hong Kong 356

Ketchum Advertising/ Los Angeles 163, 411

Kirshenbaum & Bond/ New York 573

Kohnke Koeneke/Milwaukee 472

Kopald Group, The/ Los Angeles 581

Korey Kay & Partners/ New York 27, 55, 527

Kresser Stein Robaire/ Santa Monica 287, 336

Lambesis/San Diego 272

Last Call Advertising/ New York 164

Lawler Ballard Van Durand/ Birmingham 550

Leagas Delaney/London 108, 109, 110, 111, 112, 136, 235, 273, 298

Leap Partnership, The/ Chicago 313, 436, 485

Leo Burnett/Hong Kong 350

Leo Burnett/Oslo 69

Leo Burnett Company/ Chicago 274, 528

Leo Burnett Connaghan & May/North Sydney 363

Leonard/Monahan, Providence 36, 165, 183, 240, 337, 391, 412

Livingston & Company/ Los Angeles 437

Loeffler Ketchum Mountjoy/ Charlotte 21, 22, 236, 237, 238, 239, 275, 290

Lord Dentsu & Partners/New York 241, 276
Lowe & Partners/SMS, New York 529
MacLaren Lintas/Toronto 351
Mad Dogs & Englishmen/New York 185, 258, 299, 300, 392, 393
Marc Advertising/Pittsburgh 352
Martin Agency, The/Richmond 113, 114, 137, 138, 166, 167, 168, 169, 170, 171, 172, 173, 174, 242, 243, 244, 245, 246, 277, 314, 338, 428, 438, 446, 530, 565
Martin/Williams, Minneapolis 413, 414, 447
McCann-Erickson/London 247
McCann-Erickson/San Francisco 342
McCann-Erickson/Seattle 531, 532
McCann-Erickson/Singapore 1, 3, 6
McCann-Erickson/Toronto 139
McConnaughy Stein Schmidt Brown/Chicago 394, 566
McKinney & Silver/Raleigh 115
Meldrum & Fewsmith Advertising/Cleveland 364
Merkley Newman Harty/New York 339
Meyer & Wallis/Milwaukee 140
Mezzina/Brown, New York 416
MTV/New York 486, 551
MTV Off-Air Creative/New York 34
Mullen Advertising/Wenham, MA 116, 417
Nickelodeon/New York 487
Not a Division of Omnicom Advertising/Los Angeles 395
Odiorne Wilde Narraway Groome/San Francisco 418, 419, 420, 421
Ogilvy & Mather/Auckland 117
Ogilvy & Mather/New York 278, 488, 533, 552
Ogilvy & Mather/Singapore 118
Oscar & Cooper/Bethesda 279
Pagano Schenck & Kay/Boston 30, 365
Pedone & Partners/New York 461, 462, 473, 474
Pete Smith Advertising/Minneapolis 414
Raoust & Gearhart/Hampton, VA 439
Richards Group, The/Dallas 464, 489, 553, 567, 579
Roche Macaulay & Partners/Toronto 175, 301, 302
Saatchi & Saatchi/London 490, 491, 574
Saatchi & Saatchi/New York 448
Saatchi & Saatchi/Wellington, New Zealand 429
Sandstrom Design/Portland 353
Simons Palmer Denton Clemmow & Johnson/London 248, 249
Sonnenberg Murphy Leo Burnett/Johannesburg 441
SP Lintas/London 42
StreetSmart Advertising/New York 449
TBC Advertising/Baltimore 475
TBWA Advertising/New York 119, 250, 303, 422
TBWA Wolfe Freeman/St. Louis 343
Team One Advertising/El Segundo, CA 251, 252, 253, 254, 280, 354
Trauma Unit, The/Boston 366, 367, 372
Tucker Wayne/Luckie & Company, Atlanta 368
Underdog Advertising/Boston 141
Verge/New York 396
VitroRobertson/San Diego 120, 121, 142, 143, 255
Weiss Whitten Stagliano/New York 122, 369, 370
Wells Rich Greene BDDP/New York 52, 53
Wieden & Kennedy/Amsterdam 60, 534, 535
Wieden & Kennedy/Portland 66, 73, 74, 281, 282, 304, 308, 309, 340, 371, 492, 493, 494, 536, 537, 538, 539, 540, 541, 542, 543, 544, 554, 555, 556, 557, 558, 559, 568, 569, 570, 575
Wirz Werbeberatung AG/Zurich 144
WongDoody/Seattle 256, 283, 423, 465
Young & Rubicam/Buenos Aires 78

AGENCY PRODUCERS

Amato, Steve 514
Andresevic, Jill 554
Anthony, Chris 498
Baker, Jim 491
Bannon, Dennis 497
Baran, Morty 565
Bergman, Neal 52, 53
Berriman, Tim 490
Binder, Steffi 462, 474
Bisits, Bea 481
Boyle, Jerry 448
Brimblecombe, Jane 60, 534, 535
Brown, Keith 550
Burke, Michelle 65, 67, 70, 508
Burley, Noeleen 441
Campagnoli, Pam 530
Carsillo, Roberto 78
Chambers, Alison 561
Chinich, Andrew 505, 506, 507, 545, 580
Cline, Peter 505, 545, 580
Coats, Jessica 489, 553
Cohen, Peter 449
Cosentino, Fran 495
Crawford, Laura 466
Cummins, Adrienne 56, 59, 451
Davenport, Bill 492, 493, 538, 575
Davidson, Bruce 488, 533, 552
Diedrich, Mike 485
Duggan, MaryEllen 75, 63, 511, 512
Ebel, Regina 478, 479, 501
Eddon, David 574
Emerson, Bob 499, 500
Epps, Cindy 64, 522, 572
Faircloth, Lisa 525
Flynn, Betsy 458, 459
Frame, Jim 550
Frost, Anna 548
Gerrish, Allison 483
Grylewicz, Ben 73, 541, 559, 568
Hacohen, Nancy 72, 76, 518, 519
Harding, Beth 555
Hemmert, Rick 475
Holland, Taryn 457
Hotchkiss, Sally 52, 53
Hripko, Thomas 464
Hughes, Lindsay 476, 477
Jensen, Knut E. 69
Kahn, Sylvia 496
Karsch, Roxanne 452, 468
Kay, Jill 55
Keller, Rebecca 447
Kurtzman, Anne 75, 453, 509, 510, 512
Lawless, Diana 579
Lebovitz, Jacqueline 581
Leftwich, Carol 567
Lewis, Harvey 464
Linsey, Francine 51
Low, Jack 461
Maguire, Tim 577
Mahoney, James 440
Martinez, Greg 460
McCoy, Harry 49, 50, 54, 444, 445
McDonald, Wil 482
Meschino, Jill 560
Miller, Barney 487
Moore, David 528
Mosca, Joe 517, 576
Mueller, Gary 450
Noble, Kim 524
Novak, Rachel 529
O'Brien, Mary Ellen 469
O'Toole, Elizabeth 62, 523
Olken, Linda Tesa 527
Palfrey-Rogers, Emma 471
Palumbo, Chris 49, 50
Pedone, Matt 473
Plasencia, Claudia 578
Pollitt, Sarah 480
Pompeo, Luis 78
Portaro, Donna 66, 74, 494, 539, 540, 542, 557, 569, 570
Predovich-Eisner, Shelly 563
Raab, Renee 543, 558
Rainey, Kathleen 58
Robertson, Marie 467
Robinson, Ivan 504
Schmidtbauer, Joyce 465
Segarra, Toni 584
Selis, Jeff 538, 544, 575
Shreve, Randy 446
Sitea, Olivia 546

Smieja, Jennifer 536, 537, 556
Soukup, Frank 443
Steinwede, Brad 484
Stimac, Darlene 472
Storm, Ann J. 483
Sullivan, Deborah 61, 68, 71, 520, 521, 547, 563, 571
Taub, Jay 449
Telfer, Audrey 442
Terkuhle, Abby 486, 551
Tripp, Mark 564
Van Osdol, John 502
Veal, Branson 532
Waldock, Victoria 582
Walsh, Sam 77, 513
Weiss, Lee 488, 533, 552
Weitz, Carter 466
Wellington, Bruce 573
Wickham, Maresa 469
Wiedensmith, Peter 544
Woodruff, Michelle 531
Wyville, Jon 566
Young, George 470

ART DIRECTORS

Anderson, Keith 355
Andrew, Philip 525
Angelo, David 251, 253, 280, 514
Angotti, Tony 293, 305, 560
Appleby, Bobby 587
Arghyrou, Andy 84, 123
Arnold, Rosie 190, 191
Aron, Abi 213, 288
Ayriss, David 13, 148, 151, 152, 179
Azula, Andy 236, 237, 238, 239, 275, 290
Baker, Stuart 4, 124
Baldwin, Jim 489, 553
Barrie, Bob 32, 44, 156, 157, 181, 217, 218, 267, 268, 332
Barry, Ian 39, 496
Bell, Greg 63, 75, 510, 512
Bell, Mark 418, 419
Bennett, Chuck 287
Bentley, Roger 40, 99, 100, 131, 403, 404, 426, 433
Beverley, Dave 109, 136
Blair, Stephen 139
Bleackley, Chris 429
Block, Stan 212

Bogusky, Alex 211
Boiler, John 538, 544, 575
Bokor, Greg 337
Bousman, Bruce 488, 533, 552
Bowdish, Larry 231
Boychuk, Tracy 34
Braun, Dan 303
Brazier, Paul 51
Bremner, Scott 354
Briginshaw, Paul 26
Brihn, Bob 326
Brown, Ron 83, 123
Brown, Warren 561
Burke, Brian 343
Burlison, Bryan 177
Burton, Allison 80
Butler, John 93, 129
Caballero, David 45, 584
Caldwell, Leslie 548
Calienes, Mike 586
Campbell, Walter 477
Carducci, Rob 213, 288
Carlos 490
Carrelli, Scott 497
Chasnow, Adam 38
Cheeseman, Len 429
Choo, Maggie 194, 257
Christou, Andrew 66, 74, 366, 367, 372, 539, 540, 542, 557, 569, 570
Chu, Polly 135
Clarke, Andrew 264
Cohen, Dan 291, 495
Cohen, Mark 336
Cohen, Michael 79
Cohen, Peter 449
Cole, Christopher 319
Cooke, Ronnie 357
Correa, Lucho 45
Crandall, Denise 43, 432, 498
Credeur, Darrell 315
Cronin, Markham 211
Curtin, Paul 355
Dalthorp, James 582
Davidson, Bruce 488, 533, 552
Davis, Steve 115
DeBellis, Izzy 61, 68, 71, 520, 521, 547, 571
Dektor, Leslie 488, 533, 552
Delaney, Timothy 162
DeMelio, Carol 52, 53
DeSimone, Rich 590
DeVito, Sal 212
DeVries, Audrey 288, 294

Dickey, Dave 401
DiFiore, Jeff 164
Doyle, John 20, 91, 128, 145, 146, 196, 197, 198, 199, 317
Drummond, Stacy 34
Duerr, Penny 176
Dye, Dave 136, 235, 273, 298
Eakins, Warren 60, 535
Eastwood, Matt 153
Ehringer, Sean 25, 64, 572
Engelman, Judy 591
Epstein, Pat 515, 516
Evans, Jane 484
Evans, Steve 147, 178
Fallon, Victoria 480
Farmer, Chad 272
Felton, David 34
Ferris, Ken 514
Fetrow, Mike 106, 297, 307, 389, 409
Finkle, Chuck 341, 347
Finley, Terry 230
Flagg, Danielle 370
Flora, Heidi 77, 402, 513
Fortunato, Gina 299, 300, 393
French, Neil 118
Frey, Larry 340, 554, 555
Fuller, John 436
Fuller, Mark 137
Fullwood, Chris 585
Furlong, Michael 278
Gallentine, Todd 122
Gallucci, Marc 94, 95
Galton, Martin 112, 136
Gardiner, Dave 54, 444, 445
Gausis, Peter 82
Gellos, John 397
Genell, Jim 589
Gentile, Jerry 65, 67, 70, 508
Gibson, Shane 153
Gilmore, Lara 24
Goldberg, Barney 170
Golden, Leeanna 252, 254
Goldsmith, Gary 270
Gorenstein, Rachel 334
Grace, Roy 229
Grant, Todd 361
Griak, Susan 310
Griffith, Jeff 160, 161, 182
Guan, Tan Shen 135, 390
Guidotti, Ted 595
Gulbranson, Johan 69
Guzzone, Frank 187, 188, 189, 284

Halverson, Stephanie 483
Hamilton, Bill 488, 533, 552
Hamilton, Robert 30, 365
Hanrahan, Tim 73, 536, 537, 556, 568
Hanson, Dean 105, 133, 154, 219, 220, 221, 222, 223, 269, 295, 333, 482
Harms, Sharon 210
Harper, Ty 443
Harris, Mike 123
Harrison, Chris 175
Helm, Jelly 282, 492, 493
Hemp, Joe 411
Henderson, Carol 37, 286, 289
Henderson, Jim 447
Hernandez, Dave 313, 436
Hindman, Shari 169, 171, 172
Hirsch, Andy 529
Hirsch, Paul 2, 10, 11, 12, 13, 61, 68, 71, 96, 130, 149, 150, 179, 520, 521, 547, 571
Hoffmann, Susan 534
Holden, Paul 350
Hong, Freeman Lau Siu 356
Hong, Lye Kok 192, 262
Horton, John 186, 476
Hudson, Steve 480
Huff, Greg 140
Hughes, Randy 46
Hung, Kelvin 390
Hurwit, Bruce 511
Ibarrondo, Marta 416
Jahn, Jeff 414
Jay, John C. 304, 308, 309, 543, 558, 559
Jenson, Kris 376
Jerome, Max 292, 305
Johnson, Kent 567
Johnson, Margaret 8
Johnson, Mark 329
Joiner, Erich 228, 271
Jouhar, Ashley 247
Jue, Heward 369
Kacker, Anjana 129
Kadin, Michael 395
Kalam, Ahmer 590
Karow, Bill 97, 98, 320, 546
Katalinic, Anthony 362
Keane, Jim 201, 202
Ketel, Jerry 426, 433
Keyton, Jeffrey 34
Kim, Tom 394

Kimura, Steve 195, 398
King, Eric C. 66, 74, 366, 367, 372, 539, 540, 542, 557, 569, 570
Klein, Marc 400
Kling, Jeff 399
Klonk, Debbie 158
Kong, Eddy Yu Chi 356
Koniakowsky, Wade 35
Kostyk-Petro, Maria 119, 250, 422
Ladd, Brent 385, 386, 387, 388
Lanz, Danielle 144
Leu, John 63, 75
Lichtenheld, Tom 321, 322, 323, 324, 325, 344, 431, 434, 435
Liegey, J. 214, 265, 266, 382, 383, 384
Lienke, Henriette 28, 31, 184, 296, 346, 407
Lipkin, Lisa 250, 422
Lombardi, Dante 27, 527
Low, Patrick 101
Luker, Steve 14, 15, 17, 62, 134, 227, 523
Mackechney, Tom 497
Mackler, Jonathan 166, 167
Mahoney, Jamie 244
Mapp, Steve 210
Markle, Julie 351
Marshall, Gary 108, 110, 111
Martin, Greg 125, 424, 430
Martin, Jeff 550
Matassa, Vinny 348
Matchett, Bruce 117
Mather, Ron 504
Mayeur, Gabrielle 354
Mazza, Michael 16, 19, 224, 225
McConnaughy, Tom 566
McDonald, Darryl 281, 541
McGeorge, Carolyn 242, 243, 245, 277
McKendry, Gary 278
McQuiston, Rick 494
McQuoid, Simon 374
Meagher, Bob 114, 314 338, 530
Meier, Carie 200, 318
Meng, Tham Khai 90
Midler, Rick 499
Miller, Steve 24
Milner, Duncan 505, 506, 545, 580

Mitchell, Steve 33, 306, 311, 312, 335, 410, 526, 549, 583
Moehlenkamp, Kevin 500
Mongkolkasetarin, Sakol 35
Moore, Charlotte 353, 371
Moore, Tom 278
Morrow, Sally 349
Morton, Ian 427
Mountjoy, Jim 21, 22, 236
Murray, Mike 409, 526, 549
Nardi, Mark 232
Nicholson, Amy 573
Nixon, Jeff 375
Oliver, Cathy 137
Oliver, Rob 259
Olsen, Jarl 562
Oosthuizen, Mark 528
Ozark, Andy 502
Pao, Imin 304, 308, 309
Paprocki, Joe 29, 104, 132, 215, 216, 327, 328, 360, 381
Parks, Chris 592
Parks, Ed 107
Pepper, J. Kent 377, 378
Peterson, Jason 61, 68, 71, 520, 521, 547, 571
Petillo, Katherine 550
Pirdavari, Houman 563
Poynton, Malcolm 481
Prins, Robert 163
Rabe, Rick 339
Rae, Peter 350
Ramsey, Brad 368
Rao, Rohitash 72, 76, 102, 518, 519
Redding, Lindsey 577
Reed, Dee 588
Regan, Paul 390
Reifschneider, Kurt 23
Reynolds, Terence 579
Ribble, Glenn 551
Rich, Rob 36, 165, 183, 240, 391, 412
Richards, Grant 134
Richardson, Allen 5
Richter, Robert 425
Riddle, Todd 232
Riley, Sean 137, 446
Ritter, Noel 173, 174
Robinson, Doug 85, 86, 87, 88, 126, 127
Robinson, Stuart 503
Rosen, Mike 505, 506, 545, 580

Rossouw, Sybi 92
Routson, Tom 226, 524, 564
Russell, Jay 81
Sanchez, Elvio 78
Sandstrom, Steve 353
Savage, Tiger 248, 249
Scavnicky, John 364
Schattner, Marc 1, 3, 6
Schneider, Don 478, 479, 501
Schneider, Terry 358
Schoenhoff, Gerald 301, 302
Schruntek, Mark 285, 288
Schutte, Alan 439
Schwab, Bill 316
Schwartz, Matthew 448
Sciarrotta, Joe 313, 485
Shands, Joe 208, 522, 572
Sheen, Mike 208, 209
Slomkowski, Bart 303
Smith, Colleen 81
Smith, Jud 202
Smith, Lyn 581
Sorah, Cliff 113, 138, 246, 428, 438
Soto, Jon 185, 258, 392
Souder, Kirk 578
Squier, Phillip 9
St. Clair, Steve 241, 276
Stein, Lloyd 486
Steinberg, Ellen 47, 103, 155, 180, 330, 331, 345
Stone, Steve 265
Studzinski, Nik 491
Sullivan, Tom 396
Suter, Kent 373
Sutherland, Patrick 285, 288
Sweitzer, Steve 507
Swisher, John 352
Tam, Andy 7
Tanimoto, Craig 18, 203, 204, 205, 206, 207
Taylor, Alexandra 491, 574
Tench, Hal 565
Tham, Grover 90, 264
Thomas, Steve 487
Thompson, Sean 42
Thompson, Wayne 413
Tom, Pat 437
Turner, Christopher 594
Vaglio, Gerard 159
Van Blarcom, Jennifer 593
Vendramin, Benjamin 442
Vescovo, Matt 512
Vipper, Johan 34
Vitro, John 120, 121, 142, 143, 255

Walker, Jim 532
Watson, Graham 261
Wayner, Taras 48, 279
Webb, Brad 420, 421
Weinheim, Donna 75, 509
Weinman, Keith 116, 417
Wells, Mike 260
Welsh, Megan 287
Wenneker, Mark 342
West, Robert Shaw 379, 517, 576
Westre, Susan 193, 194, 257
White, Paul 233, 234
Wilcox, Ron 141
Wilde, Michael 420, 421
Williams, Damon 41, 408
Willson, Kristy 531
Windley, Kathryn 89
Wisheart, Megan 363
Wittich, Pat 168
Wong, Tracy 256, 283, 423
Wyatt, Bob 274
York, Nic 380, 405, 406

CLIENTS

Abigail Adams Historical Society 94
Adidas 235, 273
Advanced Aerobatic Flight Training 409
Advertising Council, The/ Department of Transportation 52, 53
Akva Spring Water 20, 145, 146, 196, 197, 198, 199
All That Glitters 373
Altschiller & Company 397
American Express 278
American Hard Cider Company 95
American Isuzu Motors 16, 19, 224, 225, 226
American Lung Association of Maryland 48
American Red Cross 428, 438
American Spirit 553
Ameritech Corporate 154, 295
Ameritech Enhanced Business Services 321, 322, 323, 324, 325, 344
Amnesty International 45
Andromeda Body Piercing 396

Apple Computer 193, 194, 257, 498
Atlanta Print Production Association 368
Attila Photography School 395
Audi 115
AudioMaster 326
Austin Nichols & Company/ Wild Turkey 187, 188, 284
Australian Meat & Live-Stock Corporation 561
Back Hoe Bob 472
Barneys New York 357
Barron's 291
BBC Radio Scotland 577
BBDO 398
Beads and Rocks 166, 167
Big House, The 40, 99, 100, 131, 403, 404
Bill Hallman Shoes 141
Billy's Topless 400
BMW of North America 116, 417
Body Alarm 8
Borneo Motors/Lexus Division 101
Bornstein Memory School 163
Boston Globe, The 107
Bozell Worldwide/ Minneapolis 401
Brit's Pub 286, 289
Britches 212
British Airways 490
Britvic 58
Buena Vista Home Video 582
Bum Steer Steakhouse 466
By Invitation Only 108
California Department of Health Services 437
California Fluid Milk Processor Advisory Board 25, 64, 457, 522, 572
California Sunkist Pistachios 65, 67, 70, 508
Cartoon Network, The 318
Charles David Footwear 272
Chasnow, Adam 38
Chevys Mexican Restaurants 458, 459
Children's Cancer Research Fund 47
Children's Defense Fund 431, 434, 435
Chrysler Corporation 502
City of Hampton/Pentran 439

Clark Candy Company 342
Clemenger Adelaide 147, 178
Coalition for the Homeless 449
Coca-Cola Company, The 353, 371, 482
Coca-Cola Foods Canada 139
COI/Army 574
Columbia Sportswear 358
Combined Motor Holdings 92
Comedy Central 27, 55, 527
Converse 231
Cow & Gate 259
Crain's New York Business 28, 31, 57, 296, 346, 407, 454, 455
Crisis 42
Crystal Geyser Water Company 230
Cycle Oregon 2, 96, 130
Daffy's 285, 288, 294
Daily Grill, The 578
Daisy 375
Dennis Laminating 366, 367, 372
Diet Coke/Coca-Cola Company, The 529
Dr. Martens 10, 11, 12, 13, 148, 149, 150, 151, 152, 179, 208, 209, 320, 349
Drakes Bakeries 473
Dublin Productions 33, 311, 312, 583
Earth Communications Office 581
Earth Share 440
Eastern Veterinary Blood Bank 443
Economist, The 26, 82, 83, 84, 123, 476
Edison's Birthplace Museum 158
ESPN 73, 340, 536, 537, 554, 555, 556, 568
EyeMasters 567
Family Health Council 352
Family Life 29, 327, 328
Federal Express 499, 500
Fightertown 177
Fine Jewelers Guild 184
First Commerce Corporation 550
Frankie Ey 178
Fred Arbogast 343
Freedom Foods/RSPCA 4, 124
Frito Lay 501

Fruitopia 505, 506, 545, 580
G. Heileman Brewing Company/Henry Weinhard's Beer 489
Gametek 210, 211
General Motors of Canada/ Oldsmobile Aurora 351
Genesee Brewing Company 461, 462, 474
Golden Gate Rugby Club 418, 419
Good Guys Auto 72, 76, 518, 519
GQ 298
Grand Groomers 413
Graphic Technologies 414
Gray Cary Ware & Freidenrich 143
Great Faces 319
Guardian, The 109
Guitar Works 162
Haggar Apparel Company 355
Hanford Health Information Network 426, 433
Hanimex 504
Hannah Dee 362
Harley-Davidson 201, 348
Healthtex 242, 243, 244, 245, 277
Holeproof 481
IBM 488, 533, 552
IKEA 125
Illinois Lottery 497
India House 102
Interactive Media Corporation/Telepersonals 463
Invisible Fencing Company 39
Jim Beam Brands 155, 180
JP Morgan 270
K. James Kim, M.D. 394
KCBS Television 306
KCET 287
Keds 240
Kia Motors America 470
Kling, Jeff 399
Kraft General Foods 390
K2 Skis 256, 283, 423
Labatt Breweries of Canada 85, 86, 87, 88, 126, 127
Land Rover North America 5, 159, 229
Lane Walker Rudkin 117
Lanzera 37
Leap Partnership, The 313

Leapin' Lizards 380, 405
Lee Company, The 360, 381
Lee Printwear 329
Lever Rexona 484
Levi Strauss & Company 548
Levi Strauss & Company/ Europe SA 190, 191
Lexus 251, 252, 253, 280, 354
Liaison Condoms 153
Little Caesars 63, 75, 469, 509, 510, 511
Los Angeles County Coroner's Office Gift Shop 496
Los Angeles Times 120, 121, 142
Lotteries Commission of South Australia 374
MacTemps 317
Magnavox 265
Mamma Ilardo's 475
Martin Agency, The 314
Massachusetts Department of Public Health 49, 50, 54, 444, 445
Medicine Bow Guest Ranch 420, 421
Meijer 140
Membership Etc. 356
Mercedes-Benz Asia 192, 262
Mercedes-Benz of North America 137
Merck Sharp & Dohme 503
Mercury Communications 471
Miller Brewing Company 528
Miller Lite 485
Millers Outpost 56, 59, 451
Minnesota Brewing 307, 389, 410, 526, 549
Minnesota Department of Natural Resources 447
Miss Vera's Finishing School 160, 161, 182
Molson Breweries 467
Molson Breweries USA/ Foster's 292, 293, 305, 560
Moose Hockey 106
Motel 6 464
Mothers Against Drunk Driving 46
MTV 34, 486, 551, 562
Museum of Questionable Medical Devices 376
Mystic Lake Casino 297
Nation, The 369
National Head Injury Foundation 436

National Railway Historical Society 168
Natural History Museum, The 110, 111
NBA 61, 68, 71, 520, 521, 547, 571
NEC Computers 232
New York State Lottery 24
New Zealand AIDS Foundation 429
Nick at Nite 468
Nickelodeon 487
Nike 66, 74, 281, 282, 304, 308, 309, 492, 493, 494, 538, 539, 540, 541, 542, 543, 557, 558, 559, 569, 570, 575
Nike International 60, 534, 535
Nike Sportswear 248, 249
Nikon 103, 156, 157, 181, 214, 266, 330, 331, 345
94.5 FM/The Edge 579
91.5 KUSC Radio 411
Nissan Motor Corporation 18, 203, 204, 205, 206, 207
Normark 176
North Carolina Travel & Tourism 21, 22, 236, 237, 238, 275, 290
Northgate Mall, The 129
Norwegian Cruise Line 14, 15, 17, 62, 227, 334, 523
NSW Police Service 427
NYNEX Business to Business Directory 341, 347, 456
NYNEX Yellow Pages 452, 507
Odyssey Golf 255
Off The Street Club 425
Orange County Ad Club 35
Oregon Tourism 544
Oregonian, The 97, 98, 546
Pacific Bell 134
Pacific Science Center 23
Pagano Schenck & Kay 30
Parallel Productions 335
Parker Pen Singapore 264
Partnership for a Drug-Free America 448
People for the Ethical Treatment of Animals 44
Pepsi Cola 479
Pepsi Cola International 478
Pereaux 241, 276
Pet Shed, The 164
Pioneer Electronics USA 195

PMS Clinic 406
Poe Museum, The 113, 138
Polaroid 337
Polygram Video 279
Porsche 112, 136, 361
Porsche Cars North America 228, 271
Powerbreaker 480
Prego 460
Printbox 416
Queen Elizabeth's Foundation for Disabled People 51
Raffles Hotel, Singapore 90
Ralston Purina Company 215, 216
Reckitt & Colman 78
Reebok International 350
Residence Inn 114, 530
Richmond Ad Club 359
Richmond Symphony, The 169, 170, 171, 172
Riverside Tennis Clinic 173, 174
Roederer 254
Rootin' Ridge 385, 386, 387, 388
Royal Air Force 233, 234
RSPCA 424, 430
Saab Cars USA 89, 189, 495
Sainsbury's 186
Salvation Army, The 441
Sara Lee Foundations 250, 422
Saturn Corporation 483
Scandinavian Vehicle Distributors 525
Schaeffer's Foods 450
Schieffelin & Somerset 274
Schweppes GB 491
Schwinn 202
Seagram/Martell 118
Seattle International Film Festival 77, 513
Seattle Mariners Baseball Club 531
Seattle Post-Intelligencer 9
Seattle SuperSonics 465
Sega of America 524, 564
Seiko 514
Shakespeare 239
Shelcore 213
Shelter 185, 258, 392
Shin's Restaurant 122
Shreve Crump & Low 91, 128
Simmons 1, 3, 6

Sir Freddies's Pale Ale 382, 383, 384
Skydiving Center, The 41, 408
Snapple Beverage Corporation 573
South China Morning Post 135
Spanish Cancer Association 584
St. Joseph's 43, 432
Staples 453, 512
Star Tribune 104, 132
Stay In School 446
Stork's Landing 36, 165, 183, 391, 412
Style of Man 379
Sunset Marquis Hotel & Villas 217, 267
Technics 247
Thom McAn 299, 300, 393
Thomson Consumer Electronics/RCA 315, 316
3DO Company, The 200
Time Foto 69
Time Magazine 32, 218, 268, 332
Timex Corporation 105, 133, 219, 220, 221, 222, 223, 269
Toronto Star 175
Triumph International 144
United Distillers Australia 363
Urban Alliance on Race Relations 442
Urban Trans Ad 301, 302
V&S Vin & Sprit AB 119, 303
VH-1 310
Virtual World 93
Volkswagen 563
Volvo Cars UK 477
Walgreen Company 566
Warner Bros. Records 336
Washington State Lottery 532
Weiss Whitten Stagliano 370
Weyerhaeuser Paper Company 333
Whitbread Beer Company, The 260, 261
Whitehall International 7
Willen Dental Associates 364
Winterbrook/Africola 402
WMMR 93.9 FM 517, 576
Wool Bureau, The 339
WQHS 515, 516
Wrangler Company 246, 338, 565

Zarod Paving 365
Zoo Doo Compost Company, The 377, 378

COLLEGES

East Texas State University/Commerce, TX 80, 585
Miami Ad School/Miami 586, 587, 588
Portfolio Center/Atlanta 79, 589, 590, 591, 592
School of Visual Arts/New York 593, 594
Southern Methodist University/Dallas 81
Syracuse University/Syracuse 595

DESIGNERS

Hong, Freeman Lau Siu 356
King, Troy 41, 408
Kong, Eddy Yu Chi 356
Wa, Janny Lee Yin 356

DIRECTORS

Abramson, Neil 54, 444, 445
Avis, Meiert 578
Baldwin, Jim 553
Barnbrook, Jonathan 577
Bay, Michael 522, 572
Belefant, Brian 515, 516
Buckley, Bryan 73, 555, 568
Budgen, Frank 480
Chase, Carlton 62, 523
Chiat, Marc 524
Cone, Buddy 563
Cooke, Mary 504
Debenport, Robb 579
DeCerchio, Tom 485
Dektor, Leslie 488, 533, 552, 582
DeSalvo, Joe 559
Dublin, Rick 583
Dylan, Jesse 72, 76, 518, 519
Fairchild, Tenney 527
Fernandez, Robert 558
Fincher, David 534
Fisher, Daniel 449
Frey, Larry 554
Garfath, David 51

Gartner, James 499, 500
Godley, Kevin 507
Goodby, Jeffrey 64, 572
Gorman, Jeff 65, 67, 70, 496, 508
Gross, Ron 531, 532
Gulbranson, Johan 69
Hannant, Robert 567
Henman, Graham 528
Higgins, Thom 565
Hitchcock, Dennis 525
Holtzman, Henry 512
Hurwit, Bruce 63, 75, 511
Jarvis, Drew 442
Johns, Gary 443
Kaye, Tony 477, 554
Kellogg, David 564
Kessler, Stephen 573
Krygier, Thomas 574
Larson, Tom 526, 549
Leacock, Robert 543, 559
Marles, John 560
Matre, Tom 447
McClellan, Eric 550
McDaniel, Melodie 494, 541
McIntosh, Peter 561
Meijer, Paul 490
Miller, Barney 487
Olsen, Jarl 562
Priess, Jeff 61, 68, 71, 520, 521, 547, 571
Pritts, Rob 497, 537
Pytka, Joe 60, 66, 74, 478, 479, 492, 493, 498, 501, 535, 538, 539, 540, 542, 548, 557, 569, 570, 575
Ramsey, Greg 505, 506, 545, 580
Ribble, Glenn 551
Saarinen, Eric 502
Savidan, Murray 503
Sena, Dominic 483
Sherwood, Tony 481
Smith, David 476
Sorin, Carlos 78
Stein, Lloyd 486
Stephenson, Mike 491
Story, Mark 75, 510, 530
Tarsem 482
Tikhomiroff, Joao 584
Todaro, Frank 73, 555, 568
Tompkins, Roger 484
Weiland, Paul 514
Willis, Robin 536, 556
Wittenmaier, Charles 75, 509, 529

ILLUSTRATORS

Anderson, Ken 403
Barton, Kent 94
Bernard, Galen 231
Bileski, John 426, 433
Bottonus, Bradford 23
Bull, Michael 230
Burns, Charles 353
Cairns, Brian 143
Chan, Mike 350
Charles Anderson Design 18, 203, 204, 205, 206, 207
Clowes, Daniel 353
Cox, Paul 351
Craig, John 255
Daniels, Alan 16, 19, 224, 225
Davidson & Company 39
Dayal, Antar 140, 252
Delhomme, Jean-Philippe 357
Dominic, Joe 354
Dye, Dave 298
Ey, Frankie 147, 178
Flora, Heidi 402
Gall, Chris 95
Gudynas, Bernard 247
Hall, Peter 19, 196, 197, 198, 199
Hally, Greg 143
Hanna-Barbara Studios 318
Havlicek, Karel 140
Huerta, Gerard 316
Javier Romero Design Group 278
Kling, Jeff 399
Kolacz, Jerzy 351
Larson, Tom 410
Lee, Tom 7
Lichtenheld, Tom 322
Madill, Warren 118
Mapp, Steve 210, 211
Marsh, James 351
McCulley, Scott 414
Meagher, Bob 114
Moore, Chris 316
Ou, Dennis 350
Palm, Brad 413
Rurka, Mark 134
Sharpshooter Studios 139
Square One Studio 379
Thomssen, Kate 106
Viva, Frank 143
Wong, Shui 134
Wormell, Christopher 270
Ziering, Bob 278

PHOTOGRAPHERS

Adler, Martin 428, 438
Anderson, Ken 40, 99, 100, 131, 404
Arndt, Jim 37, 202, 246
Banfield, Liz 405
Bankhead, Jack 124
Barbour, Steve 166, 167
Bee, Alex 115
Belkowitz, Steve 379
Berman, Howard 24
Bicknell, Steve 264
Biondo, Jamie 342
Blachut, Dennis 316
Bohanon, Brian 268
Brewer, Craig 439
Bronstein, Steve 119, 303
Burnett, David 32, 332
Butler, Nathanial 107
Cailor, Jerry 292, 293, 305
Cailor/Resnick 212, 213, 229
Canzano, Beth 375
Casalini, Tom 140
Clancy, Paul 317
Clemens, Clint 228, 271, 348, 361
Crum, Lee 240
Cushner, Susie 240
Cutler, Craig 315, 354
Cwenar, Tom 352
D'Orio, Tony 274
Dailey, Richard 336
Davine, Jeff 305
Davis, Chris 41, 408
Deboar, Bruce 355
Denson, Walt 230
DeZitter, Harry 226, 237, 238, 275, 290
Douglas Brothers, The 235, 273
Dublin Productions 242, 243, 244, 245, 277
Dublin, Rick 311
Eastwood, Ryan 595
Emmite, David 589
Erickson, Jim 17, 227, 355
Escobar, Dan 25
Fagan, Dennis 385, 386, 387, 388
Family Archives 426, 433
Fehling, Ron 85, 127
Feinstein, Chris 436
Fisher, Orville 126
Ford, Graham 4, 124, 186
Fritschi, Adrian 144

Furman, Michael 116, 417
Furuta, Carl 5, 159, 215, 216
Gibson, Bernie 153
Gill, David 234
Gillette, Richard 254
Gordaneer, Chris 126
Griffiths, Ken 124
Hall, Jim 189
Hamilton, Bruce 117
Harrington, Marshall 255
Harsent, Simon 427
Hashi 20, 145, 146, 196, 197, 198, 199
Haskell, Laurie 136
Hawthorne, Dean 338
Haynes, Nigel 123
Hellerstein, Steve 28, 31
Henderson/Cartledge 377, 378
Henry, Morgan 97, 98
Holzemer, Buck 214, 266, 323, 324, 333, 344, 431, 434, 435
Huber, Vic 252, 354
Huet, John 304, 308, 309
Hunter, Tiff 260
Husebye, Terry 420, 421
Hush, Gary 10, 12, 13, 148, 149, 150, 151, 152, 179, 208, 209, 320, 349
Idea Vision 356
Imagen Retouching 177
Jackson, Nancy 86, 127
Johnson, Curtis 239
Jones, Michael 282
Kahley, Chris 241, 276
Kaikeong, Alex 118, 192, 262
Kander, Nadav 248, 249, 259
Katz, John 8
Kirkley, Kent 184
Kolhoff, Fred 187, 188, 284
Konkal, John 137
LaFavor, Mark 321, 335, 344
Lamb & Hall 89
Lampi, Joe 104, 132, 311, 319, 326, 327, 413
Lancombe, Brigette 339
Lanza, Scott 376
Lavrisha, Marko 200
Logan, Kevin 291
Lopez, Bret 354
Maisel, Jay 232
Manso, Fernando 45
Marco, Phil 139
Mark, Mary Ellen 190, 191
Max-Plank Institute for Astronomy 268

McCoy, Wade 283
McCulley, Scott 414
McGuire, Gary 398
McKechnie, Rich 86, 87, 88, 126, 127
Metcalf, Michael 218, 268
Michienzi, Shawn 18, 155, 176, 180, 203, 204, 205, 206, 207, 251, 253, 265, 280, 307, 329, 389
Miller, Brad 137
Miller, Matt 210, 211
Mohler, Chaco 283
Moran, Nancy 278
Morehead, Bryan 39
Mun's Studio 101
Muna, RJ 334, 354
Murray, Steve 236, 275, 290
Ng, Raymond 390
O'Brien, Michael 193, 194, 257
O'Neill, Terry 42
Opton, Suzanne 9
Paczkowski, Joe 105, 133, 219, 220, 221, 222, 223, 269
Pederson, Rocki 195
Perman, Craig 325, 328
Perrine, Doug 15, 17
Peterson, Kerry 103, 155, 156, 157, 180, 181
Petty, Doug 353, 373
Prosor, Larry 256, 283, 423
Quackenbush, Russ 141
Rausch, Michael 251, 252, 253, 280
Reininger, Alon 32
Reitzfeld, Peter 397
Richards, Eugene 281
Richmond, Tom 486
Ritts, Herb 14, 15, 17, 227
Rolston, Matthew 272
Ruas, Alexander 185, 258, 392
Rubin, Ilan 279, 341, 347
Ruppert, Michael 252, 354
Rusing, Rick 351, 354
Russell, Mike 125
Salzano, Jim 160, 161, 182
Saruwatari, Craig 395
Scarlett, Nora 337
Schattner, Marc 1, 3, 6
Schulten, Arthur 350
Scott, Mark 338
Seaward, Pete 14, 15, 17
Seawell, Tom 418, 419

Shaw, Mark 32
Sheehan, Chris 406
Sigurjonsson, Sigurgeir 20, 196, 197, 198
Sirota, Peggy 340
Smith, Earl 136
Smith, Richard Hamilton 409
Sports Illustrated Picture Sales 231
Stammers, Sinclair 247
Stefansson, Pall 20, 197, 198
Stein, Geoffrey 20, 91, 128, 196, 197, 198, 199
Steinbrenner, Karl 102
Stevens, Robert 115
Stewart, Holly 254, 354
Stillings, Jamey 20, 199
Stone, Pete 358
Studio 9D 374
Thijsse, Leen 199
Topelmann, Lars 2, 11, 12, 96, 130, 349, 396
Tracy, Tom 334
Tucker, Bill 425
Umland, Steve 343, 401
Vandershuit, Carl 120, 121, 142
Verdoukal, Nittin 233
Von Unwerth, Ellen 250
Weiss, Mark 400
Westmoreland, Graham 16, 19, 224, 225
White, Gary 175
White, Paul 233
White, Timothy 217, 267
Whitman, Robert 274
Wojack, James 355
Wolf, Bruce 201
Wong, CK 356
Wong, Ricky 7
Wooley, Janet 261

PRODUCTION COMPANIES

Arden Sutherland-Dodd 574
Are These My Shoes? Productions 452, 456, 468
Backyard Productions 497, 537
Barking Weasel 527
Bednarz Films 579
Blue Goose 531, 532
Bunton Films 481
Chelsea Pictures 507
Chicago Recording Company 440

Clack Sound Studio 453, 469
Clatter & Din 465
Clear Shot 464
Click 3X 505, 506, 545, 580
Coppos Films 563
Cranbrook Films 484
Crossroads Films 63, 75, 510, 511, 530, 567
Dektor Higgins & Associates 488, 533, 552, 565, 582
Dublin Productions 562, 583
Epoch Films 61, 68, 71, 520, 521, 547, 571
Farenheit Films 505, 506, 545, 580
Flite Three Recordings 475
Gartner-Grasso 499, 500
Harmony Pictures 75, 509, 529
Harris Cole Wilde 467
HKM Productions 72, 76, 518, 519, 528
HSI Productions 485, 573
Ibbetson Cherry & Dean 561
Independent Films 560
Independent Sound 450
Industrial Artists 512
Jay West Productions 473
Jodaf and Joao Daniel Films 584
Johns + Gorman Films 65, 67, 70, 443, 496, 508
Kamen Audio 469
Leo Film 69
Matre Rajtar 447
Media Lab 507
Mixed Nuts 474
Motion Pictures Auckland 525
NYU Films 449
Palomar 54, 444, 445, 494, 541
Paul Weiland Film Company 51, 480, 491, 514
Picture Park 54, 444, 445
Pirate Radio 463
Pittman Hensley 449
Plum Productions 502
Pomann Music 462, 474, 495
Propaganda Films 64, 483, 522, 534, 564, 572
Pytka 60, 66, 74, 478, 479, 492, 493, 498, 501, 535, 538, 539, 540, 542, 548, 557, 569, 570, 575
Radical Media 73, 543, 558, 559, 568

Radio Ranch 453
Real to Reel 464
Red Car 52, 53
Red Dog Films 524
Reelworks 526, 549
Ritts/Hayden 62, 523
Rolling Films 503
Sandbank Kamen & Partners 555
Smilie Films 489
Smith Hadfield 476
Sonovision 441
Sorin 78
Soundscapes 466
Soundtrack Studios 57, 454, 455
Spots Films 482, 490
Straight Cut 77, 513
Stripes 442
Thirty-Second Street 504
Tiny Films 536, 556
Tony Kaye Films 477, 554, 577
Truth 550
Wiedensmith Productions 544
Windmill Lane 578

TYPOGRAPHERS

Bistrowitz, Leslie 94
Hoza, Joe 26, 82, 83, 84, 123
Kim, Tom 394
Molloy, Kristian 427
Pavia, Joseph 241, 276

WRITERS

Aal, Scott 226
Abbott, David 83, 123
Adkins, Doug 33, 106, 297, 306, 307, 335, 389, 409, 583
Aitchison, Jim 90, 192, 262
Alexander, Joe 173, 174, 242, 243, 245, 277, 314, 338, 428, 438, 446
Alger, Wade 81
Alphin, Jeff 476
Anacker, Steve 499
Andrew, Philip 525
Aron, Abi 213, 288
Ashworth, Matt 166, 167
Astler, Craig 364
Baldacci, Roger 231

Baldwin, David 97, 98, 208, 209, 349, 546
Bales, Mike 464
Barnes, Derek 66, 74, 373, 539, 540, 542, 557, 569, 570
Barrett, Jamie 494, 541
Barry, Tony 112, 136, 298
Bassett, Steve 169, 171, 246
Bayala, Carlos 78
Becker, Jack 550
Behar, Bryan 411
Bell, Greg 63, 75
Bell, Nick 125, 424, 430
Benker, Andre 144
Berger, Dennis 500
Bickel, Keith 490
Biegel, Steve 292, 305
Bijur, Arthur 75, 453, 509, 511
Bildsten, Bruce 105, 133, 220, 221, 222, 223, 265, 269
Bitsack, Jeff 396
Blikslager, Pieter 210, 211
Borge, Oistein 69
Boswell, Michael 503
Bottonus, Bradford 23
Bradley, David 272
Braun, Dan 303
Brignull, Tony 4, 124
Brooker, Brian 385, 386, 387, 388
Brown, Ian 117
Buckhorn, Dean 32, 37, 154, 218, 268, 286, 289, 295, 326, 332, 482
Burleigh, Rob 109, 136
Burns, Scott 563
Burton, Allison 80
Calienes, Mike 586
Callen, Steve 374
Calvit, Phil 219
Camp, Tom 202
Campbell, Mike 499, 500
Carducci, Rob 213, 288
Caro, Jane 484
Carty, Tom 477
Cawley, Tim 365
Chasnow, Adam 38
Chau, Raymond 135
Cills, Ken 517, 576
Clay, Sheldon 348
Coats, David 567
Cocciolo, Harry 25, 64, 572
Cohen, Gary 5, 229

Cole, Glenn 340, 536, 544, 556
Cole, Jeff 368
Coleman, Tom 274
Collins, Simon 481
Condon, John 528
Connelly, Steve 107
Cooke, Marty 505, 506, 545, 580
Cooperrider, Stu 49, 50, 54, 444, 445
Copacino, Jim 532
Corr, David 452, 468
Cosgrove, Terry 485
Cox, Andrew 363
Coyner, Bo 361
Crandall, Court 43, 432, 578
Crawford, Laura 466
Crayton, Ed 146
Creet, Stephen 467
Crouch, Bruce 261
Daley, Blake 334
Davidson, Suzy 441
Davis, Mark 487
de Grood, Doug 215, 216, 360, 381
de Silva, Trevor 233, 234
Dean, Michael 425
DeBellis, Izzy 61, 68, 71, 520, 521, 547, 571
Delaney, Tim 235, 273
Delaney, Timothy 162
Denman, Errol 92
DeVito, Sal 212
DeVries, Audrey 288, 294
Dildarian, Steve 512
Doherty, Pat 84, 123
Dolbinski, Steve 39, 496
Duffy, Malcolm 26
Dullaghan, John 194, 257
Dunkley, Steve 440
Eastwood, Matt 153
Ebner, Ryan 56, 59, 200, 318
Eiden, Greg 358
Einstein, Harold 453
Eirinberg, Scott 394
Elhardt, Matt 311, 312
Fallon, Victoria 480
Fermor, Stuart 117
Fishlock, Paul 561
Fong, Mark 101
Foster, Richard 476
Freeman, Cliff 63, 75
French, Neil 118
Fretwell, Jason 491
Fullwood, Chris 585

Gammon, Kevin 440
Garaventi, Jim 317
Gardiner, Dave 49, 50
Garfinkel, Lee 529
Gentry, Kirt 35
George, David 448
Gibbs, Mike 103, 104, 132, 214, 266, 329
Gibson, Shane 153
Gill, Stephen P. 116, 366, 367, 372, 417
Giovagnoli, Tom 500
Givone, Tom 416
Gold, Josh 177
Gomes, Tony 316
Goodrich, Kara 165, 183, 240, 337, 391, 412
Goudie, Tom 88
Gruber, Cynthia 278
Grunbaum, Eric 18, 203, 204, 205, 206, 207
Guest, Chuck 287
Guidotti, Ted 595
Habeeb, Laurie 352
Hacohen, Dean 57, 270, 341, 347, 454, 455, 456
Hall, Charles 501
Hall, Tina 185, 258, 333, 392
Hamilton, Bill 488, 533, 552
Harper, Ty 359
Hartzell, Paul 187, 188, 189, 284, 291, 495
Haste, Dale 247
Havlena, Robert 591
Heinsma, John 10, 11, 12, 13, 149, 150, 179
Hendley, Charles 190, 191
Herbst, Ken 590
Hibbitts, Randy 470
Hieatt, Dave 112, 136
Higgins, Danny 264
Hirsch, Paul 61, 68, 71, 520, 521, 547, 571
Hogshead, Sally 8, 156, 157, 181, 380, 405, 431, 434, 435
Hoit, Craig 256, 283, 423, 465
Hudson, Steve 480
Huey, Rene 283
Huey, Ron 137, 170, 172, 565
Hughes, Dion 89, 293, 305, 560
Hughes, Mike 314
Hughlett, Neal 159
Hunt, Glen 175
Hunt, Lionel 504

Hunter, Mick 427
Hush, Michael 362
Jacobs, Chris 41, 408
James, Doug 418, 419
Jamieson, Rob 515, 516
Jeffery, Adrian 577
Johnson, Bill 46
Johnson, Ray 400
Jones, Ed 21, 22, 236, 237, 238, 275, 290
Jones, Kevin 77, 402, 513
Jorgensen, Scott 401
Kaler, Jonathan 168
Kean, Adam 491, 574
Kelly, Albert 134
Kerstetter, Bob 228, 271, 524, 564
Ketchum, Greg 498
Kiely, Kathy 473
King, Jane 475
Kinscherff, Annie 483
Kling, Jeff 399
Koelker, Mike 548
Koeneke, Steve 472
Koniakowsky, Wade 35
Kopald, Larry 581
Koppel, Joshua 497
Kostyk-Petro, Maria 250, 422
Landsberg, Steven 52, 53
Larsen, Kristine 410, 526, 549
Lasch, Steve 239
Lee, Dylan 128, 145
Leinwohl, Neil 27, 527
Leite, David 339
LeMaitre, James 66, 74, 539, 540, 542, 557, 569, 570
Lescarbeau, Mike 47, 217, 267, 330, 331, 345
Leu, John 63, 75
Levine, Alan 119
Lewis, Jeff 139
Lewis, Ken 49, 50, 54, 444, 445
Lichtenstein, Marc 475
Liegey, J. 382, 383, 384
Lipkin, Lisa 250, 422
Lipson, Larry 375
Lo, Iris 390
Locascio, David 336
Loew, Dave 592
Lombardi, Dante 55
Lovering, Joe 160, 161, 182
Low, Jack 461, 462, 474
Low, Patrick 101
Lupinacci, Ernest 418, 419

Mackechney, Tom 497
Mahoney, John 114, 530
Marcantonio, Alfredo 82
Marcus, Alan 447
Marshall, Paul 108, 110, 111
Mattig, Kimberly Anne 587
McBride, Chuck 522, 572
McDougall, Robert 442
McKinney, Raymond 113, 138, 244, 446
McMillan, David 475
Mendelis, Mark 122
Meng, Tham Khai 90
Mickenberg, Risa 573
Miller, Tom 28, 31, 184, 296, 346, 407
Moe, Erik 458, 459
Monroe, Evelyn 534
Monzon, Pablo 584
Mooney, Kevin 397
Moore, Bob 60, 535
Mouat, Maggie 429
Mueller, Gary 450
Murray, Steve 589
Nardi, Mark 232
Nelson, Jim 176, 201, 348
Nelson, Tom 85, 86, 87, 126, 127
Newton, David 123
O'Brien, Glenn 357
O'Hare, Dave 16, 19, 224, 225
O'Neill, Joe 582
O'Reilly, Terry 463
Odiorne, Jeff 420, 421
Ogilvie, Derrick 342
Olsen, Jarl 562, 563
Overall, Richard 147, 178
Paradise, Liz 115
Patterson, Katherine 210
Patti, Michael 478, 479
Payton, Andrew 241, 276
Perlman, Hank 73, 537, 555, 568
Peterson, Jason 61, 68, 71, 520, 521, 547, 571

Peterson, Matt 164
Pohl, Pete 502
Pond, Sam 460
Porter, Kim 9
Price, Rob 355
Pryce, Malcolm 1, 3, 6
Real, Jim 35
Reed, Dee 588
Regan, Paul 390
Renfro, Mike 489, 553
Resnikoff, Ben 116, 417
Rettig-Falcone, Lisa 119
Rhode, Jean 282, 353
Ribble, Glenn 551
Rice, Bob 507
Rich, Rob 36
Riddle, Todd 232
Riley, Tim 260
Riswold, Jim 281
Rivera, Rebecca 354
Robertson, John 120, 121, 142, 143, 255
Robertson, Peter 525
Robinson, Trevor 58, 471
Roddy, Kevin 279
Rosen, Tom 376
Rosenberg, David 301, 302
Rosenberg, Rick 395
Roster, Richard 186
Roufa, Michelle 75, 469, 510
Russell, Jay 81
Russell, Peter 259
Saari, Steve 141
Saltmarsh, Ron 457
Sann, Ted 479
Sarnow, Lynn 588
Schapiro, Rob 359, 443
Schapoff, Sandra 78
Schenck, Ernie 20, 91, 128, 145, 196, 197, 198, 199
Schmidt, Jim 566
Schneider, Don 501
Schofield, John 531
Schruntek, Mark 285, 288
Schutte, Alan 439

Segarra, Toni 45
Shane, David 452, 468
Sheehan, Michael 94, 95
Shiffrar, Bob 30
Shine, Marianne 129
Shine, Mike 93, 129, 451
Shuldman, Ken 514
Shurman, Rick 463
Siegel, Barbara 529
Silburn, Paul 248, 249
Silver, Eric 72, 76, 102, 452, 518, 519
Silver, Steve 252
Simmons, Kelly 379
Simpson, Steve 14, 15, 17, 62, 134, 227, 523
Sinclair, Ros 42
Skibba, Steve 195, 398, 437
Slomkowski, Bart 303
Slosberg, Rob 55, 514
Smith, Curtis 79
Smith, David 315
Smith, Jimmy 304. 308, 309, 543, 558
Smith, Pete 414
Sorensen, Eric 319
Souter, Peter 51
Southgate, Barnaby 351
Spencer, Paul 24, 310
Spiegel, Jeff 163
Sree, Kash 90
St. Clair, Steve 241, 276
Strauss, Lane 158
Sullivan, Luke 29, 44, 155, 180, 321, 322, 323, 324, 325, 327, 328, 344
Sutherland, Patrick 285, 288
Sutton, Kevin 550, 567
Swanson, Daniel 377, 378
Sweeney, Mark 230
Swisher, John 352
Szigethy, Neil 354
Taub, Jay 449
Tercek, Charlie 488, 533, 552

Thorp, Kim 429
Tilford, Todd 579
Todes, Gideon 135
Topolewski, Gary 502
Torrison, Troy 369
Treacy, Susan 299, 300, 393
Turner, Christopher 594
Turner, Graham 278
Van Blarcom, Jennifer 593
Venables, Paul 27, 527
Vincent, Scott 65, 67, 70, 508
Wachowiak, Glen 251, 253, 254, 280
Waggoner, Mark 2, 13, 96, 130, 148, 151, 152, 179
Wall, Chris 193, 194, 257
Wall, Stacy 492, 493, 538, 575
Wallis, Tim 140
Ward, Michael 278
Watzman, Jeff 453
Wayner, Taras 48
Wegner, Peter 353, 371
Wei, Dean 436
Weiss, Marty 370
Weitz, Carter 466
Weltner, Eric 420, 421
West, Brian 35
Westbrook, Bill 265
Westbrook, Tripp 137
Whalen, Geoff 486
Wieden, Ken 559
Wigert, Chris 343
Wild, Scott 40, 99, 100, 131, 320, 403, 404, 426, 433, 554
Williams, Clay 287
Wilson, Christopher 413
Wood, Tim 464
Xistris, Ted 313
Yeung, Tony 7
York, Nic 406
Young, Alan 58, 471